INVENTING 'EASTER

Easter Island, or Rapa Nui, as it is known to its inhabitants, is located in the Pacific Ocean, 3600 kilometres west of South America. Annexed by Chile in 1888, the island was first visited by Europeans in 1722, and has since attracted widespread interest owing to its intriguing statues and complex history.

Inventing 'Easter Island' examines narrative strategies and visual conventions in the discursive construction of 'Easter Island' as distinct from the native conception of 'Rapa Nui.' Beginning with a look at the geographic imaginary that pervaded the eighteenth century – a period of rapid imperial expansion – Beverley Haun discusses the forces that shaped the European version of island culture. She then goes on to consider the various representations of that culture, from the sketches and journals of early explorers to more recent texts and images, including those found in comic books and numerous forms of kitsch. Throughout, Easter Island is used as a case study of the impact of imperialism on the outsider's view of a culture. The study hinges on three key investigations – an inquiry into the formation of Easter Island as a subject; an examination of how the constructed space and culture have been shaped, reshaped, and represented in discursive contexts; and an exploration of cultural memory and the effect of foreign texts and images on perceptions and attitudes in regard to the island and its people.

Richly illustrated and engagingly written, this fascinating and provocative study will appeal to cultural theorists, anthropologists, educators, and anyone interested in the history of the South Pacific.

BEVERLEY HAUN is a postdoctoral research fellow at McArthur College, Queen's University.

BEVERLEY HAUN

Inventing 'Easter Island'

UNIVERSITY OF TORONTO PRESS
Toronto Buffalo London

© University of Toronto Press Incorporated 2008
Toronto Buffalo London
www.utppublishing.com
Printed in Canada

ISBN 978-0-8020-9888-7 (cl)
ISBN 978-0-8020-9353-0 (pa)

Printed on acid-free paper

Library and Archives Canada Cataloguing in Publication

Haun, Beverley, 1952–
    Inventing Easter Island / Beverley Haun.

Includes bibliographical references and index.
ISBN 978-0-8020-9888-7 (bound).   ISBN 978-0-8020-9353-0 (pbk.)

1. Easter Island – History.   2. Acculturation – Easter Island.
3. Easter Island – In literature.   4. Imperialism.   I. Title.

F3169.H38 2007   996.1'8   C2007-904928-1

This book has been published with the help of a grant from the Canadian
Federation for the Humanities and Social Sciences, through the Aid
to Scholarly Publications Programme, using funds provided by the Social
Sciences and Humanities Research Council of Canada.

University of Toronto Press acknowledges the financial assistance to its
publishing program of the Canada Council for the Arts and the Ontario
Arts Council.

University of Toronto Press acknowledges the financial support for its
publishing activities of the Government of Canada through the Book
Publishing Industry Development Program (BPIDP).

There is now no Native past without the Stranger, no Stranger without the Native. No one can hope to be mediator or interlocutor in that opposition of Native and Stranger because no one is gazing at it untouched by the power that is in it. Nor can anyone speak just for the one, just for the other. There is no escape from the politics of our knowledge, but that politics is not in the past. That politics is in the present.

— Greg Dening, 'Afterword,' *Cultural Memories*

'perception itself implies conceptualization'

— Bernard Smith, *Imagining the Pacific*

Sometimes things done that are culturally sanctioned are inherently evil. Our recognition of this means we're not evil and we feel better; but our recognition means we're complicit.

— Jorges de Cuchilleros, *The Invention of History*

Contents

List of Illustrations

Preface

On 19 April 2005, the Canadian Broadcasting Corporation announced that a Canadian artist had been detained on Easter Island (Rapa Nui). Montreal-based Bill Vazan had arrived on the island earlier that month to create a series of 'art' installations. His detention was the result of the accusation that he had displaced rocks of archaeological significance to create his 'land configurations.' Vazan paid a Chilean resident of Rapa Nui, Genaro Gatica, to collect stones for him to arrange in patterns on the ground at ceremonial sites around the island. He then photographed the resulting juxtapositions of his rock designs and the island's cultural monuments. As a consequence, the Rapanui court ruled that he was to destroy the thirty-six rolls of film he had shot, pay a $6,200 fine, be banned from the island for two years, and write letters of apology to the National Monuments Council, the head of the National Parks Agency, the governor of the island, and the mayor of Hanga Roa, the only village on the island.

On the same day as the CBC report, the Rapanui Information Center, a Yahoo site for conversations about the island, had a discussion thread started by José Miguel Ramírez of the Centro de Estudios Rapa Nui, Universidad de Valparaiso, explaining the island response to Vazan's actions. The Rapanui took issue with 'using a sacred island place for a personal foreign purpose' regardless of what that purpose might be, whether it is making art, producing a Hollywood movie, filming a commercial advertisement, inappropriately reconstructing an ahu platform, or destroying ceremonial sites through the grazing of imported animals. The thread ended with a clarion call to resist damaging further the culturally sacred Rapanui archaeological sites that have been disrespected for too long.[1]

Bill Vazan appeared to make the required compensations to the local authorities and was released from Rapanui custody and returned to Canada, but he does not seem to have understood the concept of respect that the islanders were asking for their material heritage. Following his return, he wrote an article published in the fall 2005 issue of *Canadian Art*. His piece was oddly titled 'Pacific Prison.' Both his written account and his published photographs indicate a dismaying lack of engagement with Rapanui cultural history or notions of the cultural integrity of Others.

> I had admitted ... that I had laid out a ground configuration of volcanic stones ... just to one side of a ceremonial area. Easter Island ... has hundreds of these stone-*rubble* mounds along its coast ... maybe my hired assistant of three days had ratted on me – they got me at my guest house ... they asked to see the rolls I had shot ... I wanted to be the first into that suitcase ... I revealed the 36 rolls of film they were after ... later ... the police would publicly destroy the film. My slight of hand arrangements of the contents of my suitcase during the inspection and the detectives' unfamiliarity with film formats, however, had left me with 80 ... colour slides. [Three days into my detention] the Prosecution lawyer presented written testimony from [my assistant] and photos of three other works ... one of the three ... contained a [part] of a toppled moai ...
>
> Normally I avoid obtaining official approval for my land configurations, as I have found it results in a great loss of time and energy. My decision to visit Easter Island was last-minute. I figured I could sidestep the bureaucracy and handle my interventions in a responsible way, hiring a local assistant as a fence against problems, curiosity and damage. If the authorities had developed the film they would have seen another seven works they had not discovered. My landworks deal with nature, history and culture, serving as signs of the importance of these concepts and pointing to the need to preserve what we can for ourselves and the future ... Despite the intent of my works to be transient, invisible and spare, they often intrude on official space. Damned if you do and damned if you don't. (Vazan 2005, 110–15)

As Vazan proclaims, the imposition of his personal agenda and the situating of his art on the sacred spaces of another culture is not an isolated act on his part, and, as the magazine article shows, did not end with his departure from the island.

In support of his intentions, if not their implications, an editorial decision was made by *Canadian Art* both to publish his article and include four photographs of his landforms from those he illegally withheld from the island authorities and smuggled back to Canada. *Canadian Art* is a publicly funded forum. In its masthead it acknowledges the financial support of the government of Canada through several agencies: the Publications Assistance Program, the Canada Magazine Fund, the Canada Council, the Ontario Arts Council, and the Ontario Media Development Corporation. What is to be made of their decision to feature photographs that the Rapanui see as violating the sacredness of their ceremonial and mortuary sites and that a legally constituted court deemed criminal?

In both the uninformed position that Vazan takes towards the stone clan platforms of the Rapanui, calling them 'rubble' mounds, and in the publication of his work in *Canadian Art*, can be seen the past failure of the academy to problematize and to voice in public conversation the very real and unequal relations of power manifest through imperial narratives, in this case about one small island that has been widely appropriated with cavalier disdain. Vazan's article, with its solipsistic title, 'Pacific Prison,' stands as a direct and very current example of contemporary understandings of Rapa Nui and how it is represented in Euro-American culture.

In this rare instance of Rapanui voices sounding on the world stage to assert control over their own ancestral structures and spaces, the concerns of the islanders have been overtly and deliberately overridden. In the very real power differential speaking through Vazan's account of his behaviour on the island and sanctioned in the public forum, *Canadian Art*, can be seen the necessity to address the sense of entitlement still extant in Canada and across so much of the globe as an imperial legacy of Europe.

The publication of Vazan's article raises questions about the relations between freedom and responsibility, when art and its celebration enact cultural privilege. This book offers a counter-narrative to challenge the continuing Eurocentric exercise of such privilege. Another instance that might enhance its necessity, more egregious in some ways, is the current reduction of the island's past to a facile rhetorical device by a number of writers in order to make it an exemplar of ecological irresponsibility. The best-known work in this genre is Jared Diamond's *Collapse: How Societies Choose to Fail or Succeed* (2005). He, like Ronald Wright, a Canadian public intellectual with a readership among environmentalists worldwide, selectively distorts or perhaps unintentionally refigures the complex relationship between the people of Rapa Nui and the land, virtually ignoring the sequencing of cultural development or the impact of outsiders who turned the entire island into a sheep station for several generations. Wright is especially of interest, as his sources are meagre and his use of them irrepressibly didactic. His book, *A Short History of Progress* (2004), is based on the Massey Lectures, a radio series presented by the Canadian public broadcaster, the CBC, in 2004, again raising questions of the relationship between freedom and responsibility. Wright and Diamond are more closely examined in the latter sections of this study.

A brilliantly intricate and well-informed novel by Jennifer Vanderbes called *Easter Island* (2003), makes an argument similar to that of Wright and Diamond. In it, a facsimile academic paper declares that Rapa Nui offers 'perhaps the only known instance in the history of mankind in which a people destroyed themselves by building monuments to the dead' (292). Fiction based on research is still fiction; the author is responsible to genre, not history. Still, Vanderbes reinforces the misapprehension of the island's heritage by outsiders. Narrative strategy that serves her novel well does not necessarily serve the interests of the people of Rapa Nui, whom she clearly admires.

Although there is some recent scholarship focused on the island's geography, flora, and fauna, and two books have been published on contemporary socio-political and cultural life on the island, the majority of work still focus on the archaeological remains of the pre-European-contact past. Within this body of work, although emphasis is placed on the history of destructive imperial exploitation and Chilean colonization of Rapa Nui, I have found no texts that challenge the imperial narrative of the island that stands as the accepted historical account of European contact. Focusing on eighteenth-century voyage texts as I have done in this book is to enter and interrogate the previously uninterrupted European imperial narrative by which Rapa Nui has become Easter Island, as it is currently named by many within the academy and bandied about in countless variations in popular representations. By troubling the accepted interpretations of past events, this book attempts to shed light on the unequal power relations embedded in the Eurocentric imperial narratives of the island and the instability of those narratives as they respond to external influences across time. My textual analyses invite resistance to the historical accounts and underscore the Rapanui right to define their past as well as their future on their own terms.

Whether what I have to say about the Eurocentricity of historic and contemporary island narratives is dismissed, challenged, or accepted, the introduction of a discordant voice into the discourse will form a supplement to the imperial narrative. My account invites both response and the possibility of alternative accounts. Rapanui constructions of their own past and sense of self are central to such alternatives. I do not presume to speak for the Rapanui, but to problematize the normalized European accounts, and perhaps to open space for the islanders' absent voices. Rapanui accounts would ideally both supplement the historical narratives and displace the currently accepted versions of the island's past, causing a rift in what Stuart Hall calls 'the power-knowledge field of force.'

This said, postcolonialism practised within Euro-American academic disciplines, whether in Canada or elsewhere, can open spaces and stand attentively to listen, but postcolonialists cannot presume that the Pacific subjects of our disciplines will either desire or choose to speak within frameworks developed for Western edification, even when they have been opened to other voices. Perhaps, instead, we will be invited to observe and participate in Pacific educational spaces of Polynesian making, as students or colleagues, within a shared dynamic. Meanwhile we must dismantle the power-knowledge fields that hold us in imperial thrall.

By providing a particular model that has universal applications, speaking both to pedagogical needs and postcolonial imperatives, my work demonstrates the influence of imperial texts beyond the literary, which are the ones postcolonialism tends normally to focus upon. My work calls into play strategies for resisting the continuing imperial influence shaping Euro-American responses to Others. It challenges the practices of the disciplines and institutions that have constructed and currently maintain the imperial narrative of Easter Island and, by implication, resonates with the Euro-narratives of other indigenous cultures, demonstrating incidents of the way such accounts have been shaped and continue to circulate. This study confirms and perhaps disturbs a continuing imperial pedagogical control within the disciplines of history and art history, anthropology, and environmental geography. The educational focus demonstrates the ways imperialism continues to teach the West to promote a Eurocentric agenda – not beside or in harmony with the inhabitants of the island, but over them. As an interdisciplinary postcolonial inquiry, it critiques from within and must breech the imperial pedagogical dynamic in order to bring about change, to facilitate the opening of a still-small space of attentiveness to Others, that in turn opens to larger spaces that transform the power dynamics of selves and Others in social and economic interaction.

As well as being a case study and a demonstration of imperial pedagogical control within the disciplines that shape the off-island narrative, this enterprise constructs a foundation for my continued interest in developing a postcolonial framework for curriculum design, teaching, and learning – a transformative pedagogical model with postcolonial testamentary practice at its core. Implicit is the need for transformation of public education and subsequent cultural transformation beyond theory to a cycle of practical application, assessment, adjustment, and reapplication. In this respect, this book may serve as the foundation for a practical course on developing postcolonial curriculum frameworks. My hope is that it can form the basis of a curriculum project, an impetus to changing understandings, attitudes, and expectations, for learning to step outside the normalized space of Euro-American cultural complicity. The implicit argument within this pedagogical idea of the possibility of individual transformations through public education begins with an altered sense of self in relation to the postcolonial island narrative. Such personal transformations are the main route to altered public iterations of the island.

When I initially embarked on this project, I assumed that my perspective, a Canadian perspective, representative of the larger Euro-American consciousness, would mean my readers would have little close or personal investment in deconstructing the discursive narratives of Easter Island. From a pedagogical point of view, this seemed an advantage. I could highlight the machinery of imperialism without having to factor in readers' personal investments in the specific culture of the Rapanui, while counting on a familiarity with Easter Island as part of their cultural capital. More than I could have anticipated, I found that the instability of textual representations of this small and isolated island in the South Pacific has generated a plethora of strange and fanciful responses, with delightful and sometimes disturbing implications. In the course of my investigation, I acquired a substantial collection of texts and images created by non-Rapanui to represent their island culture. I also amassed an extensive collection of fiction, as well as over forty comic books, and a dozen video documentaries and dramatizations. I have a startlingly large archive of images from eBay depicting T-shirts and jewellery, toys and trading cards, mugs and tumblers, house decorations and garden ornaments, all created off island.

There are enough texts and artefacts in my collection, alone, to generate further studies in cultural theory and pedagogical practice.

If this book sets readers on a course of discovery and a reconsideration of assumptions, whether about tiki coffee mugs, the future of the past, or the realization that they are inseparable, then that will have more than fulfilled my mandate to honour a place that its own people call 'Te Pito O Te Henua,' the navel of the world, the end of the earth.

Acknowledgments

Many people from around the globe have been most generous and helpful in answering questions and forwarding pieces of the puzzle that have helped me complete this project. I want to thank several members of the Easter Island Foundation who have shared their knowledge and their enthusiasm for Rapa Nui: Georgia Lee, Francis J. Morin, Antoinette Padgett, Ann Altman, and Shawn McLaughlin, as well as José Miguel Ramirez and Charlie Love who were so generous with their knowledge while I was on the island. I would also like to express my gratitude to Tom Christopher, who has shared comic book information, images, and expertise with me over the Internet.

I would like to give special thanks to Herbert von Saher of the Netherlands who was a keen correspondent throughout the project, and to my friends Michael Black of Cambridge and Peter Black of the Hunterian Art Gallery in Glasgow who helped me track down a particular picture of Queen Elizabeth I. A number of other people were also very helpful with information about the images I needed to accompany my text: Francesco Buranelli, Director of the Vatican Museums; Jennifer Ramkalawon of the British Museum; Dr Geoff Quilley, Curator of Maritime Art, and Doug McCarthy, Picture Library Manager, at The National Maritime Museum Greenwich; Dr Peter Brunt, Victoria University, Wellington; Dr Glenn E. Morris of North East Wales Institute, Wrexham Wales; Magdalene Albert, Executive Director, Canadian Institution for Historic Microreproductions (CIHM); Karla Vandersypen and Kathryn L. Beam, Curators of Special Collections for the Library University of Michigan; the Tiki artist Jamio (J.P. Odell); Thomas C. King at DC Comics; and Jim Siebold for permission to use maps from his wonderful Web collection.

Roger Simon from the University of Toronto deserves special thanks for being both a mentor and model as I have pursued this work. I would also like to express my appreciation to Kari Delhi and Robert Morgan from the University of Toronto, as well as to John Willinsky from the University of British Columbia, for their invaluable comments on the manuscript.

Family have been important in providing joy during this journey. Thank you Beatrice Winny for your love and serenity. Thank you Laura Moss for your interest and organizing help. Most importantly, thank you John Moss for your love and support and endless patience and generosity as a sounding board and partner.

Every effort has been made to get permission for images used in this project, as indicated in notes accompanying their use.

INVENTING 'EASTER ISLAND'

1 Te Pito O Te Henua: An Introduction

Fonthill, the village where I grew up in the Niagara Peninsula, has the same population as Rapa Nui – about 4,400. There is a moai, an Easter Island statue, in Fonthill in the centre of a garden three doors down from my family home. Another sits in front of a small ornament store on the main street. My grandsons in Vancouver have a plastic moai mould as one component of their Play-Doh set. Across the continent, in North Carolina, my granddaughter's favourite television character, Sponge Bob, has a friend, Squidward, who lives in an underwater moai-shaped home. Easter Island is a common part of everyday cultural capital. For example, the *Globe and Mail*, on 7 February 2004, carried a full-page ad for American Express that featured a photo of a moai on the slope of Rano Raraku, the dormant volcano where the statutes were carved. Just over the east side of the volcano, the Statue of Liberty was shown rising into view. Easter Island cultural icon meets American cultural icon in Canada's national newspaper. The caption read, 'When you earn Aeroplan Miles faster, everything gets closer.' In another section of that same day's paper, an article associated American presidential candidate John Kerry with a moai. It stated that 'his lantern-jawed looks have been compared to those massive stone heads on Easter Island.' The moai has become such a universal symbol of the long face that within six months, by 29 July 2004, the day of Kerry's acceptance speech as Democratic candidate for the presidential election, a Google search of 'John Kerry' and 'Easter Island' pulled up 277 hits. An ad that appears frequently in the travel section of the same paper also features moai as its main image. The text says, 'Book now and save up to 70% a head ... South Pacific Adventure – featuring Easter Island.'

Here, in a single newspaper, we find references to three key aspects of the imagined Easter Island that circulate in our culture: the iconic status of the moai, the positioning of the island at an extreme distance from an imagined centre occupied by the reader, and travel to the island constituted as an adventure. What is also apparent in this construction of Easter Island is that the moai have become separated from other possible traces of the island's cultural identity. The people, known as Rapanui, have been allowed to fade while the trace of the moai has been strengthened through appropriation, repetition, and distortion as a trope within Euro-American culture.

I had the opportunity in the winter of 2002, while pursuing academic work in postcolonial pedagogy, to go on 'the adventure' and travel to Easter Island (Rapa Nui) for several weeks. It was the first of two very different excursions to the island. The second occasion was as this project was nearing completion and my perspectives had been substantially altered. At the time of my visit in 2002, I had been considering from a theoretical perspective the possibilities of ethical relations with Others and the limits and potentials of cross-cultural translation. On my return to Canada, I found myself contemplating, as a white, female, Anglo-Canadian educator, the narrative positions I had assumed travelling to Easter Island, the ones I assumed while there, and the ones I was negotiating reflexively. At the same time, I became aware of narrative positions both available and unavailable to the Rapanui people. Many of them were performing roles in relation to me as a tourist in an Easter Island drama largely structured through Euro-American imaginative constructions. I recognized my cultural complicity with this selective focus on, and shaping of, the island imaginary and felt compelled to explore its origin, to examine and respond to its exclusions, and to propose ways to alter its influence.

These imperatives led me to a critical consideration of the impulses that first took Europeans to the island and of the subsequent publications meant to represent what they 'experienced.' I soon found myself engaged in an analysis of eighteenth-century imperial and Enlightenment texts and images, trying to understand the originating process by which the subjective narrative of Easter Island had acquired apparent authenticity. In those publications I focused on the textual violence that was committed towards the islanders as they were read historically, and I traced those readings to see how they became manifest in contemporary narratives of the island. The Rapanui were and still are written into specific subject positions as Others in relation to Euro-American subjects and, at the same time, erased from the scene of their own culture.

To provide a context for my investigation of how Easter Island was divided from other Pacific islands, constituted as its own subject, and brought into prominence as part of circulating cultural capital through the first four commercial and imperial expeditions to the island – the Dutch in 1722, Spanish in 1770, British in 1774, and French in 1786 – I turned to the conventions of genre. What were the historical, social, political, and textual influences on eighteenth-century travel literature through which explorers wrote their journals, collected specimens, and sketched or documented 'newly discovered' landscapes and people, to be displayed and reproduced back in Europe for an ever-increasing audience eager to understand the extent of the imperial enterprise? What cultural constraints shaped the voyagers' perceptions of the island and its people and how did those constraints, manifest in voyage texts and images, shape the thought, action, and memory, of those who read them, in a process of cultural invention that has led to unproblematized, simplistic, accepted cultural memory, today? What transformative practices for remembering might disrupt reflexive responses to current ideas of the island? How would it be possible to open a space for much more complex and nuanced narratives, offering a supplement to future engagement with Easter Island as a discursive space?

When I began this project, whenever I referred to 'Easter Island,' I placed the name in quotation marks. This was a supplementary strategy, a way of disrupting the casual acceptance of 'Easter Island' as a place or reality with the insistent reminder that it is a discursive construction, an imposed identity, and must always be considered with that awareness held open. While editing my manuscript I dropped the quotation marks around Easter Island, trusting that this text itself would keep the reader mindful of the constructed nature of the off-island name. In accordance with island custom, I use Rapanui when referring to the islanders' language and self-identification, and Rapa Nui, two words, when referring to their own name for the island, adopted in the nineteenth century. Rapa Nui means, literally, large (*nui*) dance paddle (*rapa*).

Nearing the end of my research and analysis in the autumn of 2004, I returned to the island, this time with an international cohort of Rapa Nui specialists. My experience was quite different and yet in disturbing ways it was continuous with my earlier and more naive 'adventure.' The uneasy distance between my apparently privileged academic perspective and the lives of the Rapanui seemed, if anything, exacerbated. This was perhaps because I was far better informed and in the company of experts, for whom the present is a polished lens through which to view the infinitely intriguing biocultural morphology of the island, sometimes as if it were the remains of an almost mythic organism. It was thrilling to reaffirm my project, visiting sites identified by renowned Easter Island archaeologists such as Charlie Love and Georgia Lee as locations represented in eighteenth-century texts and illustrations, and to see exactly how these had been embellished in response to forces at play in the time of their narrative origin. At the same time, I became intensely aware of the extent to which we all, whatever our focused endeavours, seemed to be working from a basic 'knowledge' of Rapa Nui as if it were, in fact, indivisible from Easter Island. It seemed more important than ever to illuminate the discontinuities between the people of the island and their rich heritage that has been imposed through the discursive invention of their world by outsiders as a geographic imaginary.

Polynesian Settlement on the Island

Keeping in mind the poststructural idea grounding this analysis, that all knowledge is subjective by virtue of its construction and practice within temporally situated and culturally located understandings of space and place, what I offer here is a brief summary of the current geographical, anthropological, and archaeological consensus about the place now widely known as Easter Island. The island is semiitropical, volcanic in origin, and little more than 166 square kilometres in size. It is located in the Pacific Ocean, 3,700 kilometres west of the coast of Chile and 4,050 kilometres north-east of Tahiti, and lies at the extreme eastern edge of the Polynesian triangle bounded by Hawaii to the north and New Zealand to the southwest. The people who originally colonized the island, arriving from elsewhere in Polynesia between 615 and 864 CE, are descended from settlers who named this place 'Te Pito O Te Henua,' meaning both the centre of the world and the end of the earth. It is now called Rapa Nui, defined in consultation with other Polynesians and in relation to another island, Rapa, within the Polynesian group.

Today, several narrative versions of the island exist. The current consensus among scholars who have made the island their specialty (see John Flenley, Georgia Lee, Grant McCall, Douglas Porteous, José Miguel Ramírez, Jo Anne Van Tilburg), as opposed to those who co-opt Easter Island references to make an argument extraneous to the island itself, is that from the time of settlement, the Rapanui developed their separate culture in relation to their past Polynesian traditions in isolation from any outside influence, until contact with Europeans in 1722.

One of the most recent and comprehensive narrative constructions of this early period, at the time I was writing this text, is offered by José M. Ramírez and Carlos Huber in *Easter Island: Rapa Nui, a Land of Rocky Dreams* (2000). Through their reading of the archaeological evidence, they suggest that the island's population peaked in the sixteenth century at between 8,000 and 10,000 people. This estimate is based on the carrying capacity of the agriculturally viable land on the island that had been cleared and put under cultivation and the population such agricultural resources could have sustained. During this period, which included the moai-building phases of the culture, it has been hypothesised that the steady increase of the island population and the limited natural resources created conditions where the island 'underwent a process of severe environmental deterioration.' Such Polynesian population increases and environmental distress are thought to have occurred on other small islands in the Pacific and are considered one of the reasons for the period of migration and settlement throughout the South Pacific. Because Rapa Nui was distant from other islands and deforestation over the first thousand years of its settlement meant there was no wood to build voyaging canoes by the time the population required more space, this migrating pattern is seen as coming to a halt at Polynesia's easternmost limit (Ramírez and Huber 2000, 24–7).

Evidence suggests that when the Polynesian colonizers arrived in large double-hulled canoes to settle the island, they brought with them domesticated chickens and the edible Polynesian rat, Kio'e, as well as a variety of plant crops to cultivate on their new island home. Dogs and pigs are understood to have been part of the stock that Polynesian colonizers transported to new islands, but neither seems to have survived the long voyage to Rapa Nui. Sedimentary pollen deposits and large root boles in the hardened lava flows on the island suggest it was originally well treed. There is also evidence of a once large migratory bird population. The island was fertile and the Polynesians, successful farmers, prospered. The Polynesian rat, however, apparently prospered too well. Tooth marks on materials found in caves suggest it ate the seeds and saplings of the native species of trees, preventing continuing natural propagation (Flenley and Bahn 2003, 160–1).

Over several centuries as the population grew, the islanders are thought to have cleared the native trees to create fields and to have used the wood for fishing boats, cooking fires, and funeral pyres. (The

Rapanui are identified as the only Polynesians to cremate their dead. With deforestation, the practice of cremation was replaced with one of burying bodies under stone cairns near the ahu, platforms that supported the moai statues, and the moai took on the role of mortuary guardians.) Eventually only the imported crop trees, such as mulberry for bark cloth and banana trees, were left standing (Ramírez and Huber 2000, 26–7). Trees are also thought to have been used whenever a moai had to be manoeuvred to an ahu somewhere on the island, but given the lengthy period of their installation, this appears to have been a statistically infrequent activity, amounting to about one annually – a significant figure in light of competing arguments that hold 'moai moving' responsible for the environmental destruction of the forests on the island.

Grant McCall, in his article 'Nissology' (2002), theorizes, through archaeological investigation and examination of climate patterns, that during the little ice age (1650–80) the carrying capacity of the island to produce enough food failed and the Rapanui population dropped from its peak of 10,000 to about half that number in a few generations. This diminishing populace may have resulted in tracts of depopulated clan-cultivated land becoming the focus of power struggles. Whatever the actual cause, there seems to have been internecine warfare and the rise of a warrior class that replaced the power base of hereditary leaders. The era of the moai ended with apparent famine and the political and artistic discourses on the island were redirected towards different forms of expression (417–20), known now as the birdman era.

The birdman era is constructed in current versions of the island political history as both a cultural renaissance and a period of continuing conflict. The concept of *mana* (power) invested in hereditary leaders was recast into the person of the birdman, apparently beginning circa 1540, and coinciding with the final vestiges of the moai period. The winner of an annual birdman contest of strength and endurance served to unite the island clans in a seasonal period of common ceremony. The clan of the winner ruled the island from one contest to the next. Conversely, this era of birdman rule has also been constructed as an era of continuing hostilities. In this version, resentment created by the birdman's clan-rule over other clans during the year of his win led to simmering resentments and retaliation during the years when a different clan ascended to leadership. During the period of birdman rule, cultural production shifted from the large-scale moai to concentrate on other materials and forms for cultural expression: stuffed bark-cloth-wrapped sculptures, petroglyphs, wooden carvings, and small portable stone carvings. Examples of each of these have been preserved in imperial museum collections (see McCall 1994, 37–40; Van Tilburg 1994, 52–3, Ramírez and Huber 2000, 25–7).

European Arrival on the Island

The era of moai carving and the honouring of hereditary leadership reflected in the moai is now thought to have ended over a century before the arrival of Europeans in 1722, at which time the moai seem to have all been standing. It was not until the 1774 visit of James Cook that the moai were reported toppled from their platforms. All journals of the eighteenth-century explorers describe the island plantations as well ordered and well grown, 'prettily laid out by line, but not inclosed [sic] by any fence' (Cook 1777, 294). Of the four European expeditions in the eighteenth century, only the Spanish did not fire guns at the island people when they came ashore to explore, although they subjected the island itself to a brief fusillade. The Dutch and the Spanish expeditions reported a vibrant culture. The British, arriving four years after the Spanish, reported a much reduced population and meagre plantings. One likely reason for this was devastation by a pandemic resulting from the encounters with the Spanish. This may also have happened after contact with the Dutch, but the islanders had forty-eight years to recover before the next foreigners arrived.

Both physician Ramón Campbell (1993) and anthropologist-adventurer Thor Heyerdahl (1958, 1976) refer to the severe respiratory pandemics that swept the island in the 1950s and 1960s while they were each resident there. These pandemics caused fatalities every year after the arrival of the annual supply ship from Chile. Rapanui immune systems did not develop resistance until after regular airline service started in 1967. A similar response to foreign disease has also been identified as killing indigenous North Americans during early contact with Europeans. According to Jared Diamond in *Guns, Germs, and Steel* (1999), death from introduced epidemics reduced Native populations to less than a tenth of their pre-contact numbers in the early years of New England settlement. He writes that throughout 'the Americas diseases introduced with Europeans spread from tribe to tribe far in advance of the Europeans themselves, killing an estimated 95% of the pre-Columbian Native American population' (78). The centuries of isolation the Rapanui experienced would have left them similarly vulnerable.

During the nineteenth century, the imperial record shows European exploration shifted to exploitation, and European and American ships sailed to the island to force the male Rapanui into several forms of labour: seal hunting, plantation work, and domestic service. Contact was characterized by bloodshed, rape, enslavement, death by imported disease, and forced emigration. Catholic missionaries arrived during this century but eventually left when they came into conflict with European sheep-farming interests, taking Rapanui with them to other Pacific islands. The era of initial missionization, in its efforts to dismiss the island cosmology and write over it with an imperial Christianity, denigrated the island culture and effectively replaced it, with devastating consequences.

The population was reduced during the nineteenth century from estimates of 4,000 to 110. Towards the latter half of the century, when the population was at its lowest, imperial interests turned to the cultural heritage of the Rapanui. In 1868, 1882, and 1889, first a British, then a German, and finally an American ship arrived for brief visits and carried off statues and artefacts for the British museum, a private German collection, and the Smithsonian Institute, laying waste to the sacred ceremonial village of Orongo at the south of the island in the process (Drake 1991, 15–17). This village has been identified through oral tradition and archaeology as the most significant ceremonial site in the last phase of pre-enslavement Rapanui culture. It is understood to have served as a common clan ceremonial site for the birdman contest that superseded the focus on the moai for some two hundred years before slavery, disease and Christian influence changed the culture forever.

The first Catholic missionary, Brother Eugène Eyraud, arrived in 1864 two years after the slave raids, and baptized the few remaining islanders (Englert 1970, 74), writing over each person's Rapanui name with a Western name from the narrative of Christianity. As Steven Fischer observed in *Easter Island Studies* (1993), 'The same Europeans and Americans who always reviled the Rapanui for being the worst thieves in the Pacific were at the same time themselves stealing the Rapanui's treasures, health, their beliefs, and even the Rapanui people' (228).

In 1888, the island was annexed by Chile, then rented out to a Scottish enterprise with the ominous name 'The Easter Island Exploitation Company,' which increased the comprehensive sheep farming. The remaining Rapanui population was concentrated into one walled compound, without direct access to a water source, and obliged to conform to the dictates of the sheep company overseers in order to survive. They were made economic slaves to the sheep ranching in exchange for goods from the company store (goods rendered necessary by the removal of the islanders from the land they relied upon for their sustenance). It was the intensive sheep farming, ending only a few decades ago, that turned the whole island into pastureland, eliminating a great deal of its biodiversity through grazing. The Easter Island Foundation (EIF) website describes what happened to the natural environment during the hundred years of sheep farming:

> The sheep (at one time there were over 70,000 of them) denuded the island. Alien trees, mostly eucalyptus, were planted for shade and windbreaks. Although a fast growing tree, eucalyptus trees shed bark, creating an acidic dry litter beneath the trees, and the roots draw the moisture of the soil away from less hardy native plants. Nothing will grow under them. By making such 'improvements' on the land, sheep masters caused the final demise of the indigenous woodland. Various birds were introduced, such as a Chilean partridge and hawks. The latter were brought in to kill off rats and sparrows (which previously had been introduced and had become pests). However, the variety of hawk that was imported lacked an interest in sparrows, and seldom encountered the nocturnal rats. Without natural enemies, pests and predators all flourished. (Easter Island Foundation 2001)

By the mid-1950s, Norwegian archaeological interest in the pre-contact culture of the island, spearheaded by anthropological popularizer Thor Heyerdahl, awakened the Chilean government to the possibility of attracting tourists to the island. An airfield was constructed in the 1960s and, in 1986, NASA extended it as an emergency landing site for U.S. space shuttle flights, enabling commercial jets to land (ibid.). The Rapanui, responding to these twentieth-century developments, have taken up new economic and cultural positions in relation to Eurocentric scholarship and tourism. They no longer refer to their island as Te Pito O Te Henua, although that is now the name of one of their two main roads in the island village, Hanga Roa, and is stencilled onto the curb at the only intersection in these roads.

The Present

The violence of an imperial legacy is strongly evident in this brief outline of European contact with the Rapanui. What is perhaps less obvious, but still troubling, is the uneasy, ongoing presence of Euro-American scholarship, popular media, and tourism that continue to write over the lives of the Rapanui and to shape the narrative of the island. The position that Europe and the colonized Americas has taken and continues to take in relation to non-Western Others is part of the ongoing postcolonial discourse within the academy. The more obvious violences of colonialism, slavery, and land and resource co-optation have been documented and engaged in both scholarly and public discourse. As part of postcolonial study, the Eurocentric mindset during the time of imperial expansion has been traced in literary and historical texts and extended to encompass the violence inherent in the very nature of writing itself. The ways in which tourism manifests itself as an extension of the discovery and acquisitions of empire has also been examined (see Harrison, Hollinshead, Huggan, Kaplan, Korte, Pratt, Rojeck, Spurr, Thomas, Urry). As postcolonial discourse moves diachronically from an examination of early exploration and conquest to the presence of colonialism in the contemporary social order, less overt manifestations of the imperial mindset come under investigation. These less overt practices of imperialism are so subtly embedded in Euro-American sociocultural practices that they do their negative pedagogical work subliminally. The appropriation of moai sculptures, for example, to serve as garden sculptures, children's toys, and Tiki party accessories, as well as logos for software developers (bitHead, see fig. 7.12) and large comic-book publishers (Dark Horse, see fig. 7.13), removes them from their cultural context, imposes an ephemeral and reductionist quality to their engagement, and erases the Rapanui from the authorship of their own cultural production. The Euro-American manufacture and sale of such cultural appropriations, without any monetary compensation to the culture who originated them, raises issues of continuing forms of imperial theft. In many ways such contemporary forms of colonialism are as sinister as the overt ones already examined, because by their very subtlety they tend to go unnoticed and thus unchallenged by the counter-discourses extant in the academy and in the public arena.

Rapanui Perspectives

The extent to which the story of Easter Island is a textual construction foregrounding Euro-American interests in its narrative is highlighted by the following Rapanui response to science and archaeology on the island, and in the following responses to a survey of Canadian students by a geography professor at the University of Victoria. At the sixth International Conference on Easter Island and the Pacific in Viña del Mar, Chile, in September 2004, two Rapanui men, Rafael Tuki-Tepano (Presidente Consejo de Cultura Rapa-Nui, Comisión de Desarrollo Isla de Pascua) and Clemente Here-veri-Te'ao (Secretario Técnico Consejo Cultura Rapa-Nui), presented their paper 'The Protection of Natural, Archaeological, and Cultural Heritage on Te Pito O Te Henua.' Its subtitle was 'A review of Scientific Studies, Emic Criticisms and Presentation of New Use Regulations for Rapanui Heritage.' They explained that Rapa Nui archaeological heritage carries a spiritual message from the past and continues to be a tangible testimony to pre-missionized traditions. The abstract of their paper reads:

> Today science and archaeology are in conflict with the ethnic world, since they are considered 'destroyers of *tapu*' [spiritual power] by interfering directly with archaeological contexts, and aggravating the situation further by providing more information to the rest of the world than to the Rapanui people themselves. Today the indigenous Rapanui ask for the preservation of the past, the transmission of knowledge, and respect of their *tapu*. The creation of the Council of Rapanui Culture (formerly the Council of Rapanui Monuments) that watches over the sacredness of Rapa Nui and the transmission of knowledge to the Rapanui people includes the development of standards to regulate and control all work of a scientific nature on Rapa Nui, such as its heritage, including Motu Motiro Hiva.

The regulations outlined by the Council are that all scholarly investigations conducted on the island, regardless of the language in which they are originally published, are also to be translated into Rapanui and Spanish and deposited with the island Council of Rapanui Culture as part of their publication process. No scholars have done so in the past.

In 'Rapa Nui: A Hyperbolic Iconography' (2004), Douglas Porteous outlines the results of a survey he conducted with third-year geography students in 1978 and again in 2003. He simply asked them, 'What three items spring to mind when you think of Easter Island?' In his article comparing the results of the survey over the twenty-five year period, he ends by saying:

> The tentative conclusions of my small longitudinal study are (a) that a sizable proportion of Canadian undergraduate geographers knows nothing

at all about Rapa Nui; (b) that the single emphasis of 1978 on archaeological themes had been challenged in 2003 by a new concentration on the
theme of environmental and cultural destruction; (c) that the moai continue to be the foremost Rapa Nui icon; and (d) that the double emphasis
on first, the gigantism of the moai, and second, the theme of island environmental destruction which presages worldwide ecocatastrophe, suggests a strong element of hyperbole in the iconic representation of Rapa
Nui to the English-speaking world. It goes without saying that the present
inhabitants are totally absent from the Rapa Nui iconic system as currently
established.

My second conclusion is really a beginning. I'd like to see the growth of
a cultural approach to Rapa Nui Studies that emphasizes both the history
of the island and the place of the island in the world here and now. There
are a dozen graduate theses to be done in this field. Over 20 years ago I
suggested that 'the single-minded pursuit of Easter Island prehistory has
resulted in an almost total neglect of the island's modern development' ...
Happily, more research is now being done on Rapa Nui history, environment, development and planning. Cultural studies approaches could be
the next frontier. (18–19)

The advantage to working within a group of texts where the limits are
finite is that it becomes readily apparent where there are gaps in scholarship that need to be filled and which questions need to be asked and
answered in order to address those omissions. As Douglas Porteous
points out, there is a significant place within the Easter Island context
for a cultural studies contribution to the existing body of work, and it is
through such a cultural and ethical space that I have directed my investigations of the explorers' journals and positioned their story in relation
to contemporary public memory and response.

With all the public attention given to such a high-profile writer as
Thor Heyerdahl in the twentieth century (whose main agenda was trying to prove that the Rapanui were from South America), it is possible
to be unaware of the scholarly pioneers of the present era. In the 1980s
and 1990s, Douglas Porteous (1991) and Grant McCall (1981, 1994)
studied the contemporary lives of the Rapanui, and Georgia Lee (1992)
has seen beyond the moai to other forms of cultural expression on the
island (petroglyphs) that pre- and postdate the moai era and are more
numerous than the moai as cultural and aesthetic expressions. By
resisting the moai era of island culture, these scholars are opening a
dynamic scholarly milieu in which their island and off-island peers and

successors may continue in an alternative to past scholarly traditions. These scholars, still working in the field, have been followed in the twentieth-first century by Carlos Mordo and José M. Ramírez who have each published overviews of the island that include sections on the culture of the island today. At the same time, as this study is grounded in postcolonial pedagogical concerns, it also inserts a voice into the more recent conversation about the island, urging those concerned with the past to realize how the context of their studies have been shaped, and joining those concerned with the present to find ways of carrying forward a reformed memory of the past that acknowledges the violences of imperialism and reinserts the voice of the Rapanui as the authors of their own story.

Reading the World

Such a project invites a rethinking of the terms for the social study of societies distant from one's own. While the analysis of European texts in relation to the invention of Easter Island holds interest for and could be situated within a number of disciplines – for example, history, geography, cultural anthropology, sociology of knowledge, eighteenth-century studies – I have approached this project as a cultural theorist. The interdisciplinarity encompassed by cultural theory creates a space for the study of cultural phenomena through literary theory, sociology, and cultural anthropology, as well as allowing me to draw upon my background as an educator.

With its focus on textual invention, this study required grounding in critical literacy and an examination of the nature of exclusionary violence embedded in word-meaning, diction, and syntax. In his book *Of Grammatology* (first published in 1967 as *De la grammatologie*), Jacques Derrida theorizes violence as an intrinsic aspect of language inherent in writing and formed at the elemental level of the trace. When we read the outside world we are actually doing so through a lens composed of the traces of 'arche-writing' where we have, as a culture, agreed on what we are seeing, an interpretation of what we see. It is the difference in consensus between cultures, about what is being seen and what values to attach to it, that enters into the widely variable responses that people from completely separate cultures may have towards the same object. The outside would not appear to us as it does without our cultural traces, our culturally specific understandings read into objects or behaviours based on temporally situated viewpoints (Derrida 1998, 71).

An extreme example of the difference in consensus can be seen in a historical episode on Easter Island during the nineteenth century. The Rapanui had the only form of writing to originate in Polynesia, a system of hieroglyphics that were carved onto wooden tablets and kept by the islanders as historical records integral to ritual ceremonies. This written language, called Rongorongo, is theorized both to antecede and to follow European contact with the islanders (see Fischer 1997). According to Thomas Croft in 1875, soon after the Catholic missions were established on the island, 'the missionaries persuaded many of their people to consume by fire' all the wooden tablets of Rongorongo in their possession, 'stating to them that they were but heathen records' (Croft 1875, 317, qtd. in Fischer 1997, 14). Fewer than two dozen tablets remain, almost all in European and American museums. Now virtually indecipherable, the memories they signify have been lost, even to the islanders who today meticulously carve replicas to sell to outsiders.

In addition to theorizing the concept of the trace and 'differance,' how the trace is shaped against other traces in order to define its boundaries, Derrida adds the term 'supplementarity,' which contributes to an understanding of the way that the trace/differance forms the basis of the text through which we read ourselves and through which we have tended to read and exclude Others. In fact, Derrida's written text is itself an example of gendered exclusion as he explains the way we use the trace/differance/supplement to define ourselves to ourselves. He writes that 'man allows himself to be announced to himself after the fact of supplementarity, which is thus not an attribute – accidental or essential – of man' (Derrida 1998, 244). Like the trace, supplementarity is neither a presence or an absence, but the play of presence and absence. 'Man *calls himself* man only by drawing limits excluding his other from the play of supplementarity ... The history of man *calling himself* man is the articulation of all these limits among themselves.' As Derrida extends his argument he notes that 'writing' will appear to us more and more as another name for this structure, for supplementarity (244–5).

Although Derrida's concept of reading/writing and the textual or narrative nature of institutions is metaphoric, it does work itself down to the level of reading actual written texts, and the nature of those texts that the West offers its readers (that it writes to itself) to form its impressions of the worlds it finds written therein. As the imperial violence of 'discovering' lands and killing, enslaving, or pushing aside the inhabitants to secure those lands and their wealth for European empires recedes into history, the violence of writing over ancestral pasts and landscapes with European names and absorbing them into a Eurocentric context continues as a legacy of imperialism. Much Eurocentric travel writing that has formed tourist narratives – as well as history and geography texts and literary works grounded in colonialism – has violently redefined and reshaped the non-West to European readers, erasing or writing over Aboriginal Others in the process. The available mainstream texts on what has come to be known throughout the English speaking world as Easter Island, follows this rewriting, as does the mapping of the island itself.

Geographical labels reposition the Aboriginal inhabitants of those global spaces, changing them from being the subjects of their own stories to being the objects or Others in Eurocentric stories. When an island was *discovered* on Easter Sunday in 1722, by the first Europeans to make contact during imperial expansion, the visit was marked by two acts of violence, renaming and gun fire. Three Dutch ships anchored off shore in sight of the island. The next day the commander, Jacob Roggeveen, and 150 men came ashore to be greeted by curious islanders. Thirty muskets were fired, killing ten islanders who ventured close enough to examine the unfamiliar clothes and firearms of the visitors (Englert 1970, 139). The Dutch renamed the location of this encounter Easter Island, and it has been *read* by that name in Euro-America ever since, combining, at first contact, the violence of negating the islanders' own identification of their land with the death of ten. Ironically, the islanders at the time of this first European contact described their location as the centre of the world, but did not have a name for the island per se, while the West has positioned Easter Island in its own narrative as the most remote inhabited place on earth.

The Spanish arrived next, in 1770, fired a cannon into the side of a volcano, and wrote out their own document claiming the island for Spain, a document which they required the Rapanui to sign with their own kind of hieroglyphic writing. Subsequent brief stops at the island by Captain James Cook in 1774 and by J.F.G. de la Perouse in 1776, who only stayed for eleven hours, have resulted in European navigators 'granting' their names to the island bays in which they anchored. Cook's Bay and Bay de la Pérouse have overwritten the islanders' names for those places in all subsequent Western charts and maps of the island.

The Postcolonial Context

The violence of renaming is one overt example of the way this Polynesian island has been constructed in text as a geographic and cultural
imaginary through a temporally situated and long-standing imperial
discourse of European exploration and expansion beyond its own geographic boundaries. In order to more fully explore the historical and
social determinants and consequences of the European construction of
Easter Island, I also frame this study within the poststructural counter-
discourse to imperialism: postcolonialism. Postcolonial theory is
largely a discourse in critical literacy emerging out of Commonwealth
literature studies that has given voice to an expression of resistance
born out of a Eurocentric discourse of exclusion. Through postcolonial
studies, scholars seek to understand the way the imperial frame of
mind has shaped Western culture, history, politics, economics, education, and travel by examining the relations of power within the imperial
project, the textual basis of that power, and the subject positions we
each inhabit in relation to it. It is a discourse grounded in social justice
and transformation as it opens space for understanding the imperial
project, examining the various forms of resistance to it, imagining a dismantling of the unequal power structures it has generated, and envi-
sioning a subsequent restructuring to achieve global harmony in
diversity.

In the literary context, postcolonial theory can be defined as a study
of colonial discursive practices and the various kinds of resistances and
evasions engaged in by writers working to decolonize the imagination.
At the same time, as emphasized by Leela Gandhi (1998), it creates a
space in the academy for non-Western critics to present their 'cultural
inheritance as knowledge' (ix), and it also serves to reveal the invisible
codings of the dominant ideology under which the Western world
lives.

One aspect of current educational theorizing in the West focuses on
the extent to which postcolonial theory might inform and reshape pedagogy. Canada, as a diverse collective of peoples sharing space as a
result of colonialism, has a vested interest in this examination. In her
keynote address, 'Postcolonial Pedagogy and Curricular Reform'
(1997), Diana Brydon creates a useful framework from which to open
up a discussion of the broad implications and possibilities for a Canadian postcolonial pedagogy. While Brydon emphasizes postcolonialism's function in trying to make sense of literary work in the world, she

also prompts educators to examine how knowledge is constructed in other fields and how it can be decolonized. The postcolonial discourse can create a space to enable a 'rethinking of national belongings and multicultural interactions,' helping to expose the binary of centre and Other that still shapes the Canadian national model (4). At the same time, Brydon points to the need to respect each other's alterity, rather than yearn for a coercive blending of diversity.

My thinking has been that a case study examining the constructed geographic and cultural imaginary of Easter Island in a Canadian educational context would, for example, provide a parallel to the Eurocentric–Aboriginal binary of centre and Other. Such a parallel holds the possibility of opening a space for the recognition of the constructed nature of, and therefore transformable power differential in, the Canadian national model. This Easter Island case study, in a travel context, could also prompt a rethinking of how, as Brydon says, 'first world countries interact with countries internationally' (4) and how the placement or displacement of a country within the current global system of power takes place (5). It could also expose the contemporary imposition of neocolonialism over the vestiges of nineteenth-century colonialism. Whether inside the classroom or in the broader public arena, this case study could have a transformative pedagogical impact.

Brydon outlines limits to the postcolonial discourse and points out that one form of postcoloniality is not appropriate to all locations. A colonial settler society like Canada, formed on the indigenous lands of the First Nations, cannot work from the same postcolonial model as a country like India that had a limited interlude of colonial administration within a much longer recorded cultural history. For this reason, a county's definition of its postcoloniality will determine the focus of its postcolonial pedagogy (5), and determine the sort of case studies that might be engaged to direct that focus.

The position of a country within the current global system of power is another consideration Brydon cites in defining what form postcolonial pedagogy should take. As Gayatri Spivak (1993) has pointed out, the United States, with its own revolutionary end to colonial rule, has seen itself as an international saviour, particularly since the end of the Second World War (275). This identity is being played out now by the United States in its stance on the 'war on terrorism.' Articulating a postcoloniality within this neocolonial location would form a daunting task dissimilar to, but with implications for, a Canadian postcolonial pedagogy.

With such vastly different locations as Canada, India, and the United

States as sites for postcolonial pedagogy, it is evident why each location must 'test its goals against the needs' of its students and its local communities. While postcolonial pedagogy is developing a complexity that allows it to articulate discrete formations for each location where it is invested, it is still an incompletely formed entity, still 'articulating its goals' which are 'still being defined' (Brydon 1997, 5). From a central academic position it can shape the whole curriculum 'from classroom interaction and curricular change to the role of the University in the world' (1). Through this process it is moving outside its original literary mandate to discover 'more nuanced understandings of what has happened and is happening in our world as the relations of the local and the global are being reconfigured' (5).

Leela Gandhi, in her introduction to *Postcolonial Theory* (1998), also speaks to postcolonialism's need for diversification in its academic 'mode of address.' She is concerned that it 'learn to speak adequately to the world that it speaks for.' Gandhi sees postcolonialism as needing 'to acquire the capacity to facilitate a democratic colloquium between the antagonistic inheritors of the colonial aftermath' (x). She sees that a way out may be achieved by 'thinking rigorously about our pasts' (9). For her, history is the discourse 'through which the West has asserted its hegemony over the rest of the world ... Western philosophy, at least since Hegel, has used the category of "history" more or less synonymously with "civilization" – only to claim both of these categories for the West, or more specifically for Europe.' Gandhi points out that 'Western Imperialist expansion has all too often been defended as a pedagogical project of bringing the "underdeveloped" world into the edifying condition of history.' In this project, history becomes the 'grand narrative on which Eurocentrism is "totalized" as the proper account of all humanity' (170–1). For Gandhi, a postcolonial engagement with the discipline of history should take as strong a place as its literary counterpart in the academy. While both literature and history are important postcolonial academic sites, an argument implicit in this project is that postcolonial discourse needs to move beyond each of them to be as all-encompassing as the imperial project against which it directs its voice.

Most of the focus of postcolonial pedagogy is in the university and there is an understandable desire to continue shaping this significant discourse at that level as it increasingly exposes the imperial web that spins us. However, there must be recognition of the fact that postcolonial study, kept as an academic discipline, cannot help but comfortably maintain, create a space for, and reproduce its own middle-class sensibilities. The academy tends to draw upon and produce participants in the middle class. Postcolonial study, for such students, may either appease ancestral guilt for colonial practices and privileges or may justify claiming a place in the same power-base created and maintained by colonial privilege. As long as postcolonialism is kept as a discourse within the academy, whether exclusive to English literature or exported to other discourses, it will maintain and reproduce for itself middle-class privilege at the level of theory. It is by developing a postcolonial pedagogy, moving from a theory to actual *practice* at the level of action for social change in primary and secondary public education, that students from all socio-economic levels will have an opportunity to be exposed to, and participate in, cultural awareness and transformation.

Broad Educational Implications of Imperialism

Edward Said, in *Culture and Imperialism* (1993), and John Willinsky, in *Learning to Divide the World* (1998), have mapped out major aspects of the relationship of imperialism to the development of Western thought in a way that implicates more than literature and history in the imperial enterprises of the West. Said has demonstrated that 'many of the most prominent characteristics of modernist culture, which we have tended to derive from purely internal dynamics in Western society and culture, include a response to the external pressures on culture from the *imperium*' (188). Willinsky has detailed just how Western culture developed in tandem with the European explorers and 'discoverers,' from the first crisis of realizing that the world existed in a form different from that depicted by the thirteenth-century Mappa Mundi, to the 'studying, classifying, and ordering' of land, flora, fauna, and humanity 'within an imperial context' giving 'rise to peculiar and powerful ideas of race, culture, and nation.' Willinsky's work is of particular interest to a mapping of postcolonial pedagogical issues because he goes on to explain how the West used its new-found knowledge to 'divide up' and 'educate the world' according to the version of it that they had constructed (2–3).

Willinsky demonstrates the consequences of how 'a few of the cognitively adventuresome scholars' of the fifteenth century recognized that in the exploits and booty of the explorers and discoverers was 'such an amassing of new evidence' that it afforded 'an opportunity for rethinking what this earth was and could now be' (24). Postcolonialists today,

having recognized the extent to which scholarship itself has been constituted within Western ideology, once again recognize the opportunity
for rethinking how we see the world and how the world could be. For
this reason there is an urgency to develop the postcolonial discourse as
widely as possible, beyond literary studies, to articulate the reforms
needed in Euro-American scholarship as well as to reform the Euro-
American vision of the world. Postcolonial scholars are grappling with
the place for, and the scope of, postcolonial discourse within the academy and beyond.

Brydon (1997) has questioned whether postcolonialism should continue to be located in university English departments and urges its connection with issues of global capitalism and poststructuralism (5).
Spivak (1993) calls for its yoking to the social sciences and the idea of
making postcolonialism a core of a transnational study of culture (277).
Because of the capacity of the postcolonial discourse to articulate and
expose the power structures of dominant Western ideology and to
mesh with other cultural discourses, it is in flux, moving from its place
as a discrete subset of academic literary studies to providing a context
and a vocabulary for a rethinking of all tertiary as well as primary and
secondary education. But in spite of its capacity to encompass the pedagogical whole, the postcolonial discourse is itself a contested site as its
theorists strive to contain its energies while they continue to refine their
insights and deconstructive techniques.

A Pedagogy of Remembrance within a Postcolonial Project

Roger I. Simon (1994) has theorized a pedagogy of remembrance that
explores ways to engage and respond to violent historic events that
form collective public memories in order to actively engage the memories of those events to work towards a transformed collective future.
His teaching strategies complement the transformative aims of postcolonial pedagogy. The first involves engaging historically situated social
memories that have been constructed by one culture and that form a
false basis of communal existence (131). Engaging such historical representations can take place at all levels from contesting the terrain of
national identities and 'the public legitimacy of institutions,' based on
Eurocentric 'social truths,' to engaging the representation of specific
episodes in local history (132). As well as proposing specific strategies
for students to engage large-scale social and historical constructions,
Simon offers a strategy for individuals to listen to their interior re-

sponses when they hear the testimony of displaced Others, such as peoples of the First Nations of Canada. Settler Canadians and more recent immigrants who have internalized colonial rhetoric and think of Canada as a new land, for example, can listen to Aboriginal testimony to find the space between their 'Canadian public memory' and the testimony they witness. Through an attentive listening, or 'summoned sensibility' – a willingness to listen openly, to respond, and to 'accept co-ownership of the testimony witness' – Canadians can reconstruct their own understanding of history (R. Simon 20001, 70–5), moving from an unconscious colonial mindset to a postcolonial one (see also Haun 2004).

I position my case study of the invention of Easter Island within this ongoing dialectic between the deconstructive practices of Derridian poststructuralism, postcolonial discourse across different disciplines engaged at different levels of education, and the discourse of transformative pedagogical practices aimed at shaping a hopeful future. I see the need for identification of the ways we are all situated in relation to imperialism and its aftermath, and the need for all curriculum to be held up to an ongoing scrutiny of the ways it is implicated in, resists, or opens up an alternative (supplementary) space to the imperium. As part of the development of such a postcolonial pedagogical space, I think there is value in identifying the contemporary and ongoing implications of imperialism by working first through a topic in which few have a close personal investment – a site where immediate identifications as victims or with guilt is less likely to impede engagement with the case study. Easter Island should offer such a case and open such a space.

Interdisciplinary Terminology and Conventions

An element from my humanities background, which has a central place in my understanding of the way the island was taken up by the eighteenth-century explorers, grows out of the discourse of the *sublime* that is part of a literary and artistic tradition extending back to the discursive traditions of classical Greece. Versions of its literary and visual currency inform the subject of Easter Island and are still extant in contemporary visual and narrative expression today. An exploration of the influence of the *sublime* on the artist who composed images of Easter Island for post-voyage publication, and on the society that read those images, informs a substantial part of the argument for the ways in which the narrative of Easter Island is so often implicated with notions of awe and mystery.

Because of the interdisciplinary nature of this project, I have also found that concepts I call upon to analyse explorer texts, concepts that are historically situated and normalized in one academic field, have been taken up as theoretical terms in another. For instance, the idea of *performance* is central to my analysis. The explorers sailed into the Pacific from within clearly defined roles and senses of entitlement shaped through their hierarchical, patriarchal, and Euro-supreme societies. The Rapanui, with their isolated geographic position, performed within the dictates of their island society where all interaction, for a thousand years, was apparently intra-island. The explorer journals and ethnographic texts that narrate the first intercultural encounters require analysis of the social performances that each group brought to their initial encounters in order to attempt to unravel the nuanced permutations of these invented narratives.

Through the sweep of Western literary tradition, the idea of human actions, reactions, equivocations, and dissemblings are understood and described through terminology associated with ideas of performance, performance spaces, and conscious or unconscious motivations and impulses dictating those behaviours. This performance terminology has travelled forward, in large part, from the British Renaissance where it is embedded in the works of William Shakespeare, best exemplified by Jaques's speech in *As You Like It* that begins, 'All the world's a stage, / and all the men and women merely players' (2.7.139–40).[1]

A complementary exploration of the ideas of performance to that in the Western literary tradition is taken up through feminist poststructural theory; specifically, for the purposes of this study, through the work of Dorothy Smith and Bronwyn Davies. I rely on Smith's ideas, in *Writing the Social: Critique, Theory, and Investigations* (1999), about the situatedness of all knowledge and therefore all practice as embedded in specific social space and place, and thus governed by specific historic relations and systems of power. I borrow and adapt Davies's 'category maintenance,' from *Frogs and Snails and Feminist Tales: Preschool Children and Gender* (1989), where she theorizes this term to describe the early childhood process of developing and maintaining one's reading of sociocultural-specific gender roles in order to fit one's assigned place in the social structure. I adapt Smith's and Davies's ideas in my analysis of the eighteenth-century encounters between European and Rapanui, engaging their terminology with that from my humanities background as I work towards an understanding of the very different specific social dynamics at odds in those encounters. I consider how the performance of each culture's specifically and locally situated social roles were misread across cultures to show how these misreadings shaped the ways each culture took up the Others in their subsequent cultural records of the encounters. Out of these analyses, subjectivity rather than narrative truth is understood as the one constant variable in all texts, both historical and contemporary.

Part of that subjective variability is located between the idea of the trace and the idea of performance. In each iteration of Easter Island or in each representation of moai (island statues), there is a slight displacement of the 'original,' or a large displacement, depending upon the other discursive variables that shape the agency of the individual retracing the subject. It is in these instabilities that the space for new meaning is opened up and change occurs and can occur, slightly shifting or redirecting both the idea of a subject and the attitudes one has available to think or rethink a subject. It is in this space of textual instability and possibility for changing performance that the final portion of this study is situated.

Responding to the Challenge

This project has a broad and a specific context. Rapa Nui, because of its small size, finite period of habitation, centuries of isolation from contact with outsiders, and the compact body of scholarly writing about it, serves as a case study for posing broad questions about the ways our knowledge of particular geographic spaces, distant from assumed centres of civilization, has been shaped. This project encompasses the way the textual construction of the geographic and cultural imaginary, during the period of imperial expansion, is consistent with the frameworks that shape thinking about the space and place of Others in, and in relation to, contemporary Western societies. At the same time, this is a case study of Rapa Nui itself, and the specific ways in which imperialism has been and continues to be positioned in relation to it. In both the broad and specific context, the imperial West takes centre stage in the story of Rapa Nui and of Easter Island that the West tells itself.

In *Learning to Divide the World* (1998), John Willinsky identifies the broad implications of the way imperialism has 'taught' the South Seas. He points out that our education system has been shaped through that same imperialism in such a way that it frames knowledge of Others through an 'anthem of detachment' sanctioned by a 'right to know others,' and we are left with the very idea of 'ourselves as knowing others better than they know themselves.' This superior knowledge has become 'part of Western identity and license.' Willinsky goes on to point out that, through this imperial education, we have come to 'know' the people of the Pacific as 'savages and primitive.' With the 'West ... turning to the Pacific as its next new world of opportunity,' educators have a special responsibility to teach with this construction in mind, to make visible the framework of imperialism that has shaped the Pacific story in the West. We need to relearn the region through a newly aroused postcolonial consciousness (262). A consideration of how education can be conducted through a framework of postcolonial immersion is the focus of the last part of my study, an exploration of possible forms of liberation from imperial knowledge constraints.

Those of us involved with education are in a position either to reinscribe established ways of knowing the world and performing our social selves or to resist those knowledges in a dance of point and counterpoint across time. I believe that formal education today can be a dynamic site for that dance. It is possible within a framework of metacognition in education at all levels, as teachers and as students, to learn to engage imperial forms of knowledge about the world at the same time as we hold open a space to critique their constructed nature. In the process of our continuing educations, we can write back to established texts and write over old narratives with new ones that will actively engage the possibilities of social justice and equity. Through this process we can work towards replacing the old paradigms of suppression and power.

There are three discrete parts to this study. The first part, which is chapter 2 examines the 'Forces at Play' that generated the explorers' texts and allowed the development of some versions of the island canonical authority while denying authority to others. From this selective shaping, I show how the idea of the island that moved forward from the eighteenth century emerged as a discrete subject, to be taken up by other discourses through the ensuing two centuries and into the present.

In the second part, made up of chapters 3 to 6, 'The Dutch,' 'The Spanish,' 'The British,' and 'The French,' I analyse the texts and images published after each expedition with particular focus on the ones that reached an English-speaking audience through translation. It is these texts that have contributed to the English language iterations of the island through intertextual responses. The course of other language manipulations in the process of inventing Easter Island, whether in Spanish, French, Dutch, or otherwise, fall outside the purview of this study, in part because the English language dominates present perceptions of the island.

In these explorer texts, I identify those historically and culturally situated perceptions that have attained staying power as narrative 'truths' about the island, its culture and people and trace them through to their continuing expression in contemporary texts. In particular, I am concerned with the inherent violence of the subjective construction of the Rapanui in these Eurocentric texts and images that shape them through cross-cultural judgment and exclusion. By an analysis of these records, I bring into focus the symbolic violence inherent in the imperial project and how that project continues to shape contemporary understanding of Rapanui culture. The nature of the dominant culture's points of view has been to suppress the views of Others. The island has been created as a subject through the 'shaped truths' of explorers and scientific researchers writing, drawing, and collecting for public consumption. While these texts were originally viewed as empirical data collection, I contest them through poststructural and postcolonial discourse to demonstrate their discursively constructed nature, a nature revealed through the influences that shaped them, as well as through the visions they conjure.

In the third part, chapter 7, 'Cultural Imaginary to Cultural Memory,' I am concerned with the active cultural memory of the island carried as part of Euro-American historical consciousness; the versions of Easter Island that have been learned and absorbed through texts and images. In this chapter I consider how the imagined island continues to be sustained through its repeated retracing at the same time as new narratives are formed that reflect contemporary concerns such as environmental sustainability.

In the final chapter, 'An Educational Supplement,' I turn to the implications of these long-term effects circulating and evolving across time both for the Rapanui and for others living within the grip of imperial cultural memory. I focus on possibilities for reshaping the imagined island in order to transform public imagination and hold public memory accountable to past deeds. I explore how to trouble the comfortable and uncontested space of power and authority of the disciplines implicated in the production of knowledge about and understanding of the island, by opening up a space from which to hold awareness of this imperial shaping at the same time as we are dismantling and renegotiating it. In such a space of postcolonial immersion, we should also be able to expose the construction and nature of the subject positions we have assumed and the ones we have created for the Rapanui as Others. To do so I bring John Willinsky's call for a postcolonial pedagogical supplement into conversation with Roger Simon's theorizing of a methodological framework from within which to consider the relationship between versions of history and personal and public transformative responses to them. Derrida's idea of the supplement is extended and given practical application through this conversation in relation to Emmanuel Levinas's ethics of responsibility in the individual encounter, and Robert Bernasconi's intersection of that ethics with the political in third party encounters.

The way Euro-Americans currently imagine Easter Island does not create space for the recognition of their culpability in the past trauma and current subjection of real people. In fact, it prevents that trauma from being presented and expressed. The perpetual retelling of the imperial story also secures the staging of a particular, limited Euro-America performance and agency. This is an agency grounded in the social repetition and rearticulation of imperial narratives about Easter Island suffused with particular interpretations and omissions of remembrance across boundaries of time, space, and identification. Intercultural relationships can be reformed when we relinquish the assumed right to consume or write over the space and culture of others, whether as scholars, tourists, or global citizens conscious of our interpenetrating social environments.

2 Forces at Play

European 'Discovery' Texts of the Eighteenth Century

Easter Island is geographically remote from other centres of population, even from other South Pacific islands. We know the island as a geographic imaginary conjured through the texts and images of authors and artists, photographers and filmmakers separate from us in time and space. Even the name Easter Island was bestowed by the world outside the island culture. It is the name Jacob Roggeveen gave the island at the point of European 'discovery' in 1722, and by which it has continued to be known in Europe, the Americas, and particularly in Chile, which annexed it (Isla de Pascua) in 1888. The inhabitants had specific names for every part of the island, but no fixed name for the island as a whole because, in their isolation, there were no Others for them to define themselves against. On the island there is a specific spot that is now, for tourists, called 'Te Pito O Te Henua,' which means the centre or navel of the world. The name Rapa Nui was given to the island by Polynesians from other Pacific islands in 1862 when Rapa Nui was used as a staging ground by Peruvian slave raiders who were gathering Polynesians and holding them there for eventual transport to servitude in Peru. Rapa Nui has been used on the island ever since for self-identification.

The subject of the island was written into textual existence for Europeans by those first Dutch explorers who visited it and chose to publish stories of their experience for profit. Later explorers added to the subject writing from within their voyage mandates, during the days of eighteenth-century imperialism in the Pacific, to narrate their experience for publication, however brief that experience may have been. In fact, none of the four eighteenth-century expeditions to the island stayed for very long. The Dutch went ashore for part of one day, the Spaniards three times over three days. The British spent two days touring the island and the French stayed ten hours. These explorers voyaging for commercial, expansionist, scientific, and, in the case of the French, philanthropic reasons, briefly visited, interacted with, and reacted to the islanders, and then presented their understanding of the physical island, the people, their agricultural production and their culture to a European audience.

The subject of the island has been rewritten and written over many times since these four eighteenth-century expeditions. While such texts and images broadcast information to readers about a seemingly fixed place, they are actually positioning a subject, a language construction, in a context of the values and interests of the describers, and, in so doing, they shape a verbal island reality in response to their own cultural values, sense of self, and perceived place in the world. Understood in this way there is no true account of Easter Island. All texts are unstable constructions. All 'information' about the island is a version filtered through the perceptions and evaluations of the writers.

Eighteenth-century texts shaped Easter Island from within several intersecting discourses: androcentrism, imperialism, Enlightenment rationalism, nationalisms, and specific class points of view. Through these intersecting discursive orbits the writers perceived, understood, classified, and shaped versions of the island and culture they explored. Most of the hegemony of these discourses probably worked below the surface of consciousness governing the reality of the explorers, absorbed and subsumed into the mariners' cultural essence, emerging as the truths of their time as they constructed their texts and images for readers and viewers.

It is not the island of Rapa Nui, or the culture of the Rapanui, but the inventing of Easter Island in explorer texts, its construction as a site of collective imaginative enquiry and as a cultural topos, that is the focus of this analysis. In chapters that follow, I will examine the explorer texts that began to circulate after the first Dutch voyage of 1722 and continue through the texts of the Spanish, British, and French expeditions that followed. Such texts increased in quantity and circulation as the century progressed and the European demand for Pacific voyage information grew. These texts invite the reader to imagine the physical and cultural landscape of Easter Island. They shape it as a separate entity divided off imaginatively from the rest of Polynesian culture.

Scholarly interest in Easter Island has tended to be focused on the archaeological past and not on the past European record of contact. Popular texts usually begin with reference to Jacob Roggeveen's 'discovery date' of 1722, starting their narratives with what would seem to be the first European publication about the island. In fact, Roggeveen's own journal was not published until 116 years after his voyage of exploration. The first European record of the island was actually provided by two separate but related publications, both transcribing the oral recollections of an anonymous sailor from the Roggeveen expedition, followed by the publication of a text by a literate German soldier, Carl Behrens, who hired on for the voyage (Anonymous 1727; Anonymous 1728; Behrens 1739). These accounts were circulated through reprints and translations, and formed the European idea of the island that the subsequent three eighteenth-century expeditions took with them, already pre-shaping their response to what they would see and how they would react. By going back to these earliest texts and tracing their influences, the European subject of Easter Island can be observed in its formation.

In the textual Easter Island of the explorers, the shaping of a people and a space can be seen against the assumptions, values, and requirements of authors constituted, first and foremost, by the imperial discourses that governed their nations and that shaped their sense of self or personal performance in relation to that nation. Edward Said, in *Orientalism* (1994), described such discursive acts as 'a dynamic exchange between individual authors and the larger political concerns of their nations and institutional sponsors in whose intellectual and imaginative territory the writing was produced' (15). Of the four voyages of discovery that produced texts, the three from the Dutch, British, and French expeditions are accompanied by images that were turned into stylized engravings according to the conventions current during each expedition. These engravings served to fix widely differing visual ideas of Easter Island in the minds of the reading public.

While more than one person from each of these voyages kept a written account of their experiences, it was the leaders of each voyage who were responsible for writing the logs that included reports about the visits to the island. And it was the expedition leaders' journals that were invested with the most authority for accurately recounting the new 'worlds' that were encountered. Their texts were preordained for publication and contested the publications by the lower-ranking Dutch mariners that preceded them, as chapter 3 on the Dutch expedition will explain in detail.

The archiving of the subject Easter Island follows a shifting temporal arc. It begins with an ever increasing reading public eager for voyage texts. Any mariner who had an exceptional story to tell about his adventures in the South Seas might be able to obtain remuneration for his narrative. Since few seamen were literate, such narratives were usually written by those in the upper echelons of the hierarchical command system. In tension with these sensational tales were two other textual urgencies growing out of the buccaneer tradition of the seventeenth century, but still lingering in the early eighteenth. One related to the official commercial reports of the leaders of expeditions who may have found sources of 'foreign' wealth they desired to keep exclusively for their companies and thus secret from the general public; the other related to the desire of nations to proclaim in print their newly acquired possessions or their primary access to new knowledge – geographical and cultural imperialism. We see these forces play out sequentially in the texts producing Easter Island, written in the context of the first four expeditions. While the publishing history of the texts from these expeditions will be examined in detail in subsequent chapters, a brief rehearsal is needed here to situate them in relation to the forces that have led to their acceptance into or rejection from the canonical archive of Easter Island scholarship.

The first three publications about the island, by low-ranking mariners on the Dutch expedition, eluded Dutch commercial authorities and were rushed into print and subsequently into translation. The official leaders' journals from this voyage, that of Admiral Roggeveen and of the ship captains in his expedition, were not released and printed until a century later. Yet with their publication, the first 'unofficial' accounts were rejected and the leaders' accounts were canonized. This investment in the authenticity of leaders' journals, as carrying the most truth about the island encounters, is bound up in two complementary value systems governing the production and authorization of knowledge texts during the eighteenth century and still extant today. One system harks back to the Middle Ages and the scholars known as 'The Schoolmen.' The other emerged from the scientific model expounded by Francis Bacon in the *New Atlantis*.

The Schoolmen, as described by Margaret Drabble in *The Oxford Companion to English Literature* (2000), were scholars who worked from the schools or universities of Italy, France, Germany, and England as Europe emerged from the 'dark ages.' They attempted to reconcile 'Aristotle with the Scriptures, and Reason with Faith' (892), cleaving to the few texts from antiquity that they valued as embodying the collective wisdom of their ancestors, the writings of the Greek philosophers and the Bible (874). In *The Frame of Order: An Outline of Elizabethan Belief Taken from Treatises of the Late Sixteenth Century* (1957), James Winny explains that the Schoolmen, whose philosophy the sixteenth century inherited, were more concerned to determine the hierarchical 'relationships and correspondences which bound together universal creation than to ascertain the true nature of any single part of it' (14). The end of their enquiry was not to know the material nature of things; it was to understand, through the relationship of one thing to another, the purpose of each thing in the whole scheme of Creation (14). As the sixteenth century gave way to the seventeenth, the graded 'steps of the hierarchies [were] never overlooked; but interest seems to have moved from the details of the design to the simple fact of its existence' (15). The medieval frame of order that the Schoolmen expounded was internalized and normalized, constituting the authoritative background shaping the understanding of experience even as new ways of understanding and knowing the world were taking form. Intellectual authority as to what constituted knowledge also followed the doctrines of the Schoolmen and looked to the credentials of the author as an indication of textual authority. The higher the rank of an individual, the greater the belief in the truth of his text.

During the Renaissance a second discourse of authority arose out of Bacon's 'scientific inquiry model,' fused with the discursive system that valued text from the 'highest authority.' Foucault, in *The Archaeology of Knowledge and The Discourse on Language* (1972), describes the parameters of this authoritative schema that merged the frame of order with the collection of facts as the 'will to knowledge' (218). This is not to say that the captains' logs met these standards of scientific rigour, but they achieved official authority by virtue of being the observations and interpretations of the 'ranking officers.' The effect of these discursive values for the emergence of the subject of Easter Island has been to honour the content of some accounts over others and, in the process, develop a selective representation and understanding of the Rapanui culture that has consequently served as the basis of contemporary narrative 'truths' about the island. Even in the fantastical distortions of Erich Von Daniken's *Chariots of the Gods?*,[1] in which he attributes the island culture to space aliens, the power of the values of the hegemonic centre assert themselves to shape the story.

Writing Variables

In each of the eighteenth-century voyage texts of the island, several writing variables intersect to shape a particular vision of the physical and cultural space. The first variable was the purpose for the voyage. The Dutch West Indies Company sought the discovery of a Pacific continent and hoped for new lands that might yield riches. The Spanish under Carlos III wished to claim the island as a strategic location for overseeing their trade routes through the Pacific to Manila, routes they felt were in jeopardy from the increased traffic of other European nations (Dos Passos 1971, 23). The British were interested in potential new commodities as well as new customers for trade goods in tandem with an expansion of knowledge and empire. The French voyage was similar to, and in some ways in response to, the British. It sailed for commercial and Enlightenment reasons, travelling very self-consciously to improve upon the work of other explorers in the mapping of the Pacific and to present the French nation, to themselves, to the rest of Europe, and to the people of the Pacific, in the best possible light. The French visit to Easter Island was, in part, a response to the impoverishment of the inhabitants reported by James Cook, published after his return to England, and then translated and published for a French audience. The French expedition was a dramatic early example of how texts – in this case that of James Cook, which was only the second voyage to gain broad public circulation – shaped future responses to the island.

A second important variable to shape the island narrative was the anticipated audience for the report. The primary audience was often the institution that bore the costs of mounting the expedition, followed by the expectation of a wider audience after the voyage journals and logs were edited and illustrated with engravings after the manner of the time, a manner that shifted during the course of the eighteenth century largely as a result of the drawings executed on the voyages of discovery. As Bernard Smith explains in *Imagining the Pacific: In the Wake of the Cook Voyages* (1992), particularly significant were those images of James Cook's voyage by William Hodges, the artist who accompanied him to Easter Island (37). These stylistic conventions that the images were shaped through, when interpreted by the engravers for publication, ultimately affected the vision the public received of the island culture. There was a considerable disjunction between the sketches made in charcoal or crayon on the island, themselves invariably shaped by the 'artistic school' of the artist, and the eighteenth-century conventions of the institutions that trained the engravers who turned those sketches into stylized illustrations for the published texts (72). As shall be shown in the chapters on individual expeditions, the impact of these artistic conventions on the perception of the island was great and has had far-reaching reverberations.

Another variable shaping the perceptions of the explorer-writers was determined by the physical needs of each expedition at the time of their arrival at the island. Even within one expedition, the initial purpose of a voyage, such as the quest for the discovery of a large continent in the Pacific, could end up competing with the practical needs of the crew by the time they arrived at the island, needs such as taking on fresh food, water, and firewood required for cooking fuel. The public purposes of the early expeditions, competing with the needs of the officers and crew by the time the ships arrived, altered the point of view of that particular voyage's valuation of the island, a point recognised at the time and commented on by the leader of the fourth voyage, Jean François Galaup de la Pérouse. In his own voyage journal, La Pérouse wrote of the British expedition that preceded his and to which he wrote back:

> ... but since man is a being who, above all others, can adapt to every situation, these people [the islanders] seemed to me to be less unfortunate than they did to Captain Cook and Mr. Forster. They [the English] had reached this island after a long and painful voyage, short of everything, sick of the scurvy; and they found no water, no wood, no pigs; a few hens with some bananas and potatoes are a very meagre comfort in such circumstances and their accounts reflect their situation. Ours was immeasurably better; our crews were in the best of health; we had obtained in Chile all we could need for several months, and all we wanted from these people was the opportunity of doing them some good: we were bringing them goats, ewes, pigs; we had seeds for orange lemon trees, cotton and maize and broadly of everything that was likely to succeed in this island. (La Pérouse 1798, 59)

The reference to Cook in the French report is an aspect of the intertextuality in relation to Easter Island that begins with the publications of the initial Dutch expedition. Each subsequent expedition speaks back to the preceding nation's texts, as well as responding to the island through its own ideologies and voyage mission, forming a layer of intertextuality to reinforce, resist or reshape those first narrations as voyage reports accumulated.

This intertextual dialogue with other European explorers served multiple purposes. In the context of the journals of exploration a site was provided where each nation could position itself hierarchically against the islanders as well as rehearse its behaviour towards them, reminding itself in the process of its own national character. As well, the commander could reaffirm his leadership and demonstrate an example of his 'national' self in relation to previous nations' accounts of island contact. The text could then serve as a document to provide an example of the nobility of purpose and refinement of nature that established the explorer's manner and actions as superior in the world both in relation to the natives of the island and to other European nations. These displays of superiority were reinforced through specific instances of self-restraint and the overall ability of the commanders to keep their own lower ranks in order. Such rehearsing of 'correct behaviour' for one's role on the public stage is described by Bronwyn Davies in *Frogs, Snails and Feminist Tales* (1989), as category maintenance, a term that she applies to gender roles but that is adaptable to cover other forms of behavioural practice within prescribed limits. It encompasses language use, physical carriage and manner as well as actions and can be practised in time and space as well as text. Written category maintenance has the added benefit of allowing modification of actual enacted behaviours through the power of the word to reshape events in the telling. The Spanish and French narratives of their encounters on the island are the strongest examples of these displays.

Against the explorer text as a self-conscious indicator and record of national character and supposed superiority can also be seen a sense of Eurocentric entitlement evident in the way each nation carries out its mission on the island. An internalized European sense of superiority is evident in the attitudes towards and treatment of islanders created by these privileging ideologies. Stephen Greenblatt in *Marvellous Possessions* (1991), characterizes this European sense of entitlement, during the age of exploration, as having 'immense confidence in its own centrality,' as having 'a political organization based on practices of command and submission,' and as having 'a willingness to use coercive violence on both strangers and fellow countrymen' (9). This entitlement can be seen in action on Easter Island against both islanders and the lower ranks of sailors and soldiers under command.

The island entered the public imagination in these eighteenth-century texts with a will to rate its potential as a site for exploitation. In each case, the subject first and foremost seems to be more about the authors than the islanders, more about Europe in the Pacific, than about the Pacific itself. The island, though acknowledged as peopled, is treated as a stage upon which text can shape desire, rehearse behaviour, form a background for monetary or noble deeds, and, in more recent texts, shine glory on the Euro-Americans who travel to the island to solve its mysteries.

Before examining these eighteenth-century texts themselves, I want to pursue a critical review of the historical traditions and contexts out of which they were produced. Literary, philosophical, religious, and geographic models, ideas, and tropes shared space and wrote over each other in the travel texts that mapped the routes of Europe into the Pacific. Together they formed the patchwork of overlapping discourses through which the explorers perceived their experience of Easter Island. These interconnecting discursive fragments embody the forces at play that shaped the explorers who in turn shaped the idea of the island in the way that they did. They are links in a discursive chain extending from antiquity through eighteenth-century constructions to modes of representing and understanding the island today.

Textual Authority Carried Forward from Antiquity

These forces at play are inexorably woven through the authority of texts. Jacques Derrida, in *Archive Fever* (1995), offers an overview into the origin of the authority bound up with the acceptance, circulation, and archiving of texts. He explains that the idea of the archive is derived from the Greek word *arkheion* that initially stood for the residence of the 'superior magistrates,' the *archons*, who 'held and signified political power' and made the law. As an aspect of their 'publicly recognized authority,' they were the guardians of official documents that were, in turn, filed in their houses (2). They ensured the physical security of the documents as well as the foundational principles out of which the documents were written, and they were also invested, through their sanctioned position, with the power to interpret those archived texts (2). Similar archiving systems are associated today with public institutions such as libraries, museums, and universities, many growing out of the long eighteenth-century period of Enlightenment and imperialism, where resident authorities, sanctioned in turn by the authority of their institutions, house and interpret the foundational and successive textual records accepted into any given discipline. Entrusted to such *archons*, these documents in effect speak, recall, call on, or impose the laws of their sphere of influence – the subjects and formal discourses they govern.

As well, such texts reveal the subvocal discourses that have shaped epistemes and, in some cases, continue to shape contemporary social and cultural world views and dynamics. It is the cultural acceptance of these institutions and their power both to commission and to accept documents for sanctioned housing or archiving that forms the basis of a text's authority and power. The building in which the texts 'dwell permanently, marks this institutional passage from the private to the public' (Derrida 1995, 2–3). Having been accepted into the archive by such institutions, the documents, which can include written texts, drawings, maps, specimens, and cultural artefacts, are kept, identified, classified, and unified into a single corpus 'under the title of the archive by virtue of a privileged *topology.*' They inhabit this sanctioned space, as Derrida says, 'where law and singularity intersect in *privilege* ... a scene of *domiciliation* ... at once visible and invisible' in a system where 'all the elements articulate the unity of an ideal configuration' (3). This consignment to a sanctioned 'accessible place' assures the 'possibility of memorization, of repetition, of reproduction, or of re-impression' (11), and through these processes of configuration and recirculation, the unity of the subject is reinforced. In the process of unification into a specific archive, a parameter forms around the subject that both contains what has been written into the subject and forms an exclusionary boundary encompassing it. While permeable and plastic, and given to transformation with each iteration over time, the formation of boundaries also controls what is accepted into the archive and what is held without. And what is held without lends the subject as strong a pedagogical influence as what is held within.

As described by Sonia Combe (1994), the nature of the archive from its inception in antiquity has always been 'a patriarchive,' and by its nature as such has never covered all the Others within or outside a given masculine society (4).The historical archive must be understood then, to have developed through time as a series of subject sites that have formed through, normalized, and perpetuated the European male, educated and comfortably classed, point of view. This point of view, inherent in the very fabric of all archived subjects, is central to the authority of the texts that influenced the Europeans travelling to Rapa Nui and is a central part of the authority with which they shaped the texts they produced to describe the island and their experience of its geography and culture.

The European Travel Archive

The discursive authority of travel and exploration archives influenced how the explorers took up the island in text as well as how the mariners' texts were taken up as they reached publication. I would argue that eighteenth-century European voyagers to the Pacific, while exploring and writing through the discursive urgencies of their own era, were still bound to the version of the world prescribed by the Schoolmen. They were venturing out of a number of lingering travel traditions that had carried forward from antiquity. Central among these were ideas about the shape of the world and about the location of an earthly paradise upon it. Subsequent ideologies and new geographic discoveries, in the centuries leading up to Pacific exploration, often accommodated these early classical perceptions rather than completely replacing them. Neil Rennie, in *Far-Fetched Facts: The Literature of Travel and the Idea of the South Seas* (1995), identifies several key texts from classical antiquity that mapped an earthly paradise onto the world through language and laid a foundation that lingered as cultural capital to shape the imaginary geography of Pacific explorers.

In the sixth century BCE, Pythagoras promoted the view, based upon philosophical principle, that the earth was 'spherical and inhabited round about,' a doctrine that was supported by both Plato and Aristotle (Rennie 1995, 1). This point of view carried forward and, in the second-century CE Ptolemy's text *Geograph* also describes a round earth. But four centuries later this idea was being refuted through new doctrines of Christianity, a religious discourse that devised its own geography from a particular interpretation of its central text, the Bible. The Alexandrian Christian, Indicopleustes Cosmas, wrote *Topographia Christiana* (1897), refuting 'globalism' with the biblical evidence that man lives on the 'face of the earth,' thus eliminating the possibility of any more world beyond the surface already known. For Cosmas, there was no point searching for an Antipodes or southern continent. His Christian world was flat (11). Cosmas was, however, in a minority within the scholarly European community of his time. Many less literal Europeans continued, according to Arthur Newton, in *Travel and Travellers of the Middle Ages* ([1926] 1967), to believe in the spherical shape of the world and in the possibility of the Antipodes – '"terra australis nondum cognita," separated from "terra firma" by a great sea and the burning heat of the sun' (8).

Classical literature, as well as classical philosophy, religion, and geography, passed on to future generations a model for travel writing as well as a vision of the world that contained, somewhere upon it, an earthly paradise. Homer's *Odyssey* is a fictional travel tale, a model of the Romance genre 'that relates improbable adventures of idealized characters in some remote or enchanted setting' (Baldick 1990, 191). The *Odyssey* introduces the questing hero Odysseus, a prototype for future sailors' self-image in the narration of his outlandish sea adventures. Odysseus's actions during his voyage exemplify a range of behaviours – actions and reactions performed during trials experienced while venturing into the unknown, trials successfully executed and reported to his own people when he returns home.

Disguise is a part of Odysseus's repertoire as he negotiates his way through the world, holding before the reader a model of travel as performance, traveller as actor engaging Others from within a variety of roles. He is not conceived as recognizably an individual self, but a heroic type, a protagonist resourcefully engaging in travel experiences. The story is not just the cataloguing of what was encountered, but his response to those encounters. This relationship between mariner and experience, modelled in this prototypic tale, will be seen to continue to inform the narrative voice of the travel tales of those exploring the Pacific several millennia in the future – not just a cataloguing of what is there, but a vicarious experience of what it is like to be there. The *Odyssey* also contains the marvellous, 'a category of fiction in which supernatural, magical, or other wondrous impossibilities are accepted as normal within an imagined world clearly separated from our own reality' (Baldick 1990, 129). Neil Rennie (1995), in identifying the central romantic and travel motifs of the *Odyssey*, describes ones quite startling in their similarity to those taken up in part by European writers travelling to the Pacific in the eighteenth century. Each new encounter of Odysseus with strangers raises the question of 'whether they are brutal and lawless savages or hospitable and god-fearing people' (4). The first are often cannibal men, like the giant Cyclops or the giant Laestrygonians, and the latter were typically 'sensual women, enforcers not breakers of the laws of hospitality.' The women threatened the travellers by tempting them to cease travelling and remain on the island of Calypso or Circe and never to return to their home again (4). Both the temptations for male sailors to stay on tropical Pacific islands enjoying female hospitality, and the fear of 'male savages' threatening that stay, merged in the accounts of eighteenth-century European sailors to the Pacific. In particular the men of Rapa Nui, some reaching six and a half feet, were identified by the first Dutch account as giants to be defeated.

The fresco illustrating the Laestrygonians attacking Odysseus's ships from the House of the Esquiline Hill, Rome, circa 50–40 BCE, is an indication of the extent to which the *Odyssey* formed a prototype for future sailors (see fig. 2.1). It provides a visual interpretation of one of his tribulations in the textual narrative. Here we are reminded of the dangers that may befall those who sail into new territory. Note the point of view. The whole scene is framed from the land, not from the perspective of the European travellers arriving by sea. This land-perspective highlights the size and vantage points of the islanders, on home territory, in the foreground as they attack the transient sailors. It is a pictorial convention used by the engraver in the publication of the anonymous sailor's first narrated account of the 1722 Dutch voyage to the South Seas (see fig. 2.2). In this engraving, the islanders also position themselves at a geographic advantage in order to attack the Europeans who have arrived with guns. Both the sloop and the larger ships are at sufficient distance from the landing party to increase the sense of vulnerability and unpredictability that informed the repertoire of sailors as they made landfall on unknown terrain.

Within the context of being a Romance, the *Odyssey* describes an elusive earthly paradise, an 'exclusive home for retired heroes at the furthest limits of the world' (Rennie 1995, 6) where 'the immortals will send you to the Elysian plain at the world's end ... in the land where living is made easiest for mankind, where ... day after day the West Wind's tuneful breeze comes in from Ocean to refresh its folk' (Homer 1945, 78). The idea of an earthly paradise was not unique to Homer. Hesiod, an approximate contemporary of Homer, describing a 'golden race of mortal men' living on 'Blessed Isles' (Rennie 1995, 5), offers another version of Elysium in *Works and Days*:

> ... like the gods they lived with happy hearts
> Untouched by work or sorrow ...
> >   and all good things
> Were theirs; ungrudgingly, the fertile land
> Gave up her fruits unaided.
> >   ... they lived with every want supplied,
> ... The son of Kronos gave [them] life
> And homes apart from mortals, at Earth's edge.
> And there they lived a carefree life, beside
> The whirling Ocean,.on the Blessed Isles. (Hesiod 1998, 62)

The Roman era saw a continuation of the Greek focus on a distant paradise. Ovid, born in 43 BCE, describes a 'Golden Age' in his *Meta-*

Figure 2.1: 'Room of the Aldobrandini Wedding: Odysseus among the Laestry-gonians.' Photo, Vatican Museums.

morphoses, a time and place with an absence of the 'features of civiliza-tion: no laws, no wars, no agriculture, no private ownership of land, no knowledge of iron or gold' (Rennie 1995, 31–3). Rennie has also traced a continuing interest in paradise through philosophy. By the fourth cen-tury CE, the scholar Servius, commenting on the *Aeneid*, stated that 'in the opinion of the philosophers, Elysium is the Blessed Isles' while Horace, in *Odes II*, wrote, 'let us seek the Fields, the Happy Fields, Islands of the Blest ... for righteous folk, ever since with bronze [Jupiter] dimmed the lustre of the Golden Age' (qtd. in Rennie 1995, 6). The con-cept of an earthly paradise as Blessed Isles was not confined to the cul-tures of Southern Europe. As early as the mid-sixth century CE, St Brendan of Ireland was said to have reached the earthly paradise some-where west of his home. This island, called St Brendan's Isle, was some-times confused with the Blessed Isles and was often marked on maps moving ever westward from the advance of geographical knowledge (5). The island was sought by others, but never found again, and became known as Perdita (ibid., 12). It continued to appear on maps as late as 1755 (Newton [1926] 1967, 162).

Figure 2.2: 'The Dutch Landing at a South Pacific Island,' not Easter Island. This engraving illustrates the anonymous Dutch sailor's account of his South Pacific adventures, *Tweejaarige Reyze door do Straat Magellanes en rondom de Wereld ter nader Ontdekkinge der onbekende Zuydlanden* (Dordrecht, Joannes van Braam, 1728) between pages 62 and 63. Courtesy of Special Collections Library, University of Michigan.

Through the cataloguing of early texts, Rennie (1995) demonstrates the way the Greek myth of the Golden Age was blended with other myths, in literature, philosophy and geography, all seeking 'to locate in the geographical present what was [perceived as] lost in a historical past' (5). The classical Golden Age became the 'counterpart of the biblical myth of Paradise, with which it was also blended, and which likewise took a geographical as well as a historical form' (5). The merging of a Golden Age ideal with the Christian concept of an earthly paradise provides necessary background to the eighteenth-century European interactions with Easter Island. The ways the island was perceived and consequently formed into a counter-narrative to the travel tropes of other Pacific 'Blessed Isles' is largely in reaction to the extent to which it disappointed those paradisial expectations and invited reconstruction as a figment of the geographic imaginary.

Texts in the Middle Ages

The desire to locate the imagined earthly paradise in the real geographical present runs through the European history of travel, exploration, and mapping. By the Middle Ages the very orientation of the earth as presented on maps, whether spherical or flat, intersected with the positioning on such maps of the location of paradise. In these images, classical traditions mixed with Christian ones to overlay a model of travel adventure with a map of the world, both combined in the service of finding an ever receding but strongly desired earthly paradise. Iain Higgins, in his 1997 essay 'Representing the New Old World: Some Medieval Europeans on the Far East,' illuminates this practice in his description of the ways Asia, the Pacific, and paradise were positioned within the medieval mind. A 'basic geographical schema inherited from Greeks and Romans' had the medieval world organized into three continents, Europe, Africa, and Asia (37–8) with the Eastern orientation at the top and the Pacific as the outer eastern edge of the map hugging the earthly paradise.

These medieval mapping conventions entered wider public currency with the advent of printing. The first world map to be printed, appearing in 1472, was a seventh-century drawing by St Isidore of Seville known as the *Etymologiarum sive Originum libri XX* (see fig 2.3). It is the first published example of the imposition of both classical and Christian concepts upon the organization of the known and unknown world, and depicts the three continents of Asia, Europe, and Africa, each surrounded by sea and all three surrounded by an ocean. This construction is known as a T-O map for the configuration of the water in relation to the continents. It is also described as a Noachid map (see fig. 2.4) because it divides the three continents among the sons of Noah, 'Shem receiving Asia, Ham Africa, and Japheth Europe' (Higgins 1997, 39). On this map as on so many during the Middle Ages, Jerusalem is centred and the earthly paradise is at the eastern extreme bordering the Pacific Ocean at the top of the map. This T-O map was also translated into three dimensions as a sphere, as seen in portraits of the Holy Roman Emperor Charles V and England's Queen Elizabeth I (see fig. 2.5). 'As they hold the 'rule of orb,' it symbolizes a righteous taking of the world in hand.' The orb or globe had a 'jewel-encrusted band circling the

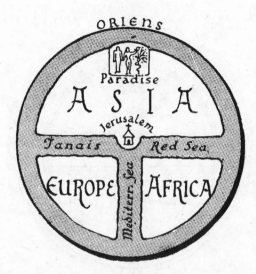

Figure 2.3: St Isidore of Seville. *Etymologiarum sive Originum libri XX*. Modern representation of seventh-century eastern-oriented map featuring paradise. Retrieved 10 June 2005 from *Cartographic Images*, 'Early Medieval Maps: Index of Early Medieval Maps, #205 Monograph,' www.henry-davis.com/MAPS/ Emwebpages/205mono. Courtesy of Jim Siebold.

sphere around the middle and over the top ... with a cross mounted on the top marking Jerusalem' (Yates 1975, 60). Jerusalem at the top would position the earthly paradise at the base. With these three dimensional globes, Europeans would now begin to situate themselves, in imagination, as living on the top of the world.

The position of paradise on maps was reinforced in text. About 1165 there began to be circulated copies of a fictitious letter that was purported to be from Prester John, a mysterious Christian king. It was addressed to the Emperor of Byzantium. The letter referred to paradise as being in the region of Prester John's kingdom in the East. By the fourteenth century that kingdom had moved in myth from a location apparently somewhere in India to somewhere in Ethiopia. This transposition was a consequence of increasing European familiarity with the East, and a failure to find the earthly paradise as more and more of the East was mapped by Europeans. At the same time the transfer speaks to the continuing desire to hold onto a possible future discovery of paradise.

Figure 2.4: St Isidore of Seville, *Etymologiarum sive Originum libri XX*, tripartite or Noachid world map. Retrieved 10 June 2005 from *Cartographic Images*, 'Early Medieval Maps: Index of Early Medieval Maps, #205,' www.henry-davis.com/MAPS/EMwebpages/205mono. Courtesy of Jim Siebold.

Because a Christian world view dominated the Middle Ages, it is understandable that the location of the earthly paradise was of geographical importance. It was the Garden of Eden on earth as well as an otherworldly hoped-for destination. 'The continued existence of the earthly Paradise was, in fact, a matter of orthodox Christian belief ... Until late into the seventeenth century, long after the great age of discovery was well under way, scholars continued to discuss the whereabouts of the terrestrial Paradise' (Manuel and Manuel 1972, 117 qtd. in Rennie 1995, 11). Throughout the Middle Ages, but especially in its last three centuries, European-mapped representations of the world continued to impose 'prevailing theological and historical ideas,' over the classical schema of three continents, creating hybrid classical-Christian topographies (Higgins 1997, 39). On such maps, Jerusalem was placed at the base of Asia in the perfect centre of a circle containing the three continents (Greenblatt 1991, 41). The earthly paradise was placed at the top of Asia bordering the Pacific Ocean. According to this scheme,

Figure 2.5: Portrait of Queen Elizabeth I holding a Christian globe, *Elizabeta D.G. Angliae Franciae Hiberniae et Verginiae Regina*. Print made by Crispijn de Passe the elder (Holland, 1596). © The British Museum RN 1868,0822.853.

'Asia, while largely unexplored, was imagined as old, its spatial distance in effect serving as an analogue to the temporal distance of Christian Europe's purported historical origins' (Higgins 1997, 39).

Yet Asia was also 'new.' Initially, it was new only to the late medieval European merchants and Christian pilgrims who travelled there and 'encountered a world unlike anything they had ever known,' but finally to those who acquired the travel texts of those merchants and pilgrims (Higgins 1997, 39). The two key texts for disseminating ideas about the East were those of the merchant Marco Polo and the travel compilations of the pilgrim persona John Mandeville, both of whose texts were transcribed in the 'vernacular' (ibid.). Marco Polo was able to travel in the Far East because of the 'rapid expansion of the Mongol Empire in the thirteenth century' (Rennie 1995, 13). That Empire brought Europe and the Far East into proximity for the first time, an event Rennie identifies as 'as important for the commerce of the Middle Ages as the discovery of America was for the Renaissance' (ibid.). By 1368, however, the Mongols had been replaced by the Ming Dynasty and access to the Far East was closed off, but not before Marco Polo had aroused an appetite for more information about it through his romantic travel narrative. In his and Mandeville's narratives, the East is described as a world unlike anything they had ever known. Polo's text remarks on 'the absolute difference – the absolute novelty of India,' and Mandeville, who did not actually travel beyond a library writes, 'We could never have believed it if we had not seen it' (Higgins 1997, 39). In both texts there is an emphasis on the kind of wonder associated with the travel romance, wonder about geography, people, and the cultures new to Europe. This emphasis on wonder continues into the Renaissance, foregrounding much sixteenth-century travel writing about the New World, and shapes the initial Dutch travel narrative about Easter Island.

Dame Gillian Beer explains in *The Romance* (1970), that the depiction of wonders and marvels in romance depends to a certain extent on having established a set distance either in time or space between the text's subject matter and its intended audience (6). According to Rennie (1995), Marco Polo did not honestly come by the romantic genre through which his adventures were narrated. On his return from Asia, he fought with the city state of Venice against Genoa and was captured and imprisoned. One of his fellow prisoners, Rustichello, was a romance writer who actually ghostwrote Polo's narrative. In the prologue to his *Travels*, it says, 'Afterwards, in the year of the Nativity of Our Lord Jesus Christ 1298, while he was in prison in Genoa, wishing to occupy his leisure as well as to afford entertainment to readers, he caused all these things to be recorded by Messer Rustichello of Pisa, who was in the same prison' (Polo 1958, qtd. in Rennie 1995, 13). L.F. Benedetto compared Marco Polo's *Travels* with Rustichello's own works and found 'many of the Romance writer's characteristic phrases and narrative patterns ... Whole sections of the *Travels* ha[d] been adapted with little revision, from an Arthurian romance' that Rustichello had written. 'If Polo travelled in the medium of Romance, it was because Rustichello knew the way ... His most important contributions are the characterization of Polo as a knight adventurer, of the Great Khan as a kind of King Arthur, and the portrayal of Polo's Orient as an exotic' realm (Rennie 1995, 14). The trope of the knight-mariner was grafted through the key text of Polo's *Travels* to that of the hero-mariner typified by Odysseus, further forming the model through which the eighteenth-century European mariners navigated their Pacific narratives.

Mandeville's Travels is another text, shaped through the romance genre, that is central in helping to understand the development of the medieval European travel writing tradition. It informed the voyage narratives that followed the discovery and exploitation of the New World in the sixteenth century and the exploration and exploitation of the Pacific in the eighteenth. *Mandeville's Travels* was originally written in the mid-1300s in French from library research rather than actual travel. It also followed the romantic convention of the knight-adventurer, Sir John Mandeville, the protagonist travelling in foreign realms and experiencing the exotic (Rennie 1995, 14). To give an indication of the influence of this text on the European travel narrative tradition, by the middle of the fourteenth century, copies of *Mandeville's Travels* circulated in English, German, Dutch, French, Latin, Spanish, Italian, Danish, Czech, and Old Irish. In fact, even today, 'some three hundred manuscripts survive' (Greenblatt 1991, 30), attesting to the wide exposure of the text as a model of travel writing before the advent of the printing press. In 1499 it was first printed by Wynkyn de Worde as *The Travels of Sir John Mandeville*. In the late sixteenth century, it was still praised and Mandeville was still being called the greatest Asian traveller in the early seventeenth century (ibid.).

The name Sir John Mandeville was actually a pseudonym for the anonymous author of *Mandeville's Travels*. The book compiles the established textual wisdom on all the places he purported to visit and presents them as having been experienced through pious Christian interaction. As a model of medieval European travel experience and behaviour, it combines the two foci evident in previous and subsequent travel narratives. The first is an awareness of the self in performance. The role of hero in the *Odyssey* becomes the role of Christian ambassador in *Mandeville*. Second to this strong sense of the role and performance of the travelling self in the *Mandeville* text is a compendium of geographic and cultural differences combined with wonder at those differences. Stephen Greenblatt (1991) explains the importance to the genre of such travel narratives being more general than specific, more wonder-full than accurate. He says that a 'purely local knowledge, an absolutely singular, unrepeatable, unique experience or observation, is neither desirable nor possible, for the traveller's discourse is meant to be useful, even if the ultimate design in which this utility will be absorbed remains opaque' (3).

That ultimate design is, of course, a pedagogical one, where the reader absorbs lessons on how to think about the self in relation to the outer world rather than to learn the particulars of a people or a region. The relaxed view of accuracy in these accounts is reflected in the texts for general audiences generated · before the late-eighteenth-century period of scientific exploration, and aspects of this 'wonder' travel discourse are in evidence in the first account of Easter Island, narrated by the anonymous sailor. It must be pointed out in passing, although the idea will be developed later, that even as the eighteenth century moves outside of the romance genre of travel tale and also embraces the 'scientific model' aimed at recording particular truths and facts about places and peoples encountered, those scientific texts were still shaped through a discursive space of imperial superiority, one that focuses power and control through language and image that always constructs and positions Others as inferior to Europeans.

Mandeville's Travels is significant for another reason: although Christian in mandate, it relied on several classical texts and helped reform the imagined Christian world from being perceived as a flat disc back into a spherical shape. Before Mandeville, as mentioned previously, the Jerusalem-centred world view positioned all the known world in relation to the Judeo-Christian centre, linking one place to another (Greenblatt 1991, 42) on a flat plane. In Mandeville, 'one place continues to be linked to another, but instead of the solidifying pull towards the centre of the circle, there is a pacing or measuring of the outer rim' (42), and with it the Pacific begins to increase in imaginative prominence. The tension between the centre and the rim is registered in *Mandeville's Travels* by 'the revealing wavering about directions when Mandeville approaches the earthy Paradise, east of the empire of Prester John and depicted as on the far edge of Asia bordered by the Pacific' (ibid.). Mandeville (1915) writes:

> And beyond the land and the isles and the deserts of Prester John's Lordship, is going straight toward the east, men find nothing but mountains and rocks, full great. And there is the dark region, where no man may see, neither by day ne by night, as they of the country say. And that desert and that place of darkness dure from this coast unto Paradise terrestrial, where

that Adam, our formest father, and Eve were put, that dwelled there but little while : and that is towards the east at the beginning of the earth. But that is not that east that we clepe our east, on this half, where the sun riseth to us. For when the sun is east in those parts towards Paradise terrestrial, it is then midnight in our parts on this half, for the roundness of the earth, of the which I have touched to you of before. For the Lord God made the earth all round in the mid place of the firmament ... Of Paradise ne can I not speak properly. For I was not there. It is far beyond. (199–200)

Displacing a world emanating from 'a perfect centre,' Jerusalem, 'Mandeville comes to imagine a world in which every point has an equal and opposite point.' Without a mystical centre, there is 'no longer a unique place of honour' (Greenblatt 1991, 42–3).

While the shift from centre to periphery was an immense conceptual change within the Christian-medieval world, that concept was still absorbed into the larger medieval construction of correspondencies whereby all known matter was organized into a hierarchical schema of order and balance. Therefore, the concept of a spherical world in Mandeville bends to the organizing principle of correspondencies and, as Greenblatt (1991) describes, when you have one landscape on the sphere, 'you always have the shadowy presence of another, when you glimpse one artefact, you conjure up its strange simulacrum somewhere else, and when you invoke one text, you hear the echo of another' (43). The search for a Southern continent to correspond to the northern landmasses begins to be imagined out of *Mandeville's Travels*, and the discovery of what seemed to be earthly paradise in the islands of the Pacific required their own non-paradisial counterpoint. This was constructed as Easter Island.

The era of limited travel drew to a close through technological innovations in the fifteenth century and provided an impetus to increased travel and travel writing. 'New developments in shipbuilding and navigation opened up previously unthinkable possibilities for [European] sea travel' (Higgins 1997, 34), and the advent of the printing press encouraged a growth in literacy and a subsequent increase in the desire to purchase texts. The expanding reading public also increased the demand for texts in regional vernaculars instead of in Latin, the language of the Church and scholarship (ibid.). At the same time, printing began to stabilize certain vernaculars that came to dominate regionally as the Renaissance progressed, becoming what we think of today as the national languages of various parts of Europe. Printing also offered the possibility of making 'one's name' through publishing, as well as making money, by 'catering to the new reading public's taste' (ibid.). Both were developments that carried forward and would shape the writing and publishing drive of Pacific explorers in the eighteenth century.

The idea of paradise at the far reaches of the Pacific was an idea of long standing for the explorers who headed for that ocean in the eighteenth century. As Alan Smith explains in *Bright Paradise: Exotic History and Sublime Artifice* (2001), 'already in possession of a sense of that distant continent drawn from ancient historians, the Bible, and what geographers had produced, they diligently integrated the "new" things they saw into the frame provided by this "old" and venerable knowledge ... thus creating a "chronotopic" device which brought together elements across both time and space' (20). Even whole new continents being added by these explorers, resulting in the creation of 'increasingly sophisticated maps of new and distant worlds, did remarkably little to disrupt what for the European mind was the oldest of global divisions' (Willinsky 1998, 137).

By the eighteenth century, European explorers were able to configure the just-discovered Polynesian islands in terms of the familiar expectation of what to find in the Pacific, thus assimilating the Asian/Pacific to the historic ideas of paradise (A. Smith 2001, 20). As the eighteenth-century explorers, particularly the British expeditions of James Cook, visited island after island in the tropical regions of the Pacific and found lush vegetation and abundant food, they continually wrote over and reinforced their understanding of paradise as being in the Pacific, or more accurately, of the Pacific as being like paradise. The diminutive planted groves of the Pacific island in the subtropics of the south-eastern Pacific, which Europeans had designated 'Easter,' stood out in stark contrast.

Integrating the 'New World'

Ideas formed in antiquity, and kept in circulation through texts and maps, continued to shape travel expectations as fifteenth-century navigational possibilities redirected European focus towards the West and a new sea route to India. Instead of such a sea route, Europeans were confronted with the West Indies and the Americas. Unlike the Pacific exploration that would follow, the first European voyagers to the region of the Americas travelled with a specific known destination in mind. As Greenblatt (1991) phrases it, they 'thought they knew where they were going and ended up in a place whose existence they had never imagined' (2, 88). Their response to the surprise of previously unimagined geography entering their world was to connect it with what they already knew, in histories of the world and constructed pasts that were understood as true within familiar narrative spaces.

It is a pedagogical tenet that we process the new by attaching it to what we already know, starting from a position of understanding and branching out, exploring, and making sense of the unfamiliar. That 'position of understanding,' our foundational knowledge, has been shaped through the extant historical and contemporary cultural discourses that inform and articulate our thinking. It is learning out of and pulling the new into a myriad of already-formed culturally determined discursive spaces that accounts for much of the distortion or nuance of our comprehension of Others. As Rennie (1995) describes it, what Europeans knew about the beginning of the world was textual, not empirical ... what they had read and believed ... the traveller discovering not a new land so much as a new location for old, nostalgic fictions about places lost in the distant past, now found in the distant present' (1), such places as paradise, such people as those perceived as primal ancestors. For example, according to Higgins (1997), 'the primacy in the medieval world of categories of thought derived from the Bible and Christian History meant that nakedness and the absence of private property, including [what a male-normative viewpoint saw as] sexual property,' were seen in America, as in the Pacific, ' not simply as different social practices, but as, in effect, prior ones' (48). Such a perception of the First Nations of the Americas and the Polynesians in the Pacific inevitably situated the European explorers as superior and they wrote that superiority into their newly acquired knowledge of the Other.

Columbus was the first to construct travel texts about the region of the Americas. He had read Ptolemy and Mandeville and, like them, travelled from within a concept of a spherical earth and a paradise positioned in the farthest extremes of the East (Rennie 1995, 17). But he was not travelling from either of the performance positions that they occupied: neither as a merchant like Marco Polo nor as a Christian pilgrim as Mandeville had purported to be. These earlier categories of medieval travellers had never thought to take possession of the new lands they encountered. Columbus travelled from within a third travel guise. It is possible to see him as Arthur Newton does, as the last to perform within the medieval spirit of the crusaders – the Paladins and the knights errant (130–41). Like the crusaders, he presumed his God backed his enterprise and he overlaid discovery-wonder with religious ideology to justify discovery-possession. And as his religion was textually constructed and language driven, so was his act of possession, an act repeated frequently by the Spanish over the next 300 years, specifically in 1770 on Easter Island.

Columbus's language-based imperialism, like all the imperialism that would follow, was enacted 'entirely *for a world elsewhere*' (Greenblatt 1991, 56):

> For Columbus taking possession is principally the performance of a set of linguistic acts: declaring, witnessing, recording. The acts are public and official: the admiral speaks as a representative of the king and queen, and his speech must be heard and understood by competent, named witnesses, witnesses who may subsequently be called upon to testify to the fact that the unfurling of the banner and the 'declarations that are required' took place as alleged. (57)

Moreover,

> Because Columbus's culture does not entirely trust verbal testimony, because its judicial procedures require written proof, he makes certain to perform his speech acts in the presence of the fleet's recorder (for a fleet which had no priest had a recorder), hence ensuring that everything would be written down and consequently have a greater authority. The papers are carefully sealed, preserved, carried back across thousands of leagues of ocean to officials who in turn countersign and process them according to the procedural rules; the notarized documents are a token of the truth of the encounter and hence of the legality of the claim. Or rather they help to produce 'truth' and 'legality' ... ensuring that the memory of the encounter is fixed, ensuring that there are not competing versions of what happened on the beach ... the institutional form secured by writing. ... The actual specific instructions for taking possession of newly discovered lands is written up 20 years later and the instructions do not include any provision for recognition of the cultural level, rights, or even the existence of the natives. (56–8)

As well as establishing a prototype for the text-based imperial acquisition of Others and their spaces, Columbus's activities in the 'New World' were taken up in sixteenth-century Italian poetry and theatre where he was portrayed as a man of prophetic vision who had imagined a New World and then proved it to be true (Rennie 1995, 20). But Columbus did not anticipate the New World. He travelled to find what he had read about in Polo, Mandeville, and the Bible. He wrote, after his third voyage, to his King and Queen, Ferdinand and Isabella, that he was convinced he had found, in the West Indies, the site of the terrestrial paradise (ibid.).

Columbus's account of his discoveries was published in 1511. With its publication, his text begins a well established tradition of 'New World' voyage narratives that follow through to European travel in the Pacific. Rennie (1995) describes the narrative of Columbus's exploits as 'the empirical discovery of the New World ... in the light of the textual discovery of the ancient world' (21), the geography and history of the New World constructed through the lost Golden Age of antiquity. But Columbus's narrative is more than that. It also partakes of the same narrative space as the romances that formed the main literary genre of the Middle Ages, tales growing out of the crusades of knights on quests for noble ladies to seek treasure in far-off lands – Columbus, Isabella, gold. In the wake of Columbus the exploration, conquest, and wealth of the Americas was so strongly tied to the narrative form of the romance quest that, by the eighteenth century, Lord Shaftesbury was able to write in the *Tattler*, '*Barbarian* Customs, Savage Manners, *Indian* Wars, and Wonders of the *Terra incognita*, employ our leisure Hours, and are the chief materials to furnish out a Library. These are in our present day what *Books of Chivalry* were, in our Forefathers' (Rennie 1995, 58). The discursive space of romance would accompany the explorers from the Americas to the Pacific.

The Romancing of *Terra Incognita*

The West Indies and then the Americas were initially engaged through classical and biblical metaphors to the extent that they could be seen as the recovery of a lost past, Eden, or the discovery of a long-hoped-for idealized space, the Blessed Isles. As well as being taken up imaginatively in relation to these two known classical and biblical places, the West Indies was also taken up through the discourse of wonder that had been the central descriptive trope during the Middle Ages for articulating the new in the East. Wonder quite naturally became, as Greenblatt (1991) describes it, the 'central figure in the initial European response to the New World' (14). The initial response of wonder to the newness of the Americas was reinforced throughout the next two centuries as their enormity was slowly added to the European mapping of the globe.

Both romances and their variant, Utopias, were literary forms that partook of the discourse of wonder. To the extent that the Americas could not be fit into a classical or Judeo-Christian geographical or historical framework, those taking the New World up in text turned to the romance genre to find a fitting mode of expression. Within this romantic genre there was still space for idealizing the landscape and people, even if not specifically along classical or biblical lines. Jonathan Lamb, in *Preserving the Self in the South Seas, 1680–1840* (2001), explains it as romance coming 'to the rescue when nothing could be made intelligible in terms of an alternative non-scriptural authority' (42). The Americas were romanticised in travel writing at the same time as romance dominated as a literary genre, with several now canonical works emerging from the era, including Ludovico Ariosto's *Orlando Furioso* (1532), Edmund Spenser's *The Faerie Queene* (1596), and Sir Philip Sidney's prose romance *Arcadia* (1590) (Baldick 1990, 192).

Among the romances written out of the 'discovery' of the New World, was the utopian subgenre. The voyage to a strange country became the 'standard model of the utopian narrative in an age when the market was redoubling the needs of navigation and fantasy' (Lamb 2001, 43–5). What merged in such responses to the New World are the idealization of the classical Golden Age and the biblical Eden, both perceived in societies in the Americas and set against the cultural development of Europe. Implicit in valuing these qualities from the past is a criticism of European culture. As early as 1516 Thomas More's *Utopia* demonstrated that these new American cultures could be used to raise questions about European society (Rennie 1995, 23). More's *Utopia* is set within a realistic framework. His imaginary traveller returns to Europe to contest urban society. The voyagers to the Americas had provided More with a method for presenting a contemporary Other society, rather than a historical one, in contrast to his own. Rennie points out that More was not interested in 'exotic cultures, ... but in civilized political systems,' in how the organization of other cultures might provide a model and a critique of European cultural structures and values (23–4).

Through the twin auspices of imperialism and commerce, this contemporary American geography provided both ideas for an idealized European social experiment and real estate for establishing one. As the sixteenth century led into the seventeenth, and the promise of idealized European settlements in North America turned into the harsh reality of pilgrim life with its mistreatment of the indigenous population as well as fellow Europeans, followed by plantation life and Africans bought and brought in as slave labour, the ever elusive notion of paradise receded from the Americas. The European vision of it shifted further round the globe.

In 1513, Captain Vasco Núñez de Balboa crossed the Isthmus of Panama and sighted the Pacific. With this new view, the imaginary geography for romances and utopian ideals found a new venue. The Pacific became the next site for the earthly paradise. And while the Pacific islands, when actually visited and mapped, were not seen as the sites of the actual Eden, they where constructed by European voyagers as idealized societies, Eden-like Utopias without many of the vices and omissions associated with European civilization. A Pacific discourse of natural lushness and ease was being developed against which deforested and extensively cultivated Easter Island would be contextualized.

As the sixteenth century progressed there was a solidification of exploration and publication by different national, commercial, and private buccaneer interests seeking wealth through exploration, conquest, piracy, and ultimately colonization. In response, the reading public increased its desire for travel texts. Stephen Greenblatt (1991) gives an indication of the vast quantities and varieties of texts that followed these New World exploits, some directed at limited audiences, some for wide public distribution:

> Journals, letters, memoranda, essays, questionnaires, eyewitnesses accounts, narrative histories, inventories, legal depositions, theological debates, royal proclamations, official reports, papal bulls, charters, chronicles, notarial records, broadsheets, utopian fantasies, pastoral eclogues, dramatic romances, epic poems – there is in the sixteenth century a flood of textual representation, along with a much smaller production of visual images that professes to deliver the New World to the Old. (145)

The explosion of travel texts continued into the seventeenth century, and, with the travel tales of Sir John Mandeville as a case in point, it was very hard, according to Michael McKeon in *The Origins of the English Novel* (1987), to tell imaginary and real voyages apart (110).[2] The travel narrative, used by voyagers and writers of fiction alike, overlapped fact and fantasy in a way that made it difficult to discern wondrous fact from realistic fiction (Lamb 2001, 46). So questionable as truth were some of the claims made in travel tales that, in reaction, a counter-narrative developed taking the same romance form. *Don Quixote*, satirizing the romance genre, was published in two parts, the first in 1605 and the second in 1615. A century later, exaggerated and fallacious travel tales were still prominent enough, and profitable enough, that Jonathan Swift satirized them in *A Tale of a Tub: A Project for the Universal Benefit of Mankind* (1704) (published eighteen years before Easter Island would enter European consciousness). Note in particular Swift's mockery of claims to veracity of such texts in the references to 999 learned and pious authors:

> The author, having laboured so long and done so much to serve and instruct the public, without any advantage to himself, has at last thought of a project which will tend to the great benefit of all mankind, and produce a handsome revenue to the author. He intends to print by subscription, in ninety-six large volumes in folio, an exact description of Terra Australis incognita, collected with great care, and prints from 999 learned and pious authors of undoubted veracity. The whole work, illustrated with maps and cuts agreeable to the subject, and done by the best masters, will cost but one guinea each volume to subscribers, one guinea to be paid in advance, and afterwards a guinea on receiving each volume, except the last. (166)

Two decades later, in 1726, just as the first Dutch text constructing Easter Island was about to be published, Swift would also publish his most famous response to travel writing excess, *Gulliver's Travels*. In a preface, his fictitious publisher declares the truth of Gulliver's tale, much as the publisher of the first exaggerated travel text about Easter Island would do in the very same year: 'There is an Air of Truth apparent though the whole; and indeed the Author was so distinguished for his Veracity, that it became a Sort of Proverb among his Neighbours at Redriff, when anyone affirmed a Thing, to say, it was as true as if Mr. Gulliver had spoke it' (The Publisher to the Reader, Swift 1726, 9).

Pacific Exploration

When Europe became aware of the Americas, that awareness involved rethinking the shape, size, and content of the world. When Europeans saw the Pacific Ocean on the other side of the American continents, they were seeing something they already knew in imagination, a body of water they had been indicating on their maps for centuries and had thought themselves sailing to when they encountered the West Indies. Because they were dealing, in imagination, with geography already known, new discursive space did not immediately manifest as European exploration of the Pacific began; instead, mariners returned to an earlier travel model than the ones that formed around the Americas when they were encountered as a previously unknown part of the world. At the same time, Pacific travel also followed on from American exploration. Like the travel writing about the East in the Middle Ages, the Pacific was a known space, but was still an unmapped region. In this sense, the Pacific discourse connected with the already known, becoming the repository for all places still lost in antiquity, a site ripe for rediscovery.

As the Pacific was mapped onto European consciousness, Old World names were written over its islands: Solomon Islands, Easter Island, the New Hebrides. At the same time, a discourse of the navigating self that had been well exercised in the mapping of the Americas in such names as Columbia, Lake Champlain, and Raleigh found the space, in the Pacific, to name islands and parts of islands after the European mariners who mapped them – Tasmania, the Cook Islands, Vancouver Island. These discursive practices of inscription to name and claim space in the Pacific into European consciousness and possession also held open a space for imagining parts of the Pacific as paradise, an aptitude still resonant today. Eva-Marie Kröller, in *Pacific Encounters: The Production of Self and Others* (Kröller et al. 1997), describes this established discourse as 'fulfilling the prophecies of existing belief systems and emulating the rhetorical and literary traditions used to convey them, rather than sustaining the shock of the unmediated new' (1). The European imaginary of the Pacific, more than that of 'perhaps any other geographical area,' has 'been a dense construct of Western discourses' (2), as it still is.

Not only were the discursive spaces for understanding and taking up the Pacific as paradise already established, but also the conquest and plunder of the Americas had set another agenda and space for performance in the initial European sailing in the Pacific. It was seen as yet another site for the generation of wealth for European individuals, trading companies, and nations. A very strong element of personal, commercial, and national greed drove the exploration in the Pacific and shaped the personal performances of those exploring it and writing about it. Buccaneers as well as commercial and national explorers sailed into the Pacific. The wealth amassed by the Spanish and Portuguese as they explored and conquered their way across the Americas gave rise to a practice of international piracy. As Jonathan Lamb (2001) describes it, the 'real object of a voyage to the South Seas between 1680 [and] 1740 as far as the participants were concerned, was not knowledge but plunder' (61) – material plunder followed by possible textual riches. The European mariners had 'the will and the ability to cross immense distance ... in the search for profit,' and part of that profit was gained at the end of the voyages through the textual representation of encounters, the broadcasting back to the reading public of 'radically unfamiliar human and natural objects' (Greenblatt 1991, 6). Seafaring buccaneers paid homage to Odysseus as they wrote texts of their adventures from within self-serving narrative personas that celebrated perceived daring and heroics against the European ships of other nations that they plundered, as well as the natives they encountered. The anonymous Dutch sailor's text about contact with the inhabitants of Easter Island partakes of the bravado of this discourse. One of these buccaneer texts also figures into the quest of Europeans to find the Island in the first place. A New Voyage Round the World (1697), written by William Dampier,[3] offered a second-hand report of a sighting, but not a visit to, a Pacific landmass that was subsequently hoped to be the imagined southern continent. The eighteenth-century commercial quest by the Dutch West Indies Company for that supposed continent led to the 'discovery' of Easter Island.

With subvocal ideas of paradise backgrounding private and national commercial ventures, the hegemony of several discursive agendas overlapped to move the European exploration of the Pacific away from overt commercialism and towards the period of scientific exploration, a space opened in the seventeenth century by Francis Bacon in his posthumously published work New Atlantis, appended to Sylva Sylvarum in 1627. In it he called for a 'college instituted for the interpretation of nature and the producing of great and marvellous works for the benefit of men' (214). The idea found fruition in England in 1660 with the founding of an organization with prescriptive instructions for knowledge gatherers and their textual records. The institution received a Royal Charter in 1662 becoming officially the Royal Society (Rennie 1995, 49).

The South Sea Bubble

Accounts of the wealth to be had in the Pacific caused the European desire for riches to be fused with the desire for wonder. In England, by

1711 the South Sea Company was formed to sell shares in Pacific wealth, even though there was no 'scheme or plan for establishing a commercial intercourse' between Britain and the countries bordering the South Sea (Burney 1803–16, 4: 486, qtd in Lamb 2001, 63). As Lamb describes it, the price of this stock rose sharply from 114 to 1,000 points between 1719 and 1720, 'engineered by means of publicity and the manipulation of the national debt, not in the least by trading profit,' and 'there ceased to be any probable connection between the price of the paper and its earning potential' (62–3). When the Bubble burst, the British suffered a crisis of conscience about its own collective greed and frenzy. Soul searching followed and a discourse of patriotism emerged from the crisis to significant effect. In reaction to the Bubble, essays were written in England that 'engaged the concept of patriotism and the duties of national preservation.'[4] These essays 'were designed to staunch the flow of corruption from the Bubble by ... defining and exemplifying an ideal of public spirit.' They were, in fact, 'strongly to influence George III and to direct ... his patronage of the Pacific exploration of the 1760s' (208), the era when James Cook made his three voyages into the South Seas, stopping on his second expedition at Easter Island.

These developments ushered in 'a period when "the views of ambition and avarice" were replaced by disinterested plans for the improvement of science and geography' (Gerrard 1994, 45; Keate 1788, v, qtd in Lamb 2001, 204). Far from being disinterested, however, this *will to knowledge* was enacted upon a stage of imperial desire that sent ships out publicly to gather knowledge and privately to ascertain the suitability of new geography, climates, plants, and other possible forms of indigenous wealth for European commerce and colonization. For example, on Cook's first expedition to Tahiti in 1769, his expedition encountered breadfruit. Sir Joseph Banks and his botanist on that voyage, Daniel Solander, described the merits of the fruit when they returned to England. 'Some nobility saw this as a plant with great potential in the British West Indies, where it could be used to feed the slaves who worked the sugar cane fields' (Gibson 1999, n.p.). The breadfruit was then imported to the West Indies to feed slaves in 1792. Timothy Fulford describes it in 'Romanticism, Breadfruit and Slavery' (1999) as the making of 'imperial capital out of natural abundance,' changing what was perceived as 'an Edenic fruit into a staple of hell.' Even today, the imperial horror of exploration serving the need to feed slaves goes unremarked in accounts of the history of breadfruit in the

Caribbean. Consider Gracefoods.com, the home of Caribbean Cuisine which says: 'The Breadfruit was originally grown in the South Seas – being a native of Polynesia. The breadfruit is a large tree that grows widely in Jamaica, but was unknown here before 1793. Its arrival is one of Jamaica's romantic stories' (Kennedy 2001, n.p.).

The shift in emphasis from overt buccaneer avarice to avarice in the spirit of scientific investigation and imperialism can be seen in the difference between the first two expeditions to Easter Island – the commercial Dutch and territorial Spanish – and the 'scientific' expeditions of the British and the French that followed. Barbara M. Stafford describes this shift in *Art, Science, Nature, and the Illustrated Travel Account, 1760–1840* (1984). Commercial voyages such as those of the Dutch West Indies Company had been conducted in some secrecy to keep the discovered wealth in the hands of those who mounted the expeditions. As the century shifted focus, the need to conceal the discovery of wealth shifted to a desire to demonstrate a nation's ability to amass knowledge. At the same time, the public interest in new knowledge increased the demand for voyage publications (25). James Cook (1777) alludes to this discursive shift in his first Pacific voyage volume when he describes 'the "veil of secrecy" that in former times had been drawn over the results of these enterprises [and] had thwarted the propagation of useful information "to every European nation; and indeed, to every nation however remote"' (iii). Andrew Sparrman, the Swedish naturalist who accompanied Cook on this first voyage to the South Pacific, also describes the increasing taste for information from 'great scientific voyages when he claims their accounts had never been more popular than in 1777' (qtd in Stafford 1984, 21). He acknowledges 'the avidity' with which voyage information was discussed and the 'eagerness' with which voyage accounts were read. As Stafford notes, this public response 'furnished undeniable proof of the era's "turn for experiment" and its "disposition to enquire"' (ibid.). The reading public's increased taste for new knowledge brought back from expedition voyages helped drive the textual construction and textual exposure of Easter Island, as did the foregrounding of the patriotism of the nations taking the exploratory risks to gather that knowledge.[5]

Both this very masculine patriotism and the imaginary geography of the Pacific share the 'same arc between the real and the fancied, the historical and the utopian,' that is implicit in the 'formation of a disinterested lover of one's country,' as well as in 'narratives of exploration' (Lamb 2001, 208). As Lamb goes on to say:

The navigation of the South Seas veers between identical extremes of public duty and private exigency, historical veracity and fantastic nullity, no
less in the period of scientific inquiry than in that of privateering and bub-
bling. Thus patriotism not only proffers an idiom in which the achieve-
ments of heroic sailors and scientists might be assessed and praised, but
also mirrors the vexing equivocality of certain experiences – of solitude, of
savagery, of landscape – so salient in maritime exploration. (ibid.)

Patriotism provides a clearly defined performance space within which
men suffered the hardships of voyages while fulfilling their duty to
king and country, a duty, which in the name of imperialism could still,
and often did, include identifying and acquiring land-based sources of
wealth, not for self but for one's developing nation-based empire.

The significance of these multiple discursive spaces in shaping eighteenth-century European perceptions of the Pacific, and on the textual
construction of Easter Island – yearning for paradise, personal heroics,
buccaneer publishing, the search for the Antipodes, commercial profit,
scientific inquiry, male national character, and strategic philanthropy –
will be elaborated upon in the chapters that follow on each expedition.
These discourses form an interlocking mesh of hegemonies that served
to erase their intended Pacific subjects (Kröller et al. 1997, 2), or if not
erase, construct them into a form suitable to the social, material and
political ends shaping their text. The 'realities of local were [rendered]
secondary to the vision imposed upon it' (1).

While the historic documents may rest unchanged, archived in sanctioned spaces, their interpretation does not remain static. A corrective
possibility is built into the dynamic of a subject once it has coalesced
into a unity. This corrective possibility or capacity to supplement an
archive with new material or to offer a new interpretation of old texts,
creates the possibility of reformation. The memorization, repetition,
and reproduction of a given archive or subject can be interrupted and
reshaped as the laws or discourses that govern its interpretation are
themselves reformed.

Derrida (1995) succinctly describes this dynamic, writing that 'an
archive ... capitalizes everything, even that which ruins it or radically
contests its power' (13). The textual history of Easter Island follows this
dictum. All possible versions of Rapanui reality are understood,
through Derridian post-structural theory, as having been constructed,
but an awareness of which versions have been constrained and which
enabled, through the temporal discursive processes that have formed,

reformed, and evaluated them, adds to an understanding of the full range of possible narratives that can be engaged in conversation about the island. In the dismissal of some accounts and the foregrounding of others some perceptions are lost, diminishing the richness of narrative diversity and what it may reveal. The consequences of the exclusion of these early works from the Easter Island canon, and the pedagogical impact of the version(s) of the island that circulate today, will be part of my examination of the explorers' texts.

3 The Dutch

1722

Six men are known to have kept journals during the Dutch expedition to the South Pacific. As a consequence of eighteenth-century Dutch trading rivalries, those journals have not all been found. Dutch mercantile interests drew up a charter in the early seventeenth century to carve the world into eastern and western halves for the purposes of their commercial enterprises. The Dutch West Indies company (WIC), formed at that time, was the sponsor of the expedition that 'found' and 'named' Easter Island, but it did not have commercial rights to trade in what it had agreed would be designated as the eastern half of the globe. According to the charters of these companies, Roggeveen's expedition, having already crossed the Pacific from east to west, should have returned home the way it had come in order to remain within its 'allowed' territory. But towards the end of its mission, having lost one ship and suffering from scurvy, Roggeveen decided to return home by going through the Indian Ocean. His chosen route went through Dutch East Indies Company (VOC) territory and when the expedition stopped at Batavia to purchase supplies, its boats were seized and the crew were arrested by their fellow countrymen. Five of the six journals were confiscated by the VOC: those of the admiral, the three ship captains, and an upper mate. The journals were apparently confiscated because their contents would have shown that the expedition had not been trading in 'eastern' waters and was only returning home through 'illicit' waters in duress. In fact, after a lengthy lawsuit, the VOC was condemned for its 'jealous actions' and forced to pay damages.[1] The sixth and only unconfiscated journal was written by a corporal, Carl

Friederich Behrens, a German from Mecklenburg who had hired on as a low-ranking military officer for the expedition (Sharp 1970, 17). Within the rigid role that these Dutch companies had written for themselves, it apparently did not occur to them that such a person would have the literacy or the personal agency to keep a journal.[2]

The publishing history following this textual confiscation is complex. The first two publications to conjure up Easter Island in their text, preceding that of Behrens, were the accounts of an anonymous sailor whose story was transcribed by an editor. The first of these unofficial accounts from the Roggeveen expedition was a fifteen-page pamphlet with two pages about Easter Island. It was printed anonymously in two different editions in Amsterdam in 1727 as *Kort en Nauwkeurig Verhall van de Reize door 3 Schepen in 't Jaar 1721 gedaan*. It is usually abbreviated in English to *The Short and Accurate Narrative* (von Saher 1993, 77). No English translations of this pamphlet appear in the body of texts known to have been published about the island in Europe until recently, when parts of it were translated, with commentary, by Dutch businessman and Easter Island enthusiast Herbert von Saher. According to von Saher's translation, an unnamed editor 'met a sailor in Amsterdam who told him the "true" story about Roggeveen's journey in his own words.' In this first publication, the 'Rapanui men were twelve feet high, the women "only" ten feet' (77). In 1728, a second account, presumably from the same anonymous sailor, was published in Dordrecht followed by later editions in 1758, 1764, and 1774. This second account was book length, 199 pages, and titled *Tweejaarige Reyze door de Straat Magellanes en rondom de Wereld ter nader Ontdekkinge der onbekende Zuydlanden*, abbreviated in English to *The Two Years Journey*. The Easter Island portion of this text, three pages long, was published in London by Alexander Dalrymple in his 1770–1 two volume collection titled *Voyages in the South Pacific Ocean* (see Appendix A). Dalrymple also published an English translation of Behrens's 1739 French account of Easter Island in his collection. This two-volume English text formed part of the ship's library during James Cook's second voyage to the Pacific. *Tweejaarige Reyze* constructs the first European representation of the island, the people, and the moai within well-established voyage narrative and illustration traditions.

The introduction to *Tweejaarige Reyze* states:

The narratives that follow were handed over to me and prepared by me for printing; I have elaborated when indicated with short historical descriptions of the countries, regions and people visited, as collected by the most trustworthy authorities on these regions. And because extraordinary matters hardly find belief in this century, amongst which the stories about the giants, as seen by my travelers, and might therefore lightly be discarded as trivial nonsense, it will become clear to you from the descriptions by men whose judgment has always been respected that in those countries people of such an exceptional length have been found in more than one region. (von Saher 1993, 78)

The 'extraordinary matters' reported by earlier explorers that 'hardly find belief in this century' point to the discursive shift from exploration for the purpose of discovering wonders in the sixteenth and seventeenth centuries, to Enlightenment exploration in the service of science and correct information based on the schema of Francis Bacon. While the editor attempts to position this text in the emerging Enlightenment discourse, the narrative of the anonymous sailor is still very much formed inside the earlier expressions of exploration where exaggeration of travel experiences heightens the projected sense of accomplishment in the narrator.

The editor positions his text within the discursive shift in European scientific scholarship in the service of imperialism during the seventeenth century that led away from the reporting and collection of the fabulous to the formation of the Royal Society in England, and, as Thomas Sprat said in the preface to his history of the Society, 'to the pursuit of knowledge in the service of humankind.' The earlier explorer impulse 'to amaze, intrigue, titillate' (Willinsky 1998, 86) is seen here as yielding to the demands of a more sophisticated audience used to European exploration and cognizant of the inaccuracies of early reports that had been corrected by more recent voyage documentation.[3] Such an audience was more inclined to question the report of marvels. At the same time, the promise to vet these reported wonders through 'descriptions by men whose judgment has always been respected,' promises the reader a narrative that allows the titillation of wonders accompanied by authorities who promise veracity – wonders proved true through scholarship. Accordingly, this second account of Easter Island also measures the height of the islanders as twelve feet in what is judged by the translator, von Saher, to be a plundered version of the account in the first pamphlet. The 'men whose judgment has always been respected' and who offer proof of the existence of such tall people are the authors of the Christian Old Testament. The text goes on to mention 'Og, the King of Bazan, Goliath and the children of Enak (in whose eyes the Israelites were as locusts)' (von Saher 1993, 78).

The Anonymous Sailor's Account and the First Illustration of Easter Island

Like the sailor's text combining elements from two disparate but overlapping narrative traditions, the illustrations that accompanied the published texts of voyages early in the eighteenth century were also the product of multiple discursive expressions. The representation of the travel experience to be pictured was combined with the desires of the traveller to have his experience constructed in a way that cast the most impressive light on his exploits. This focus, early in the century, of the male European documenting his physical presence in the Pacific, trumped his interest later in the century to focus more on the depiction and display of the Pacific landscapes and their produce that were being taken up through commerce and empire. Combined with these representational interests were the actual artistic conventions of the period and the specific conventions of woodcut artists and engravers who rendered voyage descriptions or sketches into stylized illustrations without ever leaving their workshops to travel outside their own European cities. These illustrations, like the voyage narratives, straddled dwindling and emerging discourses and crossed over the boundaries from fact to fiction.

Following the earlier explorer publications, Pacific voyage images published in the eighteenth century began as records of wonder and adventure, sharing the same discursive trajectory as their narratives. In 1722, the voyage art was not so much institutionalized and in the service of scientific travel (B. Smith 1992, 28) as it would be at the time of Cook's voyage, later in the century; instead, it was very much bound up with the discourse of wonder and in the service of the profiteer and adventurer. Jonathan Lamb in *Preserving the Self in the South Seas, 1680–1840* (2001), and Stephen Greenblatt in *Marvellous Possessions: The Wonders of the New World* (1991) each describe the ambiguities at play around the notions of truth, wonder, and the marvellous during the age of exploration. Lamb sees the narratives of the anonymous sailor as making 'explicit the division between private excitements and public standards of truth and probability' (252). He describes European audiences seeking, but not believing, 'narratives remarkable for egoisms and monstrosities' (252), and finds the popularity of travel books increasing as the age of exploration progressed not because of the truth they produced, 'for they were broadly regarded as lies,' but for their dramatizations of the 'feelings incident to the preservation of the self' (6). Such narratives provided an outlet for the titillation of the armchair Odysseus, who could experience, in imagination, the surprising dangers of exotic geography and culture and return unscathed from their duel threat.

The sailor's narrative is an example of these self-styled heroics and romance 'at the level of the ship.' In the decade preceding the Dutch expedition, Woodes Rogers, in describing sailor's narratives, lamented 'a particular Misfortune which attends Voyages to the Southsea, that the Buccaneers, to set of their Knight-Errantry, and make themselves for Prodigies of Courage and Conduct, have given such romantick Accounts of their Adventures, and told such strange Stories, as make the voyages of those who come after to look flat and insipid to unthinking people' (Rogers 1712, xvi, qtd in Lamb 2001, 57). The anonymous sailor's account is a late example of just such 'romantick Adventures,' and it can be seen as the pleasure of self-representation and aggrandizement at the expense of any humanity towards those Pacific islanders as he narrates his group encounters with Others.

Greenblatt (1991), adds another level of complexity to the voyage tale of wonder. While Lamb finds some tales 'broadly regarded as lies,' Greenblatt describes travellers' publications as recounting 'things so marvellous that experience itself can scarcely engrave them upon the understanding even of those who have in fact seen them' (21). In such texts as these, audiences are urged to believe the veracity of the travel experiences. Claims to authority for descriptions of the marvellous are vindicated through assertions of 'sober accuracy' (22).

Juxtaposition of the first printed illustration of Christopher Columbus landing in the 'New World,' published in 1493, with the first printed illustration of the Dutch landing at Easter Island, published in 1728, serves to demonstrate the well-established conventions and constructed stylized nature of explorer images from which the sailor and his editor were drawing. In the first part of the eighteenth century, the conventions for illustrating a first encounter shared a marked similarity to the 1493 woodcut illustrating Columbus making first contact in the West Indies. Not only are these images stylized in nature, rather than realistic or representational, but also they were not created by people who were present on the voyages.

The Osher Map Library website at the University of Southern Maine offers background information about the first fifteenth-century Columbus voyage publications. Eleven editions of Columbus's letters announcing his successful journey across the Atlantic were published in 1493 in Spain, Italy, France, Switzerland, and the Netherlands, with an additional six editions published in 1494–7. The Swiss letter, published in Basel in 1493, was the first to be illustrated. The woodcut image depicted in figure 3.1 from that Basel letter was not setting a new convention for discovery-expedition illustrations, but was itself styled according to existing travel illustrations. It is 'known to be a direct copy of a woodcut of a caravel (boat) from Bernhard von Breydenbach's *Peregrinatio in Terram Sanctam* (*Voyage to the Holy Land*), published in Mainz in 1486.' The rest of the illustration is schematic in nature and 'almost certainly created by a Swiss artist' (University of Southern Maine 2005).

In the woodcut, the viewer is positioned outside the framed scene much as a member of an audience looking upon a stage set. The orientation is from the south looking north at Columbus arriving from the east. Both the imposing ship and the smaller landing boat emphasize European technology in contrast to a land depicted as having no constructed artefacts. There is also a corresponding emphasis on the detailed and specifically styled clothing of the Spaniards and the naked state of the 'Indians.' The only element that both peoples have in common is the size of the objects each holds for mutual exchange. Two points about the islanders are important to note for the way they shift in future depictions of first encounters and 'new' lands. The islanders are numerous in contrast to the two Spaniards arriving in the boat, and the timidity and curiosity of many of the 'Indians' is emphasized through their physicality as they turn their bodies away from the Spaniards at the same time as they are shown as curious to know the new arrivals. The accomplishment of a single representative of the Spanish court, Columbus, accompanied by his oarsman, is emphasized in this image in relation to the vast numbers of Others with whom he is establishing trade.

Several of the elements from this 1493 picture are reprised in the first Dutch illustration, 235 years later in *Tweejaarige Reyze* (see fig. 3.2). By 1728 the technology of reproduction has shifted and the Dutch voyage illustration is a copperplate engraving rather than a woodcut, but it too is executed by an artist who was not on the voyage to Easter Island, Matthys Balen from Dordrecht.[4] His picture closely follows the description of the Dutch landing described by the anonymous sailor. It is a sufficiently significant element of the sailor's narrative to warrant a place

Figure 3.1: Christopher Columbus arriving at an island in the West Indies (Basel, 1493). Print Collection, Miriam and Ira O. Wallach Division of Art, Prints, and Photographs, the New York Public Library, Astor, Lenox, and Tilden Foundations.

Figure 3.2: Dutch landing at Easter Island. Joannes van Braam, *Tweejaarige Reyze rondom de wereld* (Dordecht 1728) frontispiece. Courtesy of Special Collections Library, University of Michigan.

of honour as the title page in the 199-page text. (Over the past fifty years, books covering several topics that include Easter Island – such as Robert Breeden's *Mysteries of the Ancient World* [1979], Kenneth Feder's *Frauds, Myths, and Mysteries* [1990], and John Spencer and Amanda Prantera's *The Encyclopedia of the World's Mystical and Sacred Sites* [2002] – often use a picture of moai from the island as their cover image, so strongly has it come to represent the mysterious.)

In the Dutch eighteenth-century illustration, like the Columbus fifteenth-century woodcut, the observer seems to be invited to view the island as rising into view on the west, the Dutch ships having approached from the northeast. Once again, the Europeans are not depicted on land but on water, making their first contact in boats smaller than their ocean going fleet. Unlike the West Indies depicted in the Columbus illustration, this island is shown to have been altered by human presence. A carved stone stands clearly to the far left of the frame surrounded by gesticulating standing and kneeling people. It is a giant slab of rock surmounted by another larger slab with a small leonine face at its centre. Its form is unrecognizable as the moai we identify with the island today (the metonym that has come to stand for the whole island), but the illustration quite faithfully reproduces the description provided by the anonymous Dutch sailor:

> Two stones of a size that surpasses belief serve them as gods. One stone was exceedingly large and lay on the earth, on top of this there was another stone of such size and height that seven of our men with outstretched arms could hardly embrace it ... it seemed impossible to us that these stones could have been moved, however strong the inhabitants were, and placed on top of the other. (von Saher 1993, 78)

This account of the moai and the accompanying illustration, like those that follow from future explorers, forcefully demonstrate the constructed nature of the island in the European record. Like so many future depictions of moai, this illustration shows a statue facing out to sea, when, in fact, they all face inward looking over the parcel of clan settlement whose fertility they are positioned to enhance.

As in the Columbus picture, there is an abundance of islanders. They dominate the Dutch in both number and proportion, depicted as menacing giants. They brandish enormous spears, prepared to attack the explorers as they come ashore. Dutch gunfire and a gunned-down islander dominate the foreground. European weapons technology is shown to triumph over size and number in this extension of the New World and incursion of a European presence into it. There is a progression seen in these two pictures, from the 1493 interest in how new Others react with timid surprise at encountering Europeans and yet offer to engage in commerce, to the domination of Others depicted as a threat to be overcome in order to gain knowledge of the Pacific, a more overt imposition of imperial vision.

In this first visual representation of Easter Island to Europeans, we have an example of an image teaching viewers how to read the island. The first constructed picture of the island demonstrates the pedagogical dynamic of explorer images to 'strengthen the position' of the individuals and societies generating the images, and shows how such images operated to take up new Others 'in ways defined by the observer' (A. Smith 2001, 20), and, I would argue, learned by the European viewer. The illustration served to arouse sympathy for the explorers and applaud their resourcefulness. It demonstrates superior power in tandem with the accompanying text that describes the Dutch killing a number of the natives who excitedly greeted them as they disembarked.

In many illustrations of European exploration into the Pacific, indigenous peoples are shown in encounters with the European explorers whose voyage accounts the pictures illustrate. The point of human encounter and the record of contact was an integral part of the picture and dominant point of the image. Even when the landscape and the atmosphere or weather dominate a canvas, as in the work of William Hodges on the second voyage of James Cook, the islanders are still a focal point of the image. But this tendency is short lived in the published images of Easter Island that follow the *Tweejaarige Reyze*. The islanders all but vanish from pictorial representation, to be replaced by a focus on landscape and moai.

These first two Dutch accounts from the anonymous sailor, although discredited as fabulous and no longer part of the canon of texts in circulation about the island, must be examined in relation to the genealogy producing the geographic imaginary of the island since they are the only accounts that describe the Rapanui as giants. This point is referred to by James Cook as he comments in an intertextual reference on the authors of Roggeveen's expedition in his own journal entries. While the Rapanui were obviously not twelve feet tall, the perception of the islanders as giants by early-eighteenth-century Dutch sailors should not be dismissed out of hand, given the average height of northern

European soldiers and sailors during the eighteenth century. John Komlos, professor of anthropometric history at the University of Munich, in an article on human height variations in time and space, describes the height of Europeans in the classes that made up soldiers and sailors as having declined from 800 CE, and as having reached its shortest in the seventeenth century. By 1789 for example, those who stormed the Bastille 'averaged five feet and weighed a hundred pounds.' Furthermore, Komlos identifies the Dutch as having 'gone from being among the smallest people in Europe' at that time to being 'the largest in the world' today (Bilger 2004, 36). Less imaginatively, perhaps, the Spanish expedition was also impressed with Rapanui height and included measurements they took while on the island:

> The men are generally of large stature, very many exceeding 8½ spans of Castile (1.80 m.; or 5 ft., 11 ins.); most of them attain 8 spans (1.69 m.; or 5 ft., 6½ ins.); and there were two out of curiosity we measured, one of 9 spans and 2 inches (1.96 m.; or 6 ft., 5 ins.); and the other 9 span 3½ inches (1.99 m.; or 6 ft., 6½ ins.), all their limbs being of proportionate dimensions. (Heyerdahl and Ferdon 1961, 1: 49)

Extrapolating from this information about the diminutive height of the Dutch sailors and the extraordinary height of the Rapanui, it is not surprising that the memory of a sailor recounting his experience of the islanders in 1722 would recall them as giants, although this notion would give way to imperial and commercial concerns in the 'official' expedition journals representing empires. The newly emerging subject of Easter Island as formed through these first explorer texts will be seen to move from this initial focus on the people to a focus on the land and finally to a focus on the cultural past of the island.

The third publication, the personal soldier's log of Carl Friederich Behrens, does not describe the Rapanui as giants. It was held for many years as the accurate account of the Dutch voyage, until 1837 when Roggeveen's own journal was found. Behrens was published in a German edition in 1739 and a French translation of the German was published in The Hague in the same year (Sharp 1970, 16). The text as a whole combines the first-hand narrative account of the voyage with borrowed material from previous publications on the area traversed as well as some areas not travelled through. It is also considered to contain some 'added invention' (ibid., 17) because it has details not included in the 'official' Roggeveen account. After these early editions, according to

Bolton Granvill Corney who translated Behrens into English from the German in 1903, it was translated and reprinted many times 'in more or less mutilated or abridged form' and can be found in 'various historical collections of voyages and travels – to wit, Harris and Campbell, the Abbé Prévost, De Brosses, Callender, Dalrymple, *The World Displayed, Nederlandsche Reisen*, Burney, and perhaps others' (Corney 1903, xxiii).

The first English version of Behrens is one of the 'more or less mutilated' accounts. It was translated into English by 1759 as the essay 'Easter Island' for inclusion in *The World Displayed; or a Curious Collection of Voyages and Travels Selected from the Writers of all Nations*, a twenty-volume endeavour with selections edited by Dr Samuel Johnson, Oliver Goldsmith, and Christopher Smart, and an introduction by Johnson. This collection was in continuous publication during the late eighteenth century with several new editions being printed over the ensuing twenty years. Given the prestige of these editors in England as eighteenth-century men of letters and the discursive power of distinguished authors/editors as an index of a work's truthfulness, it is possible to judge the authority these voyage accounts would have held for the English reading public. A search of the University of Toronto library holdings, as one central Canadian example, verifies the popularity of this collection of travel tales. It is available in a 1767 edition; a 1768 second edition; a 1775 fourth edition corrected and *'embellished with cuts'*; a 1777 fourth edition; *'illustrated and embellished with a variety of maps and prints'*; a 1778 edition; and a 1779 sixth edition *'in which the conjectures and interpolations of several vain editors and translators are expunged; every relation is made concise and plain, and the division of countries and kingdoms are clearly and distinctly noted.'*

In this limited bibliography of *The World Displayed*, we glimpse the eagerness with which the English-speaking public received texts about newness entering and altering their vision of the world, combined with an increasing preference for accuracy evidenced in the phrases, *'concise and plain,'* and *'clearly and distinctly noted.'* This pressure for accuracy from an increasingly more sophisticated audience echoes both Francis Bacon's emphasis on empirical verifiability and the reassurances of the Dutch narrator to prove extreme claims. It also points to the power of the reader to constrain or enable the writing of the text through the quality of scientific evidence the reader was now demanding. As well, it points to the power of the explorer to shape *his* experiences to generate a text within a range of discursive spaces from the exaggerated marvel to the plain-spoken cataloguing of facts observed. The Dutch expedition to Easter Island offers three textual voices that each work through a different one of these narrative performance positions. Only the sailor and Behrens were available during the eighteenth century to be taken up and responded to. An excerpt from all three is offered here to suggest the way each performs a different sense of the authoritative voice.

Anonymous Sailor:

> Thus far my narrative will gain credit, because it contains nothing uncommon, yet I must declare that all these savages are of a more than gigantic size, for the men being twice as tall and thick as the largest of our people; they measured, one with another, the height of twelve feet, for that we could easily – who will not wonder at it! without stooping have passed betwixt the legs of these sons of GOLIAH. According to their height, so is their thickness, and are all, one with another, very well proportioned, so that each could have passed for a HERCULES; but none of their wives came up to the height of the men, being commonly not above ten or eleven feet. The men had their bodies painted with a red or dark brown, and the women with a scarlet colour.
>
> I doubt not that most people who read this voyage will give no credit to what I now relate, and that this account of the height of these giants will probable pass with them for a mere fable or fiction ; but this I declare, that I have put down nothing but the real truth, and that these people, upon the nicest inspection, were in fact of such a surpassing height as I have here described. (Dalrymple [1770] 1967, 2: 113)

Behrens:

> These islanders are, in general, lively, well-made, strong, pretty slender, and very swift of foot. Their looks are mild, pleasing, modest, and submissive, and they are extremely cowardly and timorous ... They are, in general, *brown* like Spaniards; some were also found *pretty black*, and others who were *quite white*. There were others of a redish [*sic*] complexion, as if burnt by the sun. (Dalrymple [1770] 1967, 2: 94)

Roggeveen:

> These people are well-proportioned in limbs, having very sturdy and strong muscles, are generally large in stature, and their natural colour is

not black, but pale yellow or sallow, as we saw in many youths, either because they had not painted their bodies with a dark blue, or because they, being of a higher rank, were not subject to the labour of land cultivation. (Sharp 1970, 97)

For the English-language publication, the editors of *The World Displayed* (1759), with its emphasis on accuracy, chose to publish only Behrens's account. Dalrymple, with a mandate for thoroughness, published both available accounts but was critical of the obvious exaggeration in the anonymous one. Unlike the sailor's 'second-hand' account, which seemed to focus on extremes and wonders, Behrens's account of Easter Island emphasized what he observed of island life and custom as well as his perception of the reactions of the Rapanui to their encounter with the Dutch. His account stands out from other accounts in the way it offers his perceptions of the islanders' emotional responses to the situations they find themselves in when confronted with the Dutch arrival – three large ships full of small men, travelling without women.

In *The World Displayed*, the editors both translate and paraphrase Behrens's narrative, adding their editorial voice to position the Dutch violence against the islanders in an unfavourable light, which doubly shaped the response of readers to the 'discovery' of the island. The Dalrymple edition of Behrens does not editorialize within the translation, but it does precede it with a judgmental introduction to the text. He translates Behrens into English from the French translation that in turn was translated from the original German edition. Dalrymple ([1770] 1967) writes:

I have not seen the *German* original, the French translation is therefore followed: it is a very poor performance, written with much ignorance, though with the parade of knowledge ... It appears to me that the author of the French relation kept no journal, and writes from memory, but his narrative seems to be faithful in the recital of those things he saw; and in many circumstances is confirmed by the Dutch relation, which appears to be a sea-journal, to which the circumstances of description have been added, perhaps from verbal report, with some exaggeration towards the marvellous, particularly about giants; of which I am assured by a very ingenious and worthy Dutch gentleman there was no mention made in the MS journal of the voyage which he had once in his possession. (2: 85–6)

The availability of the anonymous sailor translation in English had a strong effect on the intertextual response of the British expedition of 1774. The Spanish expedition of 1770 and the French 1786 expedition, while also writing back to texts of the Dutch expedition, would have most likely read a French translation of Behrens's original German text that, as shall be shown, was less judgmental in tone than the Dutch sailor's account. On the British voyage, James Cook and the naturalists George and Johann Forster who accompanied him, responded directly to the account of Dutch interaction with the Rapanui in the Dalrymple translations, as they narrated their own experiences on the island. Cook, for example, compares his expedition experience to what he read of the Dutch, as well as comparing British behaviour on the island to that of the Dutch during their encounter. The two available Dutch accounts translated into English differ on the violence of their contact with the Rapanui. While the Behrens's account demonstrates a recognition of the need to justify the violence perpetrated by the Dutch on the islanders, the sailor's account celebrates that same violence. A reaction to this celebration carries over into the censorious tone of Cook's own narrative. The result, as will be discussed in greater detail, is that the English texts focus energy censuring the Dutch for not maintaining 'superior' European behaviour (category maintenance) while the Spanish and French texts focus more strongly on the management of their own forces in order to maintain control of their lower ranks in relation to the Rapanui.

Of the five confiscated journals from the first Dutch voyage, only two have come to light, Admiral Jacob Roggeveen's and Captain Cornelis Bouman's. Roggeveen's was found in 1836 and published in 1838 and Bouman's was found by his descendents in family papers and published in 1911 (Sharp 1970, 18–19). The first English translations were 1903 and 1993, respectively. Bolton Glanvill Corney, in his 1903 translation of the Spanish expedition accounts, included a translation of Behrens into English from the original German. He considers the Carl Behrens narrative to be 'another and better account' than the sailor narrative, and describes Behrens as presenting 'a much more sober and trustworthy account of the voyage ... bear[ing] evidence of its author having been a man of some education and social status, and an experienced traveller ...' (xxiii). But the textual authority of Behrens is short lived. When Corney (1903) moves on to a discussion of the Roggeveen journal, which he also translated, he describes it as the official account written by Mr Jacob Roggeveen, the Commodore of his 'expedition' – an account which, little known as it appears to be even at the present day, should long since have relegated the clap-trap story of the Tweejarige Reize [the sailor] to the realms of legend, and have eclipsed the claims of the more sober-minded but not wholly authentic narrative of Sergeant-Major Carl Friederich Behrens. We must now judge Roggeveen in a new and true light; and must commend his conduct of the expedition as careful and conscientious, instead of loading him, as has been done in the past, with charges of inhumanity and ruthlessness. Honour is due him as the first European to visit and explore Easter Island. (25–6)

With the emergence of these lost texts into the English-language discourse of the island, the status of the journal of Carl Behrens began to be contested. His narrative that had been sanctioned as true was now dismissed as fanciful. The evidence given in commentary for this demotion is primarily for inaccuracies in his dates and his description of the voyage route (see Sharp 1970, 17). But another factor can be seen at play in this constraining of Behrens's account. Behrens does not have the authority of Roggeveen who was a lawyer, an admiral, and an elder statesman of sixty-two when he led his expedition to search for a southern continent in the South Pacific.

The paraphrasing of Behrens in *The World Displayed*, Dalrymple's translation into English from the French translation, and Corney's translation from the German must be put into conversation with the Roggeveen journal in order to sort out the influence of these texts on the invention of Easter Island. Behrens and Roggeveen perceive and emphasize the encounters they describe differently so that it is not possible to say which is more 'true.' The point and counterpoint of the initial invention of the island can be seen in the contents of each, where Easter Island emerges as a subject through these differently nuanced narratives. Today, Roggeveen's account is referred to in texts about Easter Island as if it were the narrative that brought the island into European consciousness (see Dos Passos 1971, in particular). In this way the textual construction of the island continues to be built on texts constructed from very temporally and culturally circumscribed understandings of experience, and continues to demonstrate with this building, the tradition of inventing the island out of Euro-centred narrative authority. Each adds to an understanding of how Easter Island was formed as a subject, and how we might today imagine the interplay of the two groups, Rapanui and European, experiencing each other through their own social and cultural codes. In the privileging of the 'official' accounts with their focus on the imperial mandate, and the dismissal of Behrens's account with its emphasis on emotional responses, much of the possible complexity of a contemporary response to this past is lost.

One of the more disturbing aspects of the way the explorer texts are taken up in more contemporary accounts of the history of Easter Island is the selective way in which elements from these early texts are brought forward into the contemporary chronicles. Even texts not written for the general public that are meant as serious contributions to academic studies – such as Heyerdahl and Ferdon's *The Reports of the Norwegian Archaeological Expedition to Easter Island and the East Pacific* (1961), written in two volumes and each running in excess of 500 pages – compare the Roggeveen and Behrens accounts of the first encounter but omit any reference in either account to the shooting of islanders when the Dutch first come ashore (see vol. 1: 45–8). Such omissions, in their selectivity, distort contemporary translations of past perceptions and diminish the possibility for nuanced comprehension of the interactions and repercussions of first encounters and subsequent responses to encounter.

Jacob Roggeveen's Journal

Even before Roggeveen established the Euro-Christian epithet 'Easter' when his expedition sighted the island on Easter Sunday, 1722, the idea of it as a geographic entity had already entered public circulation. In the late seventeenth century, two separate accounts of a Pacific sandy-island sighting by the British buccaneer Captain Edward Davis, sailing on the *Bachelor's Delight* in 1687, were published in 'voyage' texts. Lionel Wafer, a surgeon who had accompanied Davis when he sighted the island, wrote about it in *A New Voyage and Description of the Isthmus of Panama* published in 1699. William Dampier, who had sailed with Davis previously, was told about the sandy island by Davis after his return form his voyage and wrote about it in *A New Voyage round the World* published in 1697 (Sharp 1970, 90).

Dampier's text went through two editions in the year it was published and a third in 1698. Rennie credits Dampier's text with reviving eighteenth-century interest in maritime travel literature and in the South Seas. When he travelled, Dampier modelled the instructions of the Royal Society that seamen, bound for far voyages, should act as botanists, zoologists, and geographers (Dampier 1697, 59). Not only did he follow their prescription, but also he acknowledged his compliance with their mandate by addressing his travel book to the Royal Society. Situated as it was in relation to this organization, the text, with its first-hand accounts of experience, took on the empirical authority of experience over philosophy for coming to terms with truths about the world.

One of the mandates of the Dutch expedition was to find Davis's 'Sandy Island' and Roggeveen's log writes back to the published descriptions of Wafer and Dampier. Roggeveen's reaction, in his text, to the inaccuracies in the Wafer/Dampier descriptions, can perhaps be seen as a strong response to the supposed authority of the Dampier account:

> But when we had approached this land to a small distance off, we saw clearly that the description of the Sandy and low island (both by Capn. William Dampier, following the account and testimony of Capn Davis, and by the diarist Lionel Wafer, whose journal of this and other discoveries the said Dampier by printing has made world renowned, and included as a distinguished adornment in his own book, comprising all his land and sea journeys) was not in the least similar to our observation, further, that it likewise could not be that land that the said discoverers testify had been seen 14 to 16 miles from them, first, stretched beyond their sight being a succession of high land, and concerning which the said Dampier judges and deems it to be the point of the unknown Southlands. That this Paaschland cannot be the sandy island appears from this, that the sandy is small and low, whereas the Paaschland in its circumference comprises 15 to 16 miles, having at the east and west point, which are situated about 5 miles from each other, two high hills which gradually slope down and at the junction of which with the plain are three to four more small heights, so that this land is of fair height, and raised above the reach of the force of the sea. That we originally, from a further distance, have considered the said Paasch Island as sandy, the reason for that is this, that we counted as such the withered grass, hay, or other scorched and burnt vegetation, because its wasted appearance could cause no other impression than of a singular poverty and barrenness, and that the discoverers had therefore given to it the name of sandy. Therefore it is to be concluded easily from the above, that this discovered Paaschland will be another land, which lies further east than that land which is one of the reasons for our expedition, or else the discoverers in their descriptions, both verbal and written, could very easily have been convinced by falsehood. (Sharp 1970, 92–3)

By asserting that the island sighted by his expedition was not at all like the island described by Davis, Roggeveen identifies himself and his nation as the discoverers of unmapped geography and he gives it the name it is still identified by in the popular press. At the same time as Roggeveen claims discovery of, and names the 'new' island, he discredits the British report of an uncharted Pacific Island and positions himself as morally superior to the authors of the British text with the statement that they 'could very easily have been convinced by falsehood.' This rather awkward expression 'convinced by falsehood,' in the Sharp translation of Roggeveen's journal, is a softened rehabilitation of the same statement translated by Corney as 'or else, the discoverers must stand convicted of a whole bundle of lies in their reports, told by word of mouth as well as in writing' (Corney 1903, 10). These two English translations of the same Dutch passage underscore the textual instability of Roggeveen's account to produce a stable meaning when processed through differing discursive positions.

As well as writing back to the British claim of sighting the island, Roggeveen's text addresses the institution with which his expedition is associated. Its three ships from the Netherlands were 'all equipped and fitted out by the Amsterdam Chamber, in accordance with the resolution of their Honourable Lords Directors of the Dutch Chartered West-India Company' (Sharp 1970, 20). Roggeveen was accountable to that institution for the results of the Pacific mission.

The focus on wealth and the desire to procure it for the company who sponsored him is evident in the text even before the mariners go ashore. Roggeveen enters in his log that he will soon 'go to land with two well-manned sloops, ... and try to see and find out what they wear and use for ornament or other thing, and also whether any supplies of greens, fruit or livestock are to be got there by barter' (Sharp 1970, 90). He then adds that some of his officers 'thought they had seen that the inhabitants had silver plates in their ears, and mother-of-pearl shells around their necks for ornament' (93). The order of interest in this preparation for a first encounter is telling: textiles, materials used for ornaments, and refreshments. The island was destined to be measured in this first instance against the potential resources it might yield – measured against the desire for tangible wealth and then found wanting or acceptable, based upon meeting this imperial standard of valuation.

Set against the desire to investigate the island as a potential source of wealth was an underlying fear of making contact with its inhabitants. Even before sighting the islanders, Roggeveen demonstrates a conflict between behaving well towards unknown Others at a first encounter and a fear of the stranger strong enough to undermine the desire for friendliness. Having anchored two miles from shore the mariners plan on the following day to 'go to land with two well-manned sloops, fittingly armed (so that in the case of hostile encounter there would be a state of defence), and showing all friendliness to the inhabitants' (Sharp 1970, 90). Through this conflicted statement Roggeveen reveals the tension between what may be described as European 'courtesy' and the fear of what such an encounter might entail; rehearsing correct behaviour and friendliness even as he positions himself to deviate from its practice.

Here, before the first encounter, is a glimpse of the world view through which Roggeveen imaginatively sees the islanders. This view has less to do with experience of the people than with European conjectures, described by Greenblatt (1991) as projecting onto the native a characteristic imperialist 'conception of their own powers of representation' (119). Roggeveen's anticipation of aggression from the islanders forms part of a self-fulfilling prophecy. It is necessary, in his evaluation, to prepare for violence and to be ready to respond in kind. Robert Young, in *White Mythologies: Writing History and the West* (1991), calls this stance by European imperialists towards people new to them an 'ethico-political violence toward the other' who is 'always to some degree seen as a threat.' The as-yet-unknown Other has to be comprehended and incorporated into a position in relation to the comprehending European self (12). In order for that position to be comfortable for the explorers, it would need to be managed, to be orchestrated. The explorers would need to feel they had the upper hand and could control the relationship. The 'natives' would be perceived to occupy a space in relation to the explorers that serves the explorers feelings of superiority and concerns for safety. This assumption of hostile first encounters is accounted for by Homi Bhabha in 'Sly Civility' (1985) from a pre-Baconian/post-Darwinian point of view, as European history inscribing the Other in a 'fixed hierarchy of civil progress' (95). Within this hierarchy, the island native, assumed to be at a lower level of civilized development, is seen as likely to be a physical threat. In order for the inhabitants to be rendered harmless, that anticipated threat would need to be neutralized whether it emerges or not.

First Contact

Before Roggeveen had the opportunity to make first contact, an islander made the first move to meet the strangers by paddling out to one of the ships. Through his experience on board, he shaped the expectations of the islanders, if not the Dutch, for future encounters. His reception was friendly, he was given freedom to explore and closely examine the fabric and the technology of the ship, and he was presented with numerous articles of material composition all unlike anything available on the island and completely new to his culture. Roggeveen, Behrens, and the anonymous sailor all describe the meeting, each constructing the encounter quite differently, foregrounding some aspects of the encounter and diminishing others as they shape their narratives. Roggeveen emphasizes the vulnerability of the lone, naked islander and how suitably impressed he is with the technology of Dutch maritime transportation and weaponry:

> In the morning Captain Bouman (because a canoe came from the land to his ship) brought to our ship a Paaschlander with his vessel who was quite naked, without having the least covering in front of what modesty forbids being named more clearly. This poor person appeared to be very glad to see us, and marvelled greatly at the construction of our ship, and what he observed about it, as the great height of the masts, the thickness of the ropes, the sails, the cannon, which he handled accurately, and furthermore at all that he saw, but particularly when his face was shown to him in a mirror, so he looked with a quick movement of the head to the back of the mirror, evidently to find there the reason for this appearance. After we had amused ourselves enough with him, and he with us, we sent him back to shore in his canoe, having been presented with two blue strings of beads round his neck, a small mirror, a pair of scissors, and other such trifles in which he seemed to take special pleasure and satisfaction. (Sharp 1970, 91)

Behrens's text shows interest in the man as an individual and as a representative of his culture. He emphasizes the intricacy of his extensive tattoos and offers a reading of his reactions to European foods, drink, clothing, ultimately describing a point of common connection in music:

> Next day we stood in with our ships to look for a harbour, whereupon one of the natives came off in a small skiff to meet us some two miles off the land. We took him aboard our vessel and gave him a piece of linen cloth to wrap about his body, for he was quite naked; and we offered him beads and other trinkets, all of which he hung round his neck together with a dried fish. He was very cleverly and regularly painted with all sorts of fig-

ures: he was of a brown tint, and had long ears which hung down as far as his shoulders as if they had been stretched to that length by being weighted, after the fashion of the Mongolian Moors. He was fairly tall in stature, strong in limb, of good appearance, and lively in mien, as well as pleasing in speech and gesture. We gave this South Lander or foreign visitor a glass of wine to drink; but he only took it and tossed it into his eyes, whereat we were surprised. I fancy he thought that we designed to poison him by its means, which is a common usage among Indians. There upon we dressed our new guest in garments and put him on a hat, but he was evidently very ill at ease in clothing. We also regaled him with food; but he was quite ignorant of the use of a spoon, knife, or fork. After he had taken his meal our musicians treated him to a specimen of each of their instruments; and whenever any person took him by the hand he began at once to caper and dance about. We were much pleased to see his enjoyment; but we did not come to an anchor that day, and therefore let him go back to the shore with the aforesaid presents to acquaint his friends in what manner he had been entertained. But he parted from us unwillingly: and held up his hands, cast his glances toward the land, and began to cry out loudly in these words, *O dorroga! O dorroga!* He was not at all disposed to return to this skiff, but preferred to remain with us that we might convey him ashore in our ship. (Corney 1903, 132–3)

The anonymous sailor is most concerned with rehearsing the superior might of the Europeans to the islanders. He constructs a text that describes a twelve-foot giant who is nevertheless no match for the prowess of the sailors. The giant is forced to board the ship and permitted to leave when it suits the Dutch. Unlike Behrens who reads a great deal from the behaviour of the islander, the sailor describes an inability to communicate:

As soon as the anchors were ready to drop, we observed at a distance a neat boat, of a very remarkable construction, the whole patched together out of pieces of wood, which could hardly make up the largeness of half a foot. This boat was managed by a single man, a giant of twelve feet high, who exerted all his strength to escape us, but in vain, because he was surrounded and taken. His body was painted with a dark brown colour. We tried with such signs and words as are used here and there among the islands in the South Seas, to get some intelligence from him, but could not perceive that he understood any thing, whereupon we permitted him to go into his boat again and depart. (Dalrymple [1770] 1967, 2: 111)

Immediately when contact is actually made between this solitary individual and the entire complement of one ship, we see each text begin to position the islander as inferior in relation to his European narrators. His nudity falls short of Dutch standards of modesty. Behrens says, 'the first present we made him was a piece of cloth to cover him.' He is described by Roggeveen as poor, not someone to meet on equal terms or attempt to know, but an amusement to beguile the time with. All of these qualifiers firmly position him as lesser in relation to the European self. This valuation is in spite of his willingness to make the first move and travel to the ship and his keen interest in the construction and mechanics of the vessel, taking special notice of 'the great height of the masts, the thickness of the ropes, the sails, the cannon, which he handled accurately.'

The inherent violence of imperial language is seen at play here. In the very process of being taken up through European text, the islander enters the narrative world in a position of inferiority to his describers, shaped into text by his writers' interpretations rather than by his actual behaviour. The textual-self, whether the author's own-self or descriptions of an Other, is inevitably positioned in relation to power when taken up in language. 'Once engaged in any kind of linguistic activity it is displaced, decentred, and variously positioned as a subject according to different systems, institutions, forms of classification and hierarchies of power' (Foucault 1972, qtd in Young 1990, 124). The first description of an 'Easter Islander' positions him as inferior to his narrators, in spite of the fact that he makes the first contact and stands before them alone and naked and unafraid, engrossed in the mechanics of their vessel, while they fear going ashore in great numbers without ample fire power.

This encounter was the first recorded contact that an islander had with a foreigner.[5] Having made the first overture and received so many gifts in response, the islander returned to shore with his presents. And as Behrens says, 'to encourage others, [we] allowed him to keep what he had got' and 'let him go back to the shore with the aforesaid presents to acquaint his friends in what manner he had been entertained.' Through the initial act of visiting the ship and receiving gifts, the Europeans established for the islanders a very specific expectation of largess connected with future contacts, contacts that the Europeans then judged harshly in spite of what they had communicated. Behrens' narrative continues, saying that the islanders beckoned to the mariners and 'made many signs that we should come on shore.' But the European fear of the Other prevented disembarking, 'as our order was not to do this, when the numbers of Indians present might be too large, this was not done' (Corney 1903, 133).

In these European representations of the Rapanui as Other, Roggeveen and Behrens, or their translators, use several different terms to describe them. During the course of the texts, they are referred to as inhabitants, as people, as Paaschlanders (Easter Islanders), and as Indians. All of these terms are written in lowercase except the single use of 'Paaschlander' and the term 'Indian.' Roggeveen's text, in its English translation, uses people when he refers to his own complement of sailors and soldiers and when he stands at a narrative distance considering the island population in general. Paaschlander is used when he comes face to face with the man who paddled out to the ships at anchor and came aboard. 'Indian' is first used when Roggeveen recounts the shooting of islanders by soldiers in his landing party: 'The Indians being completely surprised and frightened by this fled ... then another Indian tried to pull the coat of a sailor off his body' (Sharp 1970, 95). The other meaning of the term is used when Roggeveen is describing the distribution of the number of houses to the number of inhabitants: '[W]e can conclude that all the Indians make a common use of what they own' (ibid., 101).

'Indian' is the term of choice when the narrative need is to position the Other at an inferior distance from the Dutch, first in order to diminish the significance of violent acts against the islanders, and second to designate their social inferiority to European capitalism through their common sharing of property. The 1759 translation/paraphrase of Behrens uses 'Indian' repeatedly when referring to the islanders, while the 1903 translation rarely uses the term. Such textual differences speak again to the slipperiness of meaning across translations as well as time. The connection of the Pacific to the Orient, as it is cued by the use of the term 'Indian,' is evident in much eighteenth-century writing about the Pacific and points to an established textual framework for understanding Others that had been in play since Columbus's initial exploratory misconception that he had reached India when he was, in fact, encountering what came to be known as the Americas. The Orient is never far from the 'idea' of Europe and serves as a frame against which to measure the European sense of self. Edward Said in *Orientalism* (1994) demonstrates that it served as 'a collective notion' identifying Europeans 'as against all those non-Europeans' (7). Bernard Smith (1992) notes that in the eighteenth century the term 'Indian' was in 'generic usage for all non-European peoples, apart from a few old-time exotics such as Arabs and Chinese' (173). To call the islanders 'Indian' was to put into textual service, through a synecdoche, all the values, both positive and negative that defined the Orient and that positioned the European construction of self against the European construction of an Oriental Other.

Just as each of the explorers' texts wrote back to those who had travelled this route before, so in the naming of the islanders as Indians, the writers assumed a known framework, working out of what Smith describes as an 'internally structured archive' (ibid.) for their encounter with the islanders before they even met. And through this internal archive, each text constructing Easter Island affiliated itself further with other previous works, adding another layer of intertextuality, a layer familiar to the anticipated audiences for the texts, both institutional and public, all of whom would have subscribed to the same framework and understanding of what constituted Indians (Said 1994, 20). While these explorers' texts grew out of a tradition of European texts constructing the Orient, so too, as we shall see, do subsequent texts on Easter Island refer back, in an unqualified fashion, to the previous explorers' texts as documents which are taken at face value, describing rather than constructing the island culture as a European representation.

First Group Contact

After the solo visit to the ship by the first islander to make contact with Europeans, the newcomers still did not land. Many of the islanders went out to the ships, no doubt eager to replicate their compatriot's experience and to return with objects never seen before. Roggeveen writes:

> These people showed at that time their great eagerness for all that they saw and were so bold that they took the hats and caps of the sailors from their heads and jumped with their plunder overboard, for they are extremely good swimmers, as was shown by the fact that a large number came swimming from land to the ships. Also there was one Paaschlander who climbed from his canoe through the window of the Africaansche Galey. And seeing a cloth on the table, with which it was covered, having judged it as a good prize, took flight with it, so that particular care had to be taken to guard everything well. (Sharp 1970, 93–4).

In this description the inhabitants of the island are identified as thieves (a characteristic referred to in most subsequent texts on the island culture) regardless of what other interpretations might be assigned to their behaviour.[6] This judgment by Roggeveen of the islanders' behaviour against European practices needs to be examined against the experience of the islander who first boarded one of the ships alone, against the Polynesian tradition of gift exchange, and commercial exchange, and against the text of the same incident as perceived by Carl Behrens.

In Polynesian societies before the advent of European exploration and imperialism, there existed an intricate system of gifting both inter- and intra-island. On this eastern-most island of Polynesia, isolated from contact with other Polynesians, trade had only been intra-island since it was first colonized. This was a factor that no doubt contributed to the wonder, for the Rapanui, of having a large ship anchor off shore and dispense so many never-before-seen gifts to the first islander to venture out to it. Lewis Hyde, in *The Gift: Imagination and the Erotic Life of Property* (1979), describes the nature and obligations of gift exchange cultures. 'Many tribal groups circulate a large portion of their material wealth as gifts.' Food, for example is neither bought nor sold, 'even though there may be a strong sense of 'mine and thine,' food is always given as a gift' (xiv). Such transactions are governed 'by the ethics of gift exchange and not by those of 'barter or cash purchase.' The presentation of a gift establishes a relationship between the people involved, unlike the anonymity that can accompany the sale of a commodity. Also, 'when gifts circulate within a group,' their exchange creates a series of interconnected relationships and a kind of 'decentralized cohesiveness emerges' (xiv). Marilyn Strathern, in *The Gender of the Gift*, 1988, expands upon the nature of this system, as she describes 'things passing from hand to hand as gifts, not commodities, confirming sets of social relations and eliciting new ones through further acts of giving and receiving.' The gift becomes 'inseparable from these relations to other things.' (Lamb 2001, 136). Obligation is the key to this cultural system of exchange, 'the obligation to repay gifts received' as well as the obligation to give presents and the obligation to receive them' (Mauss 1990, 10–11). Ironically, the enactment of this tripartite of gift exchange is described repeatedly in the explorer narratives of Easter Island even as those narratives label the customary behaviour as theft.

When the lone islander returned to shore with so many items unique to the island culture that had been given freely by the Europeans, the response was for many other islanders to visit the ship, bearing gifts of their own for the newcomers, assuming they would come away with new things in exchange. By labelling the islanders as thieves for following their own sociocultural codes with enthusiasm, the Rapanui character is fixed negatively in the text, positioned to be forever judged as morally inferior to European social customs and mores.

Roggeveen's official report of the behaviour of the islanders on board ship can be seen in a different light when considered against the contradictory report of Carl Behrens, combined with an understanding of the practice of gift exchange in this Polynesian culture:

> Great multitudes of the inhabitants came down to meet them, bringing vast quantities of fowls and roots; many came aboard with these provisions, while the rest ran about from place to place ... very early the next morning ... the necessary preparations being made for their landing, the friendly *Indian* who had been with them before, came on board a second time bringing with him abundance of his countrymen, who to make themselves welcome, came with their canoes loaded with plenty of live fowls,[7] and roots dressed after their manner. Among them was a man whose complexion was perfectly white, in whose ears hung round white pendants as big as one's fist. This person had a very devout air, and seemed to be one of their Priests. While things were in this friendly situation, one of the Islanders was by some accident shot dead in his canoe, by a musket, which threw the rest into such consternation, that most of them leaped into the sea, in order to get the sooner to shore, while the rest who remained in their canoes, rowed with all their strength, in order to obtain a place of safety. (*The World Displayed* 1773, reproduced in the appendix of Casey 1931, 305)

Which narrative is 'correct' and why they differ is not the question. Each narrative constructs events differently and only one, Behrens, was considered as truth and responded to as such by subsequent eighteenth-century explorers. Roggeveen does not mention gifts of food brought to the ship by the islanders, nor does he mention an accidental shooting. Behrens does. Behrens's account entered recorded European history and formed the basis of the imagined island culture, only to fall out of circulation and be written over by the Roggeveen account after it was published in 1838.[8] Today, Behrens's account is discredited as fanciful and Roggeveen's is given the narrative authority as the true descriptor of historic events.

First Shore Contact

The following excerpt from Roggeveen's log is significant for its focus on and positioning of the islanders in relation to the Dutch explorers.

The constituted subject, the islanders, can be seen clearly as victims caught in processes of objectification and constraint. Out of this shaping of the violence that occurs on shore are created certain truths and understandings for students of the island reading his official account. This incident can also be seen to shape the subsequent behaviour of the Rapanui towards foreign ships when they stop at the island:

> We set out in the morning with three boats and two sloops, manned with 134 men, all armed with a musket, cartridge pouch and sword. Coming to the shore, we put the boats and sloops close to one another at their grapnels, and as protection for them left in them 20 men with arms as above, but the boat of de Africaansche Galey was also equipped with two Barkers [small cannon] forward on the bow. Having arranged all this we marched, quite close to one another, but not in order of rank, over the rocks which lay in great quantity on the sea-shore up to the level land or plain, indicating by hand that the inhabitants, who came towards us in great numbers, should give way and make room. Having arrived here, the corps de bataille of all the sailors of the three ships was formed, the Commander, Captains Koster, Bouman and Rosendaal at the front, each before his own ship's company; which corps, three rows deep, standing behind one another, was protected by half the soldiers under the command of lieutenant Nicolaas Thonnar, forming the right wing, and the left, consisting of the other half of the military, was commanded by Mr. Martinus Keerens, Ensign. After this arrangement was completed we marched forward a little, in order to give room for some of our people who were in the rear to get themselves into line, then halting so that the hindmost should come up, to our great astonishment and without any expectation it was heard that four to five musket-shots from behind us were made, with a strong shout 'it's time, it's time, fire,' whereupon as in a glance of an eye more than thirty muskets were let off, and the Indians being completely surprised and frightened by this fled, leaving behind 10 or 12 dead, besides the wounded. The Heads of this expedition, standing at the front, stopped the foremost from firing at the fugitives, asking moreover, who had given the order to shoot, and for what reason he had been moved to do this ... (Sharp 1993, 94–5)

Roggeveen takes pains to emphasize that the Dutch leaders were at the front and therefore not aware of the actions at the rear, nor able to control them. In doing so, the leaders abdicate responsibility for the behaviour of their troops and the deaths of the islanders. While Roggeveen's response to the shootings emphasizes surprise at the event with such expressions as 'without any expectation' and 'great astonishment,' his description does not express moral horror at the deaths. As well, the impulse of the troops at the front of the ranks to open fire on the islanders who were running to safety suggests that the frame of mind they carried from the ships to the shore was an expectation of violence. Even those soldiers at the head of the column and physically quite some distance from the running islanders had to be restrained from shooting, 'Heads of this expedition, standing at the front, stopped the foremost from firing at the fugitives.'

Carl Behrens's narration differs in its two eighteenth-century English translations. The first is taken from *The World Displayed*, 1759:

> The Dutch soon after followed them, and landed 150 soldiers and seamen, among whom was the Commodore in person, and the Author, who commanded the land forces; when the people crowded upon them, they had the rashness and cruelty to make their way by force, to which they were particularly prompted, by some of these *Indians*, being so curious as to lay their hands upon their arms. The *Dutch* therefore fired, and by this single discharge, many of these innocent people were killed, and among them the poor *Indian*, who had been twice on board; but though the rest were almost frightened out of their wits, yet in a few moments they rallied again; but kept at the distance of about ten yards, probably supposing they might there be safe from the muskets. Their consternation, however, was not soon over; for they still made dismal lamentations, and purchased the dead bodies of their friends, by giving for them great plenty of provisions of all kinds. In order to pacify these invaders, both the men, women, and children, presented themselves before them, with the most humble postures, how desirous they were to mollify and make them their friends.
>
> The *Dutch* affected by their submissions, did them no farther harm, and being willing to make up all differences between them, made them a present of a painted cloth sixty yards long, and also gave them a considerable quantity of coral, beads, and small looking-glasses, with which they were much pleased. (305–6)

This first English translation/paraphrase of the landing contrasts with Roggeveen's in that it is constructed from a judgmental point of view that responds negatively to the human impulses at work in the events. The 'rashness and cruelty' of the Dutch soldiers, the violent response to 'curiosity,' the death of 'these innocent people,' can all be read as additions by the editors to Behrens's description. The Dalrymple translation of 1770 does not weave a judgmental commentary into the text, but, like the 1759 publication, it does show the perception of emotional response that Behrens read in the actions of the Rapanui as they reacted to the deaths of their relatives.

> At length the landing, so much desired, was made with 150 men, soldiers and sailors; the admiral went in person, and gave me the command of a small body; I was the first who got ashore; the natives immediately came about us in such numbers, that to advance it was necessary to push the croud [sic] and make way by force. As some of them ventured to touch our arms, they were fired upon; which frightened them, and dispersed them immediately, but in a few moments after they rallied. However they did not approach so near as before, but kept constantly about ten paces distant, in the persuasion of being at that distance safe, and out of reach of our muskets.
>
> Unfortunately the discharge we had made killed several, amongst whom was the man who had come first aboard, which chagrined us much.
>
> These good people, that they might get the dead bodies, brought us all kinds of provisions: their consternation was besides very great; they made doleful cries and lamentation; all of them, men, women, and children, in going before us, carried palm-branches and a sort of red and white flag. Their presents consisted in plantains, nuts, sugar-cane, roots, and fowls; they threw themselves on their knees, placed their colours before us, and offered their palm-branches in sign of peace. They testified, by the most humble attitudes, how much they wished for our friendship. At last they shewed us their women, intimating to us that we might dispose of them and carry any of them aboard. Affected with all these demonstrations of humility and the most perfect submission, we did them no harm; on the contrary, made them a present of a whole piece of painted cloth, fifty or sixty yards long, beads, small looking glasses, &c. As they perceived by this, that our intention was to treat them as friends, they brought us soon after five hundred live fowls. (Dalrymple [1770] 1967, 92–3)

It is this second account of Behrens that was read by Cook. It is much more like Roggeveen's narration of the events without Roggeveen's specific need to position himself and his leaders to abdicate responsibility. This failure of command and the inexcusable actions of the soldiers is alluded to and censured in the Spanish and French texts that follow later in the century, as they resist identification with the actions of the

Dutch. Considering the difficulty that the Dutch had in mooring their ships and rowing ashore in smaller craft to visit the island, it is most likely that they had already brought with them the bolt of cloth they distributed to the islanders. Roggeveen, as shall be seen, constitutes the cloth as a barter payment for food. Behrens's text, suggesting that the Dutch, 'being willing to make up all differences between them, made them a present of a painted cloth sixty yards long,' invested it more as a response to the killings.

The Dutch sailor's description of the first shore contact recorded from memory and published in *The Two Years Voyage* offers a very different perception of the events. His position in the crew meant that he was not involved in any concerns about choosing trade goods to take ashore, organizing troops, or dealing with the aftermath of a violent invasion. His text is the first to use the term 'savages':

> On the 10th of April we made for the island in our boats, well armed, in order to land and take a view of this country, where an innumerable multitude of savages stood on the sea side to guard the shore, and obstruct our landing; they threatened us mightily by their gestures, and shewed an inclination to await us and turn us out of their country, but as soon as we, through necessity, gave them a discharge of our muskets, and here and there brought one of them to the ground, they lost their courage. They made the most surprising motions and gestures in the world, and greeted their fallen companions with the utmost astonishment, wondering at the wounds which the bullets had made in their bodies; whereupon they hastily fled, with a dreadful howling, dragging the dead bodies along with them, so the shore was cleared and we landed in safety. (Dalrymple [1770] 1967, 113)

As a crew member, in a top-down hierarchical command structure with little agency for independent action, his narrative does not betray any need to account for his actions. In fact, he celebrates the demonstration of power and superiority. His description of the right to land and explore is a testament to raw, unfiltered imperialism. This account was also read and reacted to by Cook.

The importance of being 'first' must not be overlooked in drawing newness into European history. One key element of contemporary accounts of Easter Island is always a description of its 'discovery.' The Spanish and French become footnotes always superseded by 'the first official text' of Roggeveen which, since its publications more than a hundred years after the 'discovery,' is the one, as noted earlier, that has been taken up and recirculated to represent the first encounter with the island, replacing the 'unreliable' Behrens's account. Roggeveen's official journal constructs events with an emphasis on the imperial mission. The deaths of the islanders evokes so little response that its mention in the text serves more as an embarrassment over a lapse of command than regret and dismay over a needless execution of 'men' on the shores of their home, men who are excitedly experiencing outsiders for the first time. As Roggeveen's narration continues, the incident is quickly written over with the pleasures of commerce:

> After lapse of a little time the Under Mate of the ship Thienhoven came to me saying that he with six men was the last, that one of the inhabitants grasped the muzzle of his musket in order to take if from him by force, whom he pushed back; then that another Indian tried to pull the coat of a sailor off his body, and that some of the inhabitants, seeing our resistance, picked up stones with a menacing gesture of throwing at us, by which by all appearance the shooting by my small troop had been caused, but that he had given no order whatever for this; then as it was not the time for taking appropriate information about this, it was postponed till a better opportunity. After the astonishment and fear of the inhabitants had abated a little, since they saw that no continuance of hostility took place ... the inhabitants who had all the time been near and about the front came back to the Chief Officers, and particularly one, who as it seemed to us had authority over the others, for giving order that all that they had, consisting of fruits, vegetables and fowls, should be fetched and brought from all sides for us, this command was accordingly received with respect and bowing of the body and at once obeyed, as the outcome testified, because after lapse of a little time they brought a large quantity of sugar-cane, fowls, yams and bananas; but we gave them to understand by signs that we wanted nothing excepting only the fowls, being about 60 in number, and 30 bunches of bananas, for which we paid them the value ample with striped linen, with which they appeared to be well pleased and satisfied. (Sharp 1993, 96)

No discomfort is registered in the speed with which the first contact, instigated by an islander, has been replaced by the shootings and by reconstituted islanders who curb their curiosity and now behave in a docile manner. The relationship between the islanders and the Europeans has been reformulated through this act of violence and show of force. The violence has gone beyond physical force, shaping an encounter that sharply limits options for response, coercing the islanders, in the words of Levinas (1961), to 'play roles in which they no longer recognize themselves, making them betray ... their own substance' (21).

Another aspect of this text that contributes to the seminal invention of the 'Easter Islander' is the absence of any attempt to portray islanders as individuals. Even the solo canoeist who comes first to one of the ships is left unnamed. Instead, we see the textual creation of an identity type, an essentialized 'Easter Islander.' The islanders are shaped along the contours of the European construction of the 'Indian' and judged against a European standard as a norm. They are positioned as inferior to that standard on several counts and written into existence through the subjective positioning power of language. The islanders, duly classified and labelled, are constituted through the text. As Foucault (1980) might say, the product of imperial textual power was being exercised over interchangeable 'Indian' bodies (73–4).

Roggeveen takes it in stride that these men should trade, even after having killed so many of them. The trifles bestowed upon the lone man aboard ship have been replaced in this transaction with the assurance that the islanders were given their due, 'we paid them ample value in striped linen,' not, in the official account of Roggeveen, as compensation for the human lives lost but as a fair exchange for the produce and chickens. While the authors of the subsequent explorer texts censure the killing of the islanders, it is never commented upon that in the account they read (Behrens's account – Roggeveen's was not available until 1837), a little cloth clears them of the deed:

> These good people, that they might get the dead bodies, brought us all kinds of provisions ... They testified, by the most humble attitudes, how much they wished for our friendship ... Affected with all these demonstrations of humility and the most perfect submission, we did them no harm; on the contrary, made them a present of a whole piece of painted cloth, fifty or sixty yards long. (Sharp 1993, 97)

Nor did they comment that no punishment was meted out to the soldiers. The shootings are always referred to in order to position the subsequent explorers as superior to those of the first expedition, superior because the leaders on subsequent visits were able to control their men. Even this murderous act is used to keep Europeans foregrounded in the texts about the island, a measurement of subsequent European self-discipline, not a remembrance of men from the island who have lost their lives. As Behrens noted in the quotation above (Dalrymple [1770] 1967, 92), the islander who made first contact was among the twelve men killed. 'Unfortunately the discharge we had made killed several, amongst whom was the man who had come first aboard, which chagrined us much.' Where Behrens's connects cloth for deaths, Roggeveen's text suggests no compensation was warranted for the islanders' lives. In his account, the cloth is a straightforward payment for food.

The textual violence of this foregrounding and superior valuation of Europeans over natives is still being re-inscribed today. One recent text from Scholastics Inc., *What You Don't Know about Mysterious Places* (2002), published for elementary-age students, presents the first shore contact as follows:[9]

> Armed with guns, Roggeveen's sailors landed on the island and were met
> by many natives who carried spears. In his journal, Roggeveen wrote that
> his men were surrounded by 'thousands' of natives. Apparently, the sail-
> ors were more than a little nervous, and they opened fire and killed nine or
> ten natives. Despite being greatly outnumbered, the Dutch Sailors left
> unharmed. (23)

The Rapanui as thieves is also still emphasized in contemporary works that focus on the island in books that continue to be written from within an imperial framework for making meaning, often with as much dramatic licence as in the following twenty-first century text:

> For the Rapanui, filching was an art form, and anything left unattended
> was immediately whisked away. We do not know how things suddenly
> turned sour. Perhaps a group of sailors were maddened by some barefaced
> larceny. Anyway the fact is that the curious bystanders were mowed down
> by musket fire and Roggeveen's man [sic] had to dash back to their boats,
> taking no more than a few provisions. (Barbier 2001, 412)

Evaluating the Island

While the islanders presented the Dutch with the foods they produced on the island, Roggeveen had an opportunity to examine the details of dress that had suggested riches when seen from aboard the ship. Even before sighting the islanders, when rising smoke seen from sea proved to the Dutch there was human life, the commercial concerns of the expedition were front and foremost. Their intent, on landing was

> to see and inquire what they wear or make use of either as ornaments or
> for other purposes ... [t]hey reported that the inhabitants there were very
> finely clad in some stuffs of all kinds of colours ... [f]urthermore some
> thought they had seen the natives to have plates of silver in their ears, and
> mother-of-pearl ornaments about their necks. (Corney 1903, 8)

But close contact proved that the native dress and ornamentation was
not as it had seemed:

> By the time we had fully investigated things, and especially their cloth
> stuffs and the dyes of them, and also the supposed silver plates and
> mother-of-pearl, it was found that they were made up of pieces patched
> together; that is, that the wraps worn on their bodies were composed of
> some field-product, sewn three or four ply in thickness, yet neat and trim,
> ... further, ... their dye is not fast, ... the colour comes off on one's fingers ...
> The plates imagined to be of silver were made out of the root of some veg-
> etable ... furthermore, the mother-of-pearl which was seen as a neck pen-
> dent is a flat shell of the same tint as the inner lip of our oysters. (Corney
> 1903, 13–15)

This evaluation of the island through commercial eyes registers disappointment in the lack of riches. It reads as if the islanders have presented a false front to the Europeans. References to 'supposed silver'
and their dye not being fast seem to have lured them ashore only to let
them down. The European imagination and desire to find wonders,
coupled with commercial avarice, lead to disappointment.

Stephen Greenblatt (1991) describes the frequency and intensity of
the appeal to wonder in the wake of the great geographical discoveries
of European nations in the late fifteenth and early sixteenth centuries
(19). But here, in the eighteenth century, we see the desire for commercial gain trumping wonder. It must be remembered that this first expedition was not mounted by a Royal Society acquiring knowledge or a
king offering philanthropy as would follow with the British and French
expeditions. Those were foci that developed later in the eighteenth century. This expedition was mounted by an investment company, driven
by new trade possibilities and seeking returns on its capital outlay. Roggeveen's assignment is ever before him. He is on a prospecting mission
and charged with finding wealth for his sponsors. While there may be
no mineral or textile wealth, he does think the island itself would make
a good plantation. 'This place, as far as its rich soil and good climate are

concerned, is such that it might be made into an earthly paradise, if it were properly worked and cultivated; which is now only done in so far as the inhabitants are obliged to for the maintenance of life' (Sharp 1993, 103). With this statement Roggeveen anticipates the arrival of the 'Easter Island Exploitation Company' in 1895, over a century and a half later.

The island, so promising from out at sea, where it could be written over with imperial desire before it was actually visited, was not found to contain any 'real' riches. This disappointment in the potential for commercial gain seems to have shaped Roggeveen's response to the most overt cultural presence on the island – the moai:

> [At] first, these stone figures caused us to be filled with wonder, for we could not understand how it was possible that people who were destitute of heavy or thick timber, and also of stout cordage, out of which to construct gear, had been able to erect them; nevertheless some of these statues were a good thirty feet in height and broad in proportion. This perplexity ceased, however, with the discovery, on removing a piece of the stone, that they were formed out of clay or some kind of rich earth, and that small smooth flints had been stuck over afterwards, which are fitted very closely and neatly to each other, so as to make up the semblance of a human figure. Moreover, one saw reaching downwards from the shoulders a slight elevation or prominence which represented the arms, for all the statues seemed to convey the idea that they were hung about with a long robe from the neck right down to the soles of the feet.[10] They have on the head a basket heaped up with flints painted white deposited on it. It was incomprehensible to us how these people cook their food, for no one was able to perceive or find that they had any earthen pots, pans or vessels. (Corney 1903, 15–16)

Behrens's description of the moai, below, in the 1903 translation from the German, is a much more 'accurate' representation of the sculptures and their platforms than is Roggeveen's and stands in counterpoint to his 'official' and authoritative report:

> The people had, to judge by appearances, no weapons; although as I remarked, they relied in case of need on their gods or idols which stand erected all along the sea shore in great numbers, before which they fall down and invoke them. These idols were all hewn out of stone, and in the form of a man, with long ears, adorned on the head with a crown, yet all

made with skill: whereat we wondered not a little. A clear space was reserved round these objects of worship by laying stones to a distance of twenty or thirty paces. I took some of these people to be priests because they showed more reverence to the gods than did the rest; and showed themselves much more devout in their ministrations. One could also distinguish these from the other people quite well, not only by their wearing great white plugs in their ear lobes, but in having the head holy shaven and hairless. One of them was with us aboard the ship as above related. They wore a head-dress of white and black feathers which were just like storks' feathers ... (Corney 1903, 136)

Roggeveen having seen the moai as clay is a perplexing conclusion to have reached. Even if the moai were made of clay, the clay would have had to be fired in order to withstand the weather. To have fired such enormous clay statues would have required the same timber for fuel that Roggeveen notes would have been needed to move them if they were carved of stone. The same impulse to be filled with wonder at the sight of carved statues should have held true if they were beholding clay statues. To successfully fire even small works of clay takes great skill, but to fire and move three-story clay figures ... ? Whether understood as carved or clay there is still missing, in this Dutch response, an acknowledgment of the moai as the engineering feat that they, in fact, are. This diminution of the accomplishment of carving and moving the moai may have been because the appearances of the other wonderful things they thought they would find on the island – silver, fine textiles – had proved to be false, or perhaps it was because they could not imagine how the sculptures had been moved. To acknowledge the extent of the moai accomplishment would have required the Dutch to position the islanders closer to themselves in the 'fixed hierarchy of civil progress.' Having come ashore and immediately shot and killed several members of the greeting party, it was perhaps best to downplay any accomplishments of the culture that would suggest an elevated level of civilization or technical accomplishment. By acknowledging the achievement of the island culture, Roggeveen might have felt he would have to face greater censure from his sponsors for taking the lives of so many islanders. In fact, on his return home he was accused of 'brutality toward the natives' and of 'failing in his quest' (Dos Passos 1971, 6).

The possibility that Roggeveen is downplaying the impressiveness of the moai is reinforced by the fact that the description of the moai is immediately followed by information about island cooking methods.

Even though the whole text on the island is divided into paragraphs, there is no paragraph break leading from the discussion of the moai to a discussion of cooking. The moai description ends with the sentence, 'They have on the head a basket heaped up with flints painted white deposited on it.' This is immediately followed by the statement, 'It was incomprehensible to us how these people cook their food, for no one was able to perceive or find that they had any earthen pots, pans or vessels.' Not only is the cooking reference without any segue to the preceding sentences about the moai, but the reference to an absence of earthen cooking pots, pans, or vessels is not connected back in any way to the oddity of this domestic omission in the face of all the clay apparently available for statue-making. This passage continues with a description of the food served after the slaying of the twelve islanders when the Dutch first came ashore: 'broiled fowl to eat very neatly wrapped round in a kind of rush, clean and hot' (Corney 1903, 16).

This menu presentation is followed by an acknowledgment that a great effort is being expended in order to keep the Dutch troops from affronting any islanders. At the same time, Roggeveen feels the need to impress upon his audience the potential for violence from the islanders that may lie beneath the surface of this encounter. To maintain the viability of the performance position of the Europeans in this encounter, Roggeveen's narrative must introduce a potential threat to help balance the actual violence committed by the Dutch:

> Though they were thanked by means of signs, we had quite enough business in hand to look after our people so as to keep order among them, and prevent any affront being offered; and also that in the event of any struggle occurring they should not allow themselves to be taken by surprise, for although these people showed us every sign of friendship, yet the experience of others has taught us that one may not put too much trust in any Indians as recounted in the Journal of the Nassau Fleet, which lost seventeen men on one occasion through the willingness of the natives of Terra de Feu to pretend to be well disposed. (Corney 1903, 16–17)

In this passage is an overt example of narrative imposition. 'Knowledge' about the islanders is being created based on the experience of other explorers and other 'Indians' rather than on any actual experience of these islanders in the most easterly part of Polynesia. This bestowing of violent power in potential is not the obvious or expected instance of the Dutch positioning themselves as powerful in relation to 'inferior' natives. Rather, the Dutch invested potential power in the natives through language in order to offset their own abuse of it. It is the islanders who were taken by surprise, but it is the Dutch who are writing the narrative. The islanders are entering imperial consciousness through this text, from the outset fixed into a position distant socially from the narrating centre. They are in the process of becoming a subject, whose discursive substance is shaped, not by the events that have transpired on the island but by the forces of the imperial framework into which they are coalescing as discursive beings. Foucault (1970) would describe this as their discursive substance being both 'constrained and enabled by the temporal space into which they are emerging' and within which they will continuously be inscribed and transformed' (32).

Even though the islanders do not behave like the 'Indians' of Terra de Feu, they are constructed through that previous experience in order to keep them in a disadvantageous subject position, bestowing violent power upon them in order to keep them fixed as untrustworthy and 'civilly' inferior. By suggesting the possibility of violence lurking just under the surface of a friendly manner, the text continues to position these Others as threatening to the European self regardless of the validity of this assumption. It also makes a more dramatic narrative for public consumption, and helps offset the violence that has already been committed by the Dutch.

As well as emphasizing the possibility of violence, by dismissing the monuments as built of clay, despite empirical evidence to the contrary, the Roggeveen text diminishes the sophisticated engineering accomplishments of the island people, a pernicious motif that echoes through writing about the people to the present day. Without material wealth or cultural accomplishment, it is easier to define the islanders as socially and politically inconsequential, erasing them from the economic equation, and focusing instead upon the profitable plantation possibilities the island itself may have for imperial enterprises.

We see in Roggeveen the beginning of a splitting off of the islanders from their land in the minds of the outsiders. People and territory emerge as a subject to be manipulated to imperial ends, subjects that can be dealt with in isolation from one another. It is possible to begin the process of establishing political control over the islanders, who have been constituted as immoral through their thievery and as potentially volatile because they are 'Indians.' By positioning them in this way they are denied the kind of personhood that would allow then to be seen as a match for the explorers. The implication of latent violence gives the right to repress and the thievery the right to dismiss. The acreage of the island itself and the positive evaluation of its latent fertility positions it as an object of knowledge quite apart from the people who live on it but who do not use it beyond the minimal needed for the 'maintenance of life.' By constituting the land as undercultivated, the narrative sets up an obligation to put it to good use, thus establishing the reasonableness of eventual acquisition and domination. The narrative also anticipates, through its devaluation of the islanders, their near extermination through slavery by 1862. Here we see the beginning of what Robert Young (1990) describes as European history shaping itself through the Hegelian dialectic. The Rapanui Other is positioned in a hierarchy in which the European 'rules, names, defines, and assigns its other,' and that Other then falls 'outside of history' as absolutely Other (2).

The split between island and islander and subsequent backgrounding of the Rapanui is part of a dividing process that continues in narrative strands about Easter Island to this day. In such texts the islanders are constructed as other than the people who carved the moai, seen as degenerated descendents of the moai carvers, or written out of existence the better to present a mystery about who could have carved and moved the moai. In some texts the islanders are entirely erased from the subject of the island and their culture. Without their presence, the geographic imaginary of the island serves as a staging ground for the exploits and theories of foreigners more interested in centring themselves in the narrative than in meeting and learning to know the Rapanui.

4 The Spanish

1770

The Rapanui, as they acted and reacted to the presence and behaviour of the Dutch, were constituted and reconstituted through the discursive perceptions of an anonymous sailor, Behrens, and Roggeveen, who measured them against European norms and codes and then embodied them in their texts. They are represented as 'hapless'; the first Rapanui encountered was judged as wanting, for his nakedness and lack of European table manners, despite his inquisitiveness and comprehension of European marine technology. Rapanui are thereafter constituted as uncontrollable thieves who evolve into a threatening presence that has to be quelled. Then their representation is as humbled natives, subdued, but with a subtext of possible threat still lurking below the surface and requiring a keen watchfulness.

The rest of the explorers' texts from the eighteenth century take up the anonymous sailor's and Behrens's narratives to reinforce, resist, or reshape the story they tell. Forty-eight years after the Dutch had arrived, the Spanish sailed to the island. The focus of this chapter is on how the Spanish wrote themselves into their own text about the newly emerged subject of Easter Island. It examines how their texts write back to Dampier's record of sighting Davis Island (or David Island as the Spanish translates into English); and it examines the vision of the island that emerged from the interplay of writing variables that produced their narratives.

The Spanish expedition first enters public textual circulation in English through 1771 newspaper articles in *Lloyd's Evening Post and British Chronicle* and the *St James's Chronicle*:[1]

Naples October 10

David Island was always judged to be farther than it is from Callao. It is now ascertained to be but 605 leagues from that port, and 680 from Chili [*sic*] ... Their approach did not seem to inspire the inhabitants with either fear or uneasiness. Their first principle is, that all men are brothers, and therefore there is no reason to be afraid of each other; Several of them jumped into the water and swam to meet the ships, offering fruits poultry etc. ... After visiting David Island, the Commandant took possession of it in the name of the King of Spain, with all military formalities that tend to command respect from his subjects. A cross was immediately erected to perpetuate the memory of that event and the island was named Saint Charles.

David Island has scarce 1000 inhabitants; their disposition is perfectly mild, but their height and strength render them fit for the strongest exercises; they are unacquainted with metals and riches, which people think they want, and consequently arts are but little cultivated among them; they have no arms nor cutting instruments, and as they are ready to part with anything they are possessed of, they as readily take anything that gives them pleasure. Men born in rude and savage climates are naturally of a ferocious disposition. A fertile soil, which leaves nothing for the inhabitants to wish for, softens their manners, and inclines them to humanity. This is without doubt, the cause of the sweet disposition of the inhabitants of David Island; they have poultry in great plenty, and enjoy those products of the earth which require little culture; they live in caves and grottoes under ground; and worship stone statues of a gigantic size. (Corney 1903, xlvii–xlviii)

In this telescoped description of the island, précised from a Spanish account, Rapanui culture is emphasized over island geography in a reversal of the Roggeveen document. The islanders are positioned within an imperial rubric of measurement composed of categories such as temperament, physical strength and proportion, artistic achievement, technology and material possessiveness, and judged against each. There is a perplexing disjunct between the note that 'arts are but little cultivated among them,' and they 'worship stone statues of a gigantic size.' Already can be seen the unwillingness of the imperial record to associate the island inhabitants with the achievement of erecting the statues.

As well, the British, mindful of their own early claim to the discovery of the island, write over its Spanish naming even as they report it.

Nowhere does the Dutch visit to Easter Island enter the mix, perhaps because the two Dutch accounts then available did not associate their discovery with Davis Island; only Roggeveen does, at a later date. Until James Cook's visit to accurately map the island, with his acknowledged superior navigational and measurement skills, there seems to have lingered some confusion and contestation as to whether Davis Island (or San Carlos in the Spanish) was, in fact, Easter Island.[2] This interplay of names and national posturing is an expression of the European imperial sense of entitlement to know and claim the world to its own ends. As well, it points to the inability of these narratives of exploration to stabilize their vision of the island while it emerged as a discursive subject through their texts.

Although James Cook refers to his awareness of the Spanish expedition shortly before his own, the actual Spanish expedition journals and letters were not translated and published in English until 1903. Three journals were kept during the expedition: one by the commodore Don Felipe; a 'fuller' journal written by Don Juan Hervé, a naval sublieutenant who occupied the position of first pilot on the *San Lorenzo*; and the 'fullest' journal written by Don Francisco Antonio de Agüera y Infanzon, sublieutenant and first pilot of the *Santa Rosalia* (Corney 1903, lxv).

The Spanish Expedition

The Spanish expedition mandate shifts from the Dutch 'discovering' new lands to a 'claiming' of lands for the Spanish Empire. This one-sided political discourse, concerning itself only with the desires of the Europeans to possess, commanded the polite fiction of willingness on the part of the inhabitants of the claimed land to comply with their absorption into the foreign empire making the claim, and to comply with their concomitant subjugation by that empire. This point of view grounds the Spanish narrative construction about their encounter with the Rapanui, as it grounded their actual interaction with the islanders. Since the emphasis of the encounter was on positive relations with the people, the roles the Spanish played out in relation to the Rapanui were benign and generous and thus well received. In fact, the Spanish expedition added to the island repertoire for 'practising newness' first experienced with the Dutch, and resulted in several aspects of this Spanish staging of imperial theatre being taken up and incorporated into Rapanui cultural activities (to be examined in the second half of this chapter). The agency that opened for Rapanui performance affected their interaction with the final two expeditions of the eighteenth century, the British and the French. These expeditions, in turn, had a direct impact on the representation of the Rapanui to a European audience. For this reason the Spanish expedition texts, although not widely circulated, nevertheless require close examination for the part their expedition played in the textual invention of Easter Island by subsequent explorers.

A copy of one of Behrens's accounts of the Roggeveen expedition is conserved in the Spanish Archives of the Indies in Seville, suggesting an awareness of the island by Captain Don Felipe Gonzalez Y Haedo in 1770, before the Spanish voyage (Dos Passos 1971, 23). As well, Manuel de Amat refers in a dispatch to the secretary of state for the Indies, that Davis Island might be explored during the calm weather:

> Observing the number, description, and character of its native inhabitants, their system of government, their weapons, or trade, and the conveniences or drawbacks which the soil offers for a permanent occupation ... No doubt the aforementioned island of *David* is one of these [islands in an extensive chain] and that of *Otaeyte* [Tahiti] will be another, together with all the rest which modern voyagers delineate, and before them the author of the *Histoire de las Navegaciones a las tierras Australes* [M. le Président Charles de Brosse] printed at Paris in the year 1756, at fol. 230 of the 2nd volume, where he describes Easter Island, which corresponds in all respects to the one now refound. (Manuel de Amat, qtd in Corney 1903, 80)

The Archives of the Indies in Seville is a large collection of books, manuscripts, and documents on the history and administration of the Spanish Empire in the Americas. In the naming of this repository the 'Archives of the Indies,' we are kept mindful of the imposition of the European Orientalist framework upon the Pacific as it was being explored, imagined through European languages, and taken through them into European cultural circulation. The Spanish, like the Dutch, 'understood' the Pacific from within this Oriental discursive space. Behrens's text and the anonymous sailor's established the discovery of the island and named it into European existence. The Spanish, as the second nation of explorers to visit, travelled there with the purpose of claiming and renaming the island for Spain. Unlike the Dutch, their expedition was not governed by any fear of the inhabitants of the island. Quite the reverse, they were more concerned about the behaviour of their own soldiers and mariners, not wishing them to repeat the violent and deadly encounter of their predecessors in this part of the Pacific.

The success of the mission to Rapa Nui was anticipated by the Spanish with a thorough mapping and renaming of every headland and cove around the island before it was actually 'claimed' in a ceremony on their last day ashore before sailing away:

> We set to work to take soundings, giving names to the points, bays, &c., as shown on the plan of the island. At half-past six in the evening we brought in to a cove which we called after [Don Cayetano] Lángara ... Then we passed on to examine the rocky islets to which we gave the name of Lángara: they lie s.w. 1/4 s. from the cape [we named] San Cristoval. (Don Juan Hervé, qtd in Corney 1903, 120–1)

Because the island is so very small, about sixty-six square miles in total, and because it had been the entire known world for the Rapanui since some time between 400 and 600 CE, the inhabitants themselves, over many generations of living there, knew and had named every small feature of their homeland. The Rapanui trace their ancestry through specific clan designations, each clan having once inhabited its own bounded region of the land space. It is difficult to walk over the island landscape in the present day without seeing in the placement of rocks for boundary markers and cooking fires, in the stone foundations of former houses, in the petroglyphs adorning smooth surfaces, and in the numerous cairns of stone assembled for domestic, agricultural, and funerary purposes, the long-established interaction of a people with their own place. The Spanish overwriting of the local names, the brisk violence of erasure, is a demonstration of what Stephen Greenblatt (1991) describes as the power of representations, in this case maps, as products and as producers, capable of decisively altering the very forces that brought them into being (6). As the Spanish text busily lists each new name conferred upon the island features, an intertextual space of island representation is opened in relation to other European texts about the island, both the Dutch texts before and most texts that have followed. Within that space circulate the various names for the island, all imposed from without and vying for ascendancy.

The Spanish name of San Carlos has never taken hold in the geographic imaginary of European historic or contemporary cultural capital about the island as a whole, but other European names have. Many

English-language books about Easter Island feature a map. On these maps, following the shoreline, are written such names as Cape Roggeveen, Cape O'Higgins, La Pérouse Bay, and Cook's Bay. The effect of these European names is the continued imposition of European reality upon a non-European space – power through language to impose a context of European history, the island brought into existence through European imperialism. Such a process is invested with a discursive violence that denies the reality of the Rapanui living their own history on the island, giving value only to European visitation and awareness of the space.

The politics of this claiming discourse required the Spanish to comport themselves during the mapping process with the utmost civility in order to win over the compliance of their future subjects. The desires for civility intersected with the national will to outperform the Dutch in their interactions with the islanders. The resulting Spanish record is doubly civil as it records these encounters:

> ... two little canoes were coming out from among them with two men in each, making for the *Santa Rosalía's* launch; so we waited for them in order that they might join our party. They gave the people of the said launch plantains, Chilli peppers, sweet potatoes and fowls; and in return our men gave them hats, *chamorretas* [trinkets], &c., and they went off contentedly with these to the shore ... We all went ashore to eat our dinner, which we carried with us for the purpose, and some hundred or so natives came to look on, offering us fruits and hens. (Hervé, qtd in Corney 1903, 121–2)

The text rehearses national civility to successfully woo the natives at the same time as it goes on to refer more than once to the steely grip of command over the Spanish soldiers and mariners that prevents the sort of disgrace committed by the Dutch:

> The officer, Don Cayetano de Lángara, issued orders to our people that no one, under pain of a severe flogging, should accept any article from the islanders without giving some equivalent in return, or something of greater value than which they received, since it was certain there was disposition to exchange articles; which was immediately put into practice ... When we had finished dinner we betook ourselves for a stroll on the island: our people were again warned to do no injury to the natives nor to their plantations ... At dusk we made back to our launches to stay the night, without our peaceful relations with the natives having been in any

way disturbed, which may be attributed to the order which the officer gave to our men not to give them any offence, backed by the threat of a flogging, without which our marines and seamen would have destroyed these poor wretches' plantations. (ibid., 122–4)

In repeated references to the control the officers exercise over their men, and in the references to eating their own food from aboard ship and engaging in fair exchange, can be seen a direct example of the way that the Spanish narrative writes back to the Dutch record, implicitly censuring the lack of control exercised by the Dutch. When we read about the Spanish bringing their own food from their ship, we are reminded of the Dutch shooting islanders and then sitting down to be fed by the survivors. The references to fair exchange conjure up images of the sixty chickens and thirty bunches of bananas the Dutch received for a bolt of cloth. The Spanish report speaks directly to Spanish imperial institutions and it speaks back to the Dutch narration. At the same time it positions the islanders as 'these poor wretches' without any power in relation to the Spanish officers, who, out of their great charity, save the 'wretches' from Spanish marines and seamen. A lack of overt references to the Dutch visit to the island suggests a desire to see San Carlos as unexplored real estate and therefore to lend greater weight to the Spanish proclamation of possession.

The islanders are, through this positioning in language, created as subjects in need of paternal aid, constituted as unable to flourish on their own. While most of the narrative focuses on the activities of the Spanish on the island, there are two paragraphs at the end of the text that imply what could be done on such an island, with such people:

They have very little wood; but if they were to plant trees there would be no lack of it; and I believe that even the cotton plant would yield, as the country is very temperate; and wheat, garden plants, pot-herbs, &c. They dye their cloaks yellow.

The number of inhabitants, including both sexes, will be from about nine hundred to a thousand souls: and of these very few indeed are women, – I do not believe they amount to seventy – and but few boys. They are in hue like a quadroon, with smooth hair and short beards, and they in no way resemble the Indians of the South American continent; and if they wore clothing like ourselves they might very well pass for Europeans. They eat very little, and have few needs: they do altogether without liquor of any kind. (ibid., 126–7)[3]

The implication for the Spanish empire is blatant in this description. The largely male 'workforce' requires a minimal amount of food and does not dissipate itself with drink. Combining that workforce with such a temperate and fertile island, it should be possible to orchestrate a cost-effective plantation to add to Spain's 'international' holdings. The journal of Don Francisco Antonio de y Infanzon, chief pilot, takes this sentiment a step further:

> They are tall, well built and proportioned in all their limbs ... their appearance being thoroughly pleasing and tallying with Europeans more than with Indians. I believe from their docility and intelligence, that it would be easy to domesticate them and to convert them to any religion which might be put before them. (Corney 1903, 96)

The term 'domesticate' commodifies the islanders, positioning them in the same discursive space as trainable animals, oxen perhaps, to work the fields. It anticipates the South American slave raids on the island that occurred during the nineteenth century.

This assessment by members of the expedition is reinforced by the desire for Pacific property relayed through the minister of state to the viceroy of Peru in the form of royal commands after the 'acquisition' of the island. One command requires action 'to forestall the suspected designs of the British, or any other foreign nation, towards establishing for themselves colonies or naval bases in the Eastern Pacific' (Corney 1903, xxvii). Another states that:

> Pending his Majesty's decision with regard to the kind of establishment to be deemed most suitable, some vessels should be dispatched to cultivate the friendship of the native inhabitants, taking them presents and using the opportunity to make a more thorough examination of the island for forming a settlement for the families and missionaries which His Majesty may decide to despatch thither. October 9, 1771. (ibid., 64–5)
>
> ... the new Island of *David* – now *Sn Carlos* – in the South Seas ... he views that useful discovery with two aims in mind – the first, to rescue the Natives from their retched state of idolatry, winning them by such discreet and gentle means as may be to a knowledge of the true God and the profession of our Catholic Religion: and the second to gain effective possession of the said island in such wise that no Foreign Nation shall occupy it. December 11, 1771. (ibid., 70–1)

Implicated in this last dispatch is the Spanish capacity, as representatives of the Catholic Church, to save the souls of the Rapanui in tandem with taking their land and pressing them into the service of the Spanish Empire. Through this agency to possess, enabled by imperialism and Christianity, the Spanish used authoritative texts to coerce Others to meet their own ends, showing complete indifference to Rapanui consciousness.

The emphasis of the Spanish voyage journals is on descriptions of good anchorage and examples of how well the Spanish behaved. Only two sentences in the Hervé journal are devoted to descriptions of the foremost cultural presence on the island, the moai atop the ahu (platforms) that dominate the landscape. The text states that 'throughout the island, but especially at the sea-beach, there are certain huge blocks of stone in the form of the human figure. They are some twelve yards in height, and I think they are their idols' (Corney 1903, 30–1). The Infanzon journal spends two pages describing the moai, but the descriptions are limited by the artistic conventions he uses as he tries to read what he sees: 'What we took for shrubs of a pyramidal form are in reality statues'; 'the only feature in the configuration of the face is a rough excavation for the eyes'; 'the mouth extends from ear to ear'; 'arms and legs are wanting.' The technology required to place the crowns on the statues 'causes wonder.' In a first step towards the future interest that would develop about the 'mystery of Easter Island,' Infanzon says: 'I even think that the stone of which the statues are made is not a product of the island, in which iron, hemp, and stout timber are absolutely unknown. Much remains to be worked out on this subject' (ibid., 93–4). In spite of spending more time on the island than any other of the four eighteenth-century expeditions, the Spanish apparently did not see the quarry at Rano Raraku from which the statues were carved, which is actually very close to the point on the island where they erected three large crosses. It must be remembered, however, that before the introduction of sheep to the island in the late nineteenth century, the moai on the slopes of the volcano Rano Raraku would have been obscured by tall native grasses.

For the purposes of the Spanish, navigational accessibility and a lengthy description of the ceremony of claiming the island were the main interest in San Carlos – strategic position and possession. The very civility of the language with which they describe their encounter, appraise the island and inhabitants, and word their royal proclamation, belies the violence of their use of authoritative texts and language to proclaim a right to ownership. Textual violence writes over the Rapanui reality with a Spanish reality shaped through Spanish names for the paper-inscribed mapping of the land; the textual authority of the Bible authorizes conversion and proposes to violate the cosmology and philosophy of the Rapanui; and text proclaims ownership through a paper-and-ink proclamation. For more than a century, issues of imperial land acquisition, human 'domestication,' and religious conversion would continue to be valorized over inquiry into the Rapanui culture.

Gifting

What is notably missing in these Spanish accounts, considering its prominence in Roggeveen, is any mention of theft. Not once in the Hervé narrative is there any suggestion of theft in the three references made to contact with the islanders that involved exchanges. Rather, the description is of gifts being given and received on both sides:

> In the cutter ... and awaiting the arrival of the ship, three of the natives swam off, painted in various colours and keeping near the boat, shouting constantly, until one of them came at last so close as to present me with a morsel of yam: I gave him some biscuit and tobacco, all of which he accepted. He carried his provisions in a basket neatly plaited of fine straw ... on board of which they climbed with much agility, shouting all the while and exhibiting much gayness of spirit. They ran about freely from stem to stern, and full of mirth, climbing about in the rigging like sailor-men. Our people played the bagpipes and fife for them, and they began to dance, evincing great pleasure. They were given ribbons, shirts, trousers, seamens' jumpers, and small gilt crosses: they accepted them with all gladness ... they gave the people of the said launch plantains, Chili [sic] peppers, sweet potatoes and fowls; and in return our men gave them hats, chamorretas [trinkets], &c., and they went off contentedly with these to the shore. (Hervé, qtd in Corney 1903, 120–1)

This description of mutual gift exchange is similar to that of Carl Behrens. It raises again the need to recognize the constructed nature of these explorer accounts, each offering a different version of 'reality.' It points to the shaping of the text to suit narrative ends, the shaping of 'truth' from a range of possibilities, and the extent to which the 'Easter Island' in textual circulation begins as a narrative invention.

Hervé describes the performance of the custom of gifting as the offering of food and acceptance of European goods in return. Infanzon comments upon gifting first from the point of being the receivers of island largess. It is a phenomenon he is unfamiliar with but accepts as an island code:

> Today great numbers of natives of both sexes came on board of the two vessels; we found them very straightforward and agreeable, most of them brought plantains, roots, chickens, &c., and readily offered the wretched scraps of clothing and other goods they had about them, until reduced to a miserable loin-cloth of fibre ... (Infanzon, qtd in Corney 1903, 96–7)

Infanzon goes on the write about the gifts of the body that women on the island are offering the mariners: 'They all of them yield with the same frankness whatever they possess, and the women go to the same length of offering with inviting demonstrations all the homage that an impassioned man can desire' (ibid., 97). Infanzon's first mention of embodied gifting reminds us of the 'unnatural' imbalance the Rapanui would have read in the all-male party of Spaniards travelling vast distances across time and space. Both groups, the Spanish and the Rapanui, were patriarchal in their social organization. In both groups women were understood from the androcentric world view to be a natural and complementary part of male reality. But within this Polynesian society, as on other Polynesian islands, women, before they married, were 'allowed' by their culture a high degree of sexual expression (Métraux 1971, 107–208; McCall 1994, 53). The Polynesian practice of gifting, bound as it is with hospitality rather than commerce, seems to have adapted itself physically to the circumstances of the visitors.

Infanzon's second reference is a brief commentary on the nature of internal-island sharing practices. While his descriptions do not mirror perfectly the notion of Polynesian gifting as outlined by Lewis Hyde, the disruption to the isolated and formalized internal island gifting practices by the introduction of sudden newness must be taken into account as a catalyst breaking down and reformulating the traditional practice in light of new stimuli. What had been the consequences of the Dutch visit forty-eight years earlier to island gifting traditions, and what behaviours had islanders rehearsed in anticipation of a subsequent visit?[4] Infanzon writes:

> The principal men as well as the women, are extremely addicted to beg,

and take with gladness whatever comes to their hands, without making any return; they show no resentment if deprived of their spoils: they are quite content with old rags, ribbons, coloured paper, playing-cards, and other bagatelles. Everything of a bright red colour pleases them greatly, but they despise black; they are so fond of taking other people's property that what one man obtains another will take from him, and he yields it without feeling aggrieved: the most he will do is to resist a little, then he loosens his hold of it and they remain friends.

It appears as if among themselves their goods are held in common, and I believe they conceal as much as they can get possession of below ground, for we never saw afterwards any of the things we gave them. (qtd. in Corney 1903, 98)

Nicholas Thomas's book *Entangled Objects: Exchange, Material Culture, and Colonialism in the Pacific* (1991), quotes C.A. Gregory on an aspect of the practice of Polynesian gifting that may apply to Infanzon's description: 'The giver acquires some sort of superiority over the receiver: a relationship of indebtedness is therefore established. Gifts are inalienable things which move between people who are mutually entangled in an array of rights and obligations, people who are "reciprocally dependent"' (14). This idea of reciprocal dependence raises the question as to who might have been first to paddle from the island out to the ships to present food? Would an understanding of the body tattoo patterns have shown them to be emissaries of each clan taking gifts of food on behalf of their relatives? Such questions about specific acts of gifting can only be musings. What is understood about Polynesian gifting practices is captured by Lewis Hyde (1979) in his statement that 'there will be an ongoing generalized indebtedness, gratitude, expectation, memory, sentiment – in short lively social feelings' (84).

Without the focus on theft in the Spanish accounts, emphasis is placed on the 'lively social feelings,' the pleasure in European music expressed by the islanders just as it was by the first islander to board a ship in the Behrens account: 'Our people played the bagpipes and fife for them, and they began to dance, evincing great pleasure.' The dancing aboard ship in response to the music is echoed in the description of the events surrounding the claiming of the island for Spain. The islanders are depicted as enthusiastically participating in the pageantry of the ceremony to take possession of the island. The Spanish formed themselves into ranks for orderly procession much as the Dutch did when they first came ashore, but with different consequences:

On the 20th, at daybreak, all the seamen bearing arms embarked in the
launches and cutters of both vessels, under Don Alberto Olaondo, Captain
of Marines, with his party of marines and those from the frigate, who
together made up 250 men ... Our commander Don José Bustillos, went
with another body of marines and seamen, and the two chaplains, who
conveyed with them three crosses to be erected on three hill-tops ... A great
number of native inhabitants received them on landing, and offered to
assist our officers in the disembarkation, which, in fact they did; and took
charge of the three crosses, which they carried up to the said hills. (Corney
1903, 125)

The Spanish ceremony of acquisition would have been read by the
Rapanui through their own social-cultural codes and taken up by them
in a range of possible responses, some of which are considered in the
second half of this chapter.

One of the features of the island remarked upon in the eighteenth
century was the absence of large tree specimens and incidence of managed groves of agricultural trees and crops such as the paper mulberry
and banana. The lack of wood was noted for its effect on the lives of the
islanders. Contemporary anthropological and archaeological studies
interpret the island's cultural past as having land distribution and
economies divided between two dominant clans, one living on the
north shore, building boats and fishing, the other living along the south
shore and raising crops. No evidence of an indigenous mammal population has been found on the island, although bone deposits in middens
suggest it did have 'one of the richest collections of sea and terrestrial
birds in the Pacific' when the Rapanui first colonized it (McCall 1994,
36). Polynesian rats and domestic chickens also found in the middens
are described through islander oral tradition as having been brought to
the island in the original human migration. Core sampling, and the discovery of centuries-old rat-gnawed seeds in caves, has recently offered
a new narrative of the island agricultural economy in the centuries
before contact with Europeans. The current theory is that over time the
forests were depleted through a combination of a high population burden on the resources of the island that necessitated clear-cutting to use
land for cultivation, and the inability of new trees to propagate because
the Polynesian rats ate the palm seeds and seedlings before new trees
could grow to maturity, bringing to an end the natural forest regeneration (Flenley and Bahn 2003, 172–3). There is also the possibility the rats
ate the eggs of shore birds, removing that source of food for the

Rapanui. Middens show evidence that fish, supplemented by the imported rats and chickens, became the main sources of protein for the human population on the island. Fishing, however, was curtailed as wood became scarce, then unattainable, for new boats or even for the repair of old boats. Without fish to trade with those who planted crops, the exchange economies between the clans would have been severely altered. Within this version of the past, the inclusion of three large pieces and three smaller pieces of wood, composing the crosses in the Spanish procession, must have been the cause of some excitement.

One can imagine the completely different point of view of the islanders as the procession made its way up the three different hills to plant the crosses. These pieces of wood were being planted on specific clan territory conferring ownership of the precious commodity to specific groups of the island community – '[they] took charge of the three crosses, which they carried up to the said hills.' The description of the pageantry continues:

> The chaplains chanting Litanies, and the islanders joining with our people in the responses, *ora pro nobis* ... the crosses being planted the party fired three volleys of musketry, and the ships replied with twenty-one guns each, to the joyful shout of *Viva el Rey.* The islanders responded with our own people; they pronounce with such ease that they repeat whatever is said to them just like ourselves ... It need not be said that the islanders were terrified at the noise of the gunfire and musketry: this must happen to people who have not used or seen such inventions. (Corney 1903, 125)

Two aspects of this description of the pageantry of possession are at odds with one another. The narration has thus far demonstrated a charitable attitude towards the islanders and it continues here to outline the ways in which they joined voluntarily into the ceremonies to procure the island, in this Spanish discourse, for Spain. At the same time as the text constructs the islanders as willing and the Spaniards as benign in their interaction, it also demonstrates Spanish firepower as a counterpoint to the music and chanting of the litanies. The 'three volleys of musketry' and the 'twenty-one gun' reply can leave no doubt in the islanders' minds about who is in charge on the island during this ritual. The recognition of the terror roused in the islanders at this display of power, preceded by the phrase 'it need not be said that the islanders were terrified,' acknowledges the effect the Spanish knew such a display would cause, even though they might not have realized the murders by Dutch firearms would still have been vivid in communal memory. Their narrative demonstrates, in this behaviour, the extent to which the Spanish were bound by their own imperial discourse to perform a ritual that they knew would cause distress. The Spanish, however, provided an alternative explanation for the firepower. 'There has in so far as it is possible been made known to and recognized by its native inhabitants their lawful Sovereign, and his powerful arm for their defence against foreign enemies' (Antonio Romero, Staff Paymaster, qtd in Corney 1903, 49). With this firepower in the Spanish construction of events, they were demonstrating protection for their newest possession even as they showed the people of that possession the power of its new masters. 'Easter Island' had become 'San Carlos.'

The islanders, who were to be virtually erased from economic appraisals of the island in the British and French accounts, are very much in evidence in the narratives from the Dutch and Spanish expeditions because they are desirable as working bodies on the potentially profitable land. The Spanish expedition stayed the longest on the island, and with their ceremonies of acquisition, music, artillery fire, procession and planting of crosses, and likely introduction of an epidemic, had a large impact on the islanders, possibly surpassing the first Dutch encounter, with death meted out by musket fire. Yet two notable French- and English-language nineteenth-century Pacific and Spanish South American histories (see Moerenhout 1837 and Parish 1852) ignore the Spanish expedition to the island (Corney 1903, xlix). Such omissions are indicative of the selective process by which some accounts were taken up while others fell away as the imaginary geography of the island continued to be shaped in European narratives after the explorers' voyages. Such omissions suggest a desire to play down the Spanish claim on the island at a time when European national imperialisms were still positioning themselves to 'acquire' new colonies and to promote the influence of one national group over another in systems of economic and political power.

Inventing the Outsiders

I have been examining, in the 'discovery' texts of the Dutch and Spanish expeditions to Rapanui, the power of imperial discourse to shape European perceptions of encounters at the island. Part of this process has been to outline the production of the subject of Easter Island by tracing the unstable and competing elements that formed its basis as it emerged into the European imagination. In the key and conflicting elements from these first two expeditions can be heard an assumption of a European right to knowledge and a European monopoly on truth. Such value-laden voyage accounts erase the story of the Polynesians 'denying the original population its history, purpose, and voice even as they create their own new subject to take its place' (Kröller 1997, 2).

The development of authoritative narratives of new Others was not confined to the imperialist agenda. In the generation of Polynesian subjects through temporal European discursive spaces, and in their examination here through contemporary European post-structural discourse, it is possible to overlook the existence of other timely and equally influential histories – ones generated by the Rapanui, themselves. Not only did the Rapanui have a complex and active culture of their own, they shielded the mysteries of that culture from their 'visitors.' Allan Smith (2001) describes a Polynesian historical preference to protect rites and mysteries of sacred culture from 'unsympathetic ... heathenish and impatient visitors' (19). As an example of a simple misreading from a Rapanui perspective, the first three expeditions all wrote of a disproportionate number of men to women and children on the island. The Europeans did not seem to have a sufficiently unfettered imagination to extrapolate from the uneven sexual representation and scarcity of children the possibility of some portions of the social groups staying in seclusion during the visits to the island. James Cook and one of his naturalists on the British expedition, George Forster, both wrote of being repeatedly denied entrance to caves in 1774. In fact, large and small caves abound in the volcanic island, and Rapanui oral tradition and archaeological evidence construct them as having been used for shelter and concealment of people and artefacts throughout the ages. More obvious demonstrations of 'unsympathetic' behaviour can be seen when Forster writes that the Rapanui 'sometimes expressed a dislike when we walked over the paved area [ahus] or pedestals, or examined the stone of which it consisted' (Thomas and Berghof 1999, 306); Infanzon states that 'the sculptured statues are called *Moày* by the natives, who appear to hold them in great veneration, and are displeased when we approach to examine them closely' (Corney 1903, 94–5). Steven Fischer interprets this as dis-ease with contact of certain sites, in *Easter Island Studies* (1993). According to Fischer, the ahu or platforms holding moai were memorials to dead ancestors and were used to expose and then hold the remains of deceased clan members. For this reason they would 'certainly have been tapu [taboo]; what was at issue was not "veneration," but the uncontrolled transmission of contagious sacred-ness' (463). Europeans, regardless of their religious affiliations, would have been familiar with sacred architecture, the sanctity of altars, and hallowed burial ground, but imperial eyes, fixed in a hierarchy of civi-lization, were often blinkered to the possibility of seeing themselves reflected in non-like Others or their practices. European constructions of Rapanui were shaped by the limitations of their own perceptions and capacity to decode the Other, and constricted by Rapanui presentations and omissions.

Cook would visit just four years after the Spanish, by which time the Rapanui had had two previous recorded encounters with European strangers. Each served to open and shape a new Rapanui discourse through which Europeans emerged as a subject for the islanders. In counterpoint to the European's assessment of the Rapanui, the island-ers were mediating their own experience with, and understanding of, the Others who were coming to their shores. Their own narratives of Others, like the European narratives in turn, emerged from their per-ception of 'foreign' reality. Through these narratives they constructed their own European imaginary apparently based on the sailing ships, and wrote the Europeans into specific subject positions within the ship context.

How these eighteenth-century encounters may have altered or added to their world view can be glimpsed in the following account recorded by Katherine Routledge in 1914, the first professional anthro-pological text to be written about the Rapanui:

> There was practically only one religious function of a general nature; it was very popular and had a surprising origin. Attention was attracted on the south coast by a particularly long stoep[5] of rounded pebbles measur-ing 139 feet, and obviously connected with a thatched house now disap-peared. That, our guides said in answer to a question, is a hare-a-té-atua, where they praised the gods.' 'What gods?' 'The men who came from far away in ships. They saw they had pink cheeks, and they said they were gods.' The early voyagers, for the cult went back at least three generations, were therefore taken for deities in the same way as Cook was at Hawaii. The simplest form of this celebration took place on long mounds of earth known as 'miro-o-orne,' or earth-ships, of which there are several on the island, one of them with a small mound near it to represent a boat. Here the natives used to gather together and act the part of a European crew, one taking the lead and giving orders to the others. A more formal cere-

mony was held in a large house. This had three doors on each side by which the singers entered, who were up to a hundred in number, and ranged themselves in lines within; in one house, of which a diagram was drawn, a deep hole was dug in the middle, at the bottom of which was a gourd covered with a stone to act as a drum. On the top of this a man danced, being hidden out of sight in the hole.

In other cases, two or perhaps three, boats were constructed inside the house, the masts of which went through the roof; these boats were manned with crews clad in garments of European sailors, the gifts from passing vessels being kept as stage properties. Fresh music was composed for every occasion, and in one song, which was quoted, much reference is made to 'the red face of the captain from over the seas.' The position of chief performer was one of great honour being analogous, on a glorified scale, to the leader of a cotillion of our own day. (Routledge 1919, 239–40)

The restaging of foreigner behaviour as filtered through Routledge is constructed as a 'religious function'; a recognition of something extraordinary or set apart, celebrated in a form of pageantry, a sacred theatrical performance. It was an opportunity to relive some of the highlights of the first encounters with outsiders and, at the same time, to rehearse the technology and architectural details of the European ships, and the embodiment of the foreigners, who had been taken up in their imaginations.[6] This is an example of what Mary Louis Pratt describes in *Imperial Eyes* (1992) as 'instances of non-European expression developed in interaction with European repertoires' (5). The dimensions and proportions of the sailing ships, studied and measured by the Rapanui aboard the explorer vessels, are reinscribed in the earthen ship-houses and *hare-a-té-atua*. The launches or sloops are depicted in the small mounds near the larger one. A two-story structure with an above and below deck was a new concept for the Rapanui. The sound of people moving about in a level below, a downstairs, finds expression through the deep hole dug in the middle, at the bottom of which was the gourd covered with a stone to act as a drum. The sound generated by the man dancing on the top of this gourd, while out of sight, must have been an attempt, with the resources to hand, to recreate the sound of dancing on the ship decks.

A carved image of a three-mast ship can be seen superimposed over the torso of a moai on the slope of the quarry at Rano Raraku, while other such images were painted in the interior of caves and still others inside the houses at the ceremonial village, Orongo. The vastness of the

Figure 4.1: Stone longboat on north shore of Rapa Nui.

ships and their capacity to hold smaller boats – floating villages and transportation within transportation, wooden ships within wooden ships – seem to have been aspects of the foreign encounters that made a strong impression. The rituals of the 'ship board' performances enabled a participatory mimicry that, in its active agency, enabled a continuing interaction with the foreigners more satisfying than passive receptive storytelling might have done. Even the garments from passing vessels are described as gifts, indicating the point of view from which the Rapanui were receiving those goods.

In September 2004, I was taken to a particular section of coast along the north shore of the island by anthropologist Charles Love. Here, as in two other north and northwest coastal locations, can be seen stone longboats fashioned in the shape of the wooden boats-within-boats that conveyed European mariners from their sailing ships to shore (see figs. 4.1 and 4.2). The explanation of these structures suggested by Love is that they are distant eighteenth-century 'cousins' to the cargo cult practices on other South Pacific islands. They are constructed on clan land where no European expeditions were ever recorded as landing. Love suggests that when Europeans visited the island in the eighteenth century, their gifts were distributed to, and trading was conducted with, those clan members who lived on the land adjacent to where the boats would come ashore. In part, this selective clan trading may account for the disparate population numbers perceived by each expedition. By building replicas of the kinds of boats that had landed and distributed largess in other clan districts, these 'stone boat' building clans apparently hoped to entice European ships to anchor off their land and

Figure 4.2: Stone longboat, facing the prow. The hills upon which the Spanish planted three wooden crosses can be seen in the background of this photograph. The bleakness of the landscape after a century of sheep, cattle, and horse grazing can be seen in the grass-dominated close-cropped vegetation. The sheep are gone, but horses and cattle remain.

exchange with them. The Rapanui describe a central aspect of the cosmology and philosophy of their culture as *mana*, understood as a powerful energy that manifests itself in the ability of an individual or clan to draw benefits. These benefits can take such forms as the capacity to grow abundant crops or catch fish, or the ability to muster a large enough workforce to accomplish a task, such as erecting a moai. *Mana* is understood to concentrate in some people and places more than in others.

Such active participation in cultural production presents an argument for the existence of the Easter Island script, Rongorongo,[7] in the island culture well before the arrival of the Europeans, a point contested by Steven Fischer in the most recent book on the subject, *Rongor-*

ongo (1997). I would suggest that written records open some, and make unnecessary other, forms of memory. With written records of island history, less need might be perceived to preserve the foreign encounters in an oral tradition, less need for telling stories about the Europeans. With the urgency to preserve specific memory satisfied through Rongorongo, the islanders would have been able to participate creatively in variations of Euro-like behaviour. Freed from the need to take up performance positions as audience and storyteller, to reprise in stories the arrival of strangers on the island, the Rapanui could engage imaginatively in their own role playing. If only in theatre productions, the earth ship performances created the ability to leave and return to the island, to practise innovation, and diversity, and to focus awareness on the undiscovered world beyond the island's shores. Theatrical performances could hold open a closed and alien world, and could allow for the embodiment by the Rapanui in the exploration of that world.

As well as the interest demonstrated in ship architecture, two other key interests emerge in Routledge's description of the land-ships. The first seems to be pleasure taken in the power dynamics and embodied organizational skills of the hierarchical command structure of the European military and mariners, and can be seen in the islanders acting 'the part of a European crew, one taking the lead and giving orders to the others.' The other seems to have been a re-enactment of the organized processional and music associated with claiming the island for Spain. The Rapanui participated in the actual ceremony and received several pieces of large wood in the form of the crosses planted on the hills of Poike in the north-east corner of the island. The Spanish claiming ceremony also folded together some other highlights of the foreigner encounters. It included an embodied organized procession accompanied by music. It featured the organizational skills of the soldiers who gave and took commands, and it involved a whole group movement choreographed in conformation.

Knowing about the land-ship performances serves to make sense of the strong desire to acquire hats and to trade for clothing items that was emphasized in the explorers' journals. Hats and particular forms and colours of clothing were already designators of rank in the island clan society, and the specialized clothing of different elements of the European ships' complements' – sailors hats, officers hats – would have been read by the islanders as also designed to denote status and therefore desirable for designating and identifying rank in their religious performances.

The desire to acquire 'stage' props makes sense of an incident that was reported by La Pérouse in 1787. Divers cut the 'cablet' of the *Astrolabe's* boat beneath the waterline and carried away its grapnel (Dunmore 1994, 66). Managing to secure the ships and boats with anchors was a key function of all the expeditions as they sought to secure their vessels in open water before disembarking to visit the island. Activity with anchors/grapnels would have been one of the repeated commands requiring obedience to orders that the Rapanui witnessed at close hand, when visiting the ships and when waiting for the crews to come ashore. What better prop for ship performances than a grapnel? The Rapanui had their own cultural needs and the land-ship rituals served one of those cultural imperatives. By mimicking the Europeans they worked them into their own story and anticipated the possible shape of future relationships; embodying their Others within their cultural repertoire they too altered their world view.

Reading Europeans through Eastern Polynesian Cultural Codes

European materials and behaviours were read on the island from within a framework of Rapanui cultural codes and understandings. Long before the description of the land-ship ceremonies recorded by Routledge, there were several details of islander behaviour recorded in European explorers' journals that suggest the emergence of a developing repertoire of island cultural conduct shaped against a reading of European behaviours. Specifically, the Rapanui seem to have read elements of their own Polynesian rituals in certain European rituals enacted on the island.

A brief explanation of some elements of Eastern Polynesian culture will serve as background to show how activities and possessions of the European voyagers could have been read by Rapanui as echoing their own traditions. Jo Anne Van Tilburg (1994) explains that 'the erect or upright pole, whether cross or flagstaff, would have been immediately recognised, by East Polynesians in particular, as a sacred sign of domination' (31). Not only the crosses and standards carried in the Spanish ceremony of possession would have fallen into this category. The very masts of the ships arriving off shore could have been read as such symbols. The heights and shapes of the masts and yardarms on the sailing ships echoed one form of Eastern Polynesian god icon. Marshall Sahlins, in *How 'Natives' Think: About Captain Cook for Example* (1995), offers several descriptions of rites associated with the Polynesian pantheon, involving wooden cross shaped icons of gods. Specifically he refers to practices in Hawaii, Tahiti and the Marquesas, all islands closely linked to the same era of migration as that of the Polynesians who went to Rapanui. In the Hawaiian rite described by Sahlins, the image of a Hawaiian god, Lonomakua, is 'a tall, cross piece affair, about three metres high, with white tapa cloth and skins of the ka'upu bird suspended from the horizontal bar' (27–8), very similar to European ship masts hung with sails. As well as the main Makahiki image, also known as the long god (*aku loa*), there were several short gods of a similar cross-shaped form (*aku poko*), apparently one in each major chiefdom division (29).

Three crosses were planted by the Spanish in a ceremony at Poike on the north-eastern tip of Rapanui, a specific geographic space on the island. These crosses could have been read on the island as 'short gods' symbolically taking up residence in a 'major chiefdom division.' Sahlins (1995) goes on to explain that 'cross-piece images of this sort were also used in the Marquesas and Tahiti as signs of truce or peace. In this reading,

'peace' entails a suspension of normal human occupations and of human control over the land, for the god now marries or takes possession of it. His domination will be signified by the tributes offered to the Makahiki image at the boundaries of each district. The ruler is immobilized by the rule that he cannot leave the place where he began the Makahiki celebrations, at least until the completion of certain purification rites following the return and dismantling of the Makahiki image. But, while the king stays put, the principal image of Lonomakua, accompanied by certain gods of sport, undertakes its clockwise or 'right circuit' of the island – that is with the land on the right. A right circuit signifies a retention of the kingdom. (28–9)

Within the context of these rituals, the Europeans can be read as the 'pink-cheeked gods' in their ships mounted by icons of peace arriving to engage in a number of activities involving celebration, claiming, purifying, and symbolic fertilization of the land.

Such a reading is born out by the reaction to the ceremony of claiming narrated by Infanzon. When the procession of Spaniards was moving towards the hills where they planted the wooden crosses and claimed the island for the King of Spain in a ceremony of Catholic imperialism, he recorded the following observations:

They seemed to me to have ministers or priests for their idols; because I observed that on the day which we erected the crosses, when our chaplains went accompanying the holy images, clothed in their cassocks and pelliz, chanting the litanies, numbers of natives stepped forward onto the path and offered their cloaks, while the women presented hens and pullets, and all cried *Maca Maca*, treating them with much veneration until they had passed beyond the rocks by which the track they were following was encumbered. (Infanzon, qtd in Corney 1903, 100)

It has already been noted that within Rapanui society, chickens provided the most valuable food as a mark of respect when given as gifts (Pollock 1993, 156). Within the Rapanui pantheon MakeMake (Maca Maca) is the creator god. Here we have islanders calling out the name of the creator god while offering gifts of respect to those carrying symbolic images of gods. The Spanish ritual continues to conform to Eastern Polynesian codes as the procession undertakes its clockwise or 'right circuit' of the bay.

On the party forming up, together with those bearing arms, we set out on the march, accompanied by the natives, who lent a willing hand in carrying the crosses, singing and dancing in their fashion as they went. We made the whole circuit of the bay with some pains, for the ground was rough and rugged, although level, a great retinue of natives collecting round us all the while as far as the foot of the rise. (Infazon, qtd in Corney 1903, 104)

Sahlins (1995) reports that the wooden icon of the god is dismantled after the ceremony, an action that conforms to this Polynesian reading and accounts for the removal of the wooden crosses from Poike. Cook notes that no crosses were in evidence when he visited the island four years after their erection.

During the British exploration of the island by Cook, a small group of explorers were taken in hand by an island elder. His actions are rendered more comprehensible when read within the context of island codes outlined above:

They left the beach at about nine o'clock in the morning, and took a path which led to the south-east side of the island, followed by a great crowd of the natives, who preyed much upon them. But they had not proceeded far, before a middle-aged man, punctured from head to foot, and his face painted with a sort of white pigment, appeared with a spear in his hand, and walked along side of them, making signs to his country men to keep a distance, and not to molest our people. When he had pretty well effected this he hung a piece of white cloth on his spear, placed himself in the front and led the way with the ensign of peace, as they understood it to be. (J. Cook 1777, 281)

The procession can be read as an escort for non-clan members travelling through another clan's territory; the white flag, as Cook surmises, denotes the request for peaceful passage. Or perhaps the raised staff procession may have been an intra-island signal to all Rapanui that these foreigners were merely visitors under island domination and supervision. The British were certainly not given the run of the island. They were escorted into houses which they found to be entirely empty and were denied entrance into any of the numerous caves on the island.

In these glimpses of Rapanui mediation of their encounters with the explorers, we are reminded of the complex and active cultural production of the islanders as well as the Europeans. Each side in these encounters produced a text of the Other, according to their cultural reading of events. The islanders' encounters with Europeans were no more unmediated experiences of newness than were the European experiences of the Rapanui. Invention came to the island through the arrival of European diversity and it was taken away from the island as a number of imaginary geographies constructed by the Europeans through their contact with the Rapanui. The interests of each group may have imposed their own sense of the world in their creations of the other, the process may have been similar, but the products are very different because of the power differential between the two constructions. The configurations of power within the European construction of Easter Island produced an archive of invention that had catastrophic repercussions for the Rapanui over time, and that continues in its different versions to both erase and misrepresent the Rapanui to the world beyond its shores to the present day. The specific contribution of the British to the European construction of the island will be the focus of the next chapter.

5 The British

In a considerably depleted condition after two years at sea, James Cook's expedition visited Easter Island in 1774 on his second Pacific voyage. Cook was commissioned on this journey by the Royal Society to explore the South Pacific in the hopes of finding the southern continent that had eluded explorers before him. He was also 'under secret orders from the British Crown' to explore with the intent of 'claiming the lands of the south Pacific for the British Empire' (Livingstone 1992, 129). In order to fulfil these twin mandates, the complement of the voyage included an artist, William Hodges, who could paint coastal views, and naturalists Johann and George Forster, who were father and son. Cook, as well as George Forster, published accounts of the voyage.

The subject of Easter Island to this point had been brought into public knowledge in Europe through the Dutch voyage narratives of the anonymous sailor and Behrens. Only brief references to the Spanish expedition in London papers offered any public information on that voyage that the British could take up as they prepared for their own visit, although I believe the Spanish expedition may have had a devastating impact, dramatically decreasing the island population through an epidemic, diminishing the agricultural production, and altering the clan power balance. This would account for a much altered cultural dynamic when Cook arrived just four years later.

In the 1770 English-language edition of the Dutch accounts before Cook's visit to the island, *Several Voyages and Discoveries in the South Pacific Ocean*, Alexander Dalrymple had challenged the authority of the Dutch texts, the sailor for exaggeration, and Behrens for inaccuracy.

Dalrymple, as a staunch supporter of the Royal Society, measured the narratives he published in his collection against the Society's guidelines for information-gathering on voyages. It was Dalrymple's collection of voyages that Cook and the Forster's read for its accounts of Easter Island. They measured their own experience of the island against these English versions of the Dutch narratives and against Dalrymple's editorial evaluations of them, and they wrote their own perceptions of the island in part as a response to those Dutch accounts in Dalrymple, as well as against what they saw on the island in the aftermath of the Spanish expedition.

As the eighteenth century progressed further into the Age of Enlightenment, with its emphasis on scientific accuracy, voyage texts were being ranked by an increasingly discerning reading public according to the degree of authority they were perceived to hold about the places they described. The exposure of fiction robed as fact in accounts such as that of the anonymous sailor was a manifestation of the reading public's increasing preoccupation with issues of authenticity and reliability. The empirical method espoused by Francis Bacon was increasingly favoured, and it widened the critical space for acts of scepticism and rigour on the part of both writers and readers. At the same time, a tradition of fictional travel literature continued to develop, separating off from the body of scientific accounts and finding space within the canon of English letters. Rather than the authority of empiricism putting an end to exaggerated accounts of the marvellous, the two kinds of texts found space to co-exist in a continuum that moved from imperially sanctioned rigorous scientific accounts, through works best called 'speculative scholarship,' to works of fiction disguised as fact.

Texts written according to the prescriptions of the Royal Society were published alongside exaggerated travel narratives that focused on exotic plants and animals or the exotic practices of newly discovered people, practices perceived as both pleasurable and painful against European norms. John Hawkesworth's edition of James Cook's first voyage to the Pacific, *An Account of the Voyages Undertaken by the Order of His Present Majesty for Making Discoveries in the Southern Hemisphere, and Successively Performed by Commodore Byron, Captain Wallis, Captain Carteret and Captain Cook, in the Dolphin, the Swallow and the Endeavour* (1773), was censured by the critics for the extent to which it was perceived to stray into this exaggerated and titillating space. Set against these two kinds of 'reporting' were the fictional accounts of travellers written both realistically, *Robinson Crusoe* (1719), and as parody, *Gulliver's Travels* (1726).

The space held open for these works of fiction in the travel genre was not uncontested. It too performed through or resisted the discursive power of imperialism. As a primary example, *Robinson Crusoe*, with its fictional exaggeration of European competence, was a manifestation of the imperial ideal, modelling desirable behaviour and the capacity of the civilized 'man' to reproduce and instil in others his values and social environment anywhere in the world he might find himself. *Gulliver's Travels*, on the other hand, parodied the values depicted in *Robinson Crusoe*, while satirizing the voyage texts produced through the imperial enterprise. The crossing and merging of discursive boundaries in these travel texts meant that for the reading public in the eighteenth century, the space between authoritative and fictional travel texts sometimes blurred. Out of this shared space began to emerge two Easter Islands, one developing from and feeding into a discursive space that celebrated the marvellous, the other developing out of and continuing to thrive in a knowledge enterprise established through imperialism. Both were to find their nucleus, not in the Dutch accounts from the first European visit to the island, but in 'authoritative' reaction to those narratives in the texts and images constructed out of James Cook's voyage.

The Imaginary Pacific

The discourse of the South Seas that developed out of European exploration of the Pacific formed in reaction to an underlying anticipation of finding paradise. As embodied in a historic, textual, geographic imaginary, 'paradise' invited a landscape of lushly flowered, perfumed, and tree-shaded islands with clear, quiet pools and refreshing gentle waterways. The trees would provide food year-round and no predatory animals would add an element of risk to lingering in the garden spaces. Depending on androcentric preferences, this earthly garden of delight could be imagined devoid of human occupation – untouched Edens, or ripe with the capacity to fulfil manly desires through abundant wealth and pliant women. As buccaneers and explorers began to venture into the Pacific and impose this trope over the islands they 'found,' other less attractive geographic possibilities emerged and began to circulate in the same discursive sphere. Through them, the idea of paradise developed a shadow-self. It was manifest in the fear of being stranded on the deserted island, forever lost in the vastness of the Pacific, or in

reaching an island, whether paradise or jungle, only to discover it pop-
ulated by cannibal Others, ready to devour the explorer before he could
consume the island prizes himself. Cook's three voyages to the Pacific
feature largely in the solidification of both aspects of this fledging discourse, a discourse not so much imagined out of the Pacific, but
imposed upon it through literary and travel tropes long in circulation in
European cultures. Neil Rennie (1995) identifies an aspect of this process as the traveller discovering in the new space of the Pacific the location of old familiar fictions, once lost in the distant past, and now
'recovered in the distant present,' and confirmed in 'the form of exotic
facts' (1).[1]

The performance space created by this Pacific discourse allowed for
the recognition of the constructed nature of European civilization that
was being both travelled away from and actively maintained aboard
the discovery ships. But at the same time the European voyagers saw
the spaces travelled to as being without any constructed civilization,
despite the Polynesian groups who were settled on most islands. There
was a failure to recognize the structures and complexities of other cultural codes.[2] What they invested the South Seas with, and how they
performed against those investments, forms part of the history of imperialism in the Pacific. This discourse not only shaped the way Europe
perceived the Pacific, it represented and produced, in image and artefact, the aesthetics of European Polynesian cultural capital, an aesthetic
that in turn informed modern European art and continues to shape
much Euro-American imagery today. Bernard Smith, in *Imagining the
Pacific* (1992), outlines just how extensive was the impact of texts and
images brought back from the Pacific for reproduction, sale, and public
display. From 1768 to 1780, 'something in the order of three thousand
original drawings were made of things, mostly from the Pacific, not
seen before by Europeans: landscapes, unknown peoples, their arts and
crafts, religious practices and styles of life' (52). In these representations, Cook's voyages, more than missions solely to gather facts,
'deeply affected conceptual thought,' and deeply influenced 'the aesthetic realm' (53).

As well as the texts and images that were reproduced and translated
for sale in Europe from the named participants in Cook's voyages, the
ships' crews had affected the aesthetic realm through their trade and
collection of natural history specimens and cultural artefacts from the
Pacific. Smith (1992) describes the sailors as collecting 'as many things
as they could from the natives of the islands they visited, knowing that

back in Europe they could command a price for them from those who were amassing collections' (219). The availability of objects from Pacific Islands 'stimulated the British market for specimens of natural history and cultural exotics. The abundant supply of Pacific artefacts encouraged demand, taste and theory' (219). John Willinsky (1998) describes these sailors and soldiers, caught up in marketing through imperialism, as approaching each destination as if it were an exhibition (81). Collection and exhibition, organization and labelling, had a disciplining effect on 'wonder' that would see it emerge in a new form as the century progressed, a form practised on Cook's voyages and further taught to European audiences.

Published Voyage Journals

The journals James Cook wrote during his second voyage to the Pacific were published in two volumes after his return to England as *A Voyage Towards the South Pole, and Round the World: Performed in His Majesty's Ships the Resolution and Adventure, in the Years 1772, 1773, 1774, and 1775.* The first volume is 378 pages with thirty-three illustrations of the Pacific. Ten are of Polynesian people and eleven are of landscapes. The rest are of natural specimens, technology, and cultural ornaments. Chapter 7, consisting of twenty-one pages, is titled 'Sequel of the Passage from New Zealand to Easter Island, and Transactions there, with an Account of an Expedition to discover the Inland Part of the Country, and a Description of some of the Surprising gigantic Statues found in the Island.' It includes a map and three illustrations of Easter Island based on sketches by William Hodges, the expedition artist, and overseen by him as they were engraved for publication by William Woolett in London. Two of the illustrations are cameo portraits, the head and shoulders of one man, and one woman. Neither person is named. The third picture is a landscape of the island, featuring an ahu with moai. These images, constructed according to specific conventions of eighteenth-century engraving, were the first of the island to gain widespread public exposure. They would also likely form the first impression for the reader, the eye drawn to the image before the text, so that when the text was read, the island and culture were already being understood through the representation of the place supplied by Hodges's images.

Five years after his circumnavigation with Cook, William Hodges was known and celebrated for his large canvases of scenes in the South

Pacific (Guest 1992, 296). Yet he was a last-minute choice for voyage painter. Joseph Banks, an aristocrat who had accompanied Cook on his first voyage, had arranged for a complement of artists to accompany Cook's second voyage, but so generous were Banks's supplies for this project that they threatened to 'capsize' the ship and he was forced to abandon his plans. He lamented to Lord Sandwich that he would not now be able to benefit the 'learned world' as much as possible with the new discoveries they were bound to make on the second voyage (Joppien and Smith 1985, 2).

The identification of Europe as the 'learned world' and the Pacific as the subject to be added to the knowledge treasury, echoes the Enlightenment will-to-knowledge and also plays into the way Easter Island was to be taken up as a mystery. Where most Polynesian islanders visited were engaged in cultural practices visible to the British visitors, even if not fully understood, the Easter Islanders had perhaps already abandoned an earlier form of highly visible cultural production, the carving and placement of moai on platforms, and were engaged in a much less overtly visible cultural production centred on the birdman competition. Each clan still had moai antiquities associated with their ancestral platforms, but had moved from a focus on producing these monuments to an island-wide annual birdman leadership contest accompanied by coming-of-age celebrations at Orongo ceremonial village – a site not visited, on record, by any of the eighteenth-century expeditions. The highly visible moai, the cultural remnants of past generations, captured the imagination of the Europeans, all the more so because the voyagers did not acquire detailed information about them, even though they had a Tahitian travelling with them who might have been able to elicit a comprehensive explanation. Unanswered questions, constructed as mysteries, have tantalized the 'learned world' determined to gain knowledge as a manifestation of power. The development and maintenance of a discursive space for taking up the island as a site of mystery, both sanctions the imaginary geography as a tantalizing site and imposes a form of oppression on the actual islanders denied association with their own cultural production.

The Pacific, at the time of the voyage, was being represented through visual allusions to the classical period of Greek antiquity. Polynesians were being depicted as if draped in togas. The classical Golden Age was merged with the biblical Eden and provided the framework through which the Pacific was shaped into images for European consumption. Central to this representation was 'Tahiti as Arcadia' (B. Smith 1992,

221). On Cook's first voyage, Joseph Banks had described Tahiti, with a proprietary twist, as 'the truest picture of an Arcadia of which we were going to be kings that the imagination can form' (*Endeavour Journal*, vol. 1: 252, qtd in ibid.). Tahiti was paradise found in the Pacific, and John Hawkesworth had worked through this vision, when writing up the account of Cook's first voyage. Through his text he established Tahiti as a tropical paradise in the British imagination (ibid., 132).

Artistic Forces at Play in the Artistry of William Hodges

William Hodges worked with this trope of Arcadia as one of the visual frameworks through which he represented the Pacific and against which he represented Easter Island. Hodges, the son of a blacksmith, owed his initial advancement to the 'philanthropic temper of the time,' where talent such as his was sought out, encouraged, and rewarded (Joppien and Smith 1935, 4). His social and artistic background warrants a close examination, because his talent and ability to advance socially through his art shaped the performance space from which he perceived and represented the island. Hodges was emerging as an artist at a point in the Enlightenment when artistic production in England was being ordered and shaped through its institutionalization. He joined William Shipley's drawing school, established in 1755 as the Society for the Encouragement of Arts, Manufacturers, and Commerce, as an errand boy, and received his first training from him. In 1758, he was apprenticed to Richard Wilson, the most famous mid-eighteenth-century master of landscape who was investigating (at the same time as he was teaching Hodges) 'the search for more rugged, erratic facts in nature,' representations of the sublime that went beyond the more prosaic landscape formulae still circulating from the seventeenth-century tradition of Claude Lorrain and Salvator Rosa (Rosenblum 1971, 191).

When Hodges left Wilson's studio in 1765, he immediately joined the Incorporated Society of Artists of Great Britain (Stuebe 1979, 7), an organization that held an annual exhibition and awarded a premium of fifty guineas for the best landscape painting (27). The prize the year before Hodges joined was a depiction of sublime aspects of Irish scenery that 'brought to England a taste for the exotic, overwhelming side of nature' (28). This celebration of the sublime added to the hegemony of the institution he had joined, an institution that greatly influenced his artistic production. Hodges also took lessons at the Duke of Richmond's Sculpture Gallery with sculptor Joseph Wilton and history painter Giovanni Battista Cipriani. The latter created some of the engravings published in Hawkesworth's *Account of the Voyages.* · Hodges' early training coincided with the revival of classical figure drawing seen in Cipriani's work, and through which the early European images of the Pacific were being produced.

The Royal Academy was formed in 1768 as Hodges was establishing his artistic career. This began an era of artistic regulation and exhibition that educated the public taste while continuing to influence the vision of the Pacific created by voyage artists. The classical draughtsmanship Hodges had learned was applicable to 'the grand style' of the Royal Academy and to the informational art required increasingly on 'Royal Society' voyages in the service of science and technology (Joppien and Smith 1985, 4). Just as there was a demand for voyage texts, there was also an audience for art exhibitions being generated through the Royal Academy in tandem with new subject matter frequently returning to British shores from exploratory expeditions. Meeting the standards of the Royal Academy was a way of achieving the approval of the highest social ranks, a heady reason for the son of a blacksmith to perform within the Academy's dictates. By doing so he could seek the approval of the upper classes and hope to be chosen to exhibit under their auspices.

When Hodges returned from the Pacific, the Lords of the Admiralty commissioned him to produce oil paintings in commemoration of the voyage and to supervise the engravings being composed from studies he had drawn (Quilley 2004, 1). He was obliged to present his Pacific vision within 'conventional superstructures,' constructed out of 'neoclassical, picturesque and romantic elements.' Through these conventions, he created 'evocative paintings of Tahiti as a South Sea Island Paradise' (B. Smith 1992, 72). It was in counterpoint to these images, but in keeping with the academy precepts of Sir Joshua Reynolds, that his images of Easter Island emerged as the ruins of antiquity, both gothic and sublime in convention and emotion.

As president of the Royal Academy, Reynolds gave an annual formal lecture to the students. These discourses were 'tantamount to a statement of policy for the young institution' and were translated into Italian, French, and German during his lifetime (Reynolds [1797] 1959, xv), suggesting the extent of his influence as a spokesperson for and an arbiter of artistic standards and expectations. Hodges would have at least known about the first three discourses and must have been present at the fourth. In them Reynolds prescribes how nature is to be composed for painting. The second discourse, 1769, advised the artist to correct what is erroneous in nature, to supply what is scant, and to add by his 'own observation what the industry of his predecessors may have yet left wanting to perfection' (27). In the third discourse, 1770, Reynolds continues: 'a mere copier of nature can never produce anything great ... Instead of endeavouring to amuse mankind with the minute greatness of his imitations, he must endeavour to improve them by the grandeur of his idea' (41–2). In the fourth discourse, 1771, shortly before Hodges left on his Pacific voyage, Reynolds emphasized that 'perfect form is produced by leaving out particularities, and retaining only general ideas' (58).

These points are pertinent to the way Hodges approached the composition of his two landscapes of Easter Island, and his other representations of the Pacific. Reynolds ([1797] 1959) states the artist 'must sometimes deviate from vulgar and strict historical truth, in pursuing the grandeur of his design.' He must take 'an allowed poetical licence' and 'must compensate the natural deficiencies of his art' (59). For '[t]he Sublime impresses the mind at once with one great idea; it is a single blow' (65). Reynolds goes on to say that in order to solve the natural deficiencies of nature, the artist should begin with a series of sketches and then combine those studies of 'various beautiful scenes and prospects' to create a grand impression (66). It was in composing his representation of Easter Island through Burke's sublime and Reynolds's sublime grandeur of design, that Hodges shaped the public imagination of the island landscape and moai, in the process erasing the island population from the place as a subject.

Although Hodges is known to have sketched many representations of the Pacific, most have been lost. For Easter Island, only the engravings published in *Cook's Journal* and a landscape painted for the Admiralty have entered the public sphere to influence perceptions of the island. What is immediately striking about both of these landscapes is the emphasis on the moai, the insignificance of living islanders in the compositions, and the foregrounding of death. Hodges can be seen through these images to be participating in an active intertextuality within several overlapping philosophical discourses finding expression in the written and visual arts in the long eighteenth century.[3] Neo-classical ideas, forms, and structures, while strongly active in the scientific and collecting side of the Enlightenment and still governing the representation of the South Seas islanders, were being challenged by Reynolds's landscape aesthetics that championed new forms for representing nature and culture, and emphasized emotion as well as reason in cultural production. The power of these artistic forces to shape Hodges's perceptions and the images of the island he produced has had a lasting impact on the way the island has been taken up as a discrete subject and the way it has been taken into other discursive spaces. In these landscapes composed by Hodges, the images of death, in the form of skeletal remains, merge with the discursive conventions of eighteenth-century European nature painting and the philosophy of the sublime to form images in reaction to the idea of the South Pacific as a paradise. Hodges both feeds out of these fledging traditions, seeing in Easter Island a site for their expression, and shapes European perceptions of Easter Island in the future through his depiction of it within the sublime. It is the more 'gothically' sublime published landscape engraving that gained such wide exposure with the reading public through the popularity of Cook's journals.

The images generated by Hodges functioned as more than a complement to the influence of the voyage texts. The art enhanced the power of the texts to reflect as well as shape the social, economic, and political practices of imperialism. Beth Fowkes Tobin, in *Picturing Imperial Power* (1999), describes such drawings and paintings as sites 'where the tensions and contradictions of colonialist doctrines and practices were negotiated, more or less successfully on an aesthetic level' (1). Hodges's painting *A View of the Monuments on Easter Island* and the three published engravings composed from his field sketches participate with the voyage texts in the European cultural production of island meaning. They cued their viewers to the socially correct ways of identifying and positioning their European selves in relation to the identities, culture, and property of Polynesians. Hodges's art was able to perform such ideological work, in part, by perceiving and depicting new land through European stylistic codes that made it familiar to its viewers and opened a space for that familiarity to take the next step towards the appropriation of the land, its resources, Polynesian labour, and culture. The new space was transformed visually into imaginative geography that was aesthetically pleasing and easy for individual viewers to absorb into their Eurocentric mapping of the globe.

Several forces in the aesthetic realm of eighteenth-century British social and political practices, examined in what follows, help reconstruct the cultural and political engagement of the images with imperialism and account for the ideological power and visual effect of Hodges's constructions of Easter Island. Some, such as the expectation of classical and biblical paradise in the Pacific, have already been explored. Others, such as the eighteenth-century aesthetic concepts of nature, the sublime, and the gothic trope of the memento mori, while evident in exploration discourse, circulated more particularly in artistic discourses taken by Hodges into his imperial images, and need to be unravelled here to see what patterns they imposed upon the social fabric of the time. The first force at play was 'travel wonder,' which, I would argue, found a new guise in Enlightenment exploration.

The Sublime Disciplining of Wonder

In *Marvellous Possessions* (1991), Greenblatt has drawn attention to the way wonder, as a travel trope from the Middle Ages onward, called 'attention to the problem of credibility' and at the same time insisted 'upon the undeniability, the exigency of the experience' (20). Wonder acted as a marker designating the new as well as mediating between the new object itself and the affective reaction to it (22). By the time of Cook's second voyage, 'wonder' at the new that had been returning to Europe with such regularity since Columbus, was well on the way to being structured and organized into specific categories and regulated responses. The new was being ordered and controlled with such systemization that wonder needed to find a space for its exercise and performance within these more regulated responses to discovery, as well as to find new outlets for its expression as it became domesticated through the structures of empire. Wonder was taken up through the discourse of the 'sublime.' Appropriate responses to the sublime, described and sanctioned by the cultural establishment, were being performed by the growing middle classes eager to develop and demonstrate indicators of their new-found social powers. Hodges, as a first generation member of the middle class, and as an artist working within the cultural establishment, both carried the discourse of the sublime on his voyage to the South Pacific, and operated from within it as he responded to and painted the landscapes of the South Pacific and the moai of Easter Island.

Order was brought to bear on the new organisms discovered in the natural world by organizing them according to the *Systema Naturae*, a taxonomy devised by Swedish doctor and botanist Carl Linnaeus, in 1735. By 1741, Linnaeus was a professor at Uppsala and had his protégés venturing on 'trade and exploration' voyages all over the world to find and add specimens to expand his taxonomy. Nineteen of his students went out on voyages of discovery. Daniel Solander, the naturalist, and Anders Sparrman, the botanist, accompanied Cook on his first and second voyages to the Pacific, respectively. As a response to the sheer numbers and varieties of new animal and vegetable forms being brought back to Europe from all over the world, Linnaeus continually revised his *Systema Naturae* and it grew from a pamphlet to a multivolume work (University of California Museum of Paleontology 2005). The space for wonder at the new in nature was largely being controlled by the weight of this regulating system, itself an exercise in imperial power. The images of tropical flowers composed as botanical illustrations as an extension of Linnaean botany, were part of a 'cultural and scientific imperialism that sought to exert control over the globe's natural resources' (Tobin Fowkes 1999, 2).

Cultural wonders that could be transported back to Europe were also caught up in developing systems of classification. Before the eighteenth century, items gleaned from exploration had been either tied to commerce and prized as forms of wealth, or collected and displayed privately as curiosities. By the eighteenth century, public natural history and cultural museums were being developed to house, consolidate, and display these disparate categories of the new in European metropolitan cultural centres. These institutional forms created a space that largely taught and regulated a sanctioned response to these marvels of other cultures.

While the external response to natural wonder was being regulated through the development of new categories to contain and convey it and while cultural wonders were collected for organized display, the internal response to wonder in the eighteenth century was also being regulated through texts that actually educated the reader in a proper response to it. It was as if the expression of wonder that 'stands for all that cannot be understood, that can scarcely be believed' as described by Greenblatt (1991, 20), needed to find a new space for its expression in the face of controlling systems for classifying new things as they emerged from continuing exploration. The development of these systems and spaces of classification gave new specimens an immediate connection to the known and removed much of their 'wondrous' gloss. The emotional exhilaration that had been experienced in the face of the new had to find another outlet for expression. The shifting in emphasis from wonder to the expression of and response to the sublime, as the century progressed, was a discursive reaction to the place wonder had held in the imagination. The sublime offered a socially sanctioned site for exercising a response to the incredible when the opportunity was provided, whether through discovery, aesthetically sanctioned sublime scenery, visited on a grand tour, or artistic creation.

The shift from spontaneous wonder to the controlled sublime is evident in the eighteenth-century revival of an anonymous text from antiquity, *On The Sublime*, attributed to Longinus and translated into French in 1674 by Nicolas Boileau-Despréaux. In a modern edition of the work (Longinus 1995), translators James Arieti and John Crossett write that Longinus developed 'a huge vogue' during the eighteenth century, roughly parallel to 'the mixed vogue and influence of Freud on the first half of the twentieth century.' As with Freud, the terminology, insights, and viewpoint of Longinus 'became such a part and parcel of both the critics and their laity that by the nineteenth century he was simply subsumed' (x). Longinus defined the sublime in relation to expressive forms of literature that have the 'power to entrance or transport' the reader, not just to persuade or please. Accordingly, whether a work is deemed sublime or not is found in its ability to reveal 'the power of the mind behind the creation.' In text, the sublime was recognized in a work that 'induces amazement, wonder or awe by virtue of its ambition, scope or its ability to convey to the reader the passion that drives it' (Pateman 1991, 169). Here is a double lesson: in criticism and in response. Longinus tells the reader what to look for as well as how to shape his or her own emotional and critical response to the sublime in literature. Even if one is not able to identify the sublime independently, this text coaches its readers in the correct performance of a response to the sublime when it has been identified for them by others. A sense of wonder, now classified in the eighteenth century as the sublime, can be induced through the right stimuli, self-monitored, or performed as a learned response to indicate a capacity for correct bourgeois sensibilities. Richard White, in 'The Sublime and the Other' (1997), ties the sublime even more closely to the bourgeois through economics. He says:

[T]he sublime may be viewed as perhaps the most excessive aspect of modern aesthetics, whose fortunes are closely linked to the rise of capitalism in the middle of the eighteenth century; and in so far as the discipline of aesthetics is considered a bourgeois creation, the ethereal category of the sublime is apparently just another front for an underlying economic shift. (126)

Longinus's sublime focused on literature. The sublime taken up by the British early in the eighteenth century expanded upon this category and emphasized the emotional and the visual as well. John Dennis's treatise *The Grounds of Criticism in Poetry*, published in 1704, focuses on feelings of elation and transcendence that the sensitive, educated reader experiences when introduced to a great work of art. 'For the sublime is nothing else but a great Thought, or great Thoughts moving the Soul from its ordinary situation by the Enthusiasm which naturally attends them' (359). In his essay, 'Pleasures of Imagination' (1712), Joseph Addison emphasized 'tasteful imaginative exertion' dependent on vision. He wrote that 'sight ... may be considered as a more delicate and diffusive kind of touch that spreads itself over an infinite multitude of bodies, comprehends the largest figures, and brings into our reach some of the most remote parts of the universe' (Addison [1712] 1975, 138). Addison's rhetoric in particular shares space with the colonial discourse and can be seen to reflect the imperial pedagogical project on the home front. Evan Gottlieb, in 'The Astonished Eye: The British Sublime and Thomson's [poem] "Winter"' (2001), describes Addison's verb choices – spreading, comprehending, and reaching – as preparing 'the reader during the early stages of Britain's imperial power, for a cognitive expansion of their borders,' to match the geographical expansion that was occurring through imperialism. Merely by using their eyes, they are told they can bring into reach 'as much of the outside world as it is possible to grasp' (44). The sublime, in this category, offered a response for the educated classes to exercise when participating in the acquisition of empire.

James Thomson's poem 'Winter,' part of a series of poems called *The Seasons* written from 1726 to 1730,[4] 'ranges over sublimely vast geographical spaces,' urging the reader to see as the poet sees (Gottlieb 2001, 45), and models moments of visionary astonishment that demonstrate for the reader how to construct sublime scenes, and how to react to those scenes with a performance of astonishment (48). The poems in *The Seasons* are also identified by Jonathan Lamb (2001) as participating in the patriotic discourse that emerged after the fiasco of the South Sea Bubble (201). So strong was the public desire for the correct practice of both patriotism and the sublime, that, as John Brewer explains in *The Pleasures of the Imagination* (1997), it became common practice, in the eighteenth century, to view natural prospects with a copy of Thomson's *The Seasons* in hand for easy reference (619).[5] In this self-conscious performance of the sublime reaction, 'the eye ... becomes docile and pliable' (Gottlieb 2001, 48), conforming to the discursive demands of the imperial subject. The passive consumption of a sublime spectacle by the imperial centre was complicit with the values and desires that made imperialism a possibility. It laid out the proper exercise of extreme emotions in controlled situations, creating the possibility for excess without the sort of abandonment that might lead to anarchy. By producing examples of the sublime, Hodges and Thomson, on the borders of the middle class, produced work according to the prescriptive imperative of this discourse where both artist and audience conformed to the aesthetic values dominant at the time.

Edmund Burke's *A Philosophical Enquiry into the origin of our Ideas of the Sublime and the Beautiful*, published in 1757, nineteen years before Cook's second voyage, was the most widely read work and most stimulating to painters at that time (Drabble 2000, 690–1). Burke added substantially to the discourse of the sublime by articulating the ways it was engaged in art and nature. In writing on the subject, like Thomson before him, he both reflected ideas circulating in the arts establishment and articulated those ideas for his readers. Like Longinus, Burke instructed his readers to identify instances of the sublime and to monitor their reactions to it. He is described by Charles Elliot (1968) as 'a defender of the established order of things' who worked closely with his influential circle of friends including Sir Joshua Reynolds (5).

So numerous are the attributes of the sublime prescribed by Burke, and influencing Hodges's Easter Island compositions, that I will identify only those that can be seen in his island landscapes and consider how these images take up, reproduce, and carry forward the sublime as a lens through which the moai and the island have continued to be viewed in one dominant branch of the imperial island discourse. For Burke ([1757] 1990) 'the sublime should impress at one blow' (31) and arouse an emotional response of astonishment, a key concept repeated by Reynolds ([1797] 1959), who declared the 'sublime impresses the mind at once with one great idea; it is a single blow' (65). The cause of such astonishment is the size, situation, and meaning of the natural or cultural object. 'In this case the mind is so entirely filled with its object, that it cannot entertain any other' (Burke [1757] 1990, 49). Burke champions obscurity over clarity in the verbal or visual depiction of the sublime as a way of having a greater effect on the imagination, saying that when 'we know the full extent of any danger, when we can accustom our eyes to it, a great deal of the apprehension vanishes' (50). He twins our ignorance of things with our admiration for them. 'Knowledge and acquaintance make the most striking causes affect but little' (52). He also equates privations, 'Vacuity, Darkness, Solitude, and Silence' with sublime terror (60), and 'difficulty' with sublime greatness. 'When any work seems to have required immense force and labour to effect it, the idea is grand.' Burke uses Stonehenge as an example, although he could be describing the ahu platforms surmounted by the moai, 'those huge rude masses of stone, set on end, and piled each on other, turn the mind on the immense force necessary for such work' (65). Making the same 'stone' connection, the sublime is the first of the layered aesthetic, social, and political hegemonies through which Hodges composed his two landscapes and communicated his vision of Easter Island to instruct his European audience.

Burke's precepts cued Hodges to feature the moai as sublime, with their astonishing size, exposed situation along the rocky shores, isolated location, and skeletal remains visible in rock cairns near the moai platforms (see figs. 5.2 and 5.4). With the vacant stare[6] of the moai and the way they resisted the imperial will to knowledge, it was understandable that Hodges would see them serving as mortuary guardians unkempt in their abandoned antiquity, emanating 'Vacuity, Darkness, Solitude, and Silence.' He takes them into the sublime by depicting them obscurely, eliminating their arms and blurring their contours. This obscuring aspect of the sublime holds the moai visually in a state that resists comprehension and the imposition of meaning – a visual mystery resisting the imperial will to possess through knowledge. The imposed obscurity holds the moai in suspension, forcing the viewer to continue to exercise sublime feelings towards them, since no other relationship is made available.

The dictates of the sublime discourse cast nature and objects as sublime, while casting people in reaction to it. In this way the sublime, as a visual category, is emptied of human occupation in order for the viewer to focus without distraction on the object arousing the sublime response. One way for Hodges to increase the sublime impact of his composition was to represent the moai in solitude, so he diminished the human presence in each scene. In the book engraving, a solitary static islander is positioned to denote scale (see fig. 5.1). In his painting for the Admiralty, three islanders are barely discernable in the distance, motes of humanity (see fig. 5.3). Erasing the Rapanui from the scene of their own cultural production is a deliberate by-product of Hodges's composition for sublime effect. Their erasure contributes to the subsequent discourse of mystery through which the moai were taken up in Western culture, a discourse that invariably asks the question, 'Who carved and

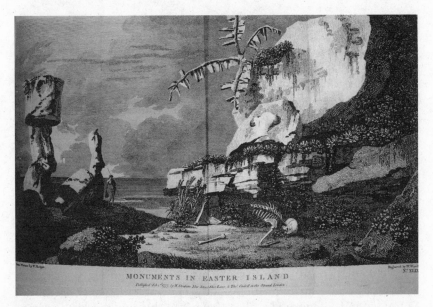

Figure 5.1: *Monuments in Easter Island*, moai landscape illustration by William Hodges, engraved by William Woollett, in *A Voyage towards the South Pole ...* (London, 1777), I, pl. XLIX, fp. 294. By permission of the Canadian Institute for Historical Microreproductions (CIHM).

moved the statues?' and answers 'No one knows.' Through these images, Easter Island was imagined into the sublime as well as the exotic, but always in relation to the stage set and never to the players. This strategy allows the viewer to be the only human presence on the island, responding to the scene with his or her own sublime response, and monitoring that response without the distraction of an invitation to engage with Others.

Death in Arcady: The Elegiac Tradition

The human bones foregrounded in Hodges's landscapes, while referencing the gothic extreme of the sublime tradition, are also elements of the elegiac tradition in Europe that contemplates death intruding into the eternal summertime of the pastoral paradise. Erwin Panofsky, in *Meaning in the Visual Arts* (1955), provides a history of the tradition of painting death in Arcadia that forms the matrix into and out of which

Figure 5.2: Ahu (moai platform), identified by archaeologist Charles Love as the site of *A View of the Monuments of Easter Island* by Hodges and turned into an engraving by Woollett. September 2004.

Hodges was responding with his composition of *A View of the Monuments of Easter Island*. Arcady, as a literary and artistic trope, has come to be associated with pastoral bliss and defined as an imaginary rural paradise. It is actually a rather sparse region of central Greece that was taken up by Ovid as a place inhabited by 'primitive savages' who were undisciplined and lived lives similar to those of beasts (299), and again taken up by Virgil who transformed it into 'an ideal realm of perfect bliss and beauty, a dream incarnate of ineffable happiness,' bounded by melancholy (297). Both poets would have been studied as part of a British grammar-school education in the eighteenth century as they were in Shakespeare's era. I mention Shakespeare because he works with Virgil's pastoral yet melancholy Arcadia in many of his sonnets and comedies. In Virgil's ideal, Arcady, human suffering, and ideal surroundings create a dissonance that, once felt, has to be resolved in a mixture of sadness and tranquillity which can be visually manifest in

Figure 5.3: *A View of the Monuments of Easter Island*, oil painting by William Hodges, commissioned by the Admiralty after the return of the expedition (ca. 1776). Courtesy of © National Maritime Museum, London. In fact, the weather, as reported in the journals, was bright and sunny while they were on the island. Stormy weather arrived as they sailed away.

twilight (300). This same dissonance is created and seeks resolution for the British voyagers when they find sparse Easter Island sharing the same South Seas as lush Tahiti. In each of Hodges's landscapes, he references Arcadian melancholy in the long shadows cast by the moai that denote the close of day. Virgil imaginatively projects the cause of melancholy either into the future or the past, creating the elegiac sentiment (301). Both past death and future bleakness are contained within Hodges's landscapes foregrounded with human bones. Virgil's 'pastoral Utopia of bliss and beauty' was positioned as distant in time and became an object of nostalgia, a haven from 'a faulty reality' and a 'questionable present' (ibid., 301). Hodges constructs it as distant in space as well as time.

Panofsky (1995) attributes to Giovanni Francesco Guercino the first pictorial rendering of death associated with Arcadia, painted in Rome between 1621 and 1623. In it, two Arcadian shepherds look upon a huge human skull lying on a 'moldering piece of masonry' inscribed with *Et*

Figure 5.4: Landscape from which Hodges composed his Admiralty painting *A View of the Monuments of Easter Island*. Note the thickness of the bodies of the moai compared to their rendition in Hodges's painting, and the way they have fallen face forward, their backs to the sea. The dark stone cylinders in the foreground are the *puka*o or red scoria (volcanic tuff) hats of the moai.

in Arcadia ego – [Death] even in paradise. The death's-head was a common feature in sixteenth- and seventeenth-century art and literature (307–8). It is a medieval memento mori recast in Enlightenment guise when used in relation to Arcadia (309). It moves from being a personal reminder of someone's death to a representation of the tenuous human condition. Variations of *Et in Arcadia ego* were produced by several other artists over the next century: Poussin produced his first *Et in Arcadia ego* in 1630, now in the Devonshire Collection at Chatworth (313). Richard Wilson, Hodges's teacher, painted *Ego fui in Arcadia* in Rome in 1755 (317), and Sir Joshua Reynolds sketched Guercino's painting into his Roman notebook, producing his own version in 1769 (295), two years before Hodges sailed with Cook.

The trope of death even in Arcadia was part of current cultural capital for Hodges. 'Remember mine end' gave form to a fear that was ever with the explorers as they navigated the Pacific, and would have been particularly emphatic in the minds of the British as they landed at Easter Island with some personal urgency. Most of the people aboard had been manifesting the early stages of scurvy for the past several weeks at sea and were looking for relief (as described in detail in the Forsters' journals). Some could barely walk. Cook navigated to Easter Island specifically to find a haven, a place to rest and replenish health, and to restock the ship. The depleted condition of Cook's voyagers at the time of their visit to the island, coupled with the inability of the islanders to share an abundance of harvest or water, positioned it in their narrative as a disappointment; an island, not of regeneration, but of potential death. Hodges projects human suffering onto the landscape as well, so that not just death is in Arcady, but the island is portrayed as death-like in the midst of an ocean of life-giving garden islands.

Hodges's Engraved and Painted Landscapes of Easter Island

Each of Hodges's pictures approaches the landscape differently, but both share the same theme. The book engraving tightly frames the composition, forcing the eye of the viewer to dwell on the skeleton in the foreground and to read the scene through its presence. Hodges interposes a representation of death to mediate the emotional response of the viewer, prompting a particular way of seeing. As well as performing a sublime response, the viewer is invited to assume the pose of the refined and contemplative subjects, the Arcadians (the Europeans who now imaginatively inhabit the South Pacific), who are recognizing the scene before them as the intrusion of death into the midst of their Pacific Eden, the whole island standing for the tomb stumbled upon by the wandering shepherds. The skeleton is positioned to be much larger than the islander who stands motionless and in shadow beside the moai. The ahu filling the right half of the frame is unrecognizable as a platform and appears to be a cliff, as if the skeleton is the discovered remains of someone who has fallen from a great height to his or her death, a visual representation of the fate of the moai culture itself. The sea appears to recede in the distance, when actually this ahu site is farther inland than most clan ahus that ring the island shore. In fact, from this viewpoint one would be looking west across the gently rolling fields (now pasture) of the centre of the island. The moai appear to be crumbling, like ancient relics. Their features are so indistinct that it is difficult to gauge in which direction they are facing, or even if they have faces. Through their visual obscurity, in the engraving, they resist being known.

The scene of the Admiralty painting is not tightly framed. It opens up as if dilating out from the skull and the quadrant to the whole island, and beyond to the edge of the sea, so that the viewer takes in the island and then moves on, leaving it behind. The painting positions the British expedition in the foreground with the quadrant placed between human bones and the cultural production of antiquity, both represented as memorials of and mementos to the past. The eye sweeps from these decipherable objects in the foreground over the whole vast landscape and vaster sea and sky, taking in all that the British viewer can survey and possess. The islanders are small static figures in the middle distance, frozen rather than active participants in their own landscape now visually measured and held. They are rendered insignificant beside the moai by their distance, and thus small size, in relation to their ancestral artefacts. The moai in effect replace the representations of people in the landscape.

Hodges has turned the moai around on their platform, their backs to the viewer, denying comprehension as they gaze over the sea. In this manipulation of the moai, he can be seen to be following Reynolds instruction to 'deviate from vulgar and strict historical truth, in pursuing the grandeur of his design.' He is also contributing to the false notion, long perpetuated, that the moai face the sea, when, in fact, they have their backs to the sea and face inward like an audience watching the lives of their clan descendants unfolding before them in daily activity and seasonal ceremony. Hodges has also erased the 'ten or twelve huts' described by George Forster as part of the landscape ([1777] 2000, 307).

With the quadrant, Hodges introduces a rhetoric of control: an angular manufactured object placed in the foreground and juxtaposed with the bones of the past and the partially toppled and broken moai, representing a culture now receding, replaced by the European presence introduced to its centre. The quadrant denotes the ability of explorers to measure, assess, define, bring under control, and exert dominion over this scene of decaying culture. While the human skull and thigh bone, like the skeleton in the engraving, remind the viewer of death even in Paradise, the quadrant reminds the Admiralty of the vastness of the imperial enterprise, foreign space now dominated by the British presence. Built into the painting is the lesson that this land is discovered, measured, and absorbed into Euro-cultural capital as the eye moves beyond it to survey the horizon.

It is through Hodges's published Easter Island engraving and the

Admiralty painting that the moai as a trope emerges, multiplies, and circulates as a sublime and a gothic subject. The vigour of the discourse of the sublime during the eighteenth century carried this reading of the moai forward into the nineteenth century, into Romanticism and also into Romanticism's outré cousin, the Gothic. The sublime in both text and image, emotion and vision, has continued to circulate through the twentieth and into the twenty-first centuries in relation to the moai of Easter Island.

Hodges's Two Published Portraits of Unnamed Rapanui

At this point in the eighteenth century, non-Europeans were being depicted as exotic through their clothing and not through their features as would be the case in the racialization of Others that occurred during the nineteenth century (Willinsky 1998, 163). Nevertheless, the exotic images formed a category against which Europeans could define themselves in ways that inevitably positioned the describers as the superior norm against which the Others were measured. There were two artistic conventions through which exotic Others might be constructed. One was allegorical, the other was ethnographic (B. Smith 1992, 79). Both had been in use since the Hellenic era whenever 'foreigners' had to be specified, and both used costumes and adornment as signifiers of difference (79). Rüdiger Joppien (1979) has shown that the illustrations of Cook's expeditions provided the basic information about Pacific 'costume' that was subsequently published in the 'great Italian and French' costume books appearing during the first third of the nineteenth century (B. Smith 1992, 75).

Hodges, trained in landscape and not portraiture, is described by Smith as not seeing people in the terms normalized for artistic depiction during the period, stereotypes such as 'noble or ignoble savages, ... but as individuals whose character and temperament showed clearly' (B. Smith 1992, 67). With Hodges, the emphasis was on landscape and monuments, not on inhabitants. Without Joseph Banks and his group of artists, as on Cook's first expedition, there was no one to provide 'an account of the figures and dresses of men' (Joppien and Smith 1985, 5). Perhaps because Hodges's portraits of Easter Islanders were cameos and not full length depictions of bodies in 'ethnic' dress, they did not enter the Western imagination as part of the peoples of the Pacific through these widely circulated costume books, resources for the depiction of Others. With the portraits of the islanders not taken up imaginatively, the landscape became the most significant of Hodges's images for tracing the emergence of the subjective island. The island space was cleared of natives in imagination to focus instead on the mysteries of what was perceived as an earlier culture and a people now vanished.[7]

As the 'Age of Discovery' unfolded, the rising middle class learned to demonstrate a facility with identifying, commenting upon, and responding to wonder through the sublime as an indicator of education, class, and banked cultural capital. Mystery about a past that did not yield immediate answers wrote over wonder at the new with wonder at the lost. Hodges offered Easter Island to be possessed by the European imagination on just such terms. Easter Island was well on the way to becoming a perpetual site and trope of mysterious wonder.

Voyage Journal Texts

Beside Cook's voyage publication containing Hodges's illustrations, several other journals were written during this expedition by William Wales, by Johann Forster, and by his son George Forster. George Forster's and James Cook's were published within six weeks of one another in 1777, while Johann's was not published until 1982.[8] Wales's journal was published in J.C. Beaglehole's multivolume edition of Cook's Voyages in the 1960s. Cook's 1777 publication sold briskly for two guineas which was considered a bargain because of the engraved illustrations (Forster [1777] 2001, 1: xxxvi). George Forster's unillustrated text did not sell as well in England, although in its German translation it became very well known (ibid., xxxvi). Johann Forster complained in an undated letter to Joseph Banks that Cook's book was out of print,[9] while George Forster still had 570 copies unsold. George Forster's book was also translated, or extrapolated in translations of Cook's voyage, into most European languages. As well, it was 'abridged, pirated, printed in excerpt – in short, everything but sold' (according to his father) (ibid.). While Cook's text was written in plain language along the rational Enlightenment ideals of the Royal Society, George Forster's text was expressed through the sentimentalism of *Sturm und Drang*, the 'Storm and Stress' movement that was a dominant discourse in the literature of Germany in the 1770s. George had grown up in radical Enlightenment circles (Liebersohn 2005, 2) and gravitated back into such circles when he returned from his voyage. He immersed himself in Goethe's *Werther* and *Götz von Berlichingen*, Lenz's

Soldaten, Claudius's *Wandsbecker Bote*, Sulzer's work on aesthetics, *Allgemeine Theorie der schönen Künste*, and Laurence Sterne's *Sentimental Journey*. The style from these texts inevitably carried over into his own journal for publication (ibid., xi). The effect of these two discursive positions and styles, plain-text rationalism and pre-Romantic sentimentalism, through which Cook and George Forster narrated their perceptions, can be seen in the excerpts from their journals below. The Rapanui are rendered more visibly as fellow human beings in the Forster text, but it is the Cook account that overpowered the Forster as the public text of record and served more vigorously to shape English-language public perceptions of the island. Through this process the cultural artefacts were emphasized over the people who produced the culture, helping to erase their contemporary presence or value from their own story, much as they were diminished in Hodges's illustrations accompanying the text.

The section of Cook's journal on Easter Island begins by situating the text in relation to the preceding Dutch and Spanish visits. Cook had read Behrens and the anonymous sailor report in Dalrymple (1771), and was aware of the recent Spanish visit which had been reported in several British newspapers. His response to the island is written with both previous European expeditions in mind, at the same time as he firmly foregrounds British seafaring accomplishments. He slots his own expedition into the ongoing European dialogue about this geographic space: 'I made no doubt that this was Davis's Land, or Easter Island as its appearance from this situation corresponded very well with Wafer's account; and we expected to have seen the low sandy isle Davis fell in with, which would have been a confirmation' (J. Cook 1777, 276). Cook constructs Davis as having found Easter Island, while Roggeveen and La Pérouse resist this connection. Here in his initial response to sighting the island, Cook reminds his readers of the British claim to first 'discovery.' In doing so, and in referring to it as Davis's Land, Cook is writing back first and foremost to his British forbearers, and to position his own expedition as verification of the earlier British discovery. At the same time as he assumes the dominant imperial posture in relation to a possible land claim, he also acknowledges the Spanish visit: 'Before I sailed from England, I was informed that a Spanish ship had visited this isle in 1769. Some signs of it were seen among the people now about us; one man had a pretty good broad-brimmed European hat on, another had a grego jacket' (279). Finally, he writes sardonically to undermine the Dutch encounter: 'They also seemed to know the use of a musket, and to stand in much awe of it, but this they prob- ably learnt from Roggeveen who, if we are to believe the authors of that voyage left them sufficient tokens' (279). Several aspects of Cook's jour- nal entries about the island echo and extend upon the experiences of the preceding expeditions. Through this textual repetition, aspects of the subject of Easter Island would become secured as truths.

As with the first two recorded European expeditions, the Rapanui instigate the initial meeting between the visitors and the islanders. 'Here a canoe conducted by two men came off to us. They brought with them a bunch of plantains, which they sent into the ship by a rope, and then they returned ashore. This gave us a good opinion of the islanders, and inspired us with hopes of getting some refreshments, which we were in great want of' (J. Cook 1777, 277–8). This dispassionate report- ing of Cook is in contrast to that of George Forster whose journal describes the same incident, but from the point of view of the ill health of the voyagers, suffering from scurvy, as they near the island:

> The expectation of a speedy end to their sufferings, and the hope of find-
> ing the land stocked with abundance of fowls and planted with fruits,
> according to the accounts of the Dutch navigator, now filled them with
> uncommon alacrity and cheerfulness ... We had no sooner thrown them a
> rope, than they tied a great cluster of ripe bananas to it, making signs for
> us to haul it up. The sudden emotions of joy in every countenance, as the
> sight of this fruit, are scarcely to be described; they can only be felt in their
> full extent by people in the same wretched situation as ourselves at that
> time. (Forster [1777] 2000, 300)

Following this initial one-sided gifting, the second contact is from an islander who, much as the first man to board a Dutch ship, is interested in examining the technology of the vessel: '[O]ne of the natives swam off to her, and insisted on coming aboard the ship, where he remained two nights and a day. The first thing he did after coming aboard, was to measure the length of the ship, by fathoming her from the taffrail to the stern; and as he counted the fathoms, we observed that he called the numbers by the same names that they do at Otaheite' (J. Cook 1777, 278). In this initial contact with an individual aboard the ship, as the Dutch and the Spanish had done before him, Cook keeps the encounter generic by leaving the islander unnamed. In general, his text gives the impression of the island as a whole and places it in a larger Polynesian context. With the reference to numbers being similar to Otaheite

(Tahiti), the connection of Easter Island with the rest of Polynesia is established and then reinforced with the following observations:

> In colour, features, and language, they bear such affinity to the people of the more western isles, that no one will doubt that they have had the same origin. It is extraordinary that the same nation should have spread themselves over all the isles in this vast ocean, from New Zealand to this island which is almost one-fourth part of the circumference of the globe. Many of them have now no other knowledge of each other, than what is preserved by antiquated tradition; and they have, by length of time, become, as it were, different nations, each having adopted some peculiar custom, or habit, &c. Nevertheless, a careful observer will soon see the affinity each has to the other. (ibid., 290)

The arbitrariness or precariousness of the version of Easter Island that grew to dominate the European imagination out of eighteenth-century travel accounts can be seen when comparing Cook's account to the narrative of George Forster about the first islander to board the ship. If Forster's publication had been positioned to dominate the public imagination, a quite different relationship with the Rapanui might have developed. The Forsters, in their respective texts, each referred to the visit to the ship of the lone man who spent the night, but they each call him by the name he uses to identify himself, Maroo-wahai.[10] Where Cook positions himself at a distance from 'one of the natives,' George Forster observes 'Maroo-wahai' from close up:

> He was of middle size, about five feet eight inches high, and remarkably hairy on the breast and all over the body. His colour was a chestnut brown, his beard strong, but clipped short, and of a black colour, as was also the hair of his head, which was likewise cut short ... his legs punctured in compartments after a taste which we had observed no where else ... At the beginning he shewed some marks of diffidence, asking whether we should kill him as an enemy (*matte-toa?*) but upon being assured of good treatment and friendship on our part, he seemed perfectly secure and unconcerned, and talked of nothing but dancing (*heeva*). It was with some difficulty that we understood him at first; but having enquired for the names by which he distinguished the parts of the body, we soon found them to be nearly the same with those which are used in the Society Isles. If we mentioned a word which he did not comprehend, he repeated it several times with a look which strongly expressed his igno-

rance. As night approached, he said he wanted to go to sleep, and complained of cold. My father gave him a large Taheitee cloth of the thickest
sort, in which he wrapped himself, saying he found it comfortably warm.
He was afterwards conducted into the master's cabin, where he lay down
on a table, and slept very quietly the whole night. (Forster [1777] 2000,
302–3)

George Forster's writing, taking its agency from within the discursive
space of the pre-romantics, engages the reader at the level of emotion,
not only fact. He perceives and represents the emotions of Maroo, and
writes him into the imagination of his reader with a degree of intimacy.
Cook writes out of an empirical discourse that promotes comparison
and categorization through observation. His description of the island
has the advantage of experience with other Polynesian societies, which
gives his observations an authoritative air over earlier accounts. The
emphasis on theft, for example, is put in a larger Polynesian context at
the same time as it is judged against European conduct. 'We presently
discovered that they were as expert thieves, and as tricking in their
exchanges, as any people we had yet met with' (J. Cook 1777, 278–9).
'[The islanders] are friendly and hospitable to strangers, but as much
addicted to pilfering as any of their neighbours' (291). Over the course
of his three voyages and the publications following each voyage,
Polynesia emerges as a generalized subject constructed as manifesting
common characteristics that can in the European imagination write
over any particular island in the South Seas. Through the foregrounding of Cook's text over those of the Forsters,' Easter Island is both positioned as Polynesian yet separated from the dominant tropes of the
discourse through its non-compliance with lushness and vegetative
fecundity so needed and admired by deprived voyagers.

Reading Each Other

The details in the journals published after the Cook voyage to Easter
Island by both Cook and George Forster, as the previous European voyage accounts show, are constructed out of and valued against European
norms of behaviour. At the same time they offer such a variety of examples of interaction with the Rapanui, particularly Forster's, that it is
possible to gain, through these texts, a sense of how the Rapanui reading of and interaction with Europeans was adapting, after the two previous European visitations to the island. Joan Seaver, in her essay

'Rapanui Crafts' (1993), opens up a discursive framework through which such a reading can be exercised. She describes the Rapanui as adapting their own economic system of reciprocity to interface with the outsiders and acquire new goods. Since European manufactured goods were outside the parameters of their reciprocal kinship exchange, they had to work out, through adaptations of their normal behaviour, the best system for acquiring them (191). They began by giving what they had and taking what they wanted, which was the basis of their island reciprocity. These actions, seen by the Dutch as theft, were recognized by the Spanish as something different and not readily labelled according to European norms of behaviour. The Rapanui adaptation of the cultural codes of exchange was described by the Spanish as begging, offering, taking and yielding. Seaver, quoting Goldman's *Ancient Polynesian Society* (1970), goes on to write that 'objects from the outside undoubtedly brought status, not only because of novelty or technical proficiency but also because the Rapanui's skill in acquiring such a treasure would have demonstrated his [or her] *Mana*, a charismatic form of power, strongly rooted in cultural and agricultural production, leadership and economic success within the island culture' (193).

The misunderstanding of each others' cultural codes that confused gifting and hospitality with begging and theft were played out in another arena of contact between the islanders and Europeans. As Marshall Sahlins explains in *How 'Natives' Think: About Captain Cook for Example* (1995), 'Things are known by their relationships to a system of local knowledge, not simply as objective intuitions' (169). As mentioned in the context of the Spanish visit, the islanders saw, in each ship of eighteenth-century Europeans, an all-male floating community; smelly, scruffy men operating within a strict hierarchical command structure and living lives completely without women and children. The Rapanui must have perceived these exclusively male groupings as abnormal and responded to their aloneness with embodied hospitality. The reports from the European explorers describes the Rapanui women responding this way, although their physical hospitality was perceived as wantonness by the Pacific explorers.

The Dutch:

The women were all clothed with red and white wraps; and each had a small hat made of straw or rushes. They sat down before us and disrobed, laughed, and were very friendly. Others called from a distance from their houses and beckoned us with the hand to come to them ... (Behrens, qtd in Corney 1903, 136)

The Spanish:

The women go to the length of offering with inviting demonstrations all the homage that an impassioned man can desire. Nor do they appear to transgress, in this, in the opinion of their men; for the latter even tender them by way of paying us attention. (Infanzon, qtd in Corney 1903, 97)

By the time of the British expedition, this physical hospitality can be read, in one way, as having been adapted to extend beyond hospitality into a form of reciprocal trade advantageous to both parties, a modification of Rapanui behaviour to assimilate a European response. It can also, through another reading, continue to be seen as hospitality.

The British:

We observed a few natives on board, who had ventures to swim off, though the ship lay about three quarters of a mile from the shore ... among them was one woman, who had arrived on board in the same manner, and carried on a particular traffic of her own. She visited several of the inferior officers, and then addressed herself to the sailors, emulating the famous exploits of Messalina. A few English rags, and some pieces of Taheitee cloth, were the spoils which she carried away with her, being fetched off by a man in the patched canoe, which was perhaps the only one in the island. Another of her country-women had visited our ship the day before, and been equally unbounded in her revels. It remained a doubt with us whether, we should most admire their success among a sickly crew, exhausted by the long continuance of a noxious diet, or their own spirit and insatiate temper. (Forster [1777] 2000, 315)

It will be recalled that this same canoe that transported the women had been used the day the British arrived to take to the ship the first island gift of hospitality, a 'great cluster of ripe bananas.' To what extent might these two separate acts, involving transmitting largess to the ship, be read as hospitality? Part of the recognition of the instability of the explorers' record, and the emergence of the subject of 'Easter Island' from their texts, is seen in the question of how such acts were read by the explorers – trade or hospitality, theft or reciprocation for a previous gift.

George Forster ([1777] 2000) records several instances of hospitality, but he is unable to connect these generous acts with the requests of the Rapanui for British goods. The British code of trade and understanding of time and space seems to have required an immediate transfer of one thing for another. The islanders can be seen to operate under a different concept of time and space, give and take. I have juxtaposed several excerpts from Forster's narrative to demonstrate the disjunct between the actions and the understandings of these two cultural codes in interaction:

... great eagerness to obtain our goods without offering any thing in return, seemed altogether to be sufficient marks of poverty. (304)

The sugar-canes were about nine or ten feet high, even in this parched country, and contained a very sweet juice, which the inhabitants presented to us very frequently, and particularly whenever we asked for something to drink. (308)

Captain Cook had not been very fortunate in trading with the people. They seemed indeed to be so destitute as to have no possessions to spare. A few matted baskets full of sweet potatoes, some sugar-canes, bunches of bananas, and two or three small fowls ready dressed, were the whole purchase which he had made for a few iron tools, and some Taheitee cloth. He had presented the people with beads, but they always threw them away with contempt, as far as ever they could. Whatever else they saw about us, they were desirous of possessing, though they had nothing to give in return. (308)

About ten or twelve people were seated at a little distance from the last [ahu] round a small fire, over which they roasted a few potatoes. These served for their supper and they offered us some of them as we passed by. We were much surprised with this instance of hospitality in so poor a country, especially when we compared it to the customs of civilized nations, who have almost entirely laid aside all tender feelings for the wants of their fellow-creatures. (310)

We had been half an hour on shore, when one of them came behind Mahine and very nimbly snatching a black cap from his head, ran off with the greatest velocity over the heaps of rugged stones, where it was impossible to follow him. (309)

The increasing heat of the day had entirely exhausted us, when we had still a considerable way to make down to the sea-side. Fortunately we passed by a native who was at work, gathering potatoes in one of the fields. We complained of great thirst to him, upon which, though he was an old man, he immediately ran to a large plantation of sugar-canes, and brought us a great load of the best and juiciest on his back. (312)

... we found Captain Cook still occupied in trading with the inhabitants, who brought him some fowls ready dressed, and some matted baskets full of sweet potatoes, but sometimes deceived him by filling the basket with stones, and only laying a few potatoes at the top. (312)

The greatest part of the natives who traded with us instantly ran off with the cloth, nut-shell, or nail which had been given in exchange for their potatoes, as if they were apprehensive that we might repent of our bargain, even though they dealt honestly with us. (312)

About the same time, as Mr. Hodges was sitting on a little eminence, and sketching a view of the country, one of the natives ran off with his hat in the same manner. (309)

In the afternoon we returned to the shore again ... I walked on the hills to the southward ... crossed a field ... I walked up to their hut, which was one of the smallest I had yet seen, and as they came about me, I sat down among them. Their whole number amounted to six or seven ... they presented me with some sugar-canes, and in return, I made them a present of a small piece of Taheitee cloth, their behaviour toward me was wholly inoffensive ... it should seem that the Dutch very wantonly fired upon the natives, who gave no provocation, and killed a considerable number of them. (315–16)

The natives continued to offer some potatoes for sale ready dressed, and, at a hut where we halted, they sold us some fish. (317)

One of our sailors, who carried my plant-bag, in which were a few nails, &c. being less careful of his bundle than the rest, a native snatched it up and ran off with it. None of us saw it, except lieutenant Edgecumb, who immediately fired his musket, loaded with small shot, at the thief, and thus gave the alarm to us all. The native being wounded threw down the bag, which our people recovered, but he fell soon after; his countrymen took him up, and fled to a little distance, till we beckoned to them to return, which almost all of them did. Though this was the only instance of firing at a native during our stay at Easter Island, yet it is to be lamented that Europeans too often assume the power of inflicting punishments on people who are utterly unacquainted with their laws. (Johann Forster, qtd in ibid., 318)

A man and a woman met us from some neighbouring houses, each with a large matted bag, of very neat workmanship, filled with hot potatoes, and placed themselves by the side of the path where we were to pass. As we came on, the man presented each of us with some of the roots, and having distributed a portion to the whole party, he ran with amazing swiftness to the head of our file to share out the rest, till he had given away the whole. He received a large piece of cloth from me, which was the only requital for an instance of hospitality, of which I never saw the like even at Taheitee. (Johann Forster, qtd in ibid. 317–18)

The natives seeing us strike into a difficult path had all left us, except one man and a little boy ... The man seeing me very faint, offered me his hand, and walking on the loose stones by the side of the path, with amazing dexterity supported me for a considerable way; the little boy going before, and picking up the stones which obstructed the path ... we continued our walk downwards, for more than two hours entirely in the dark, during which my Indian's assistance was particularly valuable to me ... I rewarded my friendly conductors with all the Taheitee cloth, and iron ware, which I had about me, and arrived safely on board with the party. (Johann Forster, qtd in ibid. 319–20)

Indeed, when I consider the wretched situation of the inhabitants, I am surprised that they parted with a quantity of provisions to us, of which the cultivation must have cost them great pains and labour. (322)

In these juxtaposed excerpts of giving and receiving/taking, it can be seen how the European point of view sees theft in the counteracts of islanders acquiring Europeans goods, like taking a hat, when it was not tied directly to a matching temporal acts of gifting. They are read doubly as theft when the hat recipient runs off after taking his goods. Yet we are also shown Rapanui running after receiving goods in an immediate temporal exchange: 'The greatest part of the natives who traded with us instantly ran off with the cloth, nut-shell, or nail which had been given in exchange for their potatoes' (Forster [1777] 2000, 312). In such acts of apparent flight we are seeing cross-cultural miscues; an attempt to operate within a foreign system and an inability to 'quite get it right' according to that foreign cultural code. There does seem to have been one actual recorded act of Rapanui deception, the stones in the basket under the potatoes. But when the Rapanui threw the beads they were given in exchange during some transactions as far away as they could, in disgust, were they not also demonstrating a feeling of deception – that they had traded in good faith and were being given something useless in return?

It is possible to see in the range of acts described in these excerpts from Forster, a series of different attempts by islanders to negotiate new ways of interacting with new people; attempts to interpret and relate to European expectations. We see instances of the Rapanui inventing the Europeans, taking them up as a new subject that needs to be understood and fitted into their known island repertoires.

Cook's Legacy

Through the journal of James Cook, Easter Island was both identified as part of and divided off from the main discursive field of Polynesia in spite of sharing many of the commonly constructed Polynesian traits. A key factor in constructing one island as inside the desirable discursive field of Polynesia and another as outside seemed to rest on its economic viability as a potential part of the British Empire. Where the Dutch and Spanish saw the possibility of plantations, the British saw no personal gain.

> No nation need contend for the honour of the discovery of this land; as there can be few places which afford less convenience for shipping than it does. Here is no safe anchorage; no wood for fuel; nor any fresh water worth taking on board. Nature has been exceedingly sparing of her favours to this spot, As everything must be raised by dint of labour, it cannot be supposed the inhabitants plant much more than is sufficient for themselves; and as they are but few in number, they cannot have much to spare to supply the wants of visitant strangers ... Such is the produce of Easter Island, or Davis Land. (J. Cook 1777, 288)

The idea of honour potentially connected with the 'discovery of land' draws upon the patriotic discourse that emerged in the aftermath of the

South Sea Bubble and betrays that ideology's direct connection of worth with commerce, in this case an island's capacity to produce wealth and a patriot's capacity to find and secure it for empire (Lamb 2001, 210). The people and their needs, and an engagement with them on the basis of their perceived needs, are not connected to a sense of honour for one's country as much as bringing glory through the acquisition of wealth and potential future wealth. A 'discovery' was not worth celebration if it could not be connected to gain. Since there is naught to barter for, the people themselves ultimately became the commodity caught up in the imperial enterprise.

Cook is not diplomatic in his dismissal of the island, but even as he writes unequivocally about the lack of merits desirable to his purposes, he is not able to let go of it as a British discovery, nor does he dismiss the place without complimenting the islanders for their generosity and the small recompense required to do business: 'Nothing but necessity will induce any one to touch at this isle, unless it can be done without going much out of the way; in which case touching here may be advantageous, as the people willingly and readily part with such refreshments as they have, and at an easy rate' (J. Cook 1777, 289). Since there was nothing to take from Rapanui, no need to set up a system of exchange, it was cast out of the economic loop for product or produce and was constructed as a site of another sort, divided off and imagined differently from the rest of the Pacific.[11] The island, in order to become part of the European economic engine had to be invented with a status that made it saleable: that is, since it was too far away to make deliberate trips to and since it did not have water to make it worth stopping at in passing, its worth had to be narrated into text. The text then became the commodity that made it a wealth-generating focus. Mystery sells, romance sells, Easter Island had no new products so it became the product itself in the metonym of the moai.

Cook's text is central in the invention of 'Easter Island' for the vision of the place that enters the public domain through his narrative. Since a key point in his text was to emphasize Dutch brutality, his narrative wrote over the first Dutch publications as offering a more authoritative and thus accurate picture of the place and its people. Cook's text, at twenty-one pages, constructed an expanded vision of the island, and in the process reinforced some aspects of the preceding publications, such as European superiority and native-friendly inferiority, while resisting or replacing others, such as the fertility of the island agricultural production. Cook also adds two key elements that get taken up by the discursive Easter Island and built upon in subsequent narratives: the separation of the eighteenth-century islanders from the inhabitants of the island who built and moved the moai, and the incorrect positioning of the moai.

The positioning of the moai as facing out to sea must grow out of Hodges's obscurely composed image of them combined with an ambiguous statement in Cook's journal that has taken firm root in the public imagination. Text reinforces image in the following statement:

> ... I rather suppose that they [ahu platforms] are burying-places for certain tribes or families ... Some of these platforms of masonry are thirty or forty feet long ... For they are generally at the brink of the bank facing the sea, so that this face may be ten or twelve feet or more high, and the other may not be above three or four ... the workmanship is not inferior to the best plain piece of masonry we have in England. ... The statues, or at least many of them, are erected on these platforms, which serve as foundations. (J. Cook 1777, 294–5)

Having described the foundations or platforms as facing out to sea, it is understandable that the mind's eye then positions the moai as also facing out to sea when Cook 'erects' them on the 'platforms.' The moai in Hodges's painting for the Admiralty, which was available for exclusive, not general viewing, adds to the impression of the statues as facing the sea. Over the intervening years up to the present, the moai of Easter Island have continued to be imagined as facing out to sea. They are surprisingly described so even by people who purport to be recounting their personal journeys to the island:

> The face of each statue is carved with a childlike lack of skill; rudiments of arms and hands are barely indicated along the sides of the round body, such that each statue resembles a squat pillar. But they must have appeared as fearsome gods when they were standing, upright and enormous, facing the limitless and deserted ocean. (Pierre Loti, 'Diary of a Cadet – 1872,' 2004, 77)

> On immense platforms lining the roadways of the island and usually placed on a slope facing the sea, stood hundreds of giant red stone images ... with sneering, proud features chiselled upon their massive faces ... From the sea Easter presents an unreal, sombre appearance – seemingly an island of the dead, guarded by sneering stone sentinels which stare out to

sea with deep sunken eyes, eyes brooding with the silence of ages and of a long-vanished race. We next rounded Cape Roggeveen and Cape O'Higgins ... (Karl Baarslag, *Islands of Adventure*, 1944, 20–1).

For ages lost in the drifts of time, some of the most mysterious eyes on earth have stared cryptically toward tiny Bikini Atoll ... Of all the strange things that the Easter Island idols have looked out upon through the ages, the strangest was preparing last week. A world with the power of universal suicide at last within its grasp, was about to make its first scientific test of that power. ('Science,' *Time Magazine*, 1 July 1946, 52)

Dutch Admiral Jakob Roggeveen beheld an astonishing sight. Unless his eyes betrayed him, his three ships were nearing a fortified land of giants in the unmapped vastness of the eastern South Pacific. His glass revealed huge coastal walls and, looming high above them, appalling helmeted figures many times the size of his crewmen. (Malcolm Burke, 'The World's Most Durable Mystery,' 1955, 123)

It is the brooding appearance of the Easter Island's statues that gives them such an air of mystery. They seem like sentinels. Standing guard over the horizon. (Charles LeBaron, 'The Giants of Easter Island,' 1978, 93)

... dotted apparently at random all over the island are huge carved statues of mysterious beings, capped with chunks of red stone ... Their long faces staring blankly across the island and across the sea, offering no answers but only inviting infinite speculation as to how they got there – and from where; whose mighty hand carved them; and, what do they mean. (L. Picknett, 'The Stone Statues of Easter Island,' 1979, 55–6)

The other key constraining element to first enter Easter Island discursive space from Cook's journal is the implied dissociation of the islanders from the creation of the moai, conjecture with far-reaching consequences. Two separate references are worded in such a way as to suggest cultural differences between the islanders Cook encounters and the people who carved and moved the moai. The first reference is: the 'gigantic stone statutes so often mentioned, are not, in my opinion, looked upon as idols by the present inhabitants whatever they might have been in the days of the Dutch; at least I saw nothing that could induce me to think so' (Cook 1777, 294). The second reference states that the moai 'must have been a work of immense time, and sufficiently shew the ingenuity and perseverance of the islanders in the age in which they were built; for the present inhabitants have most certainly had no hand in them, as they do not even repair the foundations of those which are going to decay' (296). The wording of these two sentences can be interpreted to mean that the islanders of the eighteenth century are no longer interested in the monuments and cultural activities of their ancestors, or that they are not the same people – the 'present inhabitants' are not the descendents of those who carved the moai.

The second reading of Cook's statements about the 'present inhabitants' was taken up and has been carried forward into one of the discourses of Easter Island that continues to circulate in popular culture. In it, the Rapanui were divided off from those imagined as once living on the island and identified as responsible for the creative and engineering feats still evident in the giant moai sculptures. This idea of a vanished culture drawing into focus around the image of the moai needs to erase the extant Rapanui. The apparently 'lost civilization' that created the monolithic statues on the island is then seen as the subject of interest, and through this narrative representation there develops the idea of the island's past as a site of great mystery. As the main tenet of the 'mystery of Easter island,' this fallacy provides the currency for theories of non-Polynesian origin, from Phoenicians to the people of the sunken continent of Lemuria, or from Thor Heyerdahl's hypothesis of a Peruvian origin to Erich von Daniken's assertion of visitation from another planet.

In the practice of collecting that accompanied the imperial knowledge projects, particularly into the nineteenth century, it was easier to take artefacts from the island if they did not belong to the current 'thieving population.' Even as the British of the H.M.S. *Topaze* in 1868 enlisted the aid of the Rapanui to help 'take' a moai to their ship, with supreme irony, they complained about the islanders' thieving and unhelpful ways. In response, the Rapanui told the 'collectors' that the moai they were removing from the island was called *Hoa Haka Nana Ia*. The moai was presented to Queen Victoria who had it erected in the British Museum where it rests today, with its Rapanui name *Hoa Haka Nana Ia* engraved on its pedestal, a name which translates as 'Stolen Friend' (Ebensten 2001, 48).

The mysterious origin of the moai forms the premise of many of the forty American comic books on Easter Island published from 1940 to the present. In this genre the mysterious origin is usually overlaid with the 'terror of the sublime' that originates with Hodges's skeleton-dominated scene. The visual trace of his translated experience has been extrapolated and multiplied through time in comics with titles such as *Evil on Easter Island* (1941); *The Stone Slayer* (1954); *Attacked by the Lost Tribe of Stonehead Island!* (1965); *Here Comes Thorg the Unbelievable: He Waited a Million Years to Destroy Mankind!* (1970); *Terror on the Island of Living Stone* (1985); and *A Strange Island, a Lost Culture, the Final Quest* (1997). The island and moai are appropriated as a stage for Western narratives, and each incarnation erases the Rapanui as the creators of their own cultural production.

In 1872, Pierre Loti described the moai as the work of a vanished race: 'Current opinion now admits that the Easter Island statues were not the work of the Maoris, but the work of another earlier race, now unknown' (qtd. in Dos Passos 1971, 83) . A *Time* magazine article in the science section from 1 July 1946 borrows from Percy Bysshe Shelley's 'Ozymandias' and William Blake's 'The Tyger' to present the moai, rather than the Rapanui, as bearing witness to historical events:

> For ages lost in the drifts of time. Some of the most mysterious eyes on earth have stared cryptically toward tiny Bikini Atoll. On Easter Island, outrigger of the fleets of Archipelagos that ride the Pacific Ocean, a long file of stone colossi rear cold immortal faces. No one knows what men carved these gigantic symbols, what hands, what primitive technology raised them, with what devotion or what fears. Whether they are Gods or images of human greatness, they are menacing; they are monuments to the fact that man's history can perish utterly from the earth. (52)

Gordon Cooper, in *Isles of Mystery and Romance* (1949), acknowledges the existence of the Rapanui, but dismisses their connection to the moai:

> The existing inhabitants on the island are of small significance. It is the completely lost tribe of departed builders who still hold the land and appear real. The whole air of this small spot on the earth's surface vibrates with a vast purpose which once must have been so vital and alive and is now no more. What was it? Why was it?
>
> These incredible megaliths, part of the culture of a lost and unknown race, are now in ruins; of many, comparatively little remains. The present inhabitants take little interest in them. The statues to them are accepted in much the same way as stones or crops. They know nothing about them, and care less. (45)

Unsolved Riddles of the Ages by Charles Boeckman (1965) erases the islanders before the text turns to a focus on the moai:

> With primitive adzes and picks they chiselled gigantic busts, more than 500 of them, out of the volcanic rock. They made some of these stone figures as tall as a seven-story building and as heavy as a box-car, and carried them down the side of a volcano to places miles away and set them up on stone platforms.
>
> And then, for some reason that may forever remain a mystery, one day, in the midst of their artistic labor, they dropped their stone hammers and picks and vanished forever ... the great stone figures that are scattered over it like Gargantuan soldiers of an army defeated in battle. (84)

A book published in Britain titled *Island of Secrets: The Discovery and Exploration of Easter Island* by Jack Machowski (1969), is described on its flyleaf as 'a highly researched book that will be of equal interest to the general reader.' It goes on erroneously to label Carl Behrens as a scientist accompanying an early voyage of discovery, to list Jacob Roggeveen as publishing a French edition of his journal in 1737, and to state: 'There was no doubt that these statues could only have been the work of people of a highly developed culture. But who had made them? And why were they made and amassed in such numbers on such a tiny patch of land? Many people have tried to answer these questions, but so far without success' (12). In *Easter Island: Land of Mysteries* (1976), Peggy Mann states that 'few visitors manage to make their way to this tiny volcanic triangle in the vast Southeast Pacific. But millions journeyed there in stories and dreams, ... drawn by Easter's mysterious population – not the native islanders although they have their own unique fascination, but Easter's amazing population of stone' (15).

A book published in 1977, *Ancient Mysteries*, is self-described as 'the best of archaeology and the other sciences join[ing] forces to penetrate the ageless riddles of man – and to separate the facts from fable and fiction.' The same book is reviewed with the statement, 'the research is impeccable.' The author of the book Rupert Furneaux, not only erases the Rapanui as the authors of their own culture, positioning them as minions, but constructs the sculptors of the moai in a harsh and negative light:

> The statue building seems to have been begun by an unknown race, 'the others' who forced the Polynesian migrants to work on a useless task. We

may never know who these sculptors were. They seem to have been hard, pitiless men, scornful, distasteful, alien both to the Pacific and to Peru. (Furneaux 1977, 43)

In a recent children's book designed to answer questions about mysteries, *I Didn't Know That! About Strange but True Mysteries* (1992), Tony Tallarico asks 'Who carved the giant heads?' and answers 'It's still a mystery' (3). The text on the box of a Nova video documentary, *Secrets of Lost Empires II* (2000), states:

> The mute sentinels of Easter Island are mysteries locked in stone. Nearly 1000 haunting human sculptures are the only remaining citizens of a vanished culture that existed 1500 miles from the nearest inhabited island. Weighing up to 80 tons each, the 'moai' say nothing. But, with some investigation, they speak volumes. Take a look behind the stone faces and discover how such a remote society achieved monolithic greatness – and then disappeared.

Most recently, Ronald Wright, in *A Short History of Progress* (the 2004 University of Toronto, Massey College Lectures, broadcast on CBC and published by House of Anansi), stated that 'Easter Island and Sumer wrecked their environments so thoroughly, and fell so hard, that they became effectively extinct' (83). He provides no source for this apocalyptic conflation of historical events.[12]

At the same time as such texts take up the culture of the island as a fascinating topic for investigation and an enticing topic for readers, the narrative strategies of these texts limit and constrain the Rapanui themselves. They omit evidence that clearly places the Rapanui as the authors of their own cultural production over time, instead focusing on the authorship of the moai as a mystery and emphasizing the attempts of European scholars to solve that mystery. Through this narrative positioning, which seems to find its source in the Cook journal, these texts resist the development of Easter Island discursive space that would allow the voices of the Rapanui to speak, overlaying the emergence of their own presentation of their story with Eurocentric discursive domination.

6 The French

1786

One other expedition of 'discovery' contributes to the final geographic imaginary of the island that emerged from eighteenth-century European explorers. The French expedition of La Pérouse did not survive to return to France, but it was able to send back a narrative record of its first three years of exploration. Jean-François de Galaup de la Pérouse's wide-ranging expedition was sponsored by King Louis XVI. It was mounted in relation to, and as a response to, the growing European presence in the Pacific, particularly the British presence, and the information published from the three voyages of James Cook. Bernard Smith (1960) describes Louis XVI as being among the thousands of Europeans who enjoyed reading Cook's voyages. He even had a special edition of the second voyage prepared for the education of the Dauphin (100).

The Pérouse expedition, both commercial and scientific in nature, was planned to encompass several years. It was mounted as a project of the Enlightenment, with a full complement of scholars to bring back knowledge of the Pacific world as well as to take a cornucopia of animal and plant specimens to distribute among the populations of Polynesia. The king's instructions were to dispense what the natives might need to improve their agricultural repertoire, to 'provide these islands with European articles useful to their inhabitants, and sow seed, plant trees, vegetables &c. which could in time offer new resources to European navigators crossing the ocean' (Dunmore 1994, cxxviii). La Pérouse was further advised to collect furs in trade from the northwest coast of Canada to be sold at a profit to the Chinese, and in turn trade goods acquired in China were to be brought back to France and sold for a profit at home.

All the while, detailed maps, journals, and scientific notes were to be kept. A focus on mapping the Pacific was central to La Pérouse's instructions. While much more detail than Europe had previously known about Pacific geography had been mapped by Cook's expeditions, knowledge of the region was still inferior to local knowledge of the islands and coasts. Beth Tobin Fowkes (1999) points out that after detailed mapping, future European ships would have been able to sail to Pacific land masses with advanced knowledge, for example, of whether they were landing at islands or peninsulas. They would not have to rely on local informants and would have the sense of knowing a place without having seen it (220). They would also know what sort of goods would be available at specific places for trade. Such knowledge would facilitate the capacity to bring tangibles back to Europe in regular trade cycles of 'accumulation.' One way of learning to be an empire, as shown with William Hodges's panoramic Pacific landscapes, is to imagine possession through visualization without actually seeing a place. Such imagery relies on amassing traces such as journals, logs, measurements, charts, maps, sketches, and specimens from those places (220). This visual and textual portfolio of extracted traces was condensed even further after it was sent to the centre, where it was made more abstract, mobile, combinable, and powerful (215). When published and displayed, this manipulated imperial record enabled a familiarity with a variety of imaginary Pacific Others. Exoticism, eroticism, desire, fear, nightmare, and mystery, all these impulses could be satisfied through an imaginary engagement with the Pacific.

The desire to know the world expressed through the Enlightenment will-to-knowledge and imperialism, and manifest in the willingness of the public to pay for that knowledge, meant that the French expedition travelled into the Pacific with their pens primed for publication. So powerful a commodity were the texts of the expedition considered to be that the king contracted exclusive rights to them at the return of the expedition, and only in due course would he release them for commercial publication (Dunmore 1994, cxxxviii):

Prior to his return to the port of Brest at the end of the voyage, ... Mr de la Pérouse shall collect every journal of the campaign that may have been kept on the two frigates by the officers and *gardes de la marine*, by the astronomers, scientists and artists, pilots and other persons: he shall charge them, on behalf of His Majesty, with maintaining absolute silence on the aim of the voyage and the discoveries that may have been made, and shall require thereon their word of honour. He shall moreover assure them that their journals and papers will be returned to them as soon as His Majesty shall have given His permission for this to be done. (ibid., cxlv–cxlvi)

Maps were made of the Pacific before the expedition left and Louis XVI kept one to follow its progress as reports came in from the various ports of call. Eventually it became clear that something had gone terribly wrong. The fate of La Pérouse's two ships would concern the king 'until the very eve of his execution when, as he had done on many occasions before, he enquired: "is there any news of La Pérouse?"' (ibid., xxx).

The expedition began in 1785. Three years into the voyage, while at Petropavlovsk in Kamchatka on the 'furthest end of the Russian Empire,' the first mail from France reached La Pérouse. In the mail was a directive to investigate proposed British settlement plans in New South Wales, and La Pérouse headed there immediately. In order to dispatch reports and journals to Paris before they left, one member of the voyage, the Russian-speaking vice-consul, 'young Lesseps,' was chosen to travel across country from the port to Moscow. Included in the papers he transported were La Pérouse's journal entries about Easter Island and a sketch of the French interaction with the islanders drawn by M. Gaspard Duché de Vancy. Lesseps left the expedition in September 1787 and arrived in St Petersburg on 22 September 1788. In being chosen for this mission, he became the only survivor of the expedition.

La Pérouse travelled south from Kamchatka, arriving at Samoa about two months later with members of the expedition suffering from scurvy. As part of an effort to counter the scurvy, a party went ashore to fill barrels with fresh water on the second day of their stop to trade. A crowd gathered, hostilities developed, and because the tides were too low the men could not row back to the main ships and twelve men were killed, including de Langle, the commander of the *Astrolabe*. La Pérouse, much shaken and altered in his opinion of Pacific islanders, sailed from Samoa to Botany Bay, arriving on 26 January 1788. He was able to send journals and letters that described the voyage from Kamchatka to Botany Bay back to France with a British ship, and then he travelled on to New Caledonia, Santa Cruz, the Solomons, the Louisiades, and the western and southern coasts of Australia. The two ships left Australia and were lost during a storm on reefs at Vanikoro in the

Santa Cruz group between Australia and Fiji. The fate of the expedition remained unknown for forty years (Dunmore 1994, xciii–xciv).

Because of the mysterious disappearance of the expedition, the texts that did get sent back to France were particularly sought after by the reading public. An expedition that might not have stood out from many others that sailed in this period had it returned home, became a cause célèbre because of its dramatic disappearance. The first account to be published was the journal of J.B.B. Lesseps himself, who had returned overland from Russia with what proved to be the only surviving texts from the first leg of the expedition. John Dunmore, editor of the 1994 Hakluyt edition of La Pérouse's journals, gives a comprehensive bibliography of the publication record of the voyage texts after the return of Lesseps. It demonstrates the extensive exposure these narratives had with the reading public throughout Europe and in the United States of America.

Lesseps's own account, *Journal historique de M. de Lesseps. Consul de France, employé dans l'expedition de M. le Comte de la Pérouse en qualité d'interprète du Roi*, was published in two volumes in Paris in 1790 (Dunmore 1994, 580). The National Assembly gave orders that the journal reports and charts sent back to France through Lesseps and through the British be engraved and published at the expense of the public. General Millet-Mureau of the Corps of Engineers was the editor chosen for this task. Engravings of Easter Island and the Samoan attack featured prominently in the publication. Even before the official edition of La Pérouse's journals could be published in 1797, an anonymous work of fiction describing the fate of the expedition was printed in Paris in 1795, *Découvertes dans la Mer du Sud. Nouvelles de la Peyrouse* (B. Smith 1960, 104). The Milet-Mureau editions of La Pérouse's journals followed in 1797 and 1798 in Paris, with five separate editions published in London by Hamilton, Johnson, Lemoine, Stockdale, and one anonymous publisher (Dunmore 1994, 577–81). As well, an abridged edition was published in Edinburgh and then printed in Boston for Joseph Bumstead, in 1801: *A Voyage Round the World, Performed in the Years 1785, 1786, 1787, 1788, by M. de la Pérouse: Abridged from the Original French Journal* (Gassner in La Pérouse 1969, viii). Other editions appeared in 1799 in Leipzig, Berlin, Copenhagen, and Stockholm; in 1800 in St Petersburg; in 1801 in Krakow and Amsterdam; and in 1815 in Milan (Dunmore 1994, 577–81). These numerous publications and reprintings were feeding into an appetite for voyage narratives that had been developing over the course of the eighteenth century. According to the Royal Geographical Society, by 1750, no country-house library was considered complete without a multivolume 'Collections of Travels'[1] (Nussbaum 1997, 217–18).

These accounts, that included narratives about Easter Island, responded in unison and contrapuntally to the Cook expedition texts of the island. Since their narrative agency emerged through the same overlapping discourses as the Cook voyage, in the main they added to rather than resisted the previous textual shaping of the subject, helping to solidify the European imaginary geography. Since Easter Island was the first 'primitive' country visited by the French, the text and image of La Pérouse's experience there and his perception of the island had a wide circulation and influence on its development as a subject, adding to the vision of the island published by Cook and, to a lesser degree, by Forster. At the same time as these 'official' texts and translations were being offered to the public, the mystery and romance of a lost expedition was developed through other texts and performances of a more imaginative sort. These more popular responses to the lost voyage served to develop the image of La Pérouse and of Easter Island in different directions than the Millet-Mureau editions and are described in the section below called 'Canonizing, Bowdlerizing, Essentializing.'

The Royal Instructions for the Expedition

Of the eighteenth-century European voyages to the Pacific, the texts shaping this French expedition's goals are the most overtly expressive of Enlightenment ideals. At the same time, they operate through a complementary and strongly expressed commercial-imperial discourse that was increasingly shaping voyage politics and governing expedition decisions. That Europe would carve up the Pacific was understood. Which nation would take which island, or group of islands, was still in question.

La Pérouse visited Easter Island from within a particularly complex discursive space and he wrote his account of that visit from within a correspondingly complex matrix of intertextuality. The tone for the voyage instructions emerge from twinned feelings of respect for the recently deceased James Cook and a need to honour his accomplishment as an act of fence mending with the British after French complicity with America during the American Revolution (Dunmore 1994, xx). In the king's instructions, behaviour towards natives was juxtaposed with diplomacy toward other European nations plying the same Pacific waters. Within the world stage, the French saw themselves as scholars perfecting geography, with an eye to the way such complete and accurate maps would facilitate trade:

> Captain Cook's voyages have made Europe aware of vast countries, scattered islands and groups of islands ... but although this voyager, famous for all time, has greatly increased our geographical knowledge, although the globe he travelled through in every direction where seas of ice did not halt his progress, is known well enough for us to be sure that no continent exists where Europeans have not landed; we still lack a full knowledge of the earth ... Consequently a great deal remains to be done by a nation that is prepared to undertake the completion of the description of the globe ... the advantage that can result from a voyage of discoveries, in this favourable atmosphere of a time of peace, both for the progress of national trade and for the perfecting of geography, have led me to give sympathetic consideration to the proposals that have been submitted to me for such an enterprise. (ibid., cxi–cxii)

The framework for the voyage demonstrates an extreme measure of royal control outlined in a twenty-six-page set of prescriptive instructions, divided into five parts and signed by the king: 'Plan for a Campaign of Discovery,' 'Plan of the Voyage or Proposed Navigational Routes,' 'Aims relating to Politics and Trade,' 'Operations related to Astronomy, Geography, Navigation, Physics and the various Branches of Natural History,' 'Policy to be followed towards the natives of countries where His Majesty's two frigates might land,' and 'On precautions to be taken to preserve the health of the crews.' Running throughout the instructions is a desire to be the best behaved, best loved, most generous expedition of Europeans ever mounted. What emerges in the voyage narrative about Easter Island is contempt for the islanders' lack of appreciation of the French performance of these expedition behaviours.

While the voyage is styled as one of discovery, the extent to which the published records of previous voyages were now an established part of European expedition practice can be seen in the details of the '... Proposed Navigational Routes,' written in the voice of the king:

> After this search, he will go to the latitude of 27 degrees 5 minutes on the meridian of 108 deg. West, to seek along this parallel Easter Island situated in 112° 8' of longitude. He will anchor there in order to carry out the specific objective listed in the second part of the present instructions. (ibid., cxxvi)

The mapped certainty of geographic space expressed in these proposed routes marks a discursive shift from exploration into the unknown to discover to exploration of the known to consolidate. La Pérouse's voyage was designed to refine knowledge, to exert control over the newly known, and to establish ways of making that new knowledge productive. This shift is further demonstrated in the 'Second Part, "Aims relating to politics and trade,"' in the deliberate separation of trade from study:

> The islands of the Great equatorial Ocean will present few opportunities for observations related to politics and trade: their distance would seem likely to discourage European nations from establishing any settlements on them; ... Mr de la Pérouse will devote his main attention to the study of the climate and different products of the various islands of this ocean where he effects a landing; to discovering the practices and customs of the countries' natives, their religious practices, their weapons, their seagoing craft, the distinctive character of each group, what they may have in common with other native peoples and with civilized nations, and especially what characterises each one. (ibid., cxxxv)

Cook, in his final estimation of Easter Island had pronounced it not worthy of European attention, not rich enough for trade or even succour on long voyages. With the publishing and wide distribution of his second-voyage volumes, the island was divided off in text from the map of imperial productive possibility. It was not imagined as strategically necessary or materially productive enough to warrant colonizing. The framework employed by Cook is part of the discursive matrix employed by the French. In their voyage instructions, such islands as 'Easter,' where 'distance would seem likely to discourage European nations from establishing any settlements,' are given a separate focus from commercial enterprises of imperialism, adding to the discursive dividing off of Easter Island from the rest of Polynesia. Accordingly, La Pérouse is only to study them and, in so doing, to discover their distinctive character. He is embarking upon a project in search of essentializing characteristics for each island 'group,' for the sake of knowing the new subject.

While at the same time focusing on differences between 'native peoples,' the instructions are also self-focusing in a way not seen in previous voyage texts. 'In those islands where Europeans have already landed, he will endeavour to find out whether the natives made a distinction between the different nations that visited them and he will try to identify the opinions they may have formed of each one in particular' (Dunmore 1994, cxxxvi). This French Enlightenment text seems to be the first to ask, 'How are we seen by Others?' and, by implication, 'How should we self-monitor and self-adjust to present the national image through which we desire to be seen – both by 'natives' and by other imperial nations?' The imperial education project was as much a process of learning the role of the imperial self as it was a process of learning about Others.

The power of discovery texts to make or break the reputation of exploring nations was seen in Cook's response to the behaviour of Roggeveen's voyage to Easter Island. La Pérouse's instructions were written in the self-conscious intertextuality of those two previous texts. La Pérouse sets sail aware that the narrative of encounter he would write would shape perceptions of the French as well as perceptions of the Pacific in Europe. Out of this metacognitive awareness opens a space of imperial agency from which the French act as, and can be seen as, benefactors to Polynesians in general and to the impoverished Rapanui in particular. The king's instructions make the public role of France as a benefactor clear. 'During his call at Easter Island, he will confirm whether human beings are dying out, as Captain Cook's observations and opinion seem to indicate' (ibid., cxxxvi):

> He will instruct all the members of the crews to co-exist in amity with the natives, to try to obtain their friendship by a courteous behaviour and fair dealings; and he shall forbid them, under threat of the severest penalties, ever to use force to take from the inhabitants anything they might refuse to hand over voluntarily ... He will display zeal and consideration in everything that can improve their standard of life, by supplying their country with European vegetables, fruits and other useful trees, teaching them how they should be sown and cultivated; explaining the use to which these gifts can be put, there purpose being to multiply on their own soil products that are necessary to people who draw almost all their food from the land. (ibid., cxlviii)

The instructions outline how the French were to behave on the expedition, but they did not outline how they were to think or write about their experiences. In the actual journal of La Pérouse, there is a disjunct between these 'civilized' behaviours prescribed and enacted and the attitude towards the Polynesian Others who were encountered on the actual voyage. The proscriptions of the king did not produce the version of Easter Island that entered the European imagination. The voyage narrative did.

La Pérouse's Journal

After sailing from France and rounding the southern tip of South America, La Pérouse spent three weeks at Concepción and then sailed west for Easter Island. Once there, it was an experience of exceptionally brief duration, ten hours on land, and for which he had strongly preconceived notions. He stated in his journal, 'I can only hazard guesses about these people's customs, whose language I could not understand and whom I saw for only a day, but I had the experience of earlier travellers whose accounts I knew by heart, and I could add my own reflections' (qtd in Dunmore 1994, 63). The accounts he knew by heart were from Behrens, Cook, and Forster. As well as these specific perceptions of experience on the island, La Pérouse had the theoretical commentary of Jean-Jacques Rousseau, in *A Discourse on Inequality* (1754), where the author speculated that primitive man 'unaffected by the social and economic evils of civilization, should be happy and indeed noble' (Dunmore 1994, clvi). Rousseau's theory had informed the king's instructions with the idea that 'it was not his own way of life that European man should bring to the natives, but simply new crops that could raise their standards of life without developing greed and ambition' (ibid.). La Pérouse resisted this analysis. He took up the standpoint of the previous explorers' texts instead and, with caustic wit that invites the reader to share his insider point of view, challenged Rousseau: 'No one who has read the accounts of the most recent travellers could take the South Seas natives for savages; on the contrary they have made great advances towards civilization and I believe that they are as corrupted as they can be, given their circumstances' (ibid., 66).

This opinion of La Pérouse counters the theory of the noble savage with an alternative discourse that was dominant in France at the same time and evident in La Pérouse's reference to 'civilization.' Marshall Sahlins (1976) identifies the idea of 'civilization,' in the modern European understanding of the term, as being coined in France in the 1750s and adopted shortly thereafter in England. Civilization, in this definition, had no plural. It was an ideal global ordering of all human society – a continuum that sorted self and Others by Eurocentric conceptions (10). It categorized and measured human worthiness according to the degree to which a people had achieved European ideals of technical prowess and European ideals of artistic accomplishment. It measured against its own norms the ways Others acquired and ordered knowledge; and their sex and class status. As Sahlins points out, the philosophers of civilization did not seem to notice that 'contemplation of the self in, and as, negative reflexes of the other contradicted the principles of inductive reason by which enlightenment was supposed to be acquired' (11). All human nature was seen as one and as perfectible by 'the exercise of right reason on clear and distinct perceptions' (ibid.).

La Pérouse's 'knowledge' of the islanders was formed from texts he 'knew by heart,' combined with his rejection of Rousseau and his embrace of a human hierarchy of 'civilization.' This mix informs his journal entries about the Rapanui with a patronizing tone not found in the previously published texts about the island. After some time at anchor off Easter Island, he writes:

> I flattered myself that I would have friends ashore, having showered gifts on all those who came aboard the previous day, but I had pored too much over the accounts of travellers not to know that these natives are big children who are so excited by the sight of our belongings that they cannot stop themselves trying to get hold of them. Accordingly I felt they should be controlled by fear, and I ordered quite a display for our landing which was carried out with four boats and 12 armed soldiers ... Including the crews of our rowing boats, there were 70 of us. (qtd in Dunmore 1994, 57–8)

This condescending tone, overt in La Pérouse, was normalized and imbedded in the previous texts about the island. The presumed superiority of the Dutch, Spanish, and British was not in question, as each group of explorers narrated their experiences on the island; rather, other emotional responses were paramount. Roggeveen, with no previous text about these specific islanders from which to construct or cue his response, feared possible violence. Wariness informed the tone of his perceptions. The Spanish texts were concerned about recording examples of their 'future subjects'' willing complicity with Spanish domination. The emotional response of the British narratives expressed disappointment that the island resources were not better able to fulfil their nutritional needs, and otherwise were almost matter of fact as they compared what they perceived as impoverished Polynesians with their counterparts on other islands.

With the narrative of La Pérouse, another layer of intertextuality is added to the discursive mix. The self-consciously superior tone emerges from his resistance to Rousseau's theory of the noble savage. It permeates his narrative and informs the way he engages with the islanders as he relates the details of his encounter and his observations of what he sees. To undermine 'the noble savage' point of view, La Pérouse constructs the least attractive portrayal of the islanders of any of the eighteenth-century explorer texts. In doing so, and then being lost at sea, he presents a picture that gained very wide circulation and strongly informed the present-day European imaginary of the islanders and subsequent nineteenth-century reaction to them, particularly that of the widely circulated narrative of another Frenchman, Pierre Loti.[2]

The extent to which the island La Pérouse arrives at is a mediated European textual construction, rather than actual physical geography to be explored, is demonstrated by his journal entry from the moment of his arrival: 'I sailed along the coast of Easter Island at a distance of 3 leagues ... the sky was clear ... At daybreak I made for Cook's Bay' (qtd in Dunmore 1994, 55). He experiences the island through European texts, and many themes from those texts are revisited, but each aspect of the island revisited is narrated in a tone of French superiority of vision and understanding (compared with the previous European texts), as well as in a tone of superiority to the islanders themselves. The combination of texts and theories being negotiated in La Pérouse's text distance it from his actual experience and prevent any feeling of the immediacy of actual human contact. For example, his reference to the islanders he encounters is mediated through the published engravings based on sketches by William Hodges:

> Mr. Hodges, the painter who had accompanied Captain Cook on his second voyage, has very inadequately reproduced their features. Generally speaking they are pleasing, but they vary a great deal, and do not have, like those of Malays, Chinese or Chileans, a character of their own. (ibid., 56)

The 'failure' of the Rapanui to look sufficiently different from Europeans to 'have a character of their own,' both anticipates nineteenth-century racialization of non-European Others and accounts for leaving the Rapanui out of the groups of Others that were categorized during the next century.

La Pérouse was particularly critical of Hodges's renderings of the moai:

Mr. Hodges's drawings of the statues is a very imperfect rendering of what we have seen, and Mr. Forster's conclusions, who believes them to be the work of a much larger population than exists today, do not strike me as much better; these shapeless busts, the largest of those we measured being only 14 feet 6 inches high, 7 feet 6 inches across the shoulders, 3 feet thick at the stomach, 6 feet wide and 5 feet thick at the base, could well be the work of the present population which, without exaggeration I would estimate at two thousand.

...

These colossal busts, whose dimensions I have already given and which reveal little talent for sculpture on the part of the islanders, are of volcanic origin.

...

We are certain it is a volcanic stone, very light, and that one can, with levers 5 or 5 feet in length [sic] and slipping stones underneath, as Captain Cook explains very clearly, raise a much greater weight, and that a hundred men would be enough for such a task. There would not be space around it for a greater number. And so the mystery disappears, the lapillo stone, which is not artificial, can be given back to Nature, and one concludes that, if there are no new monuments on the island, it is because equality reigns and it is not worth being the king of a people who go about naked, feeding on sweet potatoes and yams ... (ibid., 61–3)

La Pérouse's estimation of the ease with which levers could 'raise a much greater weight' was somewhat undermined by the French explorers in 1872, who found they could not move a moai to take it aboard their ship and so sawed off its head instead and transported that back to France (see fig. 6.1).

As in the earlier explorer texts, the perception of theft dominates La Pérouse's presentation of the Rapanui character. Examples of the reciprocal gifting culture described earlier are again seen acted out and misunderstood by the French. Viscount de Langle, who was distributing plants to the islanders during the one-day stop, is quoted as saying, 'These islanders are hospitable. They gave us sweet potatoes and sugar cane on several occasions, but never missed a chance to rob us when they thought it safe to do so' (qtd in Dunmore 1994, 73). Like Forster and Cook, de Langle is unable to see the reciprocal nature of exchange in the offers of food and the acquisition of European clothing. J.P. Greene, in 'French Encounters with Material Culture of the South Pacific' (2002), describes how the Rapanui had taken great care 'to

Figure 6.1: Disembodied moai head displayed in the Louvre, from the Métraux-Lavachery expedition. Gift of the Chilean government to the Musée de l'Homme, 1934–5, on loan from the Musé de l'Homme. Retrieved December 2006 from http://commons.wikimedia.org/wiki/Image:Moai_Easter_Island_ InvMH-35–61–1.jpg. Used with permission of Jastrow.

transport gifts on their heads, above the level of the water,' when they greeted the arrival of the French. He thinks it 'highly unlikely that they consciously sought to give offence,' and suggests their 'tactile and vocal interest in exotic clothing could well represent the behavior habitually displayed when any sort of bargaining, barter, or exchange was engaged in' (239). La Pérouse's response to the islanders behaviour, however, is harsh:

> It is certain that these people have different ideas about theft than we do; they clearly feel no shame about it, but they know quite well that they are committing an unfair action and immediately take flight to avoid the punishment which we would have meted out in proportion to the crime if we had had to stay on the island for any length of time, because our extreme gentleness would have had an unfortunate outcome in the end and a few blows with a rope would have made these islanders more amenable. (qtd in Dunmore 1994, 66)

While whipping may seem preferable to shooting, La Pérouse's assumption of the right to modify the behaviour of islanders on their own island is presented without self-awareness of overstepping any bounds of 'civilized' behaviour. He assumes the right to dominate and shape Others he perceives as less developed. He assumes the dynamics of this Polynesian gifting culture is theft. And he assumes a knowledge of what punishment is in proportion to this crime of theft. Such assumptions are enabled through the discursive space of imperialism to claim and master places and people new to Europe as it pursues the right to invade and impose its will throughout the Pacific. Although La Pérouse does not act on his impulses, he is operating out of a discursive space that had enabled such actions in the past and would enable their like in the next century.

In a final negative judgment of the islanders, La Pérouse identifies their interest in 'advanced' technology as an indicator of superior reasoning and then, ironically, uses this evidence of superiority to judge more harshly their perceived ingratitude to his many gifts:

> The care they took to measure my ship showed me that they did not look upon our skills in the way unreasoning beings might. They examined our cables, our anchors, our compass, our steering wheel, and came back the next day with a string to check the measurements, which gave me to think that they had discussed it on land and that some doubts remained. It low-

ered them in my esteem that they could reflect in this way – I left them a subject for thought which maybe they will not discuss, and it is that we made no use of our strength against them, although they were not unaware of our power since the mere act of taking aim with a musket made them run away; but on the contrary we only landed on their island to do good to them; we showered gifts on them, we patted all those who were weak, especially children still in their mother's breasts; we sowed all kinds of useful seeds in their fields; we left pigs, goats and ewes in their settlements, where in all likelihood they will multiply; we asked for nothing in return, and yet they threw stones at us and robbed us of everything they could carry away. As I have said it would have been unwise, in other circumstances, to behave with such softness, but I was determined to sail during the night, and I flattered myself with the thought that when they no longer saw us at dawn they would ascribe our prompt departure to the understandable displeasure we should have felt at their behaviour, and that possibly this thought might be to make them better people. Whatever foundation there might be to such idle speculation, it will not greatly concern navigators, as this island offers almost no resources for vessels and is only 25 to 30 days from the Society Islands. (ibid. 68–9)

In his role as distributor of largess on behalf of the king, La Pérouse assumes a performance position with a very specific expectation of response. When he does not receive the response he thinks appropriate, in an undercurrent of disappointment and irritation connected to the perceived lack of appreciation, he assumes the right to make strong judgments of the islanders' character and worth. He imposes with solipsistic bravado what seems to him a punishment, removing his presence from the island. He then uses the power of a text he knows will be published as further punishment to communicate his perception of their ingratitude and to promote cutting the island off from further European aid or commerce.

The Context of the Published Image

The British Admiralty had advised Cook to 'study natives in order to establish good relations with them,' and the royal instructions for La Pérouse were equally concerned with good relations. But the focus on goods and trade had previously directed human relationships more towards commerce than 'social study.' The ways in which trade drove science during Cook's expeditions and the recording of material knowledge over human knowledge, resulted in the study of 'man' being seen by contemporary social critics as lagging behind the other sciences (B. Smith 1960, 100). Bernard Smith cites two social critics of the period who were urging the development of 'anthropology,' Lord Monboddo and Johann Gottfried Herder. Monboddo published *Origin and Progress of Language* in 1773, after the publication of Cook's first voyage and while he was on his second. He wrote, 'It is really surprising that in an age, in which natural history has been so diligently cultivated, that part of it (i.e., the study of man in a state of nature), so much more interesting to us than any other, should have been neglected' (Monboddo [1773] 1967, 100). Johann Gottfried Herder published *Ideen zur Philosophie der Geschichte der Menschheit* in 1800 (*Outlines of a Philosophy of the History of Man*), a treatise that in its instructions to describe the 'varieties of our species' was one of the forerunners of the discourse constructing race as a political and social category in the nineteenth century (Russell 1997, 1). Herder concluded Book VI with the following passage, in which can be seen the roots of subsequent theories of inequality based on the authentic depiction of Others in relation to their 'natural philosophy':

O for a magic wand, which, at once transforming into faithful pictures all the vague verbal descriptions that have hitherto been given, might present man with a gallery of figures of his fellow creatures! But we are far from the accomplishment of such an anthropological wish. For centuries the Earth has been traversed with the sword and the cross, by toymen and brandy merchants: no one thought of the peaceful pencil, and it has scarcely entered the numerous herd of travellers, that words do not paint forms, particularly that which is of the most delicate, the most various, the ever changing. For a long time men sought after the wonderful and dealt in fiction: then they occasionally idealized, even when they gave figures; without considering, that no faithful zoologist idealizes, when he delineates foreign animals. And is human nature alone unworthy of that accurate attention, with which plants or animals are drawn? Yet, in modern days the laudable spirit of observation has begun to be excited towards the human species, and we have delineation of some nations, though but few, with which those of de Bry,[3] or Le Brun,[4] not to mention the missionaries, will bear no comparison; it would be a valuable present to the world, if anyone who has sufficient abilities, would collect such scattered delineations of the varieties of our species as are authentic, and thus lay the foundations of a perspicuous *natural philosophy and physiognomy of man*. Art could not easily be employed in a more philosophical pursuit ... (qtd in B. Smith 1960, 101)

Herder recognized that the stylized sixteenth-century engravings of De Bry and the classicism and grandeur of Le Brun's seventeenth-century art did not produce 'faithful pictures' of the 'varieties of our species,' and that more recent classic idealization overpowered 'accurate attention.' His point of view raised the awareness of the need for accurate pictures and more focus on the social groups of people encountered on the voyage. That need was reflected in the instructions and selection of artists to accompany the French expedition.

La Pérouse's instructions stated:

> ... he will observe the genius, character, manners, customs, bodily constitution, language, government and number of the inhabitants ... In like manner he will order the garments, arms, ornaments, utensils, tools, musical instruments, and everything used by the different people he shall visit, to be collected and classed; and each article to be ticketed, and marked with a number corresponding to that assigned it in the catalogue ... [Portraits are to be made] of the natives of the different parts, their dresses, ceremonies, buildings, boats, and vessels, and all the productions of the sea and land ... if he shall think that drawings of them will render the descriptions more intelligible. (qtd in Dunmore 1994, 37–8)

In order to produce the required images, M. Gaspard Duché de Vancy, a landscape and figure draughtsman, accompanied the expedition. One of his sketches sent back to France through Lesseps was of the French observing the monuments of Easter Island. The engraving based on de Vancy's sketch, *Insulaires et Monumens de L'Île de Pâques* (fig. 6.2), does not heed Herder's argument to move away from the eighteenth-century European propensity to depict Pacific islanders in classic form and drapery. Perhaps the desire to present the French performing as directed on their voyage, particularly since they were lost while on their mission, overrode the pressure for faithful pictures. But even if the Rapanui had been depicted in the French engraving with photographic realism, their postures and activities in the composition carry an additional textual coding beyond mere physiognomy. They are almost all shown in acts of deception and theft. Whether classically draped or not, what we do see in this widely circulated engraving is a change in attitude from the way Pacific peoples had been

Figure 6.2: *Insulaires et Monumens de L'Île de Pâques*, engraving based on de Vancy sketch, *Voyage de la Pérouse autour du monde, publié conformément du décret du 22 avril 1791* (Paris 1797).

presented by previous expeditions. Bernard Smith (1960) describes it as a shift in attitude from one of trust to one of distrust in the native character (102). No doubt this shift was amplified by the attack at Samoa later in the voyage that claimed the lives of twelve members of the expedition.

Published engravings were often composed to tell a story either of observed 'native' behaviour or to bear witness to the European encounter with the 'newly discovered.' That narrative context, shaped according to the values of the observers, taught the European audience viewing the images both how to perceive these new Others and how to think of themselves in relation to those Others. The extensive print circulation of these images carried very specific lessons about those depicted, and the reading public's repeated contact with such images had the pedagogical effect of laying down cultural capital actively maintained by continued association with expedition images in texts as well as on the stage. Over time the repetition, essentialization, and degeneration of such imagery conjured an ingrained subjective response of specific culturally taught values that could be applied to all representations of Pacific peoples.

W.J.T. Mitchell, in *Iconology* (1937), observes that there is no innocent eye or pure vision through which to see Others or their images, only 'imagination contaminated by purpose and desire' (118). In *Picture Theory* (1994), Mitchell goes on to describe the pedagogy of repetition that trains the eye to see within a learned narrative as an example of Foucault's theory of the gap between language and image being held open to allow the representation to be seen as 'a dialectical field of forces rather than a determinate' (69–70). Mitchell would describe the power of this picture of the French engaged with the 'Easter Islanders' as resting in its 'internal relations of domination and resistance,' as well as its external relations with those who view it and learn from it (324).

The Garden and the Wild: Control and Impulse

What follows is an analysis of the picture representing the visit to Easter Island in April 1786, followed by an analysis of the picture representing the attack at Samoa almost two years later in December 1787. Not only is the La Pérouse expedition image of Easter Island an engraving that needs to be read in the context of the text that accompanies it, with its emphasis on theft (an emphasis with no counterbalancing gifting in the widely circulated abridged version), but it also needs to be read in the context of what was understood as the massacre of twelve members of the expedition at Samoa. While the published journal of La Pérouse has several engravings of peoples from the northern Pacific region, the engraving of the massacre is the only other depiction of South Pacific people shown in any detail. Both of these pictures will be described to elicit what each represents as a contained field, in relation to its accompanying text and in relation to each other for the Europeans and Americans viewing them though imperial eyes in the late eighteenth and nineteenth centuries.

One of the first things to notice about the French moai picture is the artist depicted sketching the monuments (see fig. 6.2). This pictorial self-reference is described by Mitchell (1994) as cueing the viewer to see the composition as a 'metapicture,' the kind of picture that acknowledges its own self-awareness (36). In this case, the picture consciously offers a visual space of reflection on the French mission not to harm the 'natives,' and records compliance even in the face of theft. In the metapicture, the artist is depicted as a servile copyist of a passive model, while the viewer is placed in 'a position of superior visual mastery, beholding the whole scene of the pictorial production as a historical moment ... from a position (apparently) beyond history, beyond style and convention' (63). Like the 'close reading' of textual criticism theorized by Romantic poet and critic Samuel Coleridge, and practised on literary texts during much of the twentieth century, the metapicture subscribes to the idea that every painting contains within it the keys to its own comprehension. The picture invites us to ask what ways of seeing and what narratives are being elicited, and which are repressed, in the painting. It also asks what values are being promoted in the work through these commissions and omissions (91). Several aspects of the picture offer answers to these questions: the representation of the landscape, the monuments, the islanders, and the French.

In the tradition of landscape painting in Europe, distinctions can be made between the wild, unaltered natural space, often presented as grand and sublime, and the cultivated or arranged landscape that acknowledges the hand of human intervention, often soothing and pastoral. A further distinction is possible between wild space presented with or without the addition of human figures that might suggest an interpretable narrative, and shaped landscape peopled or shown empty, either with evidence of habitation, or barren, or returning to a state of wild nature. With the opening of the discourse of imperialism, these forms of landscape painting were absorbed into a complementary genre of imperial landscape that emerged in Western Europe, a visual counterpoint to the acquisition of geography remote from the imperial centre. William Hodges's landscape of Easter Island was conjured through the sublime in his painting for the Admiralty. The embrace of exotic landscapes in his Pacific works paralleled the embrace of as yet untamed foreign soil. In 'Gombrich and the Rise of Landscape' (1997), Mitchell describes the emergence of this imperial landscape genre as the moment when the Eurocentric narrative of the 'rise of landscape painting' is generalized as a master narrative for a parallel 'rise of landscape' in the world at large (104–5). From within imperialism, Europe painted for its own consumption those places that it now knew, named, controlled, or desired.

De Vancy, in his depiction of the Easter Island landscape, like Hodges before him, was apparently careful not to show any evidence of cultivation: no crops or groves planted in rows, no fields of sugar cane or yams, no chicken houses or other forms of buildings that would actu-

ally have been situated in relation to a clan platform topped with statues as can be seen in the reconstructed sketch (fig. 6.3) that depicts the
elements that would have actually been near any moai. Only barren
hills are shown in the composition of the island landscape as background to the interaction of the French and the islanders in figure 6.2.
Yet in a visit to the island, even today, it is virtually impossible to scan
any patch of ground without seeing evidence of former human habitation or cultivation, whether it is stone mulch evenly spaced in former
fields, the stone surrounds of earthen ovens, or the stone foundations of
former buildings. In this decision to erase cultivation and domestication from the landscape, the artist is deliberately eliminating the active
social dynamic and agrarian sophistication of the islanders to cast them
in his chosen narrative without the distraction of their own social production. In addition to eliminating the evidence of their daily lives, all
of the islanders are turned away from the moai as if to disassociate
them from that aspect of their culture as well. Cracks are clearly shown
on the head piece and body of the moai in the foreground suggesting
their antiquity and further separating these 'contemporary' islanders
from the earlier creation of the statues.

The barren background of the de Vancy picture frames a shrubby
foreground that provides a verdant space for a scene of human interac-.
tion. His original sketch, shows a minimum of foliage. The engraver,
following a well established painting convention of picturing men and
women sitting in park-like settings, has added extra greenery (Beckett
1994, 285). *Insulaires et Monumens de L'Île de Paques* represents the
natives, according to Bernard Smith (1960), within the conventions of
soft primitivism. He sees in the 'elegant features, serene expressions,
pale skins, and draperies,' the expression of classicism. He also sees
classic eroticism in the bare breasts and scanty clothing of the women,
but combined with these visual traditions, he sees a theme of cunning
and emphasis on the natives' aptitude for theft. 'They are in short
drawn as La Pérouse described them, as hypocrites; noble in appearance but far from noble in deed' (103).

John Greene, in 'French Encounters with Material Culture of the
South Pacific' (2002), sees in de Vancy's relation of barren landscape to
antiquities, a composition similar to those by French painter Herbert
Robert who composed many landscapes punctuated by ruins (see such
works as *Ruins on the Terrace in Marly Park, 1780,* and *Ruins of a Doric
Temple, 1783*).[5] Unlike Hodges's painting of the monuments that invites
the eye to survey the whole island and move beyond it to take in new

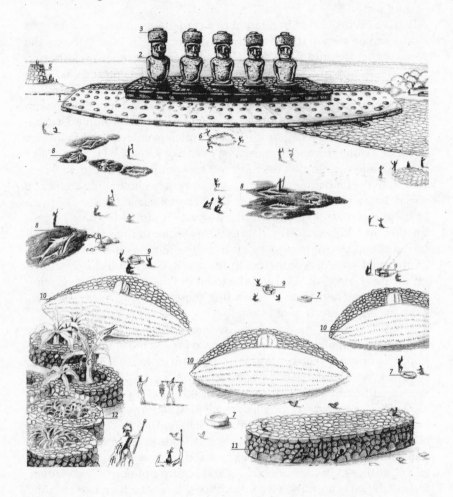

Figure 6.3: *Ceremonial Clan Site*, drawing by Te Pou Hoke, from *Easter Island: Rapa Nui, a Land of Rocky Dreams* (Ramírez and Huber, 2000). Courtesy of José Miguel Ramírez. 1. Ahu, *Ceremonial platform*, 2. Moai *Ancestor's image*, 3. Pukao *Topknot*, 4. *Cremation pit*, 5. Tupa *Tower*, 6. Paina *Ceremonial circle*, 7. Taheta *Stone basin for rainwater*, 8. *Petroglyph*, 9. Umu pae *Cooking oven*, 10. Hare Paenga *House*, 11. Hare moa *Chicken house*, 12. Manavai *Garden enclosure*.

Figure. 6.4: 'Measuring,' detail from *Insulaires et Monumens de L'Île de Pâques*, engraving based on de Vancy sketch, *Voyage de la Pérouse autour du monde, publié conformément du décret du 22 avril 1791* (Paris 1797).

horizons, de Vancy's sketch is framed to focus the eye on the activity of the humans. They are grouped in a series of vignettes, the players each acting out variations on the same scene. The four Frenchmen in the picture are placed to form a triangle where each man is facing one of the other Frenchmen. Each is therefore shown to be seeing the theft practised upon his fellows and to be passively ignoring the personal losses (see fig. 6.4).

The four Frenchmen, as Greene notes, are shown following the royal instructions to measure, record, and draw the cultures of those natives encountered on the voyage. At the same time, they can be seen to be interacting on friendly terms with them. The islanders are all shown focused exclusively on 'European material goods,' which they either

Figure 6.5: 'Mirror,' detail from *Insulaires et Monumens de L'Île de Pâques*, engraving based on de Vancy sketch, *Voyage de la Pérouse autour du monde, publié conformément du décret du 22 avril 1791* (Paris 1797).

already have in their possession, like the women looking at a mirror (fig. 6.5), or are in the process of stealing: in the foreground a woman talks to a Frenchman while a man extracts the handkerchief from his pocket (fig. 6.6); and the artist drawing the statues has just been relieved of something from his pocket (fig. 6.7), either the Frenchman recording the measurements of the statue, or his counterpart taking those measurements, is having his hat pulled away by a man hiding behind the statue (fig. 6.4) (242). Greene goes on to point out that the narrative focus of the picture is not on the statues, but on the thefts that were so strongly condemned in La Pérouse's text accompanying this engraving. The Frenchmen are situated to be aware of the thefts even as they behave as if they are not, further emphasizing 'the kindness of their mission' (ibid.). The implication is that de Vancy's instructions were to document not only the island people and culture but also to give graphic form to the islanders 'disregard for the French concept of

Figure 6.6: 'Handkerchief,' detail from *Insulaires et Monumens de L'Île de Pâques*, engraving based on de Vancy sketch, *Voyage de la Pérouse autour du monde, publié conformément du décret du 22 avril 1791* (Paris 1797).

private property,' as well as to record 'the official desire to represent the French as kindly' (243).

In their actions, the French are demonstrating self-control and personal sacrifice in the pursuit of knowledge for empire. As much power and control is conveyed in following the instruction not to retaliate as would be conveyed in the corporeal punishment of the islanders for their actions. In fact, the depiction of the islanders' lack of control is in direct counterpoint to the control exerted by the French, and each highlights the extreme of the other. Implicit in the refusal to censure the theft

Figure 6.7: 'Sketching,' detail from *Insulaires et Monumens de L'Île de Pâques*, engraving based on de Vancy sketch, *Voyage de la Pérouse autour du monde, publié conformément du décret du 22 avril 1791* (Paris 1797).

is the compliance with the royal instructions and the moral superiority of the more 'civilized' French. The French are demonstrating mastery of all they survey. Through this widely published image, the comedy of the hat being pulled away with a branch reduces the idea of male island-ers to caricatures, impish thieves, and the women to wanton accom-plices. All islander agency in the de Vancy picture is either for theft or seduction, all French agency relates to generosity and self-restraint.

With the textual work of imperialism still returning primary knowl-edge of Others back to Europe, widely circulated publications such as La Pérouse's, with its illustrated emphasis on Easter Island theft, enabled the work of the image to essentialize and set the character of the islanders forever as thieves. Mitchell (1994) describes this double coding of text and image in illustrated travel narratives as a 'suturing of discourse and representation, the sayable and the seeable, across an unobtrusive, invisible frontier.' This coding exemplifies the condi-tions that make it possible to designate and assign 'proper names, to describe, to place in grids, strata, or genealogies.' The dialectic of dis-

MASSACRE *of* DE LANGLE, LEMANON *&* TEN OTHERS *of the* TWO CREWS.

Figure 6.8: *Massacre de Mm de Langle,* engraving by Nicholas Ozanne, *Voyage de la Pérouse autour du monde, publié conformément du décret du 22 avril 1791* (Paris 1797).

course and vision, in short, is a fundamental site of imperial knowledge (69–70).

The de Vancy picture of Easter Island did not stand alone. It was one of many engravings illustrating the Milet-Mureau publication. A reader not only would have seen the de Vancy picture in relation to the negative text of La Pérouse about the islanders, but would also have seen and read it in relation to other texts and pictures of other Pacific peoples encountered on the voyage, most notably the very negative encounter with the Samoans. The engraving *Massacre de Mm de Langle, Lamanon et dix autres individus des deux equipages* by Nicholas Ozanne (fig. 6.8), reflects the hostility of La Pérouse, making 'a notable departure from the pictorial convention of the noble savage' gracefully posed in fluid draperies (B. Smith 1960, 103). Smith points out that the La Pérouse text contrasts the ferocity of the Samoans with the fertility of

their island, here 'a scene of unmitigated violence occur[s] upon a beautiful tropical beach abounding in coconut palms, bananas and breadfruit' (104). He goes on to say:

La Pérouse had described the Samoans physically as 'about five feet ten
inches, and their muscular limbs of colossal proportions gave them an
idea of their own superiority, which rendered us by no means formidable
in their eyes.' Ozanne depicts them as muscular but squat in physique.
They are not now posed in the manner of ancient marbles, their movements being swift, angular, and without grace. Both in their proportions
and their movements they are no longer invested with the neo-classical
dignity of the noble savage. Expressions are violent, the mouth open, the
eyes deep-set and dark, the hair frizzled out on all sides; while instead of
the classically draped *tapa* cloth the men are seen clothed in light grass
skirts which give them a shaggy, wild and unkempt appearance. By way
of contrast it is to be noted that the idealized family on the extreme left,
and the woman and child on the extreme right, both appear to be looking
upon the affray with considerable distaste. Both these groups, in the
greater paleness of their skins, the elegance of their hair, the drapery about
their loins, and their palpable nudity, provide a note both idyllic and erotic
amid the scene of violence. They belong to the conventions of soft primitivism from which the engraving as a whole makes such a notable
departure. For Ozanne has sought to depict the Polynesian as a violent,
treacherous, and somewhat contemptible foe. The engraving consequently occupies an important place in the European iconography of
Polynesians. (104)

Such a picture as the Ozanne engraving would have been read by its
contemporary audience as 'realism' in the sense that it was understood
to be showing the truth about things. Not a sublime representation
overpowering the viewer, but an image that, according to Mitchell,
seems to stand in for the real, serving as an eyewitness that offers a
transparent window onto a specific temporal and special reality. This
engraving, like the one of Easter Island, was encoded to be read as an
'embodiment of a socially authorized and credible "eyewitness" perspective.' Rather than the viewers being under the power of the representations, the audience was understood to be using the representation
in order to know the world and take power over it through that knowledge (Mitchell 1994, 325).

Today, there is more than one point of view to consider in trying to reconstruct the events that led to the deaths of a dozen members of the French expedition when they went ashore for water in Samoa.[6] For one hundred years there was only the La Pérouse narrative, which recounted an unprovoked attack on sixty-one Frenchmen. Like the 'Easter Islanders,' several chapters before, the male Samoans in the descriptions preceding the attack were described as thieves, and the women were described as being free with their sexual favours. The French were originally planning to leave after a day ashore, but extended their stay to take on more water. A reader could note the similarities between the behaviour of the two Pacific island groups in their first day of encounter and, by extrapolation, could wonder how the 'Easter Islanders' might have behaved if the French had stayed ashore longer.

In such a construction, the 'Easter Islanders' form part of a shared Polynesian story with shared native behaviour. This discursive strain leads to one imagined version of the South Seas as having a series of islands harbouring warriors, cannibals, and head hunters, conflating the disparate practices of far-flung peoples scattered throughout a vast region. The branching and braiding of the constructed versions of the Pacific and of Easter Island formed an 'Imperial Archive,' as described by Thomas Richards in his book of the same name, *Imperial Archive: Knowledge and the Fantasy of Empire* (1993). Through the medium of text and artefact returning from Pacific voyages, records of people, interpretations of encounters, and visions of geography were able to be categorized and combined in ways that enabled essentialized and hierarchically inferior images of Others to emerge (3). The archive supported a process that extended the ideological work of positioning Others into social categories very distant from the 'norm' of the civilized European centre, by this process teaching eighteenth-century Europeans how to read themselves in relation to Pacific 'savages.' The repercussions for the Rapanui were to be felt in the next century. This imperial archive created an immoral authority from which to enslave, and a moral certainty through which to subdue, those inferior Others.

Canonizing, Bowdlerizing, Essentializing

The loss of the French expedition and the subsequent 'authoritative' and speculative texts about its possible fate shifted European thought about the natives of the Pacific. Bernard Smith (1960) cites an example of this shift in opinion demonstrated in the fictitious *Découvertes dans la mer du Sud. Nouvelles de M. de la Pérouse. Jusqu'en 1794* (104). It was published before the Milet-Mureau edition of La Pérouse's voyage journal. In *Decouvertes*, several members of the expedition are stranded on an island after the wreck of their ship. They rehearse all the negative fates that have befallen fellow explorers at the hands of Pacific 'sauvages' and, by morning, find themselves surrounded by cannibals. Just before they are roasted they are 'saved by the timely arrival of another portion of the ship's company who had become separated from them earlier' (ibid.). This speculative narrative was joined by another, a two-act drama in German by F. Ferdinand von Kotzebue, *The Tragic Voyage of La Pérouse*, translated by Benjamin Thompson and performed in London at the Theatre Royal, Drury Lane, in 1799 (ibid., 19). Seventeen years later, a different production was being performed at the same theatre. A broadside from the collection of the Australian National Library advertises the performance of a pantomime ballet, *La Pérouse; Or, The Desolate Island*, at the Royal Theatre, Covent-Garden on Friday, 12 July 1816 (see fig. 6.9). The website for the Australian National Library describes the broadside and production as follows:

> One of the earliest broadsides in the Library's collection is for a performance at the Theatre Royal, Covent Garden, where a box could be had for seven shillings, and a place in the gallery for sixpence. On 12 July 1816, the Theatre Royal played a double bill: *School of Reform; Or, How to Rule a Husband*, a comedy featuring lords, ladies, bailiffs and jailers, and a pantomime ballet, *La Pérouse; Or, The Desolate Island* ... Thirty years after La Pérouse sailed out of Botany Bay and into history, the Theatre Royal's pantomime speculates on his survival on a desolate island. The La Pérouse pantomime offers highly decorative theatre, including original music composed by 'the late Mr Moorehead and Mr Davy,' 'a Chimpanzee (an Animal of the Defolate Ifland) played by Mafter E. Parsloe,' and the 'Natives of a Neighbouring Ifland,' extravagantly named Kanko, Umba, Pootoomora and Tangaboo. The broadside suggests that the Theatre Royal is more interested in pandering to its audience's taste for the florid and exotic, than in any credible portrayal of La Pérouse's fate. (Nugent 2000, 1)

The degeneration of the expedition narrative is overt in this move from tragedy to pantomime ballet. It is more subtle, however, than the condensed versions of the La Pérouse text that developed in the next century.

La Pérouse's voyage continued to capture the public imagination into the nineteenth century, not only in versions of his expedition and

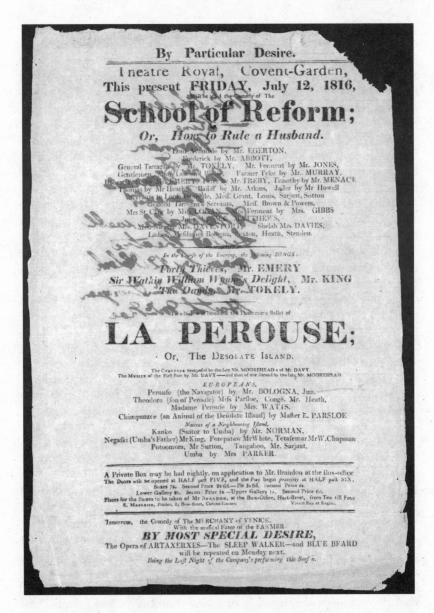

Figure 6.9: La Pérouse pantomime, broadside from the collection of the Australian National Library (London 1816). By permission of the National Library of Australia.

speculation about his disappearance but also in texts about the quest to discover his fate. By 1800, Jacque Julien Labrillardière published in both French and English one-volume versions of *An Account of a Voyage in Search of La Pérouse*. In 1875, a one-volume abridged paraphrase of La Pérouse, *Voyages and Adventures of La Pérouse*, was published by F. Valentin in Tours. A copy I studied was an English translation of the fourteenth edition of Valentin's abridgment, translated by Julius S. Gassner and published in 1969. This much published Valentin edition is notable for the license it takes with the text. Gassner writes in his introduction, that in 'producing a more readable version of the original report, Valentin omitted technical data, shortened the descriptive passages, and changed the narrative from the first person to the third' (La Pérouse 1969, x). The result for the reader is that the text that might be recognized in the first-person voice of La Pérouse, reflecting his personal negative opinion and sneering condescension towards the islanders, turns into an apparently much more authoritative third-person statement of fact.

Dunmore's 1994 translation of La Pérouse from the original French provides the following statement that, with its calculated desire to violence, cues the reader to the values of the writer:

> It is certain that these people have different ideas about theft than we do; they clearly feel no shame about it, but they know quite well that they are committing an unfair action and immediately take flight to avoid the punishment which we would have meted out in proportion to the crime if we had had to stay on the island for any length of time, because our extreme gentleness would have had an unfortunate outcome in the end and a few blows with a rope would have made these islanders more amenable. (66)

The same passage is abridged in Valentin, editing out the emotional response and stating only the even-handed sounding reference to theft: 'These people certainly do not have the same opinion of theft as we; they evidently do not consider it at all immoral. Yet they are not unaware that by stealing they are committing an injustice, since they flee as soon as they have taken something, obviously in order to avoid punishment' (La Pérouse 1969, 18). Fleeing after acquiring something, even in trade, was also an observation made by Cook. Another passage from Dunmore's translation provides the following condescending statement from La Pérouse: 'If there are no new monuments on the island, it is because equality reigns and it is not worth being the king of a people who go about naked, feeding on sweet potatoes and yams' (1994, 63). In the Valentin abridgment, this observation is softened: 'The form of government here has now declined to such an extent that they no longer have a chief of sufficient importance to merit the great amount of labor required for preserving his memory through the erection of a statue' (La Pérouse 1969, 16). The inability of the Valentin abridged version to convey the original meaning is further eroded by the omission of all passages from La Pérouse's journal that refer to the gifts of food bestowed upon the French by the islanders. At the same time all the references to French items taken by the islanders are included. The rehabilitation of La Pérouse's text to better suit the legend of a lost national hero does so at the expense of the islanders he criticized so strongly.

The more recent 1994 Hakluyt Society edition of La Pérouse as translated by Dunmore also suffers from a loss in translation, which underscores the inability of even the most authoritative publications to maintain a stable textual record. In preparing this chapter, I read the Easter Island section of the earliest copy I could find of the *Voyage de Lapérouse, rédigé d'après ses manuscrits origineaux*, published in Paris in 1831, and compared it to the Dunmore (1994) translation. The French describes the appearance of small stone structures near the statue platforms and reads as follows: 'Nous vîmes sur les bords de la mer des pyramides de pierres rangées à peu près comme des boulets dans un parc d'artillerie; et nous aperçûmes quelques ossements humains dans le voisinage de ces pyramides, et des statues qui toutes avaient le dos tourné vers la mer' (76). The key point here is the statement 'des statues qui toutes avaient le dos tourné vers la mer.' Dunmore, apparently so steeped in the erroneous textual tradition of moai facing the sea, seems to have decided that the original description of the moai with their backs to the sea must be an error. He translated the passage as: 'Along the shore we came upon several small stone cairns, similar to the way cannon balls are stored in artillery grounds, and saw human bones nearby and near the statues, all of which faced out to sea' (71).

Plagiarized Engravings: Art, Violence, and the Public Sphere

Ann Bermingham, in *The Consumption of Culture, 1600–1800* (1997), observes that the development of modern Europe as an increasingly 'literate and visual culture' came to depend more and more on expedition texts and images (12). This observation is echoed by Felicity Nussbaum (1997), in the same volume, where she describes the invention and consumption of travel books in relation to Africa. Nussbaum's statement is equally applicable to eighteenth-century voyage books about the Pacific. She refers to the printed word gaining a commodity status with collections of travel becoming extraordinarily popular, 'in spite of the fact that the same accounts were often simply reprinted or slightly altered.' Both compelling information and fantasy, 'recycled as new, produced the desire for more such travel narratives' (218). The truth of Nussbaum's observation in relation to the Pacific can be seen in the recirculation of eighteenth-century images purporting to be representations of Easter Island that have been offered for sale on eBay. Part of the research I carried out to determine the extent of the circulation and recirculation of voyage texts and images was to monitor the frequency with which they were offered for sale on eBay over a one-year period in 2004. The following four most prevalent bastardized images (figs. 6.10–6.13) that appeared with some frequency during that period, six or eight times each, are cannibalized from the Woolett engraving of Hodges's sketch and from the engraving based on the de Vancy sketch. These images are all illustrations from travel books, but seem to have left the bindings of those tomes long ago. The 'item descriptions' that accompany the offerings on eBay seldom give any pertinent bibliographical information.

The first picture, figure 6.10, is a variation on the de Vancy sketch of the French measuring the moai and the theft of the hat. All the landscape to the right of the moai has been invented, including what appears to be a Cypress tree, to balance out the moai as the centrepiece. The caption above the image, 'Manners & Customs of Nations,' may be the title of the book from which the picture was sliced. If so, the picture is adding to the image of the 'Easter Islanders' as thieves and the Europeans as benign seekers of knowledge.

The second picture, figure 6.11, may be recognizable as an inversion of and variation of the Woolett engraving of Hodges's sketch of moai, *Monuments in Easter Island* (fig. 5.1). In this picture the skeleton that foregrounded the original illustration in Cook's second voyage has been further dismantled. As well, a second islander has been added to the scene. Both people turn their backs on the monuments that are so distorted as to be unrecognizable as carved images, looking more like unusual but natural rock formations. With none of the stone suggesting architecture of any sort and the islanders being a fraction of the size of the skeleton, this image, although much altered from its source, serves to highlight death as the main feature of the island.

Figure 6.10: 'Inhabitants and Monuments of Easter Island,' book illustration, *Manners and Customs of Nations*. eBay item listed without further provenance.

The third picture, figure 6.12, was accompanied by this description: 'The print is a wood engraving printed circa 1860. The sheet measures 8 x 5 inches and is in very good condition. The image is titled "... Statues on Easter Island. Page 271." The print is a full page illustration from [a] mid-1800's volume on travel. There is nothing printed on the reverse side. The print is shown on a black background in order to show the entire sheet. This is an antique print guaranteed to be over 100 years' (eBay item 3741432807). The source of this exoticized vignette can be identified as just the moai and the native for scale from the Woolett engraving, figure 5.1.

The fourth picture, figure 6.13, is titled 'Île Vaîhou.' It takes the two moai from the de Vancy based engraving (figure 6.2), flips them to face the opposite direction to the original, and adds them to the Woolett

London, Published as the Act directs by Alex.r Hogg, at the Kings Arms, No.16. Paternoster Row.

A View *of* MONUMENTS, *&c in* EASTER ISLAND.

Figure 6.11: 'A View of Monuments, &c in Easter Island.' Illustration for publisher Alexander Hogg, described as 'for use as an illustration in a book describing the voyages of British explorer Captain James Cook' (London 1781). eBay item listed without further provenance.

engraving. The result is to marry the death associated with the British voyage picture to the more representational, but by no means more realistic, moai of the French voyage picture.

It is possible in this sequence of published images to glimpse the dynamics of the emergent visual discourse of the moai favouring Hodges's sublime vision, as he opened up a new way of seeing the statues associated with death, and then that vision circles round again picking up and repeating the new dynamic it has generated. Easter Island can be seen here to be forming its own discrete European-shaped subject. It is being identified, like the ancient Greeks, as a culture whose interest lies in its ancient artefacts, relics from a golden age that has now degenerated. Just as the ancient Greeks are no longer depicted in images of the architectural and artistic ruins of their era, so the Rapanui are not depicted in relation to their own ancient cultural relics.

While not part of the scope of this study, it would be possible to trace

STATUES ON EASTER ISLAND.

Figure 6.12: 'Statues on Easter Island' (ca. 1860). eBay item listed without further provenance.

the evolution of the moai and island images in voyage publications across the nineteenth century to determine their contribution to the process of identity construction for the geographic imaginary of the island as a cultural space. In his book *In Oceania*, Nicholas Thomas refers to the process by which a place is reformulated over time and through particular encounters (18). In these appropriated and plagiarized images we see Easter Island being reformulated, not through diverse subsequent accounts but through two well-documented encounters – the British in 1774 and the French in 1786 – reformed and recirculated to construct new imaginary representations.

This cataloguing of publication, translation, abridgement, 'correction,' and bowdlerization, as well as theatre performances that ranged from a tragedy written and performed shortly after the loss of the expe-

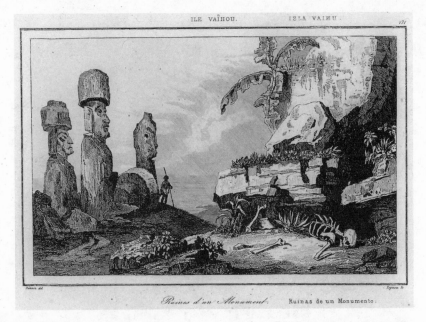

ILE VAÎHOU.   ISLA VAIHU

Ruines d'un Monument.   Ruinas de un Monumento.

Figure 6.13: 'Ile Vaîhou,' *Ruins d'un Monument* (ca. 1860). eBay item listed without further provenance.

dition to a pantomime ballet performed less than thirty years later, suggests how the lost French expedition first captured the public imagination and then degenerated as a narrative over time, both rewriting the character of the expedition leader and essentializing and diminishing the idea of the islanders in the minds of the European public. In these altered forms the French story of Easter Island was caught up in a cycle of consumption that moved away from its initial instructions and attempts to represent reality, to become appropriated and circulated as bricolage (Bermingham and Brewer 1997, 13).

The images and texts produced after the expedition was lost served to strengthen the French self-image at the expense of the 'generic' Pacific islanders who were cast in the ambiguous position of having or not having had a role in the disappearance of the mariners. (In fact, it was ultimately determined that the ships had broken up in a storm.) The frequent repetition and rewriting of narratives of righteous French character and of childlike, thieving Easter Island character, served as self-fulfilling prophecies that wrote into Euro-reality the terms and performance positions into which each group were cast and by which each came to be understood.

La Pérouse is the last of the eighteenth-century explorers to visit the island. Where the Dutch and Spanish texts both described commercial agricultural potential in Easter Island, the British account did not, and the French would now concur with that British estimation. In the European map of the Pacific, 'Easter Island' was separated from the rest of Polynesia as unproductive. Over the course of four expeditions, Europeans 'discovered' and named the island, assessed its worth to European interests, and decided to cut their discovery adrift. In the process, a new imaginary subject emerged through their texts.

7 Cultural Imaginary to Cultural Memory

Part One

The Imaginary

Eighteenth-century European explorers created Easter Island through their own world view, and versions of that view exist to the present day. They 'found,' labelled, and measured the islanders according to their own cultural imperatives, simultaneously bringing them inside of, and casting them out from, their European-centred understanding of the world. Since the extensively cultivated island was not taken up through the primary narrative of Pacific paradise, it was called into service for other purposes as the eighteenth century gave way to the nineteenth. Imperial exploration was replaced by imperial possession as the male islanders were captured for slavery, the land was taken over for sheep grazing, and the monumental cultural expressions carved in stone were extracted for European and American collections and museum display. Increasingly, as the nineteenth century gave way to the twentieth, the island was constructed as a site of impenetrable mysteries and astonishing remoteness, even though it was physically closer to Europe and the Americas by sea than the rest of the South Sea islands. Self-celebratory narratives of autobiographical adventure by twentieth-century sailors and archaeologists were reinforced with works of science fiction to sustain the idea of the island as a sublime mystery in the Euro-American imagination, with the moai as the central focus of interest. This celebration of moai reached its height with the UNESCO declaration of the whole island as an open air World Heritage museum in December 1995. Today, the statues continue their separate currency as part of circulating cultural capital, keeping the idea of moai separate from any narrative of the culture that produced them.

The textual instability of Easter Island continues with recent versions reshaping the island as a model of environmental destruction. In this new narrative, the imaginary geography continues to function as a stage for Euro-American versions of island reality projected back with textual authority to an increasingly global audience. Superlatives continue to abound as the epithet 'worst management of resources on the globe' is added to the most 'remote' and most 'mysterious' place on earth. In the island's new environmentalist incarnation, the people are once again a focus, not for theft from Europeans but for plundering their portion of planetary resources.

Eighteenth-Century Eurocentric Perception and Construction

In the four preceding chapters I examined how the commercial focus on the land by the Dutch, in 1722, as a fertile site for possible European plantations was augmented by the Spanish, in 1770, who also perceived it as a strategic site for overseeing South Pacific expansion. The Spanish described the islanders as hard workers whose energies and souls should be redirected to comply with Spanish agricultural and religious dictates. The British, arriving just four years later, apparently perceived a much-reduced people and landscape from that observed by the Dutch and Spanish. I posited the likelihood that European disease had devastated the population after the Spanish visit and that the remaining islanders had not had time to recover.[1] The French, arriving in 1786, did not describe the reduced circumstances narrated by Cook, adding weight to the likelihood of a major epidemic before Cook's arrival, but, like the British, La Pérouse dismissed the island and islanders in his report to his king.

The explorers plotted the island on their maps, defined what they judged to be the qualities and defects of the Rapanui, and evaluated the usefulness of the land and the people to their own ends. Without obvious trade resources, the island was deemed neither worthy of possession nor further study by century's end. Following these expeditions, it seems to have only found imaginative space in the gothic and sublime artwork of William Hodges and in the more people-centred, but condescending, sketch by de Vancy. Although the island had been seen initially as fertile and as a potential agricultural paradise, it was constructed away from that narrative, with the 'sublime moai' and images of death standing in for the excitement of 'Paradise Found' on other islands of the Pacific.

The first picture of the island, from the Dutch expedition, to circulate in Europe emphasized giant islanders with their spears bristling, attempting to overwhelm the explorers as they came ashore. Those 'giants' speak across half a century of imperial development to the lone island sentinel standing below a towering moai in the picture published by the British after their voyage to the island. The initial Dutch narrative of dangerous islanders fell aside and imperial print and text repositioned the moai as more significant than the culture of the people who carved them. The British print image from Cook's second voyage publication, in particular, generated and maintained a public memory of the island statuary more powerful than any memory of the islanders themselves. In fact, Hodges's and de Vancy's depiction of the moai were merged in subsequent appropriated and reconstructed images until the moai became separated from other possible traces of the island in European imagination and took on a life of their own in Western cultural production.

In the nineteenth century the Rapanui, were caught up, transported, and worked to death as slaves for empires and saw their relatives die of imported diseases and their island annexed for sheep grazing. Catholic missionaries arrived in the late nineteenth century, after slavery and disease had done their worst, and converted the remaining Rapanui to Catholicism. The population, so diminished through imperialism, continued to fade in imagination through repeated erasure in text and image in the twentieth century. Meanwhile the trace of the moai increased in strength through repetition and appropriation in Euro-American culture as a trope of the island, a metonym for Polynesia, and a universal simile for the strong jawed and long faced.

A View of the Monuments of Easter Island that Hodges composed and painted for the Admiralty and, even more influential, his landscape sketch engraved for publication seem to me to be the most culpable for all but eliminating the idea of living Rapanui from the picture of the island. I think Hodges's landscapes have had a particularly strong influence on the island imaginary in the English-speaking world. They conform to Willinsky's (1998) observation that the South Sea islands were viewed for their economic possibilities and from this perspective were often seen as uninhabited palimpsests that were already written over with their 'own buried treasure of colonial imagery.' They were uninhabited in relation to a European presence, with the indigenous populations erased or denied, written over, subsumed, and trivialized (225). Hodges's landscapes were both conceived and presented within a complex series of interlocking aesthetic discourses and social pressures shaping perception of the island against other islands visited and within the forms of representation available to artists and engravers. These aesthetic discourses worked in concert with the imperial and historic forces at play, framing the larger voyage project. The interlocking and layered aesthetic influences, exerting pressure on perception and forming a visual literacy upon which Hodges drew, included contemporary ideas for depicting the paradisial, nature and the sublime, Arcadia, antiquities, and memento mori.

Central to this examination of the eighteenth-century emergence of Easter Island has been the recognition that the very act of taking up Others in the language used to describe them automatically builds distortions and judgments into the descriptions. The language of imperialism has always positioned Europeans by 'a set of coordinates defined by race, culture, and nation,' positioning 'the West' in a top-down hierarchy in relation to the rest of the world (Willinsky 1998, 253). It is from within an understanding of this language-shaped distortion that we can recognize there is no stable narrative to write or to be read. There can only be perceptions of the island and its people shaped through the temporal cultural understandings of those who have written about them. All texts are situated documents, and all readings of those texts are filtered through the individual cultural and experiential complexities of the reader. Easter Island is geographic imaginary that can only be known through representations that create, value, and position the people, their culture, and their land in direct relation to each writer's sense of self and embedded stance within the discourses that shape his or her understanding of the world. In turn such texts have been and continue to be read and augmented through temporally and culturally nuanced readings and taken through them into memory. These texts invent Easter Island and teach us about that invention.

Learning Easter Island

So successful are these representations in teaching their versions of Easter Island that even people who make actual visits to Rapa Nui in the present do so, like their eighteenth-century counterparts, from within such well-taught lessons and firm discursive positions that they are sometimes only able to experience the space selectively through the focused and distorted lens of the imaginative space they have been educated into. Such travellers conflate textual realities and textual explanations with their empirical experience – amplifying some aspects of the culture and landscape and ignoring others, arriving and leaving with a version of island reality that conforms to their 'educated' perceptions.

Karen Michelsen of Toronto is one such traveller. She went to Rapa Nui with 'Marathon Tours' in June of 2004 to participate in several athletic events on the island: a marathon, a triathlon, and a mountain bike race. She had a day of organized 'sightseeing' followed by three days of competition, running, and biking over much of the island. Michelsen completed all three events with the highest points scored and earned the title 'First Athletic Queen of Rapa Nui.' At her awards ceremony, she listened to speeches in Rapanui by Rapanui, participated in Rapanui ceremonial dancing, and was awarded a wooden sculpture of a moai carved by a Rapanui artist. Here is her description of the island in her article for the 2004 September–October edition of *Running Room Magazine* about her experience:

> Easter Island – or as the locals call it, Rapa Nui – was discovered by the Dutch explorer Admiral Roggeveen in 1722 on Easter Sunday. Today, the island belongs to Chile. It has almost 3000 inhabitants and more than 1000 moai. Moai are giant monoliths made out of volcanic stones unique to this island. No one really knows why or when they were built or who built them. (51–2)

Karen Michelsen is perhaps an extreme case of one clinging to the mystery version of Easter Island. She spent four days on Rapa Nui where the contemporary island narrative, available in English-language brochures widely distributed on the island, describe the statues as being carved from volcanic rock or tuff, not stones, over a period of several centuries by a number of local Polynesian clans. However, she has been so well schooled in the 'mystery' of the site of her achievement that she is able to disassociate the Rapanui from those who 'built' the moai. Her intractable fix on Easter Island shows no evidence that Michelsen learned to see it through the new Euro-American narrative of ecological desolation and as an environmental warning for the planet. Her account is a clear example of the lingering power of dominant text to educate and take on a reality for the student, more real than her actual physical experience of the island and encounters with the living Rapanui.

The Moai and Mystery

After the first interest in the agricultural land for empire, subsequent textual versions of the island have always centred on the moai in some way, never opening enough space in the various discursive incarnations for the culture of the Rapanui themselves. Yet the island archaeological record and oral traditions construct a version of the past in which the culture had developed away from the moai as celebrations of hereditary rulers and turned instead to the birdman contest for establishing a yearly leader, nearly two centuries before the island was first visited by Europeans and so devastated by the slavery and disease that followed.[2]

Euro-America has written over Rapa Nui with whatever narrative has suited the agenda of the writer and the time. The emphasis on the moai, conceived within the discourse of the sublime by William Hodges, was combined with a fascination for the mysterious and exotic in France through Pierre Loti's *Reflets sur la sombre route*, published in 1899, and reprinted numerous times.[3] Loti's seems to be a key text to redirect the visual island discourse after the eighteenth century. He arrived within eight years of the Peruvian slave raids and subsequent smallpox epidemic and after Dutrou-Bornier, the rancher, had left for Australia, destined to return with 400 sheep, which would eventually overrun the island. Dutrou-Bornier had also routed many of the surviving islanders and the resident missionary Hippolyte Roussel to Mangareva to work on the Catholic mission's coco-palm plantations before he left for Australia (McCall 1994, 62). Loti arrived to find a much-reduced cultural presence on the island; the island he 'found' echoed imaginatively with the scant numbers of islanders in Hodges's painting for the Admiralty and his published engraved landscape. Loti's Romantic and lyrical style added a new dimension to the evocation of the imaginary island:

> In the middle of the Pacific Ocean, where sailors never go, there is an isolated and mysterious island; there are no other islands nearby and the island is surrounded by vast and empty rolling seas for more than eight hundred leagues in every direction. The island is planted with monstrous tall statues, carved by an unknown race of people that has either disappeared or dispersed, and its history remains an enigma. (63)
>
> ...
>
> The islanders, whose origins are shrouded in perplexing mystery, are dying out little by little, for unknown reasons, and there remain, we are

told, only a few dozen starving and timorous savages who survive on a diet of roots. In the midst of the solitude of the seas the island will soon find itself alone too, with the giant statues as its only guardians. There is nothing there, not even a spring from which to collect fresh water, and attempts to land there are hampered by breakers and numerous reefs.

...

Rapa Nui is the name by which the natives refer to Easter Island – and in the very sound of that name I hear echoes of sadness, and the darkness of night ... The darkness of the island's origins or the darkness of the sky – it is unclear what kind of darkness is implied but it is clear that the black clouds, in whose shadows the island lies before us, reflect the darkness that captures my imagination. (Altman 2004, 63–5)

The *nui* of Rapa Nui means large dance paddle. Loti's association of Nui with *nuit* (the French word for night) and therefore darkness is one straightforward example of how the variables of one writer's discursive makeup can have a powerful impact on his perceptions and representation.

In Loti's text the emphasis on the extreme deprivation of the islanders echoes Cook, and the references to the 'statues, carved by an unknown race of people' reinforces the ideas of extinction that recur in subsequent texts of the twentieth century. These distortions were introduced through a combination of Loti's Romantic aesthetic expression and through the evaluation of the island as outside any possible European economic interest. Since the island had so little to offer nineteenth-century commercial imperialist interests, its remoteness and mystery were emphasized in order to increase the domestic European market value for its textual consumption. If the island could not produce agricultural goods for Europe or its colonies, it would have to be marketed for its imaginary 'essence,' an essence created through narratives such as Loti's. To give it narrative credibility, it had to be seen in superlatives – most remote and most exotic, largest artefacts, inexplicably disappearing population. The population disappearing, according to Loti, 'for unknown reasons' is an instance of the power of the voice of imperialism to write over its own culpability. Loti's lyrical text violates the memory of the Rapanui by following European physical violence with textual erasure of the acts to cover its own traces.

This focus on the mysterious over the empirical is echoed again in an article ascribed to 'Norton' and entitled 'The Mystery of Easter Island,' published in *The Illustrated American*, 3 March 1894. Mystery continued to be emphasized early in the next century by Katherine Routledge, in 1919, with *The Mystery of Easter Island*, which sold out and went into a second printing in 1920 and was then augmented by an extensive article in 1921 in the American magazine, *The National Geographic*, volume 40. This article was also called 'The Mystery of Easter Island.' In April 1930, *Popular Mechanics* published an article by Michel Mok, 'Explore Weird Island of Death,' that is prefaced with these sentences: 'Scientists plan to invade mysterious Easter Island in an effort to solve the secret of its stone images, carved centuries ago by a forgotten race. Who were the strange men [*sic*] who lived on this most isolated spot?' A popular book, *Islands of Romance and Mystery*, by Gordon Cooper, continued the trend in 1949. The following magazine ad for Canadian Club Whiskey in figure 7.1, aimed at an American readership, was purchased on eBay. While undated, it suggests from the male attire a mid-fifties provenance. It also suggests an era when the moai had sufficient cultural currency to create space for such an ad to be recognizable to consumers.

The Easter Island mystery reached its greatest exposure in mid-century through the extensive publications by Thor Heyerdahl, following his excavations on the island and his widely circulated theories about a South American origin for the moai carvers.

Heyerdahl's focus continued to redirect the public imagination away from the Polynesian Rapanui culture for more than half a century. James Cook's certainty of the Polynesian heritage of the islanders described in his journal was overwritten as Heyerdahl's own particular version of Easter Island was broadcast through his bestselling books *Aku-Aku: The Secret of Easter Island* (1958) and *Easter Island – The Mystery Solved* (1989). In addition to these texts there were magazine articles in the mainstream press, such as *Life* and *The Saturday Evening Post* (which frequently recirculate through eBay), covering the Norwegian expedition to the island in 1950–6, as well as multimedia publicity and a book about his previous sail from South America to the Tuamotu Archipelago, the *Kon-Tiki Expedition* ([1947] 1950). The continuing emphasis on mystery taught through Heyerdahl's books was reinforced later in the century by a number of videos, all still in circulation. Their titles in themselves provide a sort of subversive subtext to Heyerdahl's deleterious influence – *In Search of Ancient Mysteries; What's Mysterious about Easter Island?; Secrets of Lost Empires, Riddles of the Monument Builders;* and *Easter Island: A Vanished Culture* – as do such recent texts as C. Boeckman's *Unsolved Riddles of the Ages* (1965); F. Mazière's *Mysteries of Easter Island* (1969); J. Machowski's *Island of Secrets* (1969); J-M.

Figure 7.1: Escape to Easter Island. 'I can thank Canadian Club for the strangest trip I've ever taken — to that weird speck called Easter Island, reads a recent letter ...' Magazine ad sold on eBay without provenance.

Schwarz's *The Mysteries of Easter Island* (1973); and J. Flenley and P. Bahn's *The Enigmas of Easter Island* (2003).

So pervasive has Heyerdahl's South American migration theory been in the latter half of the twentieth century, that many scholars, publishing texts since his bestsellers appeared, refer back to his thesis and position their scholarship in a relation of denial to his. A 1993 DNA analysis of ancient human bone on the island that identifies a Polynesian motif in the genetic code of the first islanders has meant that in more recent versions of the island imaginary, Heyerdahl's thesis has been on the wane (Hagelberg et al. 1994). It does, however, still circulate as a version of the island history through the resale of books on sites like eBay and on several websites devoted to Heyerdahl's archaeological and adventuring career. A Google search for Thor Heyerdahl in June of 2005 returned 155,000 results.

The association of the island with mystery in the titles of texts and videos points to a desire to read Rapa Nui in a particular way that invites a continuation of the exercise of wonder, which I showed to be taken from sixteenth- and seventeenth-century exploration discourse, into the eighteenth century and on into the nineteenth through the aesthetic discourse of the sublime. The casting of Easter Island moai as a mysterious wonder, as well as the quest to answer the mystery, sustains the excitement of the age of discovery and the urgency of world mastery in a different guise. It becomes a celebration of the capacity of scholars to travel vast distances, dig and delve into 'exotic' settings and find the 'answers,' at the same time as they reinscribe the supremacy of their store of knowledge and capacity to acquire it. But also revealed, in situating the wonder of the moai within the obscurity of the sublime, is the Eurocentric frustration at their powerlessness to wring knowledge out of a place and people so scourged by imperial enterprises that the details of that culture's own story have been destroyed.

The resistance of the moai to fully disclose how they were moved both holds open the space of mystery and closes down the successful quest for knowledge. There is a paradox underlying these paired desires: to experience the wonder and the lack of control its presence engenders undermines the control that knowledge is perceived to bring. Maintaining the discursive idea of mystery in connection with the island, even as solutions to that mystery are repeatedly offered, allows space for both to co-exist – a distant perpetual mystery to satisfy the imaginative questing urge.

The reinscription of the sublime, overlaying the mystery of the moai, can be seen as helping to maintain that narrative category for the statues throughout the first half of the twentieth century. A sublime response to the moai finds expression in the narratives of those who visited the island in the 1920s, 1930s, and 1940s, suggesting the extent to which they had been discursively prepared for what they experienced:

> ... I saw before me the gigantic forms of giants, which rose up out of the sunburnt grass, with the eyes, noses and mouths of a human being, but the ears extended to their shoulders. How many of these strange forms fixed their eyes upon me I could not tell. My brain simply would not act. Had I suddenly gone mad, and were these the creatures that tormented mad folk? I was petrified with fear. How long I stood staring at the images I do not know, but a cold perspiration broke out all over me and I trembled. I imagined them to be living creatures, rising out of the earth to devour me. (Bootes 1928, 199)

> From the summit of a dead volcano gigantic gods of stone leer across a landscape as desolate and forbidding as the craters of the moon. Their long ears seem attuned to the moan of the distant breakers. Their scornful faces, made animate by the sun, mock the wreckage of all that man has done, while they survey the epic futility of his glamourous past and his hopeless future. (Casey 1931, 9)

> ... the gigantic images of creatures that may have been men or gods (we don't know), done in a style which stands absolutely unique in the history of sculpture. For these stone giants with their blind eyes staring across the empty spaces of the Pacific seem the incarnation of doom. Even in the museum they will frighten you, for Dante, in all his infernal travels, never saw anything like that concentrated form of despair. (Van Loon, 1940, 75)

Consider these sublime responses to voracious leviathans, scornful, invoking despair, in contrast with the description of the moai by an American sailor, Captain Benson (1914), shipwrecked on the island in 1913. He apparently did not have, or chose not to invoke, the textual background to 'read' the moai through the literary tropes in circulation. He writes, 'Scattered all over the island are ancient colossal statues, sculptured in lava by the prehistoric inhabitants of the island' (50). Benson goes on to say, 'I am unable to judge of the significance of these statues, but it certainly is mighty interesting to come across them in the wilderness of that most isolated of islands' (ibid.).

The moai as the central object of the island mystery have interested popularists as well as archaeologists and adventurers and have been taken up in text as evidence of a lost continent and lost civilization, as evidence of extra-terrestrial visitation, as the extra-terrestrials themselves, and as surface distractions planted as decoys for various nefarious underground enterprises in comics such as *Wonder Woman*, 'The Stone Slayer!' (1954); *Kona*, 'The Island of Buried Warriors' (1965); *Uncle Scrooge Adventures*, 'The Mystery of Easter Island' (1988); and *Batman Adventures*, 'The Balance' (2003) (see figs. 7.2–7.6).

In fact, moai feature in comic book stories that send Americans to the island by boat or plane date back to 1940 with *Action Comics'* 'Three Aces in the Secret of Easter Island' and *Whiz Comics'* 1941 'Lance O'Casey on Easter Island' (figs. 7.7 and 7.8). Some arrive as shipwreck survivors. Most set off on expeditions to discover the answer to the mystery of the statues. These earliest comics do not try to base their drawings of statues on 'authoritative textual images' of the moai, nor do they concern themselves with an accurate representation of the island flora and fauna. After these early static images, moai were most often taken up in comic fiction as animate and hostile in order to maintain the terror associated with the sublime in spite of photographic and filmed representations that have removed the visual obscurity of the moai imposed through Hodges's representations. In numerous comics they rise out of the ground to reveal their legs and lumber full-bodied after American scholars, adventurers, or superheroes (figs. 7.9–7.11).[4] As well as these textual incarnations, the moai are the central focus of the UNESCO world heritage site and have been appropriated into endless forms by artists for advertising (Metropolitan Life, Sony, Smirnoff Vodka) and for mass-produced consumer items.

Today moai function as a blank slate within the Easter Island discourse, not only taking on a variety of guises in texts to function as aspects of the sublime and mysterious but also taken up as motifs for parties (tiki lights, mugs, candles, swizzle sticks) and being used as logos for software companies (bitHeads) and publishing companies (Dark Horse Comics) (figs. 7.12 and 7.13). Many of these discursive renditions of the moai circulate simultaneously and can be combined so that an 'adventure' to the island can be to experience 'remoteness' as well as to experience the 'open air museum of moai' and to respond to them with 'wonder' as, of course, great 'mysteries.'

Figure 7.2: Charles Moulton, 'The Stone Slayer!' From *Wonder Woman* #65 ©1964 DC Comics. All rights reserved. Used with permission.

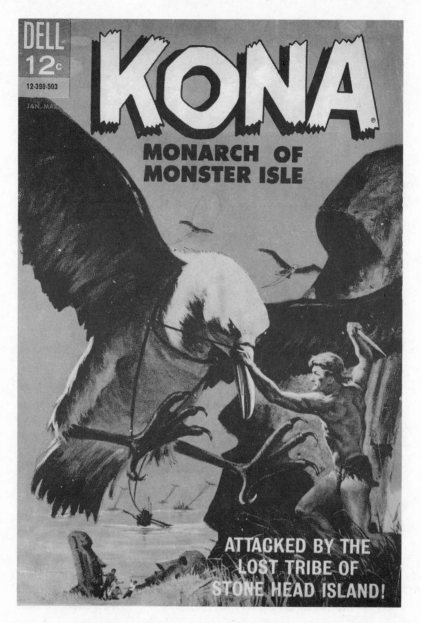

Figure 7.3: Sam J. Glanzman, 'The Island of Buried Warriors.' From *Kona, Monarch of Monster Isle* #13 (New York: Dell, January–March 1965).

Figure 7.4: Geoffrey Blum,'The Mystery of Easter Island.' From *Uncle Scrooge Adventures* (Prescott: Gladstone, January 1988).

Figure 7.5: Slott, Templeton, Burchett, and Beatty, 'The Balance.' From *Batman Adventures* #4 ©2004 DC Comics. All rights reserved. Used with permission.

Figure 7.6: Batman in chamber beneath the moai (heads), comic book illustration from Slott, Templeton, Burchett, and Beatty, 'The Balance.' From *Batman Adventures* #4 ©2004 DC Comics. All rights reserved. Used with permission.

Figure 7.7: Chad, 'Three Aces in the Secret of Easter Island.' From *Action Comics* #28 ©1940 DC Comics. All rights reserved. Used with permission.

Figure 7.8: 'Lance O'Casey on Easter Island.' From *Whiz Comics* #13. Used with permission of DC Comics.

Part Two

Moai as a Measurement of Progress against an Imperial Norm

One overt vestige of an imperial mindset extant in anthropological and economic texts is the projection of the period of moai sculpturing as the pinnacle of Rapa Nui cultural achievement. This period was normalized in eighteenth-century texts and continues uncontested in contemporary texts as the classic period or golden age of Rapa Nui culture. Terms redolent of comparisons with Greek culture as a definitive standard suggest the measurement of Others in terms of the European norm of self and achievement. Implied in this valuation of the moai phase is an implicit Western assumption of the desirability of growth and size as indicators of success for a culture, over consideration of a model, for example, that strives for environmental sustainability. At the same time as contemporary scholarship proclaims the moai phase as the golden age, often in the same essays, it is also characterized as a period of excess and concomitant depletion of natural resources for an increase of material and agricultural wealth (see Anderies 2000; Brander and Taylor 1998; Dalton and Coats 2000; Reuveny and Decker 2000).

In 'Cannibalism and Easter Island: Evaluation, Discussion of Probabilities, & Survey of Easter Island Literature on the Subject' (2005),

Figure 7.9: Edmond Hamilton, 'The Secret of Easter Island!' From *Strange Adventures* #16 ©1952 DC Comics. All rights reserved. Used with permission.

Figure 7.10: Doug Moench and Gil Kane, 'A Kingdom Lost!' From *The Mighty Thor* #318 (New York: Marvel Comics, April 1982).

Figure 7.11: V. Carrabotta and Jack Kirby, 'Back from the Dead: Terror Lurks on Easter Island!' From *Chamber of Chills* #11 (New York: Marvel Comics, July 1974).

Figure 7.12: Logo of bitHeads Computer Company, 1309 Carling Avenue, Ottawa, Canada.

Shawn McLaughlin outlines the dominant contemporary reading of archaeological evidence on the island. This reading constructs a period of distress associated with the little ice age that is believed to have brought the moai carving culture to a close. In this scenario, Rapa Nui's natural resources are believed to have been depleted before the arrival of Europeans, 'by explosive population growth, resulting in food shortage and internecine conflict' (44). This is seen to have been followed by a radical shift in politics and the development of the birdman culture, considered unique in all of Polynesia. Where the moai period is understood to have been a time of hereditary rule, the birdman period is defined by an annual contest to decide the ruler for the year based on athletic prowess. The moai are described as the conduits of *mana* (likened to positive energy transmitted from the ancestors through the moai). The abandonment of the moai and the move to a competition for leadership is seen as combined with a shift in the concept of mana being channelled through heredity, to a belief in *prowess* as an indication of the presence of mana in an individual (Drake 1991, 21). Tactile cultural expression is seen to have shifted from the creation of moai as signifiers of mana to the creation of finely detailed small-scale stone and wooden carvings. This apparent shift in governance, reflected in

Figure 7.13: Legend trademark for Dark Horse Comics.

cultural production, can be constructed as a positive step in redirecting energy from hereditary rule towards a more equitable system, and offers the birdman period as a social and cultural renaissance. To retrospectively construct the moai period through a Western lens as the peak of achievement, even in the process of explaining how it was also a period of over population that led to the downfall of the Rapanui civilization, is to impose the very values that contemporary environmental texts are trying to warn against – excessive growth over sustainability.

Against this measurement of the moai as an example of the pinnacle of technological success in Oceania stands the evaluation of the islanders' culture within the 'hierarchy of man' espoused by Jacob Bronowski and published in 1973 in his book *The Ascent of Man*. His book is based on a matching BBC-TV series that was broadcast in Britain as well as

North America. The text is described on its cover as 'one of the out-standing books of our time,' selling over a million copies. His thesis is that Europeans are superior to all others because of their 'ability to con-trol nature, not be controlled by it.' He measures Easter Island worth against Euro-temporal standards of 'development' and aesthetic expression and places the islanders at an inferior distance from that mean:

> Even so primitive a culture as Easter Island made one tremendous inven-tion, the carving of huge and uniform statues. There is nothing like them in the world ... The critical question about these statues is, why were they all made *alike*? You see them sitting there, like Diogenes in their barrels, looking at the sky with empty eye-sockets, and watching the sun and the stars go overhead without ever trying to understand them ... An earthly paradise is not made by this empty repetition, like a caged animal going round and round, and making always the same thing. These frozen faces, these frozen frames in a film that is running down, mark a civilization which failed to take the first step on the ascent of rational knowledge. (119–20)

There are many statements here that do not reflect the physical aspect of the island statues or the navigational accomplishments of the culture: 'uniform ... alike ... empty eye sockets ... watching the sun and the stars ... without ever trying to understand them.' These phrases position the moai as representatives of the Rapanui, a people constructed, in a geo-graphical mapping and navigating discourse, as the greatest pre-Renaissance navigators the world has known. To describe these few thousand islanders as a civilization in competition with great failed civ-ilizations elsewhere is facile, at best. In Bronowski's assessment, the moai are repositioned once again during the twentieth century, this time to be seen not as a great Polynesian mystery or sign of South American accomplishment but as a sign of a culture that failed to progress. It is another example of textual violence to shape another imperial agenda.

By opening a space to see the moai as a sign of failure, it is a short step to admonishing the islanders for the destruction of their environ-ment in more recent texts. In such narratives as Bronowski's can be seen the authority of European discourses to read and write the world. His represents the domination of one understanding of the world, readily able to be broadcast and learned across cultures. It is positioned through imperialism to dislodge or replace various local world views the islanders might have about themselves. Willinsky (1998) refers to this discursive pedagogical power as 'the hold of the West on the role of global authority and educator,' the language of imperialism imposing 'a set of coordinates defined by race, culture, and nation' that positions Euro-America in a top-down hierarchy in relation to the rest of the world (253). It is also a narrative that violates island history by writing over European past violence against the Rapanui and glossing over the appropriation of their island. It downplays, omits or replaces the story of imperialism.

Environmental Warnings

I referred in the introduction of this book to John Willinsky's concern that as the 'West' turns to the Pacific as the next 'new world of opportunity,' educators have a special responsibility to teach against the negative constructions of Pacific Islanders as 'primitive savages,' and to make visible the framework of imperialism that has 'shaped the Pacific story in the West' (1998, 262). Easter Island is already being pulled into curriculum and cultural capital in a new pedagogical role that once again focuses on the islanders as it is constructed increasingly as a case study of environmental degradation. Both the University of Michigan and the University of Chicago have course units that use Easter Island to teach about environmental disaster. The Michigan course on 'Global Change' has an accompanying website posting lecture material by anthropology professor Richard Ford. With grammatical and factual misconstruction, it encapsulates the degradation narrative of Easter Island in a case study:

> Cultural Evolution And Global Change: Easter Island was contacted by Dutch explorer Jacob Roggeveen in 1722. His crew found a barren volcanic island of 64 square miles surrounded by the sea. There were virtually no trees and agricultural production was marginal. The inhabitants were miserable – starving, fighting, living in caves. Yet there were some 200 standing carved volcanic statues (moai) – 2–10 meters tall, 20–50 tons; on platforms and some had heavy red stone hair caps. What they had to do with the residents was a mystery to them. Only 4 leaky, 10-foot canoes that [sic] not seaworthy served for transportation and kept the 2000 inhabitants bound to their impoverished land. The misery continued in 1774 when Captain Cook arrived. He found all statues already uprooted and the population had declined to 630.

AD 1680 Biodiversity gone – no insects, no land birds, seabird breeding ground decimated, forest destroyed (people cut, burned, and pollinators gone), soil eroded to degree it would not support crops.

Food shortage – cannibalism, no porpoises, birds decline, eat rats, famine As an example of systemic maladaptation. Eastern Islanders did not correct practices on the landscape as they progressively destroyed it and their culture. Lesson: ecological overshoot– exceeded carrying capacity of land and could not reverse it. Degraded environment, famine, warfare, social collapse, and population decline. Population crash: 1722 = 2,000; 1774 = 630; 1877 = 150 (small pox brough [sic] by sailors added to woes). (Professor Richard Ford)

The way the island is being taken up in this Michigan course posting bears little resemblance to the eighteenth-century European-voyage journal descriptions. The impressive plantations described by Roggeveen and the Spanish expeditions are replaced with 'marginal' agricultural production. The islanders first described as tall and well built are here described as miserable and starving. This narrative writes over eighteenth-century textual constructions as well as over the contemporary islanders and their adaptability. In addition to eliminating insects, it also erases the European causes for population decreases and a ravaged landscape. The island is being repositioned yet again in the public consciousness through such descriptions. It is being transformed from a UNESCO World Heritage site of celebration and mystery that emphasizes the island's pre-European contact past, involving the moving and erecting of the giant stone moai, to the premier example of deliberate self-inflicted environmental destruction and cultural extinction.

The state of the island at the end of the European sheep-ranching era in the second half of the twentieth century has often been retrofitted onto the island as it was first visited by Europeans in the eighteenth century. Grant McCall (2002) suggests that the colonial sheep-grazing development on Rapa Nui has given the island an aspect that has misled some researchers into using Rapa Nui as a metaphor for 'Earth Island' (417). It is not until the development of sheep ranching, 'using Australian grasses and trees which require annual firing to reproduce, that the island takes on its melodramatic, environmental rape aspect!' McCall urges those interested in Rapa Nui to consider it on its own terms and 'not in the imagined concepts developed elsewhere' (419–20).

The recent narrative of environmental self-destruction that features

Easter Island as a case study of environmental-cultural implosion, is being written with a selective use of past scholarship that ignores a key twentieth-century study. The nineteenth-century 'externally-induced modernization' and 'ideology of improvement,' and their effects on the island culture and physical landscape, were described by J. Douglas Porteous in *The Modernization of Easter Island* (1981). He wrote a detailed comparison of the parallels between the sheep-ranching exploitation of Rapa Nui and the matching exploitation in the Scottish highlands that preceded it. Porteous even-handedly sets his description in a context of the restricted flora and fauna species to be found on an isolated island such as Rapa Nui. He describes the original Polynesian settlers' intro-duction of new species for cultivation, and the reduction of native trees and birds through centuries of habitation and agricultural use. He then compares the method and consequences of the introduction of sheep farming on Easter Island to the highland clearances of Scotland that began in 1745. He writes that the changes to Scotland were 'sufficiently violent to aid in the destruction of a complete culture, that of the 'semi-tribal Gael,' an activity 'repeated in Easter Island a century later' by the same lowland entrepreneurs (123). Porteous's argument deserves to be quoted at length:

> In the case of Easter Island sheepranching emerged at the ultimate point of contact of two diffusion streams both emanating originally from the same British source ... Australian sheep were being taken into the Pacific, and it was from this source that Dutrou-Bornier brought the first commercial rams and ewes to Easter Island. The second diffusion reached Easter Island via the Falklands, Patagonia, and Tierra del Feugo, all of which were utilized for sheeprearing by a series of Scottish enterprises during the late nineteenth century.
>
> Meeting at Easter Island in the shape of the Branders and CEDIP, these two Scots-based sheeprearing diffusion paths were the initiators of the radical changes in settlement patterns, economy, employment and land-scape features which took place after 1870.
>
> ...
>
> Once the surviving population had been penned into the Hangaroa area, the turning of Easter Island over to the commercial production of wool and animal byproducts demanded or resulted in radical changes in the animal population, vegetation, and the built environment. (125–7)

He goes on to explain that:

The growth of sheep numbers, however, had a considerable impact on certain vegetation types. Sheep are delicate selective feeders ... Sheep readily consume the young shoots of tree species; they may strip trees of bark on the lower trunk. If allowed to roam freely, sheep will effectively prevent the natural regeneration of trees in a partially-deforested area.

Before the advent of the European it is probable that the park-like savannah, which comprised Easter Island's total non-cultivated vegetation picture, contained a fair number of trees. Polynesian legends, archaeological investigations, and pollen analysis support the case for a somewhat more arboreal vegetation type than is found on Easter Island today ...

The recency of the demise of the native woodlands is recorded in the journals of visitors. The earliest explorers were strongly divided as to the extent and nature of Easter Island woodlands. Although Forster in 1777 noted 'there was not a tree upon the island, which exceeded the height of ten feet,' we are given no indication of the extent of small trees and shrubs ... In 1868 Palmer found the boles of large trees, such as the *toromiro*, coconut, and hibiscus, decaying in several locations.

Eighteen years later, however, Cooke wrote of the existence of *toromiro* in 'considerable numbers,' but: 'all or nearly all, dead and decaying by reason of their being stripped of their bark by the flocks of sheep which roam at will all over the island.' Like much of eighteenth-century Scotland, Easter Island was finally denuded of its meagre tree cover by the depredations of the sheepmasters and their flocks. In the face of persistent grazing and gnawing, only tough grasses, lichens and mosses survive. (139–40)

This narrative of the nineteenth-century monocultural exploitation of the island environment is either omitted or downplayed in the current narrative of island environmental devastation. The increasing evidence of global warming and the concomitant increased urgency of texts warning against the Euro-American overconsumption of the planets' resources seems to give the authors of this eco-narrative dramatic license to omit imperial culpability if it suits their argument. The story of an isolated cultural self-immolation apparently makes a more dramatic point than the story of an island's devastation by imported sheep.

It is possible to follow the trajectory of the invention of Easter Island being reshaped to play a new role in this quickening environmental discourse. The trope of Easter Island's self-inflicted destruction can be seen coming into prominence in the 1990s and continuing with increasing urgency into the twenty-first century in the film *Rapa Nui* (1994) and in texts such as *A Green History of the World* (1991), by Clive Ponting; *Easter Island, Earth Island* (1992) by Paul Bahn and John Flenley and *The Enigmas of Easter Island* (2003), by John Flenley and Paul Bahn; *Easter Island: Scientific Exploration into the World's Environmental Problems in Microcosm* (2003), edited by John Loret and John Tanacredi; *A Short History of Progress* (2004) by Ronald Wright; and *Collapse: How Societies Choose to Fail or Succeed* (2005) by Jared Diamond.

Clive Ponting's (1991) first chapter is on 'The Lessons of Easter Island.' On page one he writes:

The Dutch Admiral Roggeveen, on board the *Arena* [sic], was the first European to visit the island on Easter Sunday 1722. He found a society in a primitive state with about 3,000 people living in squalid reed huts or caves, engaged in almost perpetual warfare and resorting to cannibalism in a desperate attempt to supplement the meagre food supplies available on the island. During the next European visit in 1770 the Spanish nominally annexed the island but it was so remote, underpopulated and lacking in resources that no formal colonial occupation ever took place. There were a few more brief visits in the late eighteenth century, including one by Captain Cook in 1774. An American ship stayed long enough to carry off twenty-two inhabitants to work as slaves killing seals on Masafuera Island off the Chilean coast. The population continued to decline and conditions on the island worsened: in 1877 [sic] the Peruvians removed and enslaved all but 110 old people and children. Eventually the island was taken over by Chile and turned into a giant ranch for 40,000 sheep run by a British company, with the few remaining inhabitants confined to one small village.

Ponting's version of the island's past differs in several ways from other recent versions. The texts of the Dutch expedition of 1722 did not describe warfare, cannibalism, or meager food supplies. The Peruvian slavers came in 1862 not 1877, and the population was not reduced to 110 by the slavers but by several subsequent and accumulating events such as smallpox and emigration to work in Mangareva and Tahiti to escape the conflicts created by the sheep rancher Dutrou-Bornier. Like the narrative of mystery that preceded it, the new role for Easter Island to play in environmental discourses also foregrounds the moai and erases the Rapanui as it takes their cultural production as a metonym of excess and narrates the people who created the culture into extinction. This is done to increase the dramatic effect of the story and to drive home the consequences of global deforestation at the expense of the continuing existence of these people. It does not challenge the contemporary scholarly narrative of the island with its own version; rather, it ignores the less dramatic narrative, accepted by most Rapa Nui scholars, in which the islanders abandoned their moai culture and, despite internecine wars to redistribute landholdings, developed a more sustainable birdman culture at least two generations before the arrival of the Dutch.[5]

A Short History of Progress

The University of Toronto recently hosted the 2004 Massey Lecture series by Ronald Wright, entitled 'A Short History of Progress,' in which he describes Easter Island as one of several cultures that destroyed themselves and their environment while pursuing culturally driven imperatives. The recent publicity surrounding this lecture series, its broadcast on CBC Radio's program *Ideas*, and the reviews of the subsequent book in a number of print and web sources, has raised the profile of Easter Island, in Canada, as a site of environmental degradation rather than a tourist destination for mystery and adventure or a visit to an open-air moai museum. The book, *A Short History of Progress*, was published just a few months after the Massey Lecture series. In February 2005, a Google search of the book returned 286 matches, while a Google search of Ronald Wright and Easter Island produced an impressive 69. These references are mostly reviews of the book that tend to repeat key points Wright made about Easter Island in his lecture series. Both the book and the reviews teach this relatively new version of Easter Island as a microcosm of a damaged earth and reinforce an 'appropriate' judgment to make of the island and the islanders in this environment-destroying incarnation.

Ronald Wright joins the larger trend that is removing the focus from the cultural achievement of the moai and putting it back on the land. At the same time as he turns to the land, Wright redirects the emphasis of the island culture of moai carving from a cultural achievement to an example of a past *'ideological pathology'* that destroyed the land and ended what he calls the 'mini-civilization' that developed there. An examination of the points Wright makes about the Rapanui past and the sources he uses to construct his arguments are an instructive example of the textual inventing and reinventing process of Easter Island. His new narrative destablizes the preceding narrative and continues to play a part in the imperial will-to-knowledge that, in the very process of finding fault with contemporary Western culture, reinscribes a version of the inferiority of these Others, even as it once again erases them.

A few months after giving the Massey Lectures, Ronald Wright reviewed Jared Diamond's *Collapse: How Societies Choose to Fail or Succeed* in the *Globe and Mail* (15 January 2005). He begins with a caution to the reader. 'Jared Diamond is best known for his beguiling *Guns, Germs, and Steel* (1999) ... The book was highly popular in North America, but general readers may have been unaware that few of its arguments were original and that some key "facts" were inaccurate or very selectively presented.' I highlight Wright's censure of Diamond's research because Wright, too, is inaccurate and very selective with his own representation of the island. He bases his version of Easter Island reality in *A Short History of Progress* on just two texts, *Easter Island, Earth Island* (1992) by Paul Bahn and John Flenley, and *Easter Island: Mystery of the Stone Giants* (1988) by Catherine and Michel Orliac (the same book was published in 1995 as *The Silent Gods: Mysteries of Easter Island* for the British market), part of the New Horizon series of picture books for adolescents, accompanied by text.[6] In a telling instance of synchronicity, the Orliac text was translated from the French in 1995 by Paul Bahn.

Eleven pages of *A Short History of Progress* refer to Easter Island. On those eleven pages there are several statements made by Wright to which I want to draw attention. I will discuss them in the order in which they appear in his text, and examine Wright's sources for information about the island and his interpretations of it. The reason for this examination is that some of these statements have taken on a life of their own and are being reproduced in spin-off texts, demonstrating how rapidly a new narrative about the island can develop.

Here is Wright's first statement about the island: 'On Easter Day 1722, the Dutchmen sighted an unknown island so treeless and eroded that they mistook its barren hills for dunes. They were amazed as they drew near, to see hundreds of stone images, some as tall as an Amsterdam house' (57–8). Wright offers no citation for this first statement, although it is possible to find a textual reference to the appearance of the island and its soil in Roggeveen's journal. Roggeveen does describe the island as appearing to be barren when viewed from the sea and he does describe the moai. What Wright constructs is based on only a few words from the Roggeveen original, taken out of context. In its selectivity, it does not acknowledge the positive assessment Roggeveen made of the soil after he landed on the island. The Dutch, arriving in April, were witnessing the southern hemisphere's autumn or harvest season when withered grasses and dried husks predominate in an agricultural landscape. It is understandable that Roggeveen would report 'that we originally, from a further distance, have considered the said Paasch Island as sandy, the reason for that is this, that we counted as such the withered grass, hay, or other scorched and burnt vegetation, because its wasted appearance could cause no other impression than of a singular poverty and barrenness' (Sharp 1970, 92). After landing on the island, however, Roggeveen's assessment of the fertility of the island was that 'this place, as far as its rich soil and good climate are concerned, is such that it might be made into an earthly paradise, if it were properly worked and cultivated; which is now only done in so far as the inhabitants are obliged to for the maintenance of life' (103). Far from referring to hundreds of stone images, some as tall as Amsterdam houses, Roggeveen actually wrote, 'they set fires before some particularly high erected stone images ... formed from clay or greasy earth ... all the images appeared to show that they were hung round with a long garment from the neck to the soles of the feet, having on the head a basket, in which lay heaped white painted stones' (97). His description is so far from how the moai are seen today as to make the contemporary reader wonder if Roggeveen is describing Easter Island at all. His description is also far from the one Wright attributes to him.

Here is Wright's second statement of note:

> Like Polynesians on some other islands, each clan began to honour its ancestry with impressive stone images. These were hewn from the yielding volcanic tuff of a crater and set up on platforms by the shore. ... Each generation of images grew bigger than the last, demanding more timber, rope, and manpower for hauling to the *Ahu*, or alters. Trees were cut faster than they could grow, a problem worsened by the settlers' rats, who ate the seeds and saplings ... They ate all their dogs ... There was nothing left now but the moai, the stone giants who had devoured the land. (59–61)

Several points in this theatrical quotation bear discussion. As mentioned in my introduction to this book, unlike most other Polynesian societies, the excavation of and examined contents of island middens as well as Rapanui oral traditions bear no evidence of any dogs ever being on the island. Speculation is that dogs, pigs, and some of the plants usually transported to islands for settlement did not survive the length of the original journey to Rapanui. These absent food sources are used by other writers to explain the emphasis on chickens being raised for protein as part of the islanders' diet and the elaborate and large chicken houses, *hare moa*, that number 1233 across the island (Van Tilburg 1994, 64). The archeological record does demonstrate that the Polynesian rat was introduced to the island and was a source of human protein. This animal is known throughout Polynesia for the extensive damage it causes to indigenous plant and bird life on the islands to which it was transported by settlers (48). It is theorized from centuries-old gnawed seed rinds found in caves that, without any natural predators on Rapa Nui, the rats multiplied rapidly and ate the tree seeds and saplings of the slow growing island tree species, preventing the trees from naturally regenerating (47).

Anthropological research on the island during the last twenty years has led to the current version of the island's past that argues the island trees were cleared though slash-and-burn to create fields to feed an ever increasing population as well as to be used for cooking fuel, moai moving, boats, and cremations. Rapanui are the only Polynesians believed to have cremated their dead, a practice that archaeological evidence suggests shifted to burial in and around ahu by the 1700s (Mordo 2002, 29; Ramírez and Huber 2000, 26–7). Such a practice would account for the number of skeletons found near ahu by the eighteenth-century explorers. One current theory for Polynesian migration across the Pacific islands is that overpopulation in existing settlements necessitated emigrations to new islands for the people who could no longer be accommodated in established settlements. Following this model of increase in population, and examining the evidence of early cultivation on the island, it is thought that all the arable land of Rapa Nui was under cultivation when the population reached its peak, estimated at 8,000 to 10,000 between 1400 and 1600 CE. Connecting to this theory is a strong likelihood that starvation was the main cause of the reduced population after that period. By the time of European contact, the population is thought to have fallen to about 6,000 (Ramírez and Huber 2000, 26).

In the island tradition of small wooden carvings, many depict what are known as 'Kavakava men,' sculptures that emphasize prominently outlined ribs and extended abdomens indicative of starvation (see fig. 7.14). Jared Diamond (2005) constructs these carvings as representing a significant period or incident of starvation (109). This theory rests largely on the idea that a finely balanced equation between cultivation and population would be easily upset by drought and a lack of wood

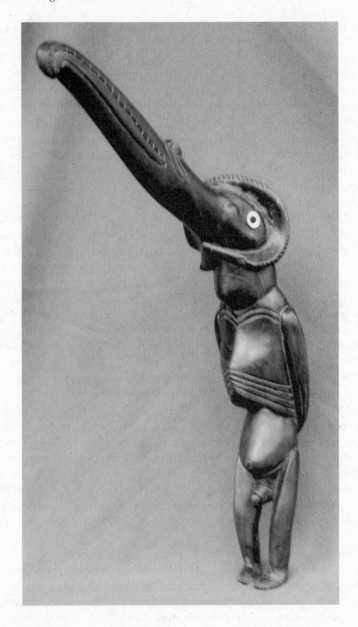

Figure 7.14: A Kavakava man/birdman, sculpture, Luis Tomas, 2004.

for large fishing boats to catch tuna and porpoise or enable a migration to a new settlement site.

It is very difficult to see the carving of moai as a contributing factor to the deforestation of the island. While the total number of moai is near 900, the archaeological consensus is that they were carved over a period of approximately 600 years.[7] A large number, 397, were never removed from the main carving quarry.

Of those that were transported, forty-six are interpreted as abandoned along the way to a particular clan platform, and 278 were erected on platforms (ahu). Over the estimated period of moai carving, if averaged out, the number of moai transported from the quarry would amount to about one statue being moved each year. This rate of moving moai seems a highly improbable explanation to account for island-wide deforestation, but Wright continues to build his case for an island devastated in that manner, without citing any source for his assertion:

By the end there were more than a thousand moai, one for every ten islanders in their heyday. But the good days were gone – gone with the good earth, which had been carried away on the endless wind and washed by flash floods into the sea ... When Europeans arrived in the eighteenth century, the worst was over; they found only one or two living souls per statue, a sorry remnant, 'small, lean, timid and miserable,' in Cook's words ... Now without roof beams many people were dwelling in caves; their only buildings were stone henhouses where they guarded their last non-human protein from one another day and night. (61)

By the time the Europeans arrived in 1722, the cultural period that focused on moai is believed to have been over for approximately two centuries. The balance between resources and population had apparently returned to a sustainable level since the Europeans' descriptions of the islanders were of tall and healthy individuals. The Spanish expedition that was the second to visit the island in 1770 reported a similar positive assessment of the soil:

A fertile soil, which leaves nothing for the inhabitants to wish for, softens their manners, and inclines them to humanity. This is without doubt, the cause of the sweet disposition of the inhabitants; they have poultry in great plenty, and enjoy those products of the earth which require little culture; they ... worship stone statues of a gigantic size. (*Evening Post and British Chronicle and the St James Chronicle*, November 1771, xlvii–xlviii)

The British expedition four years later also reported favourably on the island's agricultural product. James Cook, who was not well when he landed, stayed close to shore and did not write very much about the agricultural use of the land, saying only 'their plantations are prettily laid out by line, but are not inclosed [sic] by any fencing' (J. Cook 1777, 294; J. Cook 1968, 2: 357), and '[t]he produce is Potatoes, Yams, Taro or the Eddy root, Plantains and Sugar Cane, all excellent in its kind, the Potatoes are the best of the sort I ever tasted' (J. Cook 1968, 2: 349). William Wales, the astronomer who accompanied Cook on his second voyage to the South Pacific, did walk extensively over parts of the island and had more detailed observations to make about the land under agricultural production:

> For the greater part of the distance across the ground was everywhere covered with stones as hath been described above; but not withstanding this there were among them many large tracks of land planted with sweet Potatoes and here and there a Plantain walk [a stand of trees similar to bananas]; but I saw no fruit on any of the Trees. Towards the highest part of this end of the island the soil seemed to be much better than any I had seen before, being of a fine red earth and not covered with stones as in the other parts ... (ibid., 823)

I have used Beaglehole's Hakluyt edition of Cook's second voyage because that is the source used by Bahn who is the main source quoted by Wright. Yet nowhere in the Beaglehole edition of Cook's journals does Cook say the 'Easter Islanders' are 'small, lean, timid and miserable,' nor does Cook say it in his original journal publication. The stones described as covering the ground are currently understood to have been part of a lithic mulching system, used on the windward fields, that protected plants from the wind and held moisture in the soil (see Wozniak 1999).

None of the eighteenth-century European texts about the island describe the Rapanui as 'small, lean, timid and miserable.' Roggeveen said, 'These people are well-proportioned in limbs, having very sturdy and strong muscles, are generally large in stature, and their natural colour is not black, but pale yellow or sallow, as we saw in many youths, either because they had not painted their bodies with a dark blue, or because they, being of a higher rank, were not subject to the labour of land cultivation' (Sharp 1970, 97). The Spanish found the islanders so tall that they actually measured two of the tallest, finding one man at six feet five inches and another at six feet six-and-a-half inches (or two metres). The chief pilot, Don Francisco Antonio de y Infanzon, described them as 'tall, well built and proportioned in all their limbs ... their appearance being thoroughly pleasing and tallying with Europeans more than with Indians. I believe from their docility and intelligence, that it would be easy to domesticate them and to convert them to any religion which might be put before them' (Corney 1903, 96). George Forster describes them as 'inferior in stature to the natives of the Society and Friendly Islands, and to those of New Zeeland, there being not a single person among them who might be reckoned tall. Their bodies are likewise lean, and their faces thinner than that of any people we had hitherto seen in the South Sea' (Forster [1777] 2000, 303–4). This comparative description of the islanders by Forster is the closest to that cited in Wright. Cook did actually write about the islanders in his journal. He comments on them in an intertextual response to the anonymous Dutch sailor's description of giants in the edition of Dalrymple's *Pacific Voyages* that he took with him on his second voyage. Cook states, 'In general the people of this isle are a slender race. I did not see a man that would measure six feet; so far are they from being giants, as one of the authors of Roggewin's voyage affects. They are brisk and active, have good features, and not disagreeable countenances, are friendly and hospitable to strangers ...' (Cook 1777, 290). After reading Wright, I reread every page about the island in Cook's journal and can find no reference to 'small, lean, timid and miserable' islanders.

Wright evidently takes his description from page 170 of *Easter Island, Earth Island*, where Paul Bahn and John Flenley describe the Rapanui as 'small, lean, timid and miserable' and then attribute the reference to James Cook. The quotation allegedly by James Cook is in single quotation marks. No source is cited. Not only is the 'quotation' taken up to support Wright's argument in *A Short History of Progress*, but it is also quoted again in Jared Diamond's *Collapse: How Societies Choose to Fail or Succeed* (at page 109). Diamond, however, uses Flenley and Bahn's *The Enigmas of Easter Island* (2003). The introduction of these small, timid and miserable islanders into recent variants of the island story is quickly achieving wide dissemination and is being used to write over previous descriptions.

Again, without citation, Wright goes on to describe the islanders, by the time of Cook's visit, as caves-dwellers because they no longer have roof beams. Specifically, he says, 'Now without roof beams, many people were dwelling in caves; their only buildings were stone henhouses where they guarded their last non-human protein from one another day and night' (61). Yet the eighteenth-century texts and drawings and nineteenth-century photographs describe and depict houses, both large and small, clustered in front of clan platforms as well as farther inland where there were fields to tend.

Wright finally has the Rapanui, like the Sumerians, apparently finish themselves off. 'Easter Island and Sumer wrecked their environments so thoroughly, and fell so hard, that they became effectively extinct' (83). Again, no source is given to 'effectively' erase the Rapanui. In Wright's descriptions of Easter Island, the contemporary scholarship that theorizes more than three hundred years of birdman-based culture following on from the moai-based cultural period, is not contested, but ignored, in his version of the destruction of the island to suit his thesis. He does not describe the consequences of what 150 years of sheep, cattle, and horse grazing have done to the island flora. Nor does he comment on the vibrancy and resilience of contemporary life on the island. Instead, he uses his moai-environmental equation to finish off the culture: 'In the case of Easter Island, the statue cult became a self-destructive mania, an ideological pathology' (129).

Wright's use of the island to promote his thesis, in the process writing over the islanders, is little different in kind from that of former Euro-American uses of the island and narratives about it. Grant McCall (2002) sums up this imperial grasp of the island:

> The Dutchman Jakob Roggeveen came to Rapanui in his quest for commercial development on a global scale. James Cook explored small islands for the growth of the British Empire. The sheep ranch development on Rapanui, was inspired by Australian technology of the 1870s, French commercial development in Tahiti and, eventually, the needs of the textile mills of England! In the twentieth century, Rapanui continued to be a colony of Chile as that South American country sought to establish itself in the wider Pacific, only permitted the place to become a civil territory with its inhabitants have [sic] normal citizen rights in 1966, that coming from the exigencies of the cold war and the desire of the USA to establish a secret base on the island, which it did from 1966 to 1970. (420)

As previously stated, the archaeological and ethnographic evidence of the island is currently read to suggest the culture shifted from its focus on hereditary rule and the moai to an annual birdman leader chosen by athletic accomplishment. How the culture might have continued to alter and develop in isolation was stopped when Europeans arrived and shot, raped, enslaved, or killed a large portion of the population and then devastated much of the rest through smallpox, leprosy, and flu epidemics. Further cultural changes were brought about through missionization, the concentration of all island clans into one space, Hanga Roa, as well as the destruction of the island biodiversity through intensive sheep ranching.

The authority of high-profile narratives such as Wright's to write over previous and contemporary scholarly versions of the island can be seen in a brief sampling of reviews of his book that repeat his thesis. The first, to emphasise the pedagogical nature and influence a review can exert, is in McMaster University's student newspaper, *The Silhouette* of 2 December 2004:

> Wright has been able to make sound interpretations of fallen civilizations and relativize [sic] them to the present by building on his archaeological [sic] background, including his recent excavations [sic] at Easter Island and South America. Essentially, he attempts to dig up answers to the universal questions that he feels called to personally respond to: 'where do we come from, who are we, and where are we going.' If his calculations are correct, we are headed in the a fatal direction, but this time it will be globally catastrophic ... For one who has long discounted the logic of a circular history formula to explain human progress, I was intrigued to find so many shocking similarities. For instance, the compelling tale of the Easter Islanders who used up their natural capital and then prayed to their gods for aid, much like the Mayans and other civilizations who appear to recognize but do not heed the limits of their growth and exploitation. (Nash 2004)

In *Quill and Quire* (December 2004), Bronwyn Drainie says, 'Wright takes us to Easter Island, a formerly abundant place rich in trees and provenance, where tending to the cult of the moai, the 30-foot-high stone carvings of the gods, destroyed the forests and the land forever.' While Darren Shore in Concordia's *The Link* (11 January 2005) writes, 'From Mexican jungle ruins where the great Maya built their own decline, to once green Mesopotamian deserts where we irrigated the land to death, to the desolate misery of Easter Island where we razed the last tree, civilizational [sic] shipwrecks point at our repeated experiments in self-destructive development, now on a global scale.'

Hamilton Ontario's online magazine about healthy cities, *Raise the Hammer*, has a 28 November 2005 review by Ben Bull in which he states:

> Wright reflects on our inability to engage in long-term planning – to look out for our future – by citing the example of Easter Island. Here, where people literally cut off from the world, they steadfastly chopped down every tree in their quest to build bigger and higher temples to a god that could do nothing to save them from themselves.
>
> In the end, the trees were all gone, the soil was ruined, and the monuments destroyed. The last signs of civilization were a few rotted canoes made from poor quality timber: all that was left. (Bull 2005)

The textual instability of the island story, shifting with each iteration, combined with a high degree of intertextuality, creates a layering of repertoires for understanding the island – the collective memory is like a cupboard full of competing text fragments. The result is a bricolage of island interpretations reassembled in different configurations to meet different ends.

Collapse: How Societies Choose to Fail or Succeed

Jared Diamond, in *Collapse: How Societies Choose to Fail or Succeed* (2005), is similar to Wright in his presentation of the Rapanui pre-European contact population as an example of a culture responsible for their eco-cultural collapse. He provides a detailed thirty-two-page examination of the environmental degradation of the island during the pre-contact period of Polynesian habitation, attributing the collapse to the population increase and land clearance outstripping the island's carrying capacity. While not writing overtly from a position of European superiority, he nevertheless betrays the Eurocentricity of his narrative when he almost ingenuously describes moai transportation, saying, 'how did all those Easter Islanders, lacking cranes, succeed in carving, transporting, and erecting those statues? Of course we don't know for sure, because no European ever saw it being done to write about it' (99). The bias of his thesis towards islander self-destruction is evident when read contrapuntally to Porteous's description of the sheep-grazing era. Thirty-two pages into a forty-page chapter called 'Twilight at Easter Island,' Diamond writes two paragraphs about European colonization of the island. He begins with, 'the sad story of European impacts on Easter Islanders may be quickly summarized,' and continues: 'Grazing by the company's sheep, goats and horses caused soil erosion and eliminated most of what had remained of the native vegetation, including the last surviving hauhau and toromiro individuals [trees] on Easter around 1934' (112).

Diamond proclaims, without specific citation, that 'in place of their former sources of wild meat [sic], islanders turned to the largest hitherto unused source available to them: humans, whose bones became common not only in proper burials but also (cracked to extract the marrow) in late Easter Island garbage heaps' (109). Two pages later he refers to cannibalism a second time, again without citation:

> I don't want to portray the social developments on the Easter after 1680 as wholly negative and destructive. The survivors adapted as best they could, both in their subsistence and in their religion. Not only cannibalism but chicken houses underwent explosive growth after 1650; chickens had accounted for less than 0.1% of the animal bones in the oldest middens that David Steadman, Patricia Vargas, and Claudio Cristino excavated at Anakena. (111)

Diamond writes of human bones becoming 'common' in garbage heaps, as cannibalism 'underwent explosive growth' without offering any documented evidence of this dietary change. In 'Cannibalism and Easter Island' (2005), Shawn McLaughlin reviews the existing literature, reporting that almost all of it is based on oral tradition.[8] In one paragraph, however, he does deal with tangible evidence that might be interpreted as proof of cannibalism:

> Ramírez (personal communication, 2004) relates interesting but inconclusive osteological evidence on Easter Island: 'classic cuts on the surfaces' of bones 'closer to the extremes could indicate cutting meat instead (to separate long muscles).' He describes burnt human bones in a 'cooking context' and he examined the skull of a 6- or 8-year-old child with 'clear marks around the foramen magnum,' though he couldn't say those marks 'indicate taking the brain to be eaten.' In evaluating human remains found at Ahu _O Rongo in 2001, Polet (2003) reports cut marks on the ulna of a 10-year-old. 'These cut marks,' Polet says, 'suggest that the corpse was defleshed with a sharp object prior to cremation and interment. They might result from a ritual treatment of the deceased before transfer from the original burial location to the *ahu*. On the other hand, they could also point to cannibalistic or sacrificial practices.' (44)

In McLaughlin's survey, these inconclusive instances of cut marks are the only tangible indicators of what could be interpreted as instances of cannibalism. All other references are from island legends and ambiguities of language. For example, a cave on the western edge of the island is known as Ana Kai Tangata, which can translate as 'man eat cave.' McLaughlin points out that in the vernacular of Rapanui this could either mean 'cave where men eat' or 'cave where men are eaten.' He goes on to say:

> However, the word 'kai' has both ancient and modern etymologies – meaning either 'to tell' or 'to eat,' respectively. So the name could actually mean 'cave where men tell stories.' (Maybe even stories about cannibalism, but seriously ...) There are even some who believe that Ana Kai Tangata got its name simply because the mouth of the cave looks like it's swallowing people when they enter it. And Fischer (1992) speculates that the name might relate to 'a legendary East Polynesian chief, Kai Tangata' – also known on Aotearoa (New Zealand), Hawai'i, and Rarotonga. (38)

My point here is not to try to prove or disprove cannibalism but to point out the flimsy basis on which to make such an extravagant claim in the first place in order to bolster a serious thesis. To assert the practice of cannibalism when tangible evidence is so slight, repositions the discourse of this Pacific island into the early European vision of the Pacific as alternating between being a paradise and a hell. This current environmental debate is still being framed by the earlier conventions. Easter Island is still being positioned as a counter-narrative to the lush tropical Pacific.

Diamond is not alone in contemporary responses to the island that re-engage the vision of the Pacific as paradise and hell. The 'Taboo Tiki' artist J.P. Odell combines the two to create an image of paradise *as* hell in *The Devil's Paradise* (fig. 7.15), offered for sale on eBay and through the 'Tiki Taboo and Kustom Kulture Art' website. He explains, in personal correspondence, his interpretation of moai in his work as follows:

> ... I would be honored to lend you the use of the artwork for your needs. Let me take a moment and say I am flattered that you picked up on the element of what I was attempting to communicate with 'The Dark side Tiki.' It is indeed a Euro-American *interpretation* of Polynesian/tribal cultures. I make up my own names of tiki gods, tiki temples and create my own stories of rituals and folklore, knowing none of it can be found in the real

Figure 7.15: *The Devil's Paradise*, acrylic painting by J.P. Odell. 'There's a place hidden deep within the raging volcanic fury of Mt. Kilauea, a "sin"-tillating hellfire and brimstone palace fit for Pele herself, a "Devil's Paradise," if you will. Thieves, murderers, cannibals, deviants of all walks of life were cast away to this wasteland to serve their remaining days in solitude and desolation. Oh, what spoils the madness of mankind can bring!' Courtesy of the artist.

world. I know it is sort of an American stereotype in the sense that all tribal cultures are savage and practice dark magics. This stereotype was probably forged in part by the American film industry of 1930's and 1950's. That era of Hollywood films seems to be largely responsible for the highly embellished story telling of non-American cultures. I admire those authors and film makers of this era for their creativity, although this type of creative storytelling is considered stereotyping and politically incorrect today. I intentionally incorporate this 1930's through 1950's American interpretation of Polynesian culture into my work, which makes it Pop Art in a sense. Anyway I don't want to go on about myself, just wanted to say as an artist I am happy to hear I am successfully communicating these ideas to the viewer. Thanks so much:)! (5 June 2005)

In this replay of earlier assumptions, what are the consequences of this imagined Easter Island? The images of Odell have Internet circulation, while Diamond's *Collapse* is a text given considerable mainstream authority through the Pulitzer Prize awarded to his previous book, *Guns, Germs, and Steel* (1999). *Collapse* might be expected to have wide ranging influence given that *Guns, Germs, and Steel* has already sold over a million copies. *Collapse* has the pedagogical power to shape an authoritative version of island reality carried in memory about the Easter Island culture and people.

There is a certain irony to 'Easter Islanders' no longer being constructed as inferior to the 'forgotten race of moai builders' but now being acknowledged as the authors of their own cultural production. They have been resuscitated only to become representatives of the rest of the earth's population heading into self-destruction. Here the islanders do not fall outside the Hegelian measure of the world but are taken up as a bad example of human folly. In times like these when the geopolitical dialectic is in great flux, and when that instability is combined with physical evidence of our self-induced pollution and global warming, there is an attraction to 'narratives of certainty,' even if their vision is bleak. To pen a text of planetary doom with instructions for survival forms one such compelling narrative and offers concrete direction.

We are seeing, in the environmental focus on Easter Island, the re-emergence of a site of knowledge-construction that is moving away from the enduring myth of the island as a last earthly frontier of mystery and sublime wonder, or as the UNESCO celebration of a great 'past' civilization, and back into the dichotomy of Pacific paradise turned to hell. Because of its geographic distance from an assumed centre, Easter Island is able to be maintained as an imaginary geographic and cultural space open for whatever narrative imposition serves the purpose of that centre. It is the very instability of the invented Easter Island that allows it to be transformed into different versions to suit the zeitgeist of the time. From Roggeveen's assessment that it could be made an earthly paradise to Jared Diamond's description of timid and miserable cannibals, there is evidence of the inherent violence of language as it shapes judged versions of Others. Marshall Sahlins, in 'Cosmologies of Capitalism' (2000), describes this practice as an expression of 'the globalized expansion of Western Capitalism,' making the colonized and 'peripheral' peoples of the world the 'passive objects of their own histories and not its authors.' 'Tributary economic relations' have turned their cultures into 'adulterated goods' (416).

The Rapanui continue to be represented by the textually manipulated adulterated goods of Easter Island. The images from this virtual space that achieve reproductive power form cultural capital and are authorized to stand as truth about the Other they represent. They are both maintained and multiplied as well as transformed, as Stephen Greenblatt (1991) argues, into 'novel and often unexpected forms' (6). They circulate to serve pedagogical ends, teaching readers and viewers how to see the island Others in relation to themselves or rendering them invisible, depending upon the agenda of the times.

When contemporary Rapanui attempt to monitor, evaluate and develop their tourism potential against their available physical and semiotic resources, they find themselves doubly displaced. First, they are a culture whose own historical record, hieroglyphic Rongorongo, was destroyed through the imperial project.[9] Second, through their deep colonization and missionization, they have largely a European geographic and narrative imaginary of themselves against which to see their reflection and identify themselves globally, historically, and culturally. Euro-America historically established, and continues to circulate, the dominant semiotic resources that are available to the Rapanui, restricting the vision of Rapa Nui they can present to the world in an effort to win tourist attention. On my visit to the island in 2002, I observed two different carvers consulting photographs of Rapa Nui antiquities (wooden carvings) from European and American collections represented in Thor Heyerdahl's *The Art of Easter Island* (1976). In both cases the carvers referred to the photographs in order to copy the carvings depicted as well as to show me, the tourist, that they were creating 'authentic' reproductions. The authority of the imperial archive overrode their own personal creativity and signalled to them what value system to use in relation to me.

8 An Educational Supplement: Pedagogy and Remembrance

In this chapter I want to explore strategies for engaging forms of knowledge about the world while at the same time holding open a space so we are aware of our subjectivity and the constructed nature of the subjects we study. By maintaining such an opening or supplemental space as we connect with text and image, we can write back to established texts and write over old narratives with new ones that will actively engage transformative possibilities of social justice and equity. Within this dynamic, we can work towards uprooting old paradigms of suppression and power and change ourselves, our performances, and our view of and engagement with Others in the process.

Learning to 'Remember Otherwise': Education and Cultural Memory

In the very act of being created through language, a new subject such as Easter Island enters the narrative world in an imposed relationship because it is shaped into text through culturally formed interpretations. Since the subject is only ever possible in language, it is through language that subjects are limited or expand through interlocking systems of discursive possibility or power. That power inevitably promotes the dominant culture's points of view as it shapes a subject for its own archive, through and within its own grand narratives, in the process writing over the viewpoints of cultural Others. But this process can be interrupted. By coming to know the mechanics through which power positions us when engaging texts, we can learn to resist rather than reinscribe the power dynamics that inform our subjectivity and the subjective Others we engage through language. It is within this archive of subject-knowledge, where we construct ourselves and Others, that it is possible to hold open a supplemental space from within which to think differently about a subject, even as we engage its existing narratives. Formal education today can be a dynamic site for learning and practising that resistance.

The implications of the long-term effects circulating and evolving across time for the Rapanui and off-islanders within the grip of imperial cultural memory must be addressed in order to consider how one might frame a post-imperial pedagogical space wherein transformative practices of remembrance might be envisioned to engage with Easter Island, and to move towards a reshaping of its shared cultural memory. To do so I will bring John Willinsky's call for a postcolonial pedagogical supplement in *Learning to Divide the World: Education at Empire's End* (1998) into conversation with Roger Simon's theorizing of a methodological framework – *The Touch of the Past: Remembrance, Learning, and Ethics* (2005) – from within which to consider the relationship between versions of history and personal and public transformative responses to them. In order to present a practical example of a transformative response in relation to the Rapanui, I will also work with Emmanuel Levinas (1998) theorizing of an ethics of individual responsibility towards one's Other and Robert Bernasconi's (1999) call for such an ethics to be pulled into larger political engagements with 'the third parties.'

By thinking Willinsky through Simon, and Levinas through Bernasconi, I want to explore how one might engage aspects of Easter Island within a pedagogical ideology that acknowledges the imperial framework continuing to subsume education and thus collective and individual vision in Euro-Americans. Following Willinsky, I propose a postcolonial supplementation to buttress and redistribute the weight of that existing framework. The call here for supplementation rather than replacement is because, before such an imperial structure can be dismantled, the people that fortify it need to engage in a process of pedagogical transformation to reach the point where they will be able to reform and support a rebuilt postcolonial institution. A key part of that postcolonial process of transforming cultural memories is to refigure our relationship with the situated historical record. Simon's (2005) ideas for 'remembering otherwise' meld seamlessly with a postcolonial revision as we reflect on new 'terms for the relationship between history and public life' in a process to broaden perspectives, and rethink assumptions and organizing frameworks, while at the same time generating 'the bases for new thoughts and actions' (2).

Imperial Implications in Euro-America and in Rapa Nui

European imperialism grew out of a complex economic exploratory desire for expanded commerce that bound up land, people, raw materials, and cultural goods in complementary and competing relations focused on individual and national wealth. This early impulse to explore and acquire joined forces with a belief in a right to knowledge and was also bound up with the Christian adjuration to collect souls. All three, commerce, knowledge, and Christianity, developed over time within, and operated out of, a patriarchal and Euro-supremacist overview. This imperialism has been played out on a world stage from a position that values life in a top-down male hierarchy rather than within any valuation of common humanity or equality.

Commerce, knowledge, and the Christian quest for paradise all converged in the eighteenth-century exploration of the Pacific. Initially, Easter Island failed the tangible commercial and paradisial test of imperialism, but in the nineteenth century the island and people experienced the full impact of imperial violence when they were pulled into the economic and Christian loops, losing men to slavery, land to sheep, and their cultural sense of self to a Roman Catholic identity. The constructions of islanders in imperial-contact texts, as inferior in relation to their European describers, was reinforced and mirrored back to the Rapanui by the succession of missionaries who wrote over the island cosmology and spirituality with a 'right' version, teaching the Rapanui their inferior selves and place in the newly imposed order.[1] The sheep ranchers' concentration and management of the remaining Rapanui on a fraction of their former island reinforced the lessons of the Church. At the same time as imperialism worked to destroy nineteenth-century Rapanui culture, it also had an interest in trying to reconstruct and perpetuate the cultural past. The Euro-American Easter Island is still in textual play, still performing a pedagogical function to shape versions of the island imaginary and to shape the subjective responses of those who engage the idea of the island.

One of the less-contested imperial versions of the culture can be seen in public museum displays of artefacts from Easter Island, offered as evidence of the accomplishment of imperial exploration and contact. David Hanlon, in 'The Chill of History: The Experience, Emotion, and Changing Politics of Archival Research in the Pacific' (1998), critiques such displays for failing to account for the local histories of 'production, meaning, and relationships' that inform these artefacts, as well as

ignoring the entangled local and European histories of 'their acquisition and transfer across physical and cultural space.' He points out that
such histories have been ignored or dismissed to suit imperial ends,
replaced by the imperial narratives that stand in for the island stories
'to justify European understandings of hierarchy, race, difference, evolution, and progress' (33). Extensions of these museum displays are
found in videos and textual versions of the island's past, as well as
innumerable appropriated moai, reproduced as mass-produced market
commodities. All circulate as objects of unproblematized exchange,
either in and of themselves or taken up to serve the purposes of other
discursive spaces.

While the effect of imperialism's physical violence on those it con-
quers is obvious, the impact of the display of explorer-collected artefacts, the textual violence of the imperial archive, and the contemporary
textual and image constructions are sometimes not so clear. This less
tangible destruction or subversion of other cultures through text and
image often goes unrecognized and unchallenged because of the extent
to which the West has been schooled from within imperial texts. Such
texts and images have both shaped the vision of, and blinded their readers to, aspects of their actions that would be and are visible from outside
the imperial thrall. John Willinsky (1998) expressed this state of affairs
when he asked, 'What comes ... of having one's comprehension of the
world so directly tied to one's conquest of it?' (3). The answer is that this
vantage point from which Euro-Americans comprehend the world, the
space of imperial power and privilege, is as comfortable and normalized as home. For many it remains unproblematized. Even when reading or viewing documents of historic violence and greed against Others,
many Euro-Americans do not feel negatively implicated in these actions
of distant generations and therefore do not feel an obligation to remember the historic trauma they engendered. They do not acknowledge that
their contemporary privilege is constructed on Others' past and continuing losses. Or, worse, if they do acknowledge the loss they do not
acknowledge any corresponding obligation to own, memorialize, or
resist past acts of inhumanity. It is into this unreflective space that Roger
Simon (2005) calls for practices of 'remembering otherwise' (4).

From Postcolonial Supplementation to Postcolonial Immersion

The broadest focal point of this study is the culpability of the imperial
project in relation to Easter Island, and its continuing circulation as a

historically situated yet unstable text with the possibility of far-reaching pedagogical impact that constrains and limits thought, action, and memory of all those who engage with its idea both on and off the island. Recognition of this impact is the first step to obviating its effects through a counter-project of curriculum supplementation and 'insurgent forms of remembrance' (Simon 2005, 10). Such a counter-project begins in an awareness of the way subject discourses are constructed and shape a historically situated social memory of Others archived as cultural capital. Specifically, when imperialism is the project to be countered, postcolonialism is the post-structural discourse to frame the task (Willinsky 1998, 256). Working within postcolonial discourse to teach historical records can open an examination of the violent story that shapes the imperial archive and gives it such insidious authority. But an awareness of the historical and continuing impact of imperialism is only a first step. Simon's (2005) pedagogy of remembrance can be engaged within such an aware space to address the need for a response to unproblematized narratives such as Easter Island by recognizing we are not released from the obligation of remembering past injustices and violences just because it was not our generation or our culture who committed the traumatic actions (1). As Simon points out, we all, in our attempts to maintain our humanity, must acknowledge and resist past acts of inhumanity and connect across historically structured differences of time and place (2).

Willinsky's postcolonial supplementation, enveloping Simon's pedagogy of remembrance, is best positioned, not as part of a unit of study on Easter Island, but like language-immersion programs, as the framework through which all course subjects are taken up. Easter Island is a discrete case study of imperialism that could be engaged within such a framework. The idea of postcolonial immersion is that it constitutes the ideal learning situation for unsettling the hegemonic hold of the current educational structure. All subjects can be filtered through its lens until it becomes the learner's second nature to read with a postcolonial inflection.

Postcolonial immersion also helps to prepare the state of mind for more than just reaction to injustices of the past. It can help set the conditions for the possibility of personal transformation and transformative action that can change the way we respond in the present and the future. To paraphrase Simon's (2005) description of transformative practices in the public sphere, taking up the texts of course subjects through the language of postcolonial immersion would challenge the normalized way of framing them. A postcolonial reassessment inter-rupts the conventional ways of organizing or seeing a subject, opening space for engagement that will carry forward an altered way of under-standing the subject and narrating it to others (7).

For example, to take up the subject of Easter Island within an evolv-ing postcolonial sensibility should mean that the unproblematized per-formance positions normally assumed in relation to moai are no longer possible. A new space would open to govern engagement with the sub-ject that would interrupt and counter the thoughtless indifference con-stantly reinscribed into the Euro-American constructed norm and appropriated form of the moai. Rather than standing in for Easter Island, or as elements of Tiki decor, the imperially formed moai images would be perceived through traces of the past that invoke an awareness of the violence of the island's imperial history and thus a transforma-tion of one's way of negotiating that history, of travelling through and participating in the human story across time. Outlined in Appendix B, are practical steps to implement Willinsky's call for the postcolonial supplementation needed to position teachers and students within a potentially transformative pedagogical space that can become, with time, an educative site of postcolonial immersion.[2]

An active awareness of the constructed nature of our response and of the constructed nature and instability of imperial texts and images enables them to be engaged differently. The self-conscious supplement checks the formerly unproblematized response to imperial texts, always adding a 'tag' that prompts a post-imperial response. Therefore postcolonial immersion creates a stage for an alternative engagement and response, and that alternative can become the new norm, creating the opportunity for a pedagogical process of altered historical memory and future transformation of personal subjectivity and response. Altered (supplemented) memories of the imperial past would also serve to reshape contemporary and future responses to cultural Others, synergizing altered collective cultural identity and agency.

Responding to Rongorongo

In what follows I take up the idea of Rongorongo, the Rapanui hiero-glyphics, to engage with it as a trace of the traumatic past. At the same time, I want to explore a pedagogical space of postcolonial supplemen-tation, working within it to develop an ethically transformed response to the culture of Others. I take up the memory of Rongorongo through my encounter with it as a tourist visiting the island. My viewpoint, then, is of a tourist/student seeking to enact the gift of testimony by elaborating a possible pedagogy of ethical tourism based in the memory of Rongorongo. My exploration can serve as a model for classroom-based projects.

Because the circulation and recirculation of versions of Easter Island has been the focus of this study, I have often turned to the Internet to gauge the extent of and permutations of this subject. I use an Internet site here to situate my initial response to the idea of Rongorongo as I explored the narratives about it after my return from my first visit to the island in 2002. The website, Rongorongo.org, has, perhaps, a problematic heading for the English-language reader, a meaningless untranslatable repetition of sound accompanied by the interpretable idea of the existence of this mystery at a site in virtual space, a site on the Web at which the nature of Rongorongo may be revealed. In a direct reading of the word Rongorongo, the meaning remains elusive, nothing more than an exotic sound sequence to the English ear.

To help understand what Rongorongo is you need to imagine that you are holding a tablet of wood perhaps forty-five centimetres long and twelve wide. It is as smooth as satin to the touch and tapers from one and a half centimetres in thickness down to a soft edge around its perimeter. Inscribed on the surface of the tablet are fine rows of hieroglyphics. Many of the glyphs can be discerned as recognizable figures such as human beings holding objects and different kinds of flora and fauna. Other images appear as abstractions or geometric shapes. Each drawing seems to represent a word or idea rather than an alphabetical phoneme. After examining the first row of hieroglyphs you will notice that the second row, and all alternate rows, are upside down in relation to the first. You recognize it as text but its meaning eludes you. You have no power to access it, no access to its power.

Rongorongo are the hieroglyphs of the Rapanui, the only Polynesian people recognized as inventing a system of writing. It appears to consist of a base of 120 separate hieroglyphs arranged in combinations that seem to make over 2,000 complex symbols. Island tradition attributes the origin to Hotu Matua, identified as the leader of the original settlers. While no one reads Rongorongo today, it is still written. The Rapanui narrative concerning the place of Rongorongo in their culture was recorded by ethnologist and anthropologist Katherine Routledge in *The Mystery of Easter Island* (1919). She describes her informant's story of the schools and ritual behaviour by which writing on the island

was passed down through the generations until the slave raids of 1862.
These raids are reported to have brought an end to the social class of
male scholars who were described as teaching Rongorongo to their
male students in a continuous line of scholarship over the entire history
of the island, *history* being the appropriate term in this narrative. Juan
Tepano, Routledge's informant, described schools established on clan
lands across the island and annual oral testing days held when all the
scholars and their pupils were gathered to be evaluated by a pair of
Rongorongo 'quality and accountability officials' who ensured that
established standards were maintained by both teachers and students
alike (243–54). According to Tepano, in Rapa Nui's highly stratified and
class-conscious society, only the males of the royal family (descendants
of Hotu Matua), clan chiefs, and scholar-priests were privy to the significance of the Rongorongo characters and able to possess the tablets
and read them.

Today, everyone on Rapa Nui has access to contemporary Rongorongo tablets and great pride is invested in them. Members of both sexes
of the island's indigenous adult population, numbering about a thousand people, spend their days preparing Rongorongo tablets, smooth-
ing the wood and inscribing it with row on row of the fine small
hieroglyphics in order to sell them to tourists. The tablets they make
range from tiny pieces to be worn as pendants around the neck to large,
metre-long tablets designed for prominent display on a wall. Very close
and patient work is needed to inscribe the numerous Rongorongo
images on the wooden and sometimes stone tablets. Anyone on Rapa
Nui has access to and may carve the glyphs. But no one can read them.

Racial and gendered violence is reinscribed in every mute creation of
a new tablet, repeatedly producing texts that cannot be read, and yet in
that *unreading*, retelling the violent legacy of European contact. Rongorongo writing stands as a metonym for the history of Rapa Nui, but it
also enacts a site of witnessing – the untranslatable as immemorial past.
Because its meaning is lost, its untranslatability must be a metonym for
memory instead, standing in for the memorial connections that bind
the past to the future (Simon 2000, 9).

In my initial exposure to the idea of Rongorongo and its reproduction
on Rapa Nui as a student/tourist travelling to 'learn a new culture,' I
was imbedded in an already-given linguistic system, my intent shaped
within the established parameters of my own community's outlook on
the world. I was already within the history of Western tourism and its
multiple and intertwined texts and performance spaces where the

desire to acquire the culture and landscape of an Other is constituted, even before my decision to travel was formulated. 'We cannot step beyond the historical encoding of the world, beyond a "white mythology" that holds many of us in its educated grasp' (Derrida 1982, 223). We can, however, develop an alternative response to Others by consciously attending to the discord created when competing discourses overlap.

As I 'supplement' the experience I had on the island with a postcolonial response, I recognize that my travelling identity was produced in the West, carried with me to the geographic travel destination, and formed in the space from which I negotiated my experience of the site and the people being visited. In the process, I imposed that narrative on those Others and positioned them in roles that served as responses to my tourist–subject position. As I read myself against these cultural Others, I recognise that I was constantly reaffirming my Anglo-Canadian identity in relation to them through those reading practices, and that an aspect of that affirmation of self had as its cost 'the expulsion of otherness' (Britzman 1998, 85). I was continuing to normalize and reinscribe imperial narratives.

Sidestepping One's Reality

The first impulse when recognizing that one's own imperial narratives are drawn tightly around the self in a cloak of exclusion is to initiate a project of recovery and to attempt to enfold the Other. An uneasy paradox of such Euro-American projects to recover that which has been expelled, however, is that we continue to perform violence against Others by forcing them, through our reclamation, into our own dominating narratives. We continue to privilege our system of values and to follow our agenda. In order to move towards a space where we can connect with others rather than just reading them into our narratives, we must refuse, as Drucilla Cornell says in *The Philosophy of the Limit* (1992), 'the idea that what "reality" is can ever be reduced to our conception of it' (178). An ethical moment can be realized in opening the self to the community and to individuals of the Others' culture, but not in internalizing a translation of that culture and taking it home for presentation to one's own community, as an essentialized or commodified version of those Others.

There appears to be no such thing as a neutral tourist stance in relation to Others. The writing of Emmanuel Levinas, however, offers a potential site from which to consider ways of opening the closed Euro-American narrative through a responsiveness to the Other that avoids the violence of knowing the Other by translating him or her into oneself. It offers the paradox of an asymmetrical relationship, an awakening to the Other that is not knowledge about the Other, not just a cataloging of this particular individual as an 'individual within a genus,' but a responsiveness to the proximity of another like me, beside me or face to face (Levinas 1998a, 168). Levinas begins his explanation of an ethical way of responding to an individual Other by focusing our attention on the need to shatter the 'subject's illusion that he is the meaning-giving centre' (Cornell 1942, 72). He takes us back to Hegel's absolute knowledge where 'thought completes itself by equaling and interiorizing the other [and] culture triumphs over things and men,' establishing a process that confirms a Western identity in which the subject, 'in his identity, persists without the *other* being able to challenge or unsettle him' (Levinas 1998b, 181; emphasis in original). This perpetuates a state Levinas refers to as 'the unity of the one' (184). He then asks if it is not possible to know the Other without reducing him to the same, without seeing him as either part of the same unity of the Western 'whole,' or as remaindered outside that whole. He demonstrates that it should be possible to avoid reducing the Other to the self-same because the Other has an absolute character – is an individual Other just as I am an individual in an 'irreducible fashion,' and thus has an otherness and a separation that resists all synthesis, prior to all unity (185).

Levinas, then, has us hold on to two concepts at once (a familiar concept residing in the concept of the supplement), the recognition of the Other as a fellow human being and the recognition of the individuality of the Other. In a recognition of the self in the Other it becomes possible to respond to, and be responsible towards, the *self* in the Other as well as the *alterity* of the Other. The 'face to face' double recognition arrests the move to synthesis (185). At this point, however, we need to recall Derrida who shows us that behind Hegelian unity, and Levinas' notion of 'prior to all unity,' there are other pre-existing unities that take us back to the arche-writing/the trace/difference, and, therefore, we cannot actually go to a place prior to all unity because we cannot step out of the narratives, the play of the trace, through which we are constituted. We can create and consciously hold open an imaginary space, however, at the same time as we hold before us an awareness of the normative exclusionary discourses we are constituted by. We can hold open a space for the difference of the Other to co-exist. Such is a neces-

sary part of ethical tourism, both to be aware of the Eurocentric impe-
rial/tourist discourse that has been informing our travelling position/
performance and also to stand separate from that narrative as we
respond ethically to Others through and during our travels.

Derrida's (1982) version of the 'supplement' can be called on here to
help envision an idea of the 'between' space the ethical traveller must
inhabit. The supplement, as its name implies, is a surplus to something
already existing and creates the fullest measure of presence by being
added on (144). The supplement adds onto, but only with the intention
of replacing or intervening; it insinuates itself in-the-place-of (145). The
inflexion of the supplement varies from moment to moment, creating a
space of double signification. Each of the two significations (in the case
of an ethical tourist, the Western travel signification and the space held
open for responding to the Other) is by turns effaced or becomes dis-
creetly vague in the presence of the Other whether it adds or substitutes
itself, 'the supplement is exterior,' outside that to which it is super-
added, alien, and other to the main discursive space it joins (145), but
stitched to and combining with it to form a new between-space.
Through its difference from the main discourse that it supplements, it is
able to change the shape of, alter the intent of, the main, a fluid counter-
discursive space of consciously and purposefully directed agency.

Recognizing the need for an ethical response to Others should
prompt the creation of an ethical supplement that, through its presence,
will tend to shift one's discursive positions, helping to acknowledge
sameness and respect alterity; to identify and dis-identify with Others;
and to experience the wonder of the Other's difference. Ideally, knowing of the need for an ethical supplement will create a conscious awareness that resists separation from the supplement once it has been
created. Imagining an ethical supplement as an adjunct to one's existing travel narrative will help create a pedagogically transformative
space in anticipation of actual travel, as well as creating a space to
inhabit during travel that will shift the parameters of one's tourist experience. Through its presence the Euro-American will no longer inhabit
the normative centre, but will occupy a translated space, a hybrid sensibility – *the space between*.

While travelling consists of a series of one-on-one encounters in
which the potential to respond ethically is repeatedly possible, the narrative of tourism (a narrative with applications beyond that activity)
requires that the opening of a supplemental space for the ethical
encounter be imagined beyond the individual encounter and theorized

as a third-party notion of ethical behaviour. Third-party ethical behaviour allows an ethical response to the summons by colonized communities, and those living with the repercussions of former colonization, to the witness of past traumas and present injustices. Robert Bernasconi, in his essay, 'The Third Party: Levinas on the Intersection of the Ethical and the Political' (1999), addresses the fact that the 'main thrust of Levinas's account is to resist the reduction of ethics to politics,' the totality of interrelationships. He points out that it is 'precisely within the context of political society,' in this case manifested through the travel experience, 'and not in an ethical realm abstracted from it – that Levinasian ethics has its impact' (80).

Levinas introduces the third party into the face of the Other to exempt the face to face from being a closed couple where the rest of humanity is eliminated from ethical encounters. He describes the third party as looking at me in the eyes of the Other, displacing the self-sufficient 'I-thou' (Bernasconi 1999, 78). The third person emerges next to the Other and is also a neighbour; as such he or she also falls within the purview of the *I*'s responsibility. Levinas asks, who comes first in this plurality and introduces the question of justice (1998a, 166)? Since the third party is already located within the one on one encounter, 'the passage from ethics to politics is immanent' (Bernasconi 1999, 78). The ethical can reorient the political nature of the tourist experience 'through a point of intersection between the political and the ethical that can be achieved by seeing them in relation to each other through a layering of meaning' (ibid., 80). Within an ethically responsive tourist narrative my responsibility to the Other does not allow me to put aside 'my responsibility to the others of the Other.' 'My relation to the Other in his or her singularity and my relations to the other Others are conjoined in a single structure, because the presence of the face is also the presence of the third party' (ibid., 79). Within this plural form of ethical response, the tourist must respond beyond the present serial encounters with individual Others met while travelling. As the tourist learns of injustices from the imperial past, she is called by the third party or by communal summons to respond to those injustices from the past that need to be remembered.

The Responsibility of the Ethical Student/Tourist

The ethical response for Levinas is described as at the moment of an actual encounter in the present. It is through such an encounter that one is able to see the face of the Other, and hear the voice of the Other, both of which enable a response to the self-same of the Other and at the same time, the recognition of the alterity of the Other that resists being absorbed into oneself – the Other's irreducible exteriority (Cornell 1992, 72). The tourist, preparing for an ethical response to Others during a planned future encounter, will find it useful to have a catalyst to the recognition of sameness and alterity that will help open the space for the ethical encounters to come in a future present. In the case of Rapa Nui, Rongorongo can serve as that catalyst, a metaphor of the Other's absent past, which can call the Euro-American traveller to a symbolic mourning of the loss of Rongorongo, now 'irreducibly exterior' to any efforts to call it back, to possess it, to know it, or to make meaning of it.

With Rongorongo there is no possible memory except of violence. Euro-American anthropology, archaeology, and linguistics have been unable to bring back the meaning of the historical knowledge held captive in the Rongorongo tablets. No matter how strong the desire to 'advance learning' or draw *all* into an 'absolute knowledge,' 'the West' has reached the limit of its narcissism with the realization it cannot bring Rongorongo back into history. Imperialism destroyed the living Rongorongo 'Rosetta Stones' when the Euro-Peruvians, unable to see themselves in the Rapanui, ranked their economic gain above the lives and work of the scholar-priests, and enslaved and worked them to death or exposed them to lethal disease in two short years. Precisely because Europe and the Americas still have Rongorongo tablets in their museums, but cannot decode their meaning, its loss makes a dramatic impression, defying the desire to know all and possess all. The possibility of opening a space for an ethical response in the present and the future is situated in remembering the untranslatable Rongorongo. The very work of holding a space open by acknowledging the loss of the meaning of Rongorongo embodies a rebellion against the Hegelian system that denies the value of respecting people outside its circle, both collectively, and as individuals in personal encounters.

Simon's (2000) idea of hope in the present is illuminating in relation to the idea of Rongorongo as a catalyst or metonym for the Rapanui Others' absent past. Hope is usually situated in a continuing present and focused on an altered future. Simon, working with the idea of hope, positions it in relationship to remembrance in ways that can be adapted for the tourist wanting to honour the memory of historical loss. His work gives direction to possible tourist practices that might be able to encompass an ethics of responsibility. Simon introduces hope as a reason for positioning oneself to experience the violent historical memories of Others. He suggests hope, though oriented toward the future, must be reconstituted as a structural condition of the present; 'a condition rooted in a conception of what it means to be positioned in-the-present' (Andrew Benjamin qtd. in Simon 2003, 3). In Simon's idea, hope is sustained in a continuing present when one recognizes that existing discursive norms do not include a space for 'a hopeful remembrance.' This discourse of hope, practised as a response to the loss of historical memory represented by Rongorongo, opens a space allowing for a move beyond the shock of hearing about the loss to an affirmation of the need to learn a supplemented version of the historical record. In this concept of hope, 'tradition is recognized as that which must be rethought' (Simon 2005, 112) The untranslatability of Rongorongo can be positioned in relation to hope in the present through both a memorialization and a transformative recollection.

Rongorongo can be memorialized by actually bringing into view that which has been erased. Through being made aware of the way its reading was lost, we are able to 'attach ourselves' through ethical identification to this remembrance, 'thus securing the personal and communal importance of the eternal act of remembering' (Simon 2003, 4). Rongorongo is brought into memory through the 'collective rituals' of its reinscription, inscribing the Rongorongo. To watch the Rapanui inscribing ancestral writing they cannot read, if viewed knowingly by the tourist in connection to the deaths and loss of people and historical record, can mobilize an affective response wherein hope is affirmed. New inscriptions of Rongorongo onto tablets confront past loss and speak to the continuation of life in the present (4–5). Most importantly, such a process, whether experienced in person as a tourist, or through a documentary film, speaks to the cracking open of the present, to the notion of futurity as something other than the sameness of an external present. To attempt to achieve this purpose, Rongorongo can also be positioned within the context of a transformative recollection. In this context, hope names the present's inherent incompleteness, the always untranslatable text of Rongorongo, and holds the present open, always unfinished (Benjamin qtd. in ibid., 5). Here also, remembrance enacts a transformation which unsettles the present, acting as a supplement to the discursive position of the tourist in which she recognizes the past as one of her own concerns in the present (ibid.). The Rongorongo, physically present, yet 'unspeaking' evokes a questioning response. As soon as a tourist hears of or researches the reasons for the untranslatability, she recognizes the culpability of Euro-American imperialism in the loss.

Hope resides here in a supplemental position to disrupt the continuity of the central discourse through which Western tourists are constituted. The Hegelian system of knowledge is recognized as unable to provide the space for remembrance without the supplement of hope. Simon (2003) describes such a space of remembrance as a 'social process,' one within which a tourist can find space to admit accounts of the past so that she can transform her 'present and future actions in ways that do not reduce the terms of this admittance to projections' of her own identity and desires (5).

The ethical tourist, by challenging her normative Western travel discourse, by holding open a between space through the addition of a hopeful supplement, can be awakened to an attending to her attending (Simon 2003, 12). Here Simon uses Levinas's understanding of 'the *kavannah*,' as a way of describing a self-conscious state where one is both aware of the self and aware of, and responsive to, an existence beyond oneself (ibid., 7). This state of encompassing dual consciousnesses, one's own and an awareness of one beyond oneself, corresponds to the frame of mind needed for the between-space of the ethical tourist, created by the awareness of the need for the ethical supplement – a space where one holds oneself open to the summons of the Other and the past traumas of the Other. Here Levinas's thought opens the possibility of a social practice, a relationality to the 'necessities of the present,' 'a concern for the self in regard to how self might answer for its responsibility to and for others' (ibid., 12).

When one witnesses the Rapanui inscribing Rongorongo and learns of the past genocide that means it can no longer be read, there is a desire to respond to the violence of this knowledge as well as to the cultural wonder of the hieroglyphs themselves. Simon (2003) proposes that the way to return the gift of this knowledge, 'to return the receipt of the problem of inheritance initiated by the movement of testament, is to give it to someone else' (13).

I did not go to Rapa Nui aware of the trauma the people had endured in the name of imperialism. I travelled only knowing my culture's popular story of the mysteries of the island. Having witnessed the consequences of that imperialism, however, I returned to consider the implications of my experience within the context of ethical encounters. In so doing I have theorized a framework for ethical tourism based on the work of Levinas, Derrida, and Simon. It is a framework that can be positioned within the larger education framework of Willinsky's post-colonial immersion. This framework creates a between-space for the traveller to inhabit self-consciously, through the addition of an ethical supplement to the imperial narrative. Within that space, it is possible to be open to and formulate responses to traumas from the past that one witnesses through travel, responses that should be carried back from those travels to be shared. The idea of ethical tourism is my answerability to that witness. Through it I speak of what I have witnessed, 'speaking specifically so as to teach others what it is that it has taught' me (Simon 2003, 3).

Iorana

The word for hello and goodbye in Rapanui is the same, *iorana*, a term that stands between the past and the future. I have argued that the eighteenth-century invention of Easter Island may be taken up through practices of remembrance within a context of postcolonial immersion to both transform us in the present and carry hopeful change into the future. But, while focused on the European imperial record and its continuing deleterious pedagogical influence in Euro-America, this project cannot help but recognize implications for the Rapanui as well. It raises questions worth addressing in further studies, preferably written by members of the Rapanui community, specifically focused on the impact of the imperial record upon the contemporary Rapa Nui population. Such studies could examine the consequences for the islanders of the off-island trend away from moai celebration, in which the people themselves are obscured, distorted, or erased, to moai as a reflection of environmental devastation, wherein the people are still being obscured, distorted, or erased. What will the current narrative of environmental destruction do to the Rapanui self-image? What are the Rapanui doing to counter this off-island shifting narrative overlay?

What are and will be the consequences of such contemporary cultural developments on the island as the annual *Tapati* festival competition, a Rapa Nui communal re-memory and elaboration of old and new cultural practices? Also, what will be the consequences for the new proactive island cultural regulations to tie access to heritage sites to islanders' access to subsequent scholarly publication? Will 'Euro-American' scholarship comply with the regulations and trade the translated research for geographic access to sites or continue to operate on imperial principles? In the Rapanui public school system, what will be the cultural impact of the Rapanui language immersion program, now, in 2005, at grade four, as it progresses through the otherwise Spanish school curriculum and combines with these other cultural developments to work towards reclamation of a Rapanui voice and heritage? These questions and the call for a Rapanui scholarly investigation of and response to them, speaks to Stephen Greenblatt's (1991) observation that there has been 'almost no authentic reciprocity in the exchange of representations between Europeans and the people of the New World, no equality of giving and receiving' (121).

These questions also speak back to Douglas Porteous's (2004) call for 'the growth of a cultural approach to Rapa Nui Studies that emphasizes both the history of the island and the place of the island in the world here and now' (18). Several projects complementary to mine suggest themselves in this category. A study of nineteenth-century historic imperial texts and images would form the most obvious study in a direct continuum, followed by a study of contemporary popular texts and images, and a study of contemporary academic texts. Texts about the island written in the twentieth century lend themselves to several different investigations. A lengthy investigation could be made of the impact, on and off the island, of the work of Thor Heyerdahl, as could the scope and influence of the textual island as it has been taken up in fiction, particularly science fiction. The impact of extravagant 'coffee-table books' could form another investigation. Studies such as these could be framed from within cultural theory and postcolonial theory to investigate other pedagogical influences in shaping perceptions of the island. Finally if this study achieves its desired goals, it might perhaps be used as an exemplar for the reclamation of other discrete places that have suffered from comparable impositions, distortions, and violence.

As with every instance of imperial violence, Rapa Nui should not be subsumed into a generalized epistemic account of imperial expansion. Rapa Nui has the right to its own voice, its own story on its own terms. To recognize elements in the cultural swirl about Others that are inherently violent in their construction is to confront our own complicity. Hearing the story of the Rapanui may open possibilities of response to other imperial violences, expanding the boundaries of the human community outwards from Te Pito O Te Henua, the navel of the world, the end of the earth.

Appendix A: *The Anonymous Sailor*

An Historical Collection of the Several Voyages and Discoveries in the South Pacific Ocean 1770. Edited and Translated by Alexander Dalrymple[1]

'EXTRACT of the DUTCH RELATION, many Digressions in the Original, entirely foreign to the subject, are left out.'

'UPON the 6th day of April, being in lat. 27°. S, and long. 268°, we discovered an island, hitherto unknown to any European, for which reason, according to the usual custom on the first discovery of any unknown land, we christened it by the name of EASTER ISLAND, it being the anniversary of our Saviour's Resurrection, on that very day that we arrived there. As soon as the anchors were ready to drop, we observed at a distance a neat boat, of a very remarkable construction, the whole patched together out of pieces of wood, which could hardly make up the largeness of half a foot. This boat was managed by a single man, a giant of twelve feet high, who exerted all his strength to escape us, but in vain, because he was surrounded and taken. His body was painted with a dark brown colour. We tried with such signs and words as are used here and there among the islands in the South Sea, to get some intelligence from him, but could not perceive that he understood any thing, wherefore we permitted him to go into his boat again and depart. Two days afterwards the whole sea was covered with the savage inhab-

---

1 Dalrymple, ed., *An Historical Collection of the Several Voyages and Discoveries in the South Pacific Ocean 1770 (Printed for the Author)* ([1770] 1967), vol. 2: 111–13. Eighteenth-century spelling from the original has been retained in this extract.

itants of this island, who came swimming round the ship in such multitudes, that we neither could, nor did we think it adviseable to land. They clambered like cats up the ship's sides with the utmost assurance, and came aboard, where they did not appear to be in the least afraid of us, but they seemed very much surprised at the large nets and extent of our ships and rigging, and could not conceive the meaning of all that they saw; but their curiosity was chiefly engaged by the great guns, which they could not enough admire, and which they frequently struck their hands upon, to try if they could not lift them up, and carry them off; but when they saw that such logs by such an attempt were too heavy for them, and could not be moved, these overgrown fellows stood abashed, and were, in appearance very much out of humour. They no sooner came aboard, than we immediately found that they were naturally as thievish and nimble-fingered as the inhabitants of those islands to which voyagers have affixed the name of the ISLANDS OF THIEVES, from the great propensity of the people to rob and steal, if they were not beaten from it. Rusty nails, old iron, and whatever they could catch or lay hold on, was equal to them, with which they jumped over immediately. They attempted with their nails to scratch the bolts out of the ship, but these were too fast for them. These huge fellows came at last aboard in such great numbers, that we were hardly capable to keep them in order, or keep a watchful eye upon their motions, and the quickness of their hands; so that fearing they would become too many for us, we used our best endeavours to get rid of them in a friendly way, but they not seeming inclinable to leave us, we were obliged to use harsher methods, and drive these savages out of the ships by force.

'On the 10th of April we made for the island in our boats, well armed, in order to land and take a view of this country, where an innumerable multitude of savages stood on the sea side to guard the shore, and obstruct our landing; but as soon as we, through necessity, gave them a discharge of our muskets, and here and there brought one of them to the ground, they lost their courage. They made the most surprising motions and gestures in the world, and viewed their fallen companions with the utmost astonishment, wondering at the wounds which the bullets had made in their bodies; whereupon they hastily fled, with a dreadful howling, dragging the dead bodies along with them, so the shore was cleared, and we landed in safety.

'These people do not go naked, as many other savages do; every person is clothed in different colours of cotton and worsted, curiously woven, or stitched; but nothing misbecomes them more than their ears, which are abominably long, and in most of them hang upon the shoulders, so that though they themselves look upon this as the greatest ornament, they appeared very uncouth to us, who were accustomed to such, the more so, as there were in them such extravagantly large holes and openings, that we could easily put our hands through them.

'Thus far my narrative will gain credit, because it contains nothing uncommon, yet I must declare that all these savages are of a more than gigantic size, for the men being twice as tall and thick as the largest of our people; they measured, one with another, the height of twelve feet, for that we could easily – who will not wonder at it ! without stooping have passed betwixt the legs of these sons of GOLIAH. According to their height, so is their thickness, and are all, one with another, very well proportioned, so that each could have passed for a HERCULES; but none of their wives came up to the height of the men, being commonly not above ten or eleven feet. The men had their bodies painted with a red or dark brown, and the women with a scarlet colour.

'I doubt not that most people who read this voyage will give no credit to what I now relate, and that this account of the height of these giants will probable pass with them for a mere fable or fiction; but this I declare, that I have put down nothing but the real truth, and that these people, upon the nicest inspection, were in fact of such a surpassing height as I have here described. In this all the most famous voyagers, who have ever navigated these seas, agree with me, men of veracity, whose narrations none can mistrust, without doing them an injury; who in their journals unanimously agree that in the countries adjacent to, and in the SOUTH SEA, giants have been found of a height far superior to us, and exactly agreeing with that of theses islanders, as I shall further make appear in the following chapter.

'After the inhabitants of EASTER ISLAND had made trial of the strength of our weapons, as we have before related, they began to use us in a more civil manner, and brought us from their huts all kinds of vegetables, sugar-canes, with yams, plantains, and a great quantity of fowls, which came very a-propos, and tended to refresh us greatly.

'What I have seen of the worship and idols of these savages is very wonderful. Two stones, of a largeness almost beyond belief, served them for gods; the one was broad beyond measure, and lay upon the ground; upon this stood the other stone, which was of such extent and height that seven of our people with outstretched arms would hardly have been able to encircle it; so that it appeared to me, and all others, impossible that this stone could have been lifted up and placed upon the other by the inhabitants of these islands, how large and strong so ever they might be; for, besides the thickness, it was fully as high as three men. About the top of this stone there was cut or carved the shape of a man's head, adorned with a garland, which was set together in the manner of inlaid work, made of small stones, in a manner not very improper. The name of the largest idol was called TAURICO and the other DAGO.'

Appendix B: Postcolonial Immersion

Three initial steps come into play when considering a move from an imperial pedagogical model into a postcolonial model. They consist, one, of identifying the subject positions of the teachers and students involved in any specific educational endeavour; two, of recognizing the power dynamics at play in the teacher–student relationship largely as a consequence of those subject positions; and, three, only then of moving into postcolonial course work by identifying the form of imperialism relevant to the context (in Canada's case, the Eurocentric assumptions underlying the curriculum in question). By establishing the internally and externally persuasive discourses that constitute us, and by acknowledging the power dynamics and performance positions of all involved in the educational process before beginning to actually focus on course content or on a case study, it should be possible to lay the groundwork for enacting ethical student–teacher relationships and then directing mutual energies to the work of re-educating imaginations and public memories.

Willinsky calls on Derrida's idea of the 'supplement' to help envision the 'between' space the postcolonial student must inhabit. As its name implies, the supplement is a surplus to something already existing that creates the fullest measure of presence by being added on with the intention of replacing or intervening (Derrida 1998, 144–5). As Willinsky notes, we cannot wait for a wholesale rewriting of the existing educational system before we begin to teach from a postcolonial point of view, and the addition of such a postcolonial supplement is a way to convert any existing curriculum, no matter how imperially oriented, or Eurocentric (255).

The inflexion of the postcolonial supplement would vary from moment to moment, creating a space of double signification. Students and teachers shaped through a Eurocentric education system would hold open a space for responding to the curriculum from a postcolonial point of view, while retaining conscious hold of how their understanding of their various Others has been constructed, and remembering it is an illusion that the way they understand the world represents any underlying truth or reality. Whether it 'adds or substitutes itself, the supplement is exterior,' outside that to which it is super-added, alien and other to the main discursive space it joins (Derrida 1998, 145), but stitched to it, combining with it to form a new between-space. Through its difference, in this case from the main educational discourse that it supplements, it is able to change the shape of and alter the intent of the main. Creating a space at the start of a course for students and teachers alike to engage in metacognitive reflexivity, and then adding to that space a postcolonial supplement that can be inflected to encompass themselves as well as the curriculum, will enable the participants to transform Eurocentric pedagogical experiences into postcolonial ones.

Transformative Practices

For practices of postcolonial supplementation to become the normalized site of postcolonial immersion, the act of double signification is the key concept to carry forward. It must be stressed that the site and idea of supplementation are exterior enablers. It is the individual subject's conscious act and continuing engaged practice that leads to a personal transformation and changed way of participating in and understanding the constructed world. Simon (2005) adds to this point that remembering differently 'resides not in the monuments, images, and texts themselves, but in our engagement with them (153). When engaging versions of history and our own social practices from within a framework of postcolonial immersion, the supplement enables us to read our sense of history and our personal responses self-consciously. We can monitor our 'usual' response at the same time as we remember that these normalized responses have been learned and are not innate. This recognition of the constructed nature of our response and of the constructed nature and instability of imperial texts and images enables them to be engaged differently. The self-conscious supplement checks the formerly unproblematized response to imperial texts, always adding a 'tag' that prompts a post-imperial response. Therefore postcolonial immersion creates a stage for an alternative engagement and response, and that alternative can become the new norm, creating the opportunity for a pedagogical process of altered historical memory and future transformation of personal subjectivity and response. Altered (supplemented) memories of the imperial past would also serve to reshape contemporary and future responses to cultural Others, synergizing altered collective cultural identity and agency.

Within a formal educational context, a pedagogy of postcolonial immersion cannot thrive in a hierarchy of teacher-to-student subject transmission, but only in a shared space of engagement where teachers facilitate and participate in students' encounters with cultural instances of the imperial narrative across time, space, place, and culture(s). Simon (2005) differentiates between these two approaches, passive transmitted spectacle and active engagement. In the first we are cast as the receptive audience for a spectacle of the past that does not summons the spectator to action or change, while the second requires participatory forms of remembrance that are transformative by nature because they require active engagement with, and active response to, events from the past and therefore carry the hope of change into the future (137–41). At the same time, Simon cautions against organizing a 'pedagogy of remembrance' in a formulaic way, recognizing that transformation is most likely to occur through the sharing of personal responses achieved through individual and group engagement with materials from the past (147). This practice does not call for a series of encounters with texts and images to be orchestrated by a teacher, but for individuals to actively pursue a personal engagement with historical texts, to formulate a private response and then to share that response with a group in fellowship (154). It is through the active engagement in processes of remembrance and in the personal and shared responses that normalized imperial-narratives can be dismantled and then carried forward in new versions that expose their full implication with past and continuing forms of violence, bearing an educative legacy to those who come after (133). For students to engage with a trace of the traumatic past they would need to participate in acts of research to assemble the story counter-discursive to the imperial record. Such acts of research and assembly in a postcolonial context hold within the possibility of being pedagogically transformative. A more detailed explanation of how we might engage in practices to transform our historical memories is described by Simon as 'historiographic poetics' (153).

Using 'Easter Island' as an example, teachers and students together would conduct research and collect detailed historiographic references in a reading, writing, and sharing process that would immerse them in traces from the past that demand a response. It is key in this potentially transformative practice for students and teachers to write responses to the past, creating something new as they are touched by what they discover. Yet, at the same time, historiographic poetics must not just be seen as a written response but also as a performance, elaboration, and interpretation that enacts the gift of testimony by creating a community of memory that gives voice to, and witnesses, the testimony again (Simon 2005, 154). Since, as students will discover, the Rapanui historical text written in Rongorongo was largely destroyed and the transmission of its meaning was interrupted and ended through imperial violence, there are no translatable Rapanui histories of the island past. Examples of Rongorongo do remain – undecipherable. They are unable to offer up their intended meaning, but stand as powerful traces of the past, that both demand and require our attention. Out of a researched connection with these *Rongorongo* boards and imperial historic texts, students and teachers could mount a presentation of the record of the past to the present. Such work is described by Simon as a collage of citation and a finite set of testamentary texts and images that in their arrangement and juxtaposition can invoke the past and write back to it in a cycle that turns us to our responsibility (154). This personal and social practice could stage a renewal of the lost Rapanui voice, altering the present way of remembering and responding and carrying that alteration forward (155).

Notes

Preface

1 José Miguel Ramírez, 'Art, Vandalism or Just Disrespect?' Centro de Estudios Rapa Nui, Universidad de Valparaiso. Retrieved 19 April 2005 from http://groups.yahoo.com/group/easterislandinfo/messages/1901?viscount =100.

1. Te Pito O Te Henua

1 The idea is also strongly presented in *The Merchant of Venice*, 'I hold the world but as the World, Gratiano – / A stage, where every man must play a part, / And mine a sad one' (1.1.76–8) and 'Bring us to this sight and you shall say / I'll prove a busy actor in their play' (3.4.62). It also runs throughout *Hamlet*. In fact, *Hamlet* is a key work in the English canon that extensively explores the performance of social roles from the symbolic to the subversive. These range form the deliberate socially prescribed performance of Polonius within the Royal Court, through the attempt of Hamlet to take on alternative roles and his inability to perform them, to the inability to resist performing within roles defined, not by the self, but by social and familial forces seen in Ophelia.

2. Forces at Play

1 The copy I acquired through eBay was a twenty-sixth printing of the fifth English language publication of the book. The five publishers listed in the printing history are Putnam, Souvenir Press, Universe Book Club, six-part National Enquirer serialization, and Bantam.

2 See also Adams (1983).
3 William Dampier spent 1679 to 1691 as a pirate, 'plundering ships in the
   West Indies and Central America, and eventually making his way across the
   Pacific to the Philippines, the East Indies, and Australia.' He published his
   journal, dedicated to the president of the Royal Society, in 1697. His works
   were subsequently often included with the publications of more explicitly
   scientific expeditions, because his observations of people, places, and natural history were perceived as astute. From 'Voyages: Scientific Circumnavi-
   gations 1679–1859,' An Exhibition of Rare Books from the Linda Hall
   Library of Science, Engineering, and Technology, Kansas City Missouri.
4 See the essays of Viscount Henry St John Bolingbroke's, written in the persona of Calib D'Anvers as *The Craftsman: Being a Critique of the Times* (1727).
5 Several key earlier voyage texts increasing such texts' subsequent popularity were W. Dampier, *A New Voyage round the World* (1697); John Hawkesworth, *An Account of the Voyages Undertaken by the Order of His Present
   Majesty for making Discoveries in the Southern Hemisphere, and Successively Performed by Commodore Byron, Captain Wallis, Captain Carteret and Captain Cook,
   in the Dolphin, the Swallow and the Endeavour* (1773); and L.A. Bougainville.
   *Voyage autor du monde, par la frégate du roi la Boudeuse et la flûte l'Étoile; en
   1766, 1767, 1768* (1771).

3. The Dutch

1 Herbert von Saher, fellow of the Easter Island Foundation, personal correspondence with author, 23 March 2004.
2 The literacy and journal keeping of 'low-ranking' Behrens is not unique to
   eighteenth-century Pacific travel writing. Ordinary seaman Heinrich Zimmerman, a 'jack of all trades from the Palatine,' was aboard the *Discovery* on
   James Cook's third voyage when Cook was killed in Hawaii. He kept notes
   in German on the experience, including decipherable transcriptions of the
   Hawaiian language that recorded the Hawaiian's impressions of Cook as
   the Hawaiian god Lono. Much like Behrens, Zimmerman was overlooked
   by the admiralty when it tried to sequester all shipboard records of the expedition to prevent other accounts from reaching print before the official-
   sponsored version of Cook and his successor on the voyage, James King. In
   fact, Zimmerman managed to precede the official publication with *Reise um
   die Welt mit Captaine Cook* (1781) (Beaglehole 1968, lxxxix).
3 The Dutch journals of the officers emerged more decidedly from this newer
   discursive space, but because of their confiscation, they did not influence
   the eighteenth-century perception of the island.

4 Matthys Balen is described by Benezit in the *Dictionnaire critique et documen-taire des peintres, sculpteurs, dessinateurs et graveurs* (Paris: Librairie Gruend, 1976) as a 'Flemish [?] painter from Dordrecht, 1684–1766.' Karla Vander-sypen, curator of the Special Collections Library, University of Michigan, thinks he should be described as Dutch, not Flemish. She goes on to say that as his name is followed by the abbreviation 'inv.' (i.e., 'invenit,' it means he was the inventor or original artist, rather than 'fec.' (i.e., 'fecit,' meaning the one who made the image at hand). Based on this information, Vandersypen assumes that Balen made the original image from which the engraving in the book was engraved, but that he was not himself the engraver. No engraver is identified on this plate, or on any of the other four plates in the book. Balen's name as 'inv.' appears as well on three of the other plates (Vandersyper, personal correspondence with the author).

5 It is worth noting at this point in the analysis of the first European text about Easter Island that, at the same time as it was being written, a mirror narra-tive was being developed on the island about the strangers who had mate-rialized off shore. As assumptions and evaluations were being made by Europeans about the islanders, assumptions and evaluations were being made on the island about the strangers. While it is not the purpose of this study to examine the island narrative, certain of its key elements will be con-sidered against the European actions and cultural objects that shaped so sig-nificant a response within the island culture. We shall see, for example, that as cultural objects were being acquired for eventual display in European private collections and museums, European objects were being collected for individual and community display, ceremony, and spectacle on the island.

6 Extensive discussions of the different perceptions of reality in many indige-nous cultures of the Pacific Islands and Pacific Rim and the notions of prop-erty, gifts, and giving within those realities can be found in Mauss (1966), Hyde (1979), and Ross (1992).

7 Within Rapanui society, chickens provided the most valuable food as a mark of respect when given as gifts (Pollock 1993, 156).

8 The Behrens's paraphrased narrative was still representing the island textu-ally in English as late as 1931 as seen in the Robert Casey text *Easter Island Home of the Scornful Gods*, even though the Bolton Granvill Corney transla-tion form the German had been available since 1903.

9 This book is published for a wide 'Commonwealth' readership in London, New York, Toronto, Auckland, Sydney, Mexico City, New Delhi, Hong Kong, and Buenos Aires.

10 Grant McCall, author of *Rapanui Tradition and Survival on Easter Island* (1994), must have misread this statement as a literal description when he writes:

'The huge stone figure, towering over the Dutch, with its red topknot, draped with a cape from shoulder to base, astonished the visitors' (32).

4. The Spanish

1 *Lloyd's Evening Post and British Chronicle*, no. 2249, 29 November to 2 December 1771, 529. The same announcement appeared in the *London Chronicle*, no. 2335, 28 November to 30 November 1771, 526; and in the *St James's Chronicle* of even date, no. 1680.
2 One conjecture by Alfred Métraux is that Davis Island is possibly Mangareva (Métraux 1957, 32).
3 The statement that there are only about seventy women in a total of nearly a thousand souls suggests a lack of imagination about the possibility that women and children were being kept secluded or protected during the visit of the Spanish to the island.
4 See Grant McCall's book *Rapanui: Tradition and Survival on Easter Island* (1994) for speculation on the breakdown of the gifting tradition in the wake of the eighteenth-century expeditions to the island.
5 A stoep (stoop) is a South African Dutch term for a veranda or porch.
6 This description by Routledge is echoed in another source of ethnographic information about the island. Ramón Campbell, a physician from Chile who resided on Rapanui for several years in the 1960s, investigated Rapanui musical history. His essay 'The Performing Arts of Rapanui' (1994) identifies a tradition of singing called Koro 'ei and Koro 'ate 'atua 'koro. They are described as songs sung by large groups of people as a form of worshipping the gods in honour of past events, and songs that alluded to the sporadic navigations of the eighteenth century, and to the slave raids of the nineteenth century (187).
7 Rongorongo is the name given to the hieroglyphs of the Rapanui who are the only Polynesian people known to have invented a system of writing. It consists of a base of one hundred and twenty separate hieroglyphs arranged in combinations that make over 2,000 complex symbols. The Rapanui describe this writing as having originated on the island in 400 CE with Hotu Matua, the leader of the original settlers.

5. The British

1 This layering of ancient European tropes such as paradise, or the lost city of Atlantis, found a base in the invention of 'Easter Island' in its textual guise as the Lost Continent of Mu. For examples of twentieth-century books con-

tinuing to promote the marvellous 'Easter Island,' see Pauwels and Bergier (1972), Lee and Moore (1975), Childress (1988), and Hancock and Faiia (1998).

2 A discussion of the eighteenth-century discourse on civilization as a counterpoint to the concept of the 'noble savage' is in chapter 6, 'The French.'

3 The 'long eighteenth century' is a term used to describe the period from about 1650 to 1850, Milton to Keats, or roughly from the end of the Renaissance to the beginning of the Industrial Revolution. Retrieved 16 April 2006 from *Rutgers University*, 'Eighteenth-Century Resources,' www.andromeda.rutgers.edu/~jlynch/18th/.

4 '*The Seasons*, one of the most popular (and frequently reprinted and illustrated) of English poems, was immensely influential, offering both in style and subject a new departure from the urbanity of [Alexander] Pope and developing in a highly distinctive manner the range of topographical poetry ... Thomson contributed greatly to the vogue for the picturesque and his landscapes were influenced by those of Claude Poussin ...' (Drabble 2000, 979). This work also influenced Hodges.

5 Richard Wilson painted a series of illustrations of the 'Solitude' from *The Seasons* by James Thomson. The earliest dates from 1762 during Hodges's apprenticeship to him and can be seen to be referenced in Hodges's painting of *Pickersgill Harbour* executed in New Zealand in 1773 (Stuebe 1979, 24). Hodges's aggrandized natural landscapes exceeded the 'scope of his own painting master' in a continuum that 'would reach its climax some seventy years later in the engulfing vortices of Turner's storms' (Rosenblum 1971, 210).

6 The eyes sockets of the moai were not carved out until they were mounted upon their ahu. The majority of the moai seen in photographs are those buried up to their necks in the quarry and these have no eye sockets at all. The eye sockets were carved at the ahu and provided with eyes of white coral with red scoria irises that seem only to have been inserted into the carved sockets for ceremonial occasions, since they were not commented upon by the explorers. Broken coral eyes have been found during excavations around the ahu. The empty sockets of the moai standing on ahu have a particularly haunting appearance. (Personal observation and discussion of the island with José Ramírez, 2004.)

7 In eighteenth-century England, antiquarians were busily recording the surviving stone elements of their own previous incarnations as Celts and Romans, see Rosemary Sweet, *Antiquaries: The Discovery of the Past in Eighteenth-Century Britain* (2004). These micro-historical investigations on local British soil were not viewed as evidence of the failure of contemporary

social cultural production, but recognized as vestiges of past cultural difference, now superseded by contemporary beliefs, practices, and icons. Yet the floating historians of the discovery voyages in the Pacific were not able to see the parallel of ancient and contemporary development on Rapanui.

8 The reasons for the lengthy delay in publishing can be found in *The Resolution Journal of Johann Reinhold Forster 1772–1775* (Hoare 1982), and in *A Voyage Round the World* by George Forster (Thomas and Berghof [1777] 2000).

9 Cook's journal publication was sold through presubscription. Like John Newbery's edited volume *The World Displayed* (1759), which contained the Behren's text, Cook's *A Voyage towards the South Pole* went into multiple printings over the years following the voyage and then continued to stay before the public eye in numerous abridged versions up to and including today.

10 Wahai could be Tahai, a place name, just north of where Cook landed. Maroo is likely Miru, the name of an island clan. 'Maroo-wahai' is explaining where specifically in his world he is from and of which clan he is a member.

11 As suggested above, one likely reason for the very reduced circumstances of the Rapanui during the Cook visit may have been devastation by a epidemic resulting from the recent visit of the Spanish. This may also have happened after the Dutch visit, but the islanders had forty-eight years to recover from its effects before the next foreign visit. If a pandemic brought by the Spanish had ravaged the island population, the effects would still have been noticeable only four years later. Both physician Ramón Campbell, in his essay 'The Performing Arts of Rapanui' (1993), and Thor Heyerdahl in *Aku-Aku* (1958), refer to the pandemics that swept the island in the 1950s and 1960s while they were residents there. These pandemics caused fatalities each year after the arrival of the annual supply ship from Chile. Such assaults upon the Rapanui immune systems did not stop until regular air travel began after 1967. Such a response to foreign disease was also experienced by the Aboriginals in North America during early contact with Europeans. Death from introduced epidemics are estimated to have reduced their populations to less than a tenth of their pre-contact numbers in the early years of New England settlement. The isolation of the Rapanui population would have given it a similar vulnerability.

12 Wright used an adolescent picture book, *Easter Island: Mystery of the Stone Giants* (1995), by Catharine and Michel Orliac and *Easter Island, Earth Island* (1992) by Paul Bahn and John Flenley, in which they conclude a discussion of palaeo-environmental and archaeological research with a speculative and

somewhat apocalyptic vision. These appear to be his only sources for information on the island. His thesis about moai-based environmental destruction is appraised in chapter 7, 'Cultural Imaginary to Cultural Memory.'

6. The French

1 From the *Records of the African Association 1788–1831*, ed. and intro. by Robin Hallet for the Royal Geographical Society (London: Thomas Nelson, 1964), 10.

2 Pierre Loti was part of a French expedition to the island, aboard the *Flora*, to 'acquire' a moai in 1872. He wrote in *Reflets sur la sombre route* about his impressions of the place in relation to the text of La Pérouse and his own experiences. One of his assertions was that no one knows who carved the moai.

3 Theodor De Bry, a Frankfurt goldsmith, engraver, printseller and bookseller, started in 1590 to produce a series of volumes with stylized engravings that chronicled many of the earliest expeditions to the Americas.

4 Charles Le Brun (1619–90) was the dominant painter and art theorist of Louis XIV's reign. He went to Rome in 1642 working under Classicist Poussin. In 1662 he was raised to the nobility and named *Premier Paintre du roi*. As director of the Academie, he imposed a codified system of orthodoxy in matters of art, providing the official standards of artistic correctness formulated on the basis of the Classicism of Poussin. Much like Reynolds would do in the next century, he gave authority to the view that every aspect of artistic creation could be reduced to teachable rule and precept. Many of the leading French artists of the next generation trained in his studio. (Pioch 2002)

5 For online images of these works, see www.hermitagemuseum.org.

6 Several suggestions have been postulated for the attack on the French shore party: retaliation for the 'accidental' killing of a Samoan aboard one of the French ships the day before, the slighting of a chief who was thrown overboard the previous day, or, most likely, the extensive trading with one island group and the refusal to trade with another group, even as it was their water that was being taken for the ship stores.

7. Cultural Imaginary to Cultural Memory

1 Extrapolating from the thesis popularized by Jared Diamond (1999) that '[t]hroughout the Americas diseases introduced with Europeans spread from tribe to tribe far in advance of the Europeans themselves, killing an

estimated 95% of the pre-Columbian Native American population,' it is plausible that the large numbers of human bones on ahus, and the evidence of farmland lying fallow, were the direct result of the ravages of an epidemic. The isolation of the Rapanui population from contact with outsiders would have given it a similar vulnerability to foreign germs (78).

2 The year 1540 is currently considered to be the start of the new social order of the birdman competition based on the age of archaeological evidence at the ceremonial site of Orongo (Drake 1991, 32).

3 Editions from first and third printing are available through online second-hand booksellers as I write. Tom Christopher, the vice-president of the Easter Island Foundation, writes, 'It was reprinted in 1926 again by Caimann-Levy. A Spanish translation of the Ile de Paques portion appeared in 1903 along with works [by] Gana and Ballesteros. Dos Passos in *Easter Island* had the first English translation in 1977. A reprint entitled *Journal d'un aspirit de la Flore* was published in 1988, another one in Spanish in 1998, and of course [Ann Altman's] translation last year. In addition Loti's drawings and romantic notions of the island were widely published in *Globus, L'Illustration, Harpers' Weekly*' (personal correspondence, 2005).

4 See *House of Mystery,* 'The Stone Sentinels of Easter Island' (1958); *Tales to Astonish,* 'Where Creatures Roam: This Is Thorg' (1960); *The Mighty Thor,* 'A Kingdom Lost!' (1962); *Where Monsters Dwell,* 'I Was Trapped by the Things on Easter Island' (1973).

5 See Van Tilburg (1994, 52) for a more detailed explanation of this version of Rapa Nui history.

6 The New Horizon Series includes such titles as *Ancient Egypt, Ancient Greece, The Celts, The Aztecs, Mummies, Dinosaurs, Vampires,* and *Voodoo.*

7 For a detailed description of 'The Statue Project, ' an archaeological survey that divided the island into forty-five quadrants, see Van Tilburg (1994). There are a total of 397 statues in the main quarry; 54 moai were not carved in the main quarry, but in small regional quarries; 2 are still in a small quarry; 269 are on ahu; 9 are incorporated into enlarged ahu; 46 outside the quarry are interpreted as having been abandoned in transport. These categories as well as a designation called 'other' total 887 moai that had been recorded as of 1994.

8 For a recent example of references to 'Easter Island' cannibalism, see *The Journal and Letters of Captain Charles Bishop on the North-West Coast of America, in the Pacific and in New South Wales, 1794–1799,* reproduced by permission of the Hakluyt Society in the *Rapa Nui Journal* 19, no. 1 (May 2005). Bishop was the guardian on this voyage of a ten-year-old boy, the son of his late captain. The islanders who swam out to the ship, he wrote, 'solicited me

often to let him go on shore ... Upon this defeat one of the Women took him in her arms and gave him her Breast, casting a look of so benign and Gentle a description that I am well persuaded they would have taken care of him, and that it was not, for the unkind supposition of their being cannibals suggested by some of the Crew, that they wished to have him onshore. In confirmation of this idea I observed that they had not a weapon, or a Scar or a spot or Blemish on their skins; and if they were cannibals they would certainly have wars, which I believe is not the case.' Attached to this last sentence is a footnote from the Hakluyt publication that writes over the captain's opinion with an alternative one positioned within the Pacific paradise/hell discourse. It reads, 'The islanders engaged in both war and cannibalism, the latter sometimes the result of "a simple liking for human flesh that could impel a man to kill for no other reason than his desire for fresh meat (Métraux 1957, 103)." In this light even the wet-nursing of chubby young Learne can appear sinister' (Bishop 2005, 63).

9 Rongorongo, the only written record of any Polynesian group, was destroyed in two ways. The first was by South American colonizers who, through the Peruvian slave raids, killed all the high-ranking priests who were the literate element of the Rapanui society. The second was by the Catholic missionaries who considered the Rongorongo tablets vestiges of a pagan past and had the Rapanui destroy those they still had in their possession. Today, Rongorongo tablets are often positioned in a context that downplays the accomplishment of developing such a script by emphasizing its conception as a response to the signing of the Spanish Proclamation of 1770 rather than celebrating it as a Rapanui cultural development (see Fischer 1997).

8. An Educational Supplement

1 See Ann Altman's translation of nineteenth-century Roman Catholic missionary texts in *Early Visitors to Easter Island, 1864–1877* (2004).

2 For a fuller explanation of these ideas, see Beverley Haun, 'From Praxis to Practice: Prospects for Postcolonial Pedagogy in Canadian Public Education' (2004).

Bibliography

Adams, Mark, and Nicholas Thomas. 1999. *Cook's Sites: Revisiting History.* Dunedin, NZ: University of Otago Press.

Adams, Percy G. 1983. *Travel Literature and the Evolution of the Novel.* Lexington: University Press of Kentucky.

Addison, Joseph. [1712] 1975. *Essays in Criticism and Literary Theory.* Edited by John Loftis. Northbrook: AHM Publishing.

Ahmed, Sara. 2002. 'Strange Encounters: Embodying Others in Postcoloniality.' In *Embodying Strangers.* London: Routledge.

Altman, Ann M., ed. 2004. *Early Visitors to Easter Island, 1864–1877.* Los Osos: Bearsville Press.

Anderies, J.M. 2000. 'On Modelling Human Behaviour and Institutions in Simple Ecological Economic Systems.' *Ecological Economics* 35: 393–412.

Anderson, Benedict. 1991. *Imagined Communities: Reflections on the Origin and Spread of Nationalism.* 2nd ed. London: Verso.

Ankersmit, F.R. 2001. 'The Sublime Dissociation of the Past: Or How to Be(Come) What One Is No Longer.' *History and Theory* (October): 295–323.

Anonymous. 1727. *Kort en Nauwkeurig Verhall van de Reize Door 3 Schepen in 't Jaar 1721 gedaan.* Amsterdam: n.p.

Anonymous Sailor. 1728. *Tweejaarige Reyze Door De Straat Magellanes En Rondom De Wereld Ter Nader Ontdekkinge Der Onbekende Zuydlanden.* Dordrecht: n.p.

Anthony, Pagden. 1993. *European Encounters with the New World: From Renaissance to Romanticism.* New Haven: Yale University Press.

Antze, Paul, and Michael Lambek, eds. 1996. *Tense Past: Cultural Essays in Trauma and Memory.* New York: Routledge.

Apple, Michael W. 2000. 'The Shock of the Real: Critical Pedagogies and Rightist Reconstructions.' In *Revolutionary Pedagogies: Cultural Politics, Insti-*

tuting Education, and the Discourse of Theory, edited by Peter Pericles Trifonas. New York: Routledge.

Ariosto, Lodovico. [1532] 1983. *Orlando Furioso.* Translated by Guido Waldman. New York: Oxford University Press.

Arnold, Caroline. 2000. *Easter Island: Giant Statues Tell of a Rich and Tragic Past.* New York: Clarion Books.

Ashcroft, Bill, Gareth Griffiths, and Helen Tiffin. 1989. *The Empire Writes Back: Theory and Practice in Post-Colonial Literatures.* New York: Routledge.

Attridge, Derek, Geoffrey Bennington, and Robert Young. 1989. *Post-Structuralism and the Question of History.* New York: Cambridge University Press.

Augé, M. 1995. *Non-Places: Introduction to an Anthropology of Modernity.* London: Verso.

Baarslag, Karl. 1944. *Islands of Adventure.* London: Travel Book Club.

Bacon, Francis, the Right Honourable. Verulam Viscount St Alban. 1627. *New Atlantis: A Worke Unfinished,* Published with *Sylva Sylvarum or a Natural History in Ten Centuries.* London: n.p.

– [1651] 1658. *Sylva Sylvarum or Naturall History in Ten Centuries: Whereunto Is Newly Added the History Naturall and Experimentall of Life and Death or of the Prolongation of Life. Hereunto Is Now Added an Alphabetical Table of the Principall Things Contained in the Ten Centuries.* 7th ed. London: W. Rawley, Dr. of Divinity one of his Magesties Chaplains.

Bahn, Paul G., and John Flenley. 1992. *Easter Island, Earth Island.* New York: Thames and Hudson.

Baldick, Chris. 1990. *The Concise Oxford Dictionary of Literary Terms.* Oxford: Oxford University Press.

Balfour, Henry. 1917. 'Some Ethnological Suggestions in Regard to Easter Island, or Rapanui.' *Folklore* 28: 356–81.

Barbier, Jean Paul. 2001. *Vanished Civilizations.* New York: Assouline Publishing.

Barclay, H. 1899. Vere. *Easter Island and Its Colossal Statues, Plus Separate Map, Plates I–Iii, and Two Sketches.* Adelaide: Royal Geographical Society of Australia.

Barrell, John. 1990. 'The Public Prospect and the Private View.' In *Reading Landscape,* edited by Simon Pugh. Manchester: Manchester University Press.

Barthel, Thomas S. 1978. *The Eighth Land: The Polynesian Discovery and Settlement of Easter Island.* Honolulu: University of Hawaii Press.

Beaglehole, J.C., ed. 1968. *The Voyage of the Endeavour.* 4 vols. Cambridge: Cambridge University Press.

Beasley, H.G. 1923. 'Rapa Nui: A Stone Image.' *Man* 23, no. 71.

Beckett, Sister Wendy. 1994. *The Story of Painting*. New York: Dorling Kindersley.

Beer, Gillian. 1970. *The Romance*. London: Methuen.

Behrens, Carl. 1739. *Histoire de l'expédition de trois vaisseaux, envoyés par la Compagnie des Indes Occidentales des Provinces Unies aux Terres Australes in Mdcxxi*. Den Haag: n.p.

– 1759. 'Easter Island.' In *The World Displayed; or, a Curious Collection of Voyages and Travels Selected from the Writers of All Nations*, edited by John Newbery. Vol. 9. London: n.p.

Beilharz, Peter, ed. 2001. *A Bauman Reader*. Malden, MA: Blackwell.

Benhabib, Seyla. 1999. 'Sexual Difference and Collective Identities: Towards a New Global Constellation.' *Journal of Women in Culture and Society* 24, no. 2: 1–24.

Benhabib, Seyla, and Drucilla Cornell. 1987. *Feminism as Critique: Essays on the Politics of Gender in Late-Capitalist Societies. Feminist Perspectives from Polity Press*. Cambridge: Polity Press.

Benjamin, Jessica. 1998. 'The Shadow of the Other Subject: Intersubjectivity and Feminist Theory.' In *The Shadow of the Other: Intersubjectivity and Gender in Psychoanalysis*. New York: Routledge.

Benjamin, Walter. 1969. 'The Task of the Translator.' In *Illuminations*. New York: Schocken Books.

Bennett, Tony. 1994. 'The Exhibitionary Complex.' In *Power/Culture/History*, edited by Nicholas B. Dirks. Princeton: Princeton University Press.

Benson, Captain. 1914. *Captain Benson's Own Story*. San Francisco: James H. Barry Co.

Berg, L.D., and R.A. Kearns. 1996. 'Naming as Norming: Race, Gender and the Identity Politics of Naming Places in Aotearoa/New Zealand.' *Environment and Planning D: Society and Space* 14, no. 1: 99–122.

Berkeley, George. [1721] 1953. 'An Essay Towards Preventing the Ruin of Great Britain.' In *Philosophical Writings*, edited by A.A. Luce and T.E. Jessop. Vol. 6. London: Nelson.

Berkeley, University of California, Museum of Paleontology. 1996. 'Carl Linnaeus (1707–1778).' Retrieved 10 June 2005 from www.ucmp.berkeley.edu/history/linnaeus.html.

Bermingham, Ann, and John Brewer, eds. 1997. *The Consumption of Culture, 1600–1800: Image, Object, Text*. London: Routledge.

Bernasconi, Robert. 1999. 'The Third Party. Levinas on the Intersection of the Ethical and the Political.' *Journal of the British Society for Phenomenology* 30, no. 1: 76–87.

Bhabha, Homi K. 1990. *Nation and Narration*. London: Routledge.

– 1994. *The Location of Culture*. London: Routledge.

Bhattacharyya, Gargi, John Gabriel, and Stephen Small. 2002. *Race and Power: Global Racism in the Twenty-First Century*. New York: Routledge.

Bierbach, Annette, and Horst Cain. 1993. 'The Rapanui Pantheon.' In *Easter Island Studies*. Oxford: Oxbow Books.

– 1996. *Religion and Language of Easter Island: An Ethnolinguistic Analysis of Religious Key Words of Rapa Nui in Their Austronesian Context*. Berlin: D. Reimer.

Biesta, Gert. 1998. 'Say You Want a Revolution ... Suggestions for the Impossible Future of Critical Pedagogy.' *Educational Theory* 48, no. 4: 499.

Bilger, Burkhard. 2004. 'The Height Gap.' *New Yorker*, 5 April: 38–45.

Bishop, Charles. 2005. 'The Journal and Letters of Captain Charles Bishop on the North-West Coast of America, in the Pacific and in New South Wales, 1794–1799.' *Rapa Nui Journal* 19, no. 1: 61–3.

Blake, William. [1794] 1927. *Songs of Experience*. London: E. Benn.

Blunt, Alison, and Gillian Rose. 1994. *Writing Women and Space: Colonial and Postcolonial Geographies*. New York: Guilford Press.

Boeckman, Charles. 1965. *Unsolved Riddles of the Ages*. New York: Criterion Books.

Boler, Megan. 1999. 'The Risks of Empathy: Interrogating Multiculturalism's Gaze.' In *Feeling Power: Emotions and Education*. New York: Routledge.

Bolingbroke, Vicount Henry Saint-John. 1721. *The Craftsman: Being a Critique of the Times*. London: n.p.

Bootes, Henry. 1928. *Deep Sea Bubbles: or the Cruise of the Anna Lombard*. London: Ernest Benn Limited.

Bordo, Jonathan. 1992–3. 'Jack Pine – Wilderness Sublime or: The Erasure of the Aboriginal Presence from the Landscape.' *Journal of Canadian Studies* 27, no. 4: 98–128.

Borofsky, R. 1997. 'Cook, Lono, Obeyesekere, and Sahlins.' *Current Anthropology* 38: 255–82.

– ed. 2000. *Remembrance of Pacific Pasts: An Invitation to Remake History*. Honolulu: University of Hawaii Press.

Bougainville, L.A. 1771. *Voyage Autor Du Monde, Par La Frégate Du Roi La Boudeuse Et La Flûte L'étoile; En 1766, 1767, 1768*. Paris: n.p.

Bourdieu, Pierre. 1979. *Distinction: A Social Critique of the Judgement of Taste*. Cambridge: Harvard University Press.

– 1981. 'On Symbolic Power.' In *Language and Symbolic Power*. Cambridge: Harvard University Press.

– 1986. 'The Forms of Capital.' In *Handbook of Theory and Research for the Sociology of Education*, edited by J.G. Richardson. New York: Greenwood Press.

Bourget, Marie-Noelle, Lucette Valensi, and Nathan Wachtel, eds. 1990. *Between Memory and History*. London: Harwood.

Brander, J.A., and M.S. Taylor. 1998. 'The Simple Economics of Easter Island: A Ricardo-Malthus Model of Renewable Resource Use.' *American Economic Review* 88: 119–38.

Breeden, Robert L., ed. 1979. *Mysteries of the Ancient World*. Washington, DC: National Geographic Society.

Brewer, John. 1997. *The Pleasures of the Imagination*. New York: Farrar, Straus and Giroux.

Britzman, Deborah. 1991. *Practice Makes Practice: A Critical Study of Learning to Teach*. Albany: State University of New York Press.

– 1995. 'Beyond Innocent Readings: Educational Ethnography as a Crisis of Representation.' In *Continuity and Contradiction: The Futures of the Sociology of Education*, edited by William T. Pink and George W. Noblit. Cresskill, NJ: Hampton Press.

– 1998. *Lost Subjects, Contested Objects: Toward a Psychoanalytic Inquiry of Learning*. Albany: State University of New York Press.

Bronowski, Jacob. 1973. *The Ascent of Man*. London: Macdonald Futura Publishers.

Brown, J. 1979. Macmillan. *The Riddle of the Pacific*. New York: AMS Press.

Brydon, Diana. 1997. *Curricular Reform and Postcolonial Studies*. Keynote Address at Red Deer College Alberta. Available online from www.publish .uwo.ca/-dbrydon/red_deer.html.

Buber, Martin, and Franz Rosenzweig. 1994. 'Rosenzweig's "Scripture and Word" and Buber's "On Word Choice in Translating the Bible" and Everett Fox on "Translating the Bible."' In *Scripture and Translation*. Bloomington: University of Indiana Press.

Bull, Ben. 2005. 'Review: A Short History of Progress.' *Raise the Hammer*, 28 November.

Burke, Edmund. [1757] 1968. *Edmund Burke on Taste, on the Sublime and Beautiful, Reflections on the French Revolution, a Letter to a Noble Lord*. Edited by Charles W. Elliot. Harvard: Harvard Classics.

– [1757] 1990. *A Philosophical Enquiry into the Origin of Our Ideas of the Sublime and Beautiful*. Edited by Adam Phillips. Oxford: Oxford University Press.

Burke, Malcolm K. 1955. 'The World's Most Durable Mystery.' *Reader's Digest* 123–6.

Burney, James. 1803–16. *A Chronological History of the Discoveries in the South Sea*. 5 vols. London: Luke Hansard.

Cahudry, Lubna Naizer. 2000. 'Researching My People.' In *Working the Ruins:*

Feminist Poststructural Theory and Methods in Education, edited by Elizabeth St Pierre and Wanda S. Pillow. New York: Routledge.

Calder, Alex, Jonathan Lamb, and Bridgit Orr, eds. 1999. *Voyages and Beaches: Pacific Encounters, 1769–1840.* Honolulu: University of Hawaii Press, 1999.

Campbell, Ramón. 1993. 'The Performing Arts of Rapanui.' In *Easter Island Studies,* edited by Steven Fischer. Oxford: Oxbow Books.

Carroll, Allen. 1892. 'The Easter Island Inscriptions and the Way in Which They Are Translated.' *Journal of the Polynesian Society* 1: 103–6 and 233–53.

– 1898. 'The Mystery of Easter Island, Its Statues, Platforms and Stonehouses, &C.' *Science of Man* (Sydney) 1: 246–7.

– 1900. 'Easter Island and Its People.' *Science of Man (Sydney)* 3: 159–60.

– 1907. 'Easter Island.' *Science of Man* (Sydney) 9 and 10.

Carswell, John. 1960. *The South Sea Bubble.* London: Cresset.

Casey, Robert Joseph. 1931. *Easter Island: Home of the Scornful Gods.* London: Elkin Mathews and Marrot.

Caughie, John, and Annette Kuhn. 1992. *The Sexual Subject: A Screen Reader in Sexuality.* New York: Routledge.

Cervantes Saavedra, Miguel de. [1605] 2003. *Don Quixote De La Mancha.* Translated by Edith Grossman, and edited by Harold Bloom. New York: Harper Collins.

Chakrabarty, Dipesh. 2000. 'Introduction: The Idea of Provincializing Europe and Translating Life-Worlds into Labor and History.' In *Provincializing Europe: Postcolonial Thought and Historical Difference.* Princeton: Princeton University Press.

Chard, Chloe. 1996, 'Crossing Boundaries and Exceeding Limits: Destabilization, Tourism, and the Sublime.' In *Transports: Travel, Pleasure, and Imaginative Geography, 1600–1830,* edited by Chloe Chard and Helen Langdon. New Haven: Yale University Press, 1996.

Charola, A. Elena, Robert J. Koestler, and Gianni Lombardi. 1990. 'Lavas and Volcanic Tuffs.' *Proceedings of the International Meeting, Easter Island, Chile, 25–31 October 1990.* Edited by A. Elena Charola. Rome: Iccrom.

Chatterjee, Partha. 1993. *The Nation and Its Fragments: Colonial and Postcolonial Histories.* Princeton: Princeton University Press.

Childress, David Hatcher. 1988. *Lost Cities of Ancient Lemuria and the Pacific.* Stelle, IL: Adventures Unlimited Press.

Chrisman, Laura, Benita Parry, and English Association. 2000. *Postcolonial Theory and Criticism: Essays and Studies.* Cambridge: D.S. Brewer.

Chubb, Lawrence John, and Constance Richardson. 1971. *Geology of Galapagos, Cocos, and Easter Islands; with Petrology of Galapagos Islands.* Edited by Honolulu Bernice Pauahi Bishop Museum. New York: Kraus Reprint.

Churchill, William. 1912. *Easter Island, the Rapanui Speech and the Peopling of Southeast Polynesia*. Carnegie Institution of Washington. Publications, No. 174. Washington, DC: Carnegie Institute of Washington.

– 1978. *Easter Island, the Rapanui Speech, and the Peopling of Southeast Polynesia*. New York: AMS Press.

Churchward, James. 1926. *The Lost Continent of Mu*. Albuquerque: Brotherhood of Life.

Clark, Bouverie F. 1899. *Reporting Calling at Sala-Y-Gomez and Easter Islands*. Adelaide: Royal Geographical Society of Australia, South Australia Branch.

Clark, Liesl. 'Easter Island.' Narrated by Stacey Keach. *Secrets of Lost Empires II*. Written and produced by Liesl Clark. Boston: WGBH, 2000. Video cassette.

Clark, S.H. 1999. *Travel Writing and Empire: Postcolonial Theory in Transit*. New York: St Martin's Press.

Clifford, James. 1988. *The Predicament of Culture: Twentieth-Century Ethnography, Literature, and Art*. Cambridge, MA: Harvard University Press.

– 1997. *Routes: Travel and Translation in the Late Twentieth Century*. Cambridge, MA: Harvard University Press.

Clifford, James, George E. Marcus, and School of American Research. 1986. *Writing Culture: The Poetics and Politics of Ethnography*. A School of American Research Advanced Seminar. Berkeley: University of California Press.

Colley, Linda. 1992. *Britons: Forging the Nation, 1707–1837*. New Haven: Yale University Press.

Combe, Sonia. 1994. *Archives interdites: Les peurs françaises face à l'histoire contemporaine*. Paris: Albin Michel.

Connerton, Paul. 1989. *How Societies Remember*. Cambridge: Cambridge University Press.

Cook, James. 1777. *A Voyage Towards the South Pole, and Round the World: Performed in His Majesty's Ships the Resolution and Adventure, in the Years 1772, 1773, 1774, and 1775*. 2 vols. London: W. Strahan and T. Cadell.

– 1955–68. *The Journals of Captain James Cook on His Voyages of Discovery*. Edited by J.C. Beaglehole. 3 vols. Cambridge: Hakluyt Society.

Cook, Terry. 2000. *Archival Science and Postmodernism: New Formulations for Old Concepts*. Available online from http://www.mybestdocs.com/cook-t-postmod-p1-00.htm.

Cooke, George H. 1899. *Annual Report of the Board of Regents of the Smithsonian Institution for the Year Ending June 30, 1897*. Washington, DC: Smithsonian Institution Press.

Cooper, A.A., 3rd Earl of Shaftesbury. 1710. *Soliloquy: Or, Advice to an Author*. London: n.p.

– 1716. *Several Letters Written by a Noble Lord to a Young Man at the University.* London: n.p.

Cooper, Gordon. 1949. *Isles of Romance and Mystery.* London: Lutterworth Press.

Cornell, Drucilla. 1992. *The Philosophy of the Limit.* New York: Routledge.

Corney, Bolton Granvill. 1917. 'Notes on Easter Island.' *Geographical Journal* (London) 50: 57–68.

– ed. 1903. *The Voyage of Captain Don Felipe Gonzalez to Easter Island, 1770–1771.* Vol. 13. Cambridge: Hakluyt Society.

Cosmas Indicopleustes. 1897. *Topographia Christiana* 6ad. Translated by J.W. McCrindle. London: n.p.

Cowell, A. 1999. 'The Apocalypse of Paradise and the Salvation of the West: Nightmare Visions of the Future in the Pacific Eden.' *Cultural Studies Routledge London* 13, no. 1: 138–60.

Croft, Thomas. 1875. *Two Letters Accompanying the Presentation of 25 Photographs of Hieroglyphics at Alia from Easter Island.* Proceedings of the California Academy of Sciences.

Cunningham, Hilary. 1998. 'Colonial Encounters in Postcolonial Contexts.' *Critique of Anthropology* 18, no. 4: 205–33.

Dalrymple, Alexander, ed. [1770] 1967. *An Historical Collection of the Several Voyages and Discoveries in the South Pacific Ocean.* 2 vols. in 1. New York: De Capo Press.

Dalton, O.M. 1904. 'On an Inscribed Wooden Tablet from Easter Island (Rapa Nui) in the British Museum.' *Man* 4, no. 1.

Dalton, T.R., and R.M. Coates. 2000. 'Could Institutional Reform Have Saved Easter Island?' *Journal of Evolutionary Economics* 10: 489–505.

Dampier, William. 1697. *A New Voyage Round the World.* London: James Knapton.

Davies, Bronwyn. 1989. *Frogs, Snails and Feminist Tales: Preschool Children and Gender.* Sydney: Allen and Unwin.

– 2000. 'The Subject of Poststructuralism.' In *A Body of Writing: 1990–1999.* Walnut Creek, CA: Alta Mira Press.

de Cuchilleros, Jorges. 1984. *The Invention of History.* Translated by Manuel de Medeiros. Madrid: Prado Editores.

Defoe, Daniel. 1719. *The Life and Strange Surprising Adventures of Robinson Crusoe of York, Mariner.* London: n.p.

Del Casino, Vincent, and Stephen Hanna. 2000. 'Representations and Identities in Tourism Map Spaces.' *Progress in Human Geography* 24, no. 1: 23–46.

Dening, Greg. 2001. 'Afterword: On the Befores and Afters of the Encounter.' In *Cultural Memory: Reconfiguring History and Identity in the Postcolonial Pacific,* edited by J.M. Mageo. Honolulu: University of Hawaii Press.

Dennis, John. [1704] 1971. *The Grounds of Criticism in Poetry.* Menston: Scholar Press.

Derrida, Jacques. 1978. *Writing and Difference.* Translated by Alan Bass. Chicago: University of Chicago Press.

– 1982. 'White Mythology: Metaphor in the Text of Philosophy.' Translated by A. Bass. *Margins of Philosophy.* Chicago: University of Chicago Press.

– 1995. 'Archive Fever: A Freudian Impression.' *Diacritics* 25, no. 2: 9–63.

– 1998. *Of Grammatology.* Translated by Gayatri Chakravorty Spivak. Baltimore: Johns Hopkins University Press.

Descartes, René. 1911. *Philosophical Works.* Translated by Elizabeth Haldane and G.R.T. Ross. 2 vols. Cambridge: Cambridge University Press.

Diamond, Jared. 1999. *Guns, Germs, and Steel: The Fates of Human Societies.* New York: Norton.

– 2005. *Collapse: How Societies Choose to Fail or Succeed.* New York: Viking.

Dimitriadis, Greg, and Cameron McCarthy. 2001. *Reading and Teaching the Postcolonial: From Baldwin to Basquait and Beyond.* New York: Teachers College Press.

Diprose, Rosalyn. 2001. 'Here I Am by the Grace of the Other and Feminism is in Disgrace: Levinas and Postcolonialism.' *Studies in Practical Philosophy* 3, no. 1: 1–9.

Dirks, Nicholas B., Geoff Eley, and Sherry B. Ortner, eds. 1994. *Culture/Power/History: A Reader in Contemporary Social Theory.* Princeton: University of Princeton Press.

Dos Passos, John. 1971. *Easter Island; Island of Enigmas.* Garden City, NY: Doubleday.

Drabble, Margaret, ed. 2000. *The Oxford Companion to English Literature.* 6th ed. New York: Oxford University Press.

Drainie, Bronwyn. 2004. 'A Short History of Progress.' *Quill and Quire* (December).

Drake, Alan. 1991. *Easter Island: Ceremonial Center of Orongo.* El Cerrito, CA: Easter Island Foundation.

Dreyfus, H.L., and P. Rabinow, eds. 1982. *Michel Foucault: Beyond Structuralism and Hermeneutics.* Chicago: University of Chicago Press.

Dunmore, John, trans. and ed. 1994. *The Journal of Jean-François De Galaup De La Pérouse, 1785–1788.* 2 vols. London: The Hakluyt Society.

Duran, Eduardo, and Bonnie Duran. 1995. *Native American Postcolonial Psychology.* Albany: State University of New York Press.

Earp, T.W. 1945. *French Painting from the Seventeenth Century to To-Day.* London: Avalon Press, and Collins.

'Easter Island.' *The London Packer or Lloyd's New Evening Post,* 25 April 1777.

Easter Island Foundation. 2001. 'Visitor Guide: A Short History of Easter
    Island.' Retrieved June 2005 from http://islandheritage.org/eihistory.html.
Ebensten, Hanns. 2001. *Trespassers on Easter Island*. Key West: Ketch and Yawl
    Press.
Edge-Partington, James, and Charles Heape. 1901. 'On the Origin of the
    Stone Figures and Incised Tablets from Easter Island.' *Man* 1, no. 7: 9–10.
Edney, Mathew. 1993. 'The Patronage of Science and the Creation of Imperial
    Space.' *Cartographica* 30, no. 1: 61–7.
Edward, Dayes. 1980. 'William Hodges.' In *The Works of the Late Edward Dayes*,
    edited by E.W. Brayley. London: n.p.
Edwards, Edward. 1808. 'William Hodges.' In *Anecdotes of Painters Who Have
    Resided or Been Born in England: With Critical Remarks on Their Productions*.
    London: n.p.
Elias, Norbert. 1976. 'Introduction: A Theoretical Essay on Established and Out-
    sider Relations.' In *The Established and the Outsiders: A Sociological Enquiry into
    Community Problems*. London: Sage.
Ellen, R.F. 1984. *Ethnographic Research: A Guide to General Conduct*. New York:
    Academic Press.
Elliott, Charles. 1968. 'The Satirist Satirized.' In *Twentieth Century Interpreta-
    tions of 'Gulliver's Travels,'* edited by Frank Brody. Englewood Cliffs: Pren-
    tice Hall.
Englert, Sebastián. 1970. *Island at the Center of the World: New Light on Easter
    Island*. Translated and edited by William Mulloy. New York: Scribner.
– 2001. *Exhibition English Translation*. Rapa Nui: Sebastian Englert Anthropo-
    logical Museum.
Ernst, Max. [1934] 1976. *Une Semaine De Bonté: A Surrealistic Novel in Collage*.
    Translated by Stanley Appelbaum. New York: Dover Publications.
Farington, Joseph. 1979. 'William Hodges.' In *The Diary of Joseph Farington, July
    1793–December 1794*, edited by Kathryn Cave. Vol. 1. New Haven: Yale Uni-
    versity Press.
Feder, Kenneth. 1990. *Frauds, Myths, and Mysteries: Science and Pseudoscience in
    Archaeology*. Mountainview: Mayfield Publishing.
Feld, Steven, and Keith H. Basso, eds. 1996. *Senses of Place*. Santa Fe: School of
    American Research Press.
Fentress, James, and Chris Wickham. 1992. *Social Memory*. Oxford: Blackwell.
Ferdon, Edwin N. 1966. *One Man's Log*. London: Allen and Unwin.
Fernández de Oviedo y Valdés, Gonzalo. 1959. *Historia General y Natural de las
    Indias / Gonzalo Fernandez De Oviedo: Edicion y Estudio Preliminar De Juan Perez
    De Tudela Bueso*. Edited by Juan Pérez de Tudela y Bueso. 5 vols. Madrid: Edi-
    ciones Atla.

Fischer, Steven R. 1997. *Rongorongo: The Easter Island Script. History, Traditions, Texts.* Oxford Studies in Anthropological Linguistics 14. Oxford: Clarendon Press.

– 1993. *Easter Island Studies.* Oxford: Oxbow Books.

Fitzpatrick, Peter, and Eve Darian-Smith. 1999. *Laws of the Postcolonial: Law, Meaning, and Violence.* Ann Arbor: University of Michigan Press.

Flenley, John, and Paul G. Bahn. 2003. *The Enigmas of Easter Island: Island on the Edge* 2nd ed. Oxford: Oxford University Press. Previously published as *Easter Island, Earth Island.*

Ford, Richard. 2005. *Cultural Evolution and Global Change.* Course Lecture Case Study. Regents of the University of Michigan. Retrieved 2 June 2005 from http://www.globalchange.umich.edu/globalchange2/current/lectures/cult ural_evolution/.

Forster, George. [1777] 2000. *A Voyage Round the World in His Majest's Sloop Resolution Commanded by Captain James Cook 1772, 3, 4, 5.* Edited by Thomas Nicholas and Oliver Berghof. 2 vols. Honolulu: University of Hawaii Press.

Foster, Robert John. 1995. *Nation Making: Emergent Identities in Postcolonial Melanesia.* Ann Arbor: University of Michigan Press.

Foucault, Michel. 1970. *The Order of Things: An Archaeology of the Human Sciences.* London: Tavistock Publications.

– 1977. *Language, Counter-Memory, Practice.* Translated by D.F. Bouchard and Sherry Simon. Ithaca, NY: Cornell University Press.

– 1980. *Power/Knowledge: Selected Interviews and Other Writings, 1972–1977.* Translated by Colin Gordon. Brighton, Sussex: Harvester Press.

– 1982. 'Afterword: The Subject and Power.' In *Michel Foucault: Beyond Structuralism and Hermeneutics.* Edited by H.L. Dreyfus and P. Rabinow. Chicago: University of Chicago Press.

Freeman, M. 1993. *Rewriting the Self: History, Memory, Narrative.* London: Routledge and Kegan Paul.

Freidman, Jonathan. 1992. 'The Past in the Future.' *American Anthropologist* 94: 837–59.

Freire, Paulo. 1998. *Pedagogy of Freedom: Ethics, Democracy, and Civic Courage.* Lanham, MD: Rowman and Littlefield.

Freund, Philip. 1947. *Easter Island, a Novel by Philip Freund.* New York: Beechhurst Press.

Fulford, Timothy. 1999. 'Romanticism, Breadfruit and Slavery.' North American Society for the Study of Romanticism. Retrieved 10 June 2005 from www.rc.umd.edu/features/conferences/archive/3d.html.

Furneaux, Rupert. 1977. *Ancient Mysteries.* New York: Ballantine.

Furniss, Elizabeth. 1999. *The Burden of History: Colonialism and the Frontier Myth in a Rural Canadian Community.* Vancouver: UBC Press.

Fuseli, Henry. 1910. 'William Hodges.' In *A Dictionary of Painters from the Revival of the Art to the Present Period,* edited by Matthew Pilkington. London: n.p.

Gandhi, Leela. 1998. *Postcolonial Theory: A Critical Introduction.* New York: Columbia University Press.

Ganguly, Keya. 2001. *States of Exception: Everyday Life and Postcolonial Identity.* Minneapolis: University of Minnesota Press.

Garman, Samuel. 1908. *Reports on the Scientific Results of the Expedition to the Eastern Tropical Pacific, in Charge of Alexander Agassiz, by the U.S. Fish Commission Steamer 'Albatross,' from October, 1904, to March, 1905, Lieut. Commander L.M. Garrett, U.S.N., Commanding.* Bulletin of the Museum of Comparative Zoology at Harvard College 52, no. 1. Cambridge, MA: Printed for the Museum.

Garth, John S., et al. 1985. *On a Small Collection of Brachyuran Crustacea from Easter Island Obtained by the Scripps Institution of Oceanography Downwind Expedition of 1958.* Occasional Papers of the Allan Hancock Foundation. N.S. No. 3. Los Angeles: Allan Hancock Foundation University of Southern California.

Geary, Patrick J. 1994. *Phantoms of Remembrance: Memory and Oblivion at the End of the First Millenium.* Princeton: Princeton University Press.

Geiseler, Wilhelm, and William S. Ayres. 1995. *Geiseler's Easter Island Report: An 1880s Anthropological Account.* Asian and Pacific Archaeology Series No. 12. Honolulu: Social Science Research Institute University of Hawaii at Manoa.

Gerrard, Christine. 1994. *The Patriotic Opposition to Walpole: Politics, Poetry and National Myth, 1725–42.* Oxford: Clarendon Press.

Gibson, Arthur C. 1999. *Breadfruit (Artocarpus).* Botony Textbooks UCLA. Retrieved 10 June 2005 from www.botgard.ucla.edu/html/botanytextbooks/economicbotany/Artocarpus/.

Gil López, Olga. 1995. *Adiós Rapa Nui.* Córdoba, Argentina: Ediciones Argos.

Giroux, Henry. 1992. *Border Crossings: Cultural Workers and the Politics of Education.* New York: Routledge.

– 2000. 'Postmodern Education and Disposable Youth.' In *Revolutionary Pedagogies: Cultural Politics, Instituting Education, and the Discourse of Theory,* edited by Peter Pericles Trifonas. New York: Routledge.

Glesne, Corrine, and Alan Peshkin. 1992. *Becoming Qualitative Researchers: An Introduction.* New York: Longman.

Goethe, Johann Wolfgang (von). [1729] 1991. *The Sorrows of Werther.* Translated by Daniel Malthus. Revolution and Romanticism 1789–1834. New York: Woodstock Books.

– [1773] 1991. *Götz Von Berlichingen*. Translated by Charles E. Passage. Prospect Heights: Waveland Press.

Goldman, I. 1970. *Ancient Polynesian Society*. Chicago: University of Chicago Press.

Gonzalez de Haedo, Don Filipe. 1908. *The Voyage of Captain Don Felipe Gonzalez in the Ship of Line San Lorenzo, with the Frigate Santa Rosalia in Company, to Easter Island in 1770–1771: Preceded by an Extract from Mynheer Jacob Roggeveen's Official Log of His Discovery and Visit to Easter Island in 1722*. Translated by Bolton Granvill Corney, and edited by Bolton Granvill Corney. Vol. 13. Cambridge: Hakluyt Society.

Gosden, Chris, and Chantal Knowles. 2001. *Collecting Colonialism: Material Culture and Colonial Change*. New York: Berg.

Gottlieb, Evan. 2001. 'The Astonished Eye: The British Sublime and Thomson's "Winter."' *Eighteenth Century: Theory and Interpretation* 42, no. 1: 43–56.

Grace, Sherrill. 2001. *Canada and the Idea of North*. Montreal: McGill-Queen's University Press.

Greenblatt, Stephen. 1991. *Marvellous Possessions: The Wonders of the New World*. Chicago: University of Chicago Press.

Greene, John Patrick. 2002. 'French Encounters with Material Culture of the South Pacific.' *Eighteenth-Century Life* 26, no. 3: 225–45.

Gregory, C.A. 1982. *Gifts and Commodities*. London: Academic Press.

Grewal, Inderpal. 1996. *Home and Harem: Nation, Gender, Empire, and the Cultures of Travel*. Durham, NC: Duke University Press.

Grewal, Inderpal, and Caren Kaplan. 1994. *Scattered Hegemonies: Postmodernity and Transnational Feminist Practices*. Minneapolis: University of Minnesota Press.

Grosvenor, Gilbert M., ed. 1979. *Mysteries of the Ancient World*. Washington, DC: National Geographic Society.

Guest, Harriet. 1992. 'The Great Distinction: Figures of the Exotic in the Work of William Hodges.' In *New Feminist Discourses: Critical Essays on Theories and Texts*, edited by Isobel Armstrong. London: Routledge.

Gutting, Gary. 1989. *Michel Foucault's Archaeology of Scientific Reason*. Cambridge: Cambridge University Press.

Hagelberg, Erika, Silvia Quevedo, Daniel Turbon, and J.B. Clegg. 1994. 'DNA from Ancient Easter Islanders.' *Nature* 369: 25–6.

Hakluyt, Richard. 1599–1600. *The Principal Navigations, Voyages, Traffiques and Discoveries of the English Nation: Made by Sea or Overland, to the Remote and Farthest Distant Quarters of the Earth, at Any Time within the Compasse of These 1600*

Yeres: Divided into Three Severall Volumes According to the Positions of the Regions Whereunto They Were Directed. 12 vols. London: George Bishop, Ralph Newberie, Robert Barker. Microform.

Hamilton, E., and H. Cairns, eds. 1961. *Plato the Collected Dialogues.* Princeton: Princeton University Press.

Hancock, Graham, and Santha Faiia. 1998. *Heaven's Mirror: Quest for the Lost Civilization.* London: Michael Joseph.

Hanlon, David. 1999. 'The Chill of History: The Experience, Emotion, and Changing Politics of Archival Research in the Pacific.' *Archives and Manuscripts: The Journal of the Australian Society of Archivists* 27, no. 1: 8–21.

– 2003. '"Beyond the English Method of Tattooing": Decentering the Practice of History in Oceania.' *Contemporary Pacific* 15, no. 1: 19–40.

Harley, J.B. 1992. 'Deconstructing the Map.' In *Writing Worlds,* edited by Trevor Barnes and James Duncan. London: Routledge.

Harrison, John Park. 1874a. 'Exhibition of Photographs and Implements from Easter Island.' *Journal of the Royal Anthropological Institute of Great Britain and Ireland* (London) 3: 177–8.

– 1874b. 'The Hieroglyphs of Easter Island.' *Journal of the Royal Anthropological Institute of Great Britain and Ireland* (London) 3: 370–83.

– 1874c. 'Note on Easter Island Writing.' *Journal of the Royal Anthropological Institute of Great Britain and Ireland* (London) 3: 528 and plate 27 opposite.

Harrison, Julia. 2003. *Being a Tourist.* Vancouver: UBC Press.

Haun, Beverley. 2003. 'The Rise of the Aboriginal Voice in Canadian Adolescent Fiction 1970–1990.' In *Windows and Words: A Look at Canadian Children's Literature in English,* edited by Aïda Hudson and Susan-Ann Cooper. Ottawa: University of Ottawa Press.

– 2004. 'From Praxis to Practice: Prospects for Postcolonial Pedagogy in Canadian Public Education.' In *Home-Work: Postcolonialism, Pedagogy and Canadian Literature,* edited by Cynthia Sugars. Ottawa: University of Ottawa Press.

– 2006. 'Introduction.' In *Rapa Nui, Island of Memory* by Georgia Lee. Los Osos, CA: Easter Island Foundation.

Hawkesworth, John, ed. 1773. *An Account of the Voyages Undertaken by the Order of His Present Majesty for Making Discoveries in the Southern Hemisphere, and Successively Performed by Commodore Byron, Captain Wallis, Captain Carteret and Captain Cook, in the Dolphin, the Swallow and the Endeavour.* N.p.

Hawley, John C. 2001. *Encyclopedia of Postcolonial Studies.* Westport, CT: Greenwood Press.

Herder, Johann Gottfried. 1800. *Outlines of a Philosophy of the History of Man.* Translated by T. Churchill. London: Printed for J. Johnson, by Luke Hamsard.

Herrmann, Anne, and Abigail J. 2001. Stewart. *Theorizing Feminism: Parallel Trends in the Humanities and Social Sciences*. 2nd ed. Boulder, CO: Westview Press.

Hesiod. 1988. *Theogony and Works and Days*. Translated by M.L. West. Oxford: Oxford University Press.

Heyerdahl, Thor. 1950. *The Kon-Tiki Expedition: By Raft across the South Seas*. Translated by F.H. Lyon. London: Allen and Unwin.

– 1958. *Aku-Aku: The Secret of Easter Island*. Harmondsworth: Penguin Books.

– 1976. *The Art of Easter Island*. London: Allen and Unwin.

– 1989. *Easter Island – The Mystery Solved*. New York: Random House

Heyerdahl, Thor, and Edwin N. Ferdon, Jr., eds. 1961. *The Reports of the Norwegian Archaeological Expedition to Easter Island and the East Pacific (1955–1956)*. 2 vols. London: Allen and Unwin.

Higgins, Iain. 1997. 'Representing the New Old World: Some Medieval Europeans on the Far East.' *Pacific Encounters: The Production of Self and Other*, edited by E. Kröller et al. Vancouver: Institute of Asian Research, University of British Columbia.

Hoare, Michael E., ed. 1982. *The Resolution Journal of Johann Reinhold Forster 1772–1775*. Vol. 4. London: Hakluyt Society.

Hobbes, Thomas. [1651] 1968. *Leviathan 1651*. Edited by C.B. Macpherson. Hamondsworth: Penguin.

Hollinshead, K. 1994. 'The Unconscious Realm of Tourism.' *Annals of Tourism Research* 21: 387–91.

Homer. 1945. *The Odyssey*. Translated and edited by E.V. Rieu. Harmondsworth: Penguin.

Horace. 1967. *Odes of Horace*. Translated by J. Michie. Harmondsworth: Penguin.

Hough, Walter. 1889. 'Notes on the Archaeology and Ethnology of Easter Island.' *American Naturalist* (Philadelphia) 23: 877–88.

Hovde, Karen. 1998. 'Index to Rapa Nui Journal 1988–1996.' *Behavioral and Social Sciences Librarian* 16, no. 2: 27–55.

Huggan, Graham. 2001. *The Postcolonial Exotic: Marketing the Margins*. New York: Routledge.

Hulme, Peter. 2000. *Remnants of Conquest: The Island Caribs and Their Visitors, 1877–1998*. Oxford: Oxford University Press.

Hutcheon, Linda. 1995. 'Post Always Rings Twice: The Postmodern and the Postcolonial.' *Material History Review* 41: 4–23.

Hyde, Lewis. 1979. *The Gift: Imagination and the Erotic Life of Property*. New York: Vintage.

In Search of Ancient Mysteries. 1989. Translated by Rod Serling. Star Classics. Videocassette.

Inda, Jonathan Xavier, and Renato Rosaldo. 2001. *The Anthropology of Globalization: A Reader*. Oxford: Blackwell.

Isin, Engin F. 2002. *Being Political: Genealogies of Citizenship*. Minneapolis: University of Minnesota Press.

James, Fentress, and Chris Wickham. 1992. *Social Memory*. Oxford: Blackwell.

Janmohamed, Abdul R. 1994. 'Some Implications of Paul Freire's Border Pedagogy.' In *Between Borders: Pedagogy and Politics of Cultural Studies*, edited by Henry Giroux and Peter McLaren. New York: Routledge.

Janssen, Marco A., and Marten Scheffer. 2004. 'Overexploitation of Renewable Resources by Ancient Societies and the Role of Sunk-Cost Effects.' *Ecology and Society* 9, no. 1: 6–20.

Johnson, Samuel, Oliver Goldsmith, and Christopher Smart. 1759. *The World Displayed; or a Curious Collection of Voyages and Travels Selected from the Writers of all Nations*. 21 vols. London: Printed for J. Newbery and J. Hoey.

Jolly, Margaret. 1992. 'Spector of Inauthenticity.' *Contemporary Pacific* 4: 47–72.

Jones, Alison. 1991. *'At School I've Got a Chance': Culture/Privilege: Pacific Islands and Pakeha Girls at School*. Palmerston North, NZ: Dunmore Press.

– 1997. 'Teaching Poststructuralist Feminist Theory in Education: Student Resistances.' *Gender and Education* 9, no. 3: 262–9.

– 1999. 'The Limits of Cross-Cultural Dialogue: Pedagogy, Desire, and Absolution in the Classroom.' *Educational Theory* 49, no. 3: 299–316.

Jones, Alison, Phyllis Herda, and Tamasailau M. Suaalii. 2000. *Bitter Sweet: Indigenous Women in the Pacific*. Dunedin, NZ: University of Otago Press.

Joppien, Rüdiger. 1979. 'The Artistic Bequest of Captain Cook's Voyages.' In Robin Fisher and Hugh Johnston, eds., *Captain Cook and His Times*. Seattle: University of Washington Press.

Joppien, Rüdiger, and Bernard Smith. 1985. *The Art of Captain Cook's Voyages*. Vol. 2. New Haven: Yale University Press.

Kaplan, Caren. 1996. *Questions of Travel: Postmodern Discourses of Displacement*. Durham, NC: Duke University Press.

Kaplan, E. Ann. 1997. *Looking for the Other: Feminism, Film, and the Imperial Gaze*. New York: Routledge.

Kappeler, Susan. 1986. *The Pornography of Representation*. Cambridge: Polity Press.

Keate, George. 1788. *An Account of the Pelew Islands*. London: H. Wilson.

Kellner, Douglas. 2000. 'Multiple Literacies and Critical Pedagogies.' In *Revolutionary Pedagogies: Cultural Politics, Instituting Education, and the Discourse of Theory*, edited by Peter Pericles Trifonas. New York: Routledge.

Kennedy, Grace. 2001. 'Breadfruit.' Grace Foods. Retrieved 10 June 2005 from www.gracefoods.com/Blackhistory/Breadfruit.asp.

Kincaid, Jamaica. 1988. *A Small Place*. New York: Penguin.

Kjellgren, Eric, JoAnne Van Tilburg, and Adrienne Lois Kaeppler. 2001. *Splendid Isolation: Art of Easter Island*. New York: Metropolitan Museum of Art; New Haven: Yale University Press.

Klein, Bernhard, and Jürgen Kramer. 2001. *Common Ground? Crossovers between Cultural Studies and Postcolonial Studies*. Trier: WVT Wissenschaftlicher Verlag Trier.

Knauft, Bruce M. 1999. *From Primitive to Postcolonial in Melanesia and Anthropology*. Ann Arbor: University of Michigan Press.

Kohli, Wendy. 1995. 'Postmodernism, Critical Theory and the New Pedagogies.' In *Postmodernism, Postcolonialism and Pedagogy*, edited by Peter McLaren. Albert Park, Australia: James Nicholas Publishers.

Korte, Barbara. 2000. *English Travel Writing from Pilgrimages to Postcolonial Explorations*. New York: St Martin's Press.

Kritzman, L.D., ed. 1988. *Michel Foucault, Politics Philosophy and Culture: Interviews and Other Writings, 1977–1984*. New York: Routledge.

Kröller, Eva-Marie, et al., eds. 1997. *Pacific Encounters: The Production of Self and Others*. Vancouver: Institute of Asian Research at the University of British Columbia.

La Pérouse, Jean-François de Galaup, comte de. 1798. *The Voyage of La Pérouse Round the World, in the Years 1785, 1786, 1787, and 1788, with the Nautical Tables [Microform] / Arranged by M.L.A. Milet Mureau ... ; to Which Is Prefixed, Narrative of an Interesting Voyage from Manilla to St. Blaise ; and Annexed, Travels over the Continent, with the Dispatches of La Pérouse in 1787 and 1788, by M. De Lesseps ; Translated from the French ; Illustrated with Fifty-One Plates*. 2 vols. London: Printed for John Stockdale.

– 1969. *Voyages and Adventures of La Pérouse*. Translated by Julius S. Gassner. Honolulu: University of Hawaii Press.

Labone, M. 1996. 'The Roaring Silence on the Sociology of Leisure.' *Social Alternatives* 15: 30–2.

Lamb, Jonathan. 1999. 'Re-Imagining Juan Fernandez: Probability, Possibility and Pretence in the South Seas.' *Double Vision: Art Histories and Colonial Histories in the Pacific*, edited by Nicholas Thomas and Diane Losche. Cambridge: Cambridge University Press.

– 2001. *Preserving the Self in the South Seas, 1680–1840*. Chicago: University of Chicago Press.

Langdon, Robert, and D.T. Tryon. 1983. *The Language of Easter Island: Its Development and Eastern Polynesian Relationships*. Monograph Series, No. 4. Laie, Hawaii: Institute for Polynesian Studies.

Lavie, Smadar, Kirin Narayan, and Renato Rosaldo. 1993. *Creativity/Anthropology*. Ithaca, NY: Cornell University Press.

Lazarus, Neil. 1999. *Nationalism and Cultural Practice in the Postcolonial World*. New York: Cambridge University Press.

LeBaron, Charles. 1978. 'The Giants of Easter Island.' *Reader's Digest: The World's Last Mysteries*. Montreal: Reader's Digest Association.

Lee, Georgia. 1992. *Rock Art of Easter Island: Symbols of Power, Prayers to the Gods*. Los Angeles: Institute of Archaeology, University of California Los Angeles.

Lee, Georgia, Edward Stasack, and Easter Island Foundation. 1999. *Spirit of Place: The Petroglyphs of Hawai'i*. Los Osos, CA: Easter Island Foundation; Bearsville and Cloud Mountain Presses.

Lee, John, and Barbara Moore. 1975. *Monsters among Us: Journey to the Unexplained*. New York: Pyramid Books.

Lesseps, J.B.B. 1790. *Journal historique de M. De Lesseps, Consul De France, employé dans l'expédition de M. Le Comte de la Pérouse en qualité d'interprète du Roi*. 2 vols. Paris: n.p.

Levinas, Emmanuel. 1961. *Totality and Infinity*. Edited and translated by Alphonso Lingis. Pittsburgh: Duquesne University Press.

– 1998a. 'Diachrony and Representation.' Translated by Michael B. Smith and Barbara Harshav. In *Entre Nous: Thinking-of-the-Other*. New York: Columbia University Press.

– 1998b. 'The Philosophical Determination of the Idea of Culture.' Translated by Michael B. Smith and Barbara Harshav. In *Entre Nous: Thinking-of-the-Other*. New York: Columbia University Press.

Lewis, Gail. 1998. *Forming Nation, Framing Welfare*. New York: Routledge in association with the Open University Press.

– 2000. *'Race,' Gender, Social Welfare: Encounters in a Postcolonial Society*. Cambridge: Polity Press.

Liebersohn, Harry. 2005. 'A Radical Intellectual with Captain Cook: George Forster's World Voyage.' *Common-Place: The Interactive Journal of Early American Life* 5, no. 2: 8.

Lingus, Alphonso. 1994. *The Community of Those Who Have Nothing in Common*. Bloomington: Indiana University Press.

Linton, John Palmer. 1870a. 'Observations on the Inhabitants and the Antiquities of Easter Island.' *Journal of the Ethnological Society* (London) 1: 371–7.

– 1870b. *A Visit to Easter Island, or Rapa Nui*. London: Proceedings of the Royal Geographical Society.

– 1870c. 'A Visit to Easter Island, or Rapa Nui, in 1868.' *Journal of the Royal Geographical Society* (London) 40: 167–81.

Livingstone, D.N. 1992. *The Geographical Tradition: Episodes in the History of a Contested Enterprise*. Oxford: Blackwell.

Login, George M., ed. [1518] 1989. *The Utopia of Sir Thomas More*. New York: Cambridge University Press.

Longinus. 1985. *On the Sublime*. Translated by James A. Arieti and John M. Crossett. Toronto: Edwin Mellon Press.

Loret, John, and John T. Tanacredi, eds. 2003. *Easter Island: Scientific Exploration into the World's Environmental Problems in Microcosm*. London: Kluwer Academic/Plenum Publishers.

Loti, Pierre. 1899. *Reflets sur la sombre route*. Original ed. Tirage numéroté limité à seulement 100 ex. ed. Paris: Calmann-Levy.

– 2004. 'Diary of a Cadet – 1872.' Translated by Ann Altmann. *Early Visitors to Easter Island 1864–1877*, edited by Ann Altmann. Los Osos: Bearsville Press.

Loti, Pierre, and Louis Marie Julien Viaud. 1971. 'Young Pierre Loti's Account.' In *Easter Island; Island of Enigmas*, edited by John Dos Passos. New York: Doubleday.

Luke, Harry, Sir. 1952. 'The Red Hats of Rapa-Nui.' *Listener* 48, no. 1221: 24.

MacGregor, Rob. 1992. *Indiana Jones and the Interior World*. Auckland: Bantam.

Machowski, Jacek. 1969. *Island of Secrets: The Discovery and Exploration of Easter Island*. London: Hale.

Mackenzie, J.M. 1986. *Imperialism and Popular Culture*. Manchester: Manchester University Press.

Mageo, Jeannette Marie. 2001. *Cultural Memory: Reconfiguring History and Identity in the Postcolonial Pacific*. Honolulu: University of Hawaii Press.

Mandeville, John. [1499] 1915. *The Travels of Sir John Mandeville*. Edited by A.W. Pollard. Cotton Manuscript 1725 ed. London: Macmillan.

Mann, Peggy. 1976. *Easter Island: Land of Mysteries*. New York: Henry Holt.

Manuel, F.E., and F.P. Manuel. 1972. 'Sketch for a Natural History of Paradise.' *Daedalus* 101, no. 1: 83–128.

Martinsson-Wallin, Helene, and Societas Archaeologica Upsaliensis. 1994. *Ahu, the Ceremonial Stone Structures of Easter Island: Analyses of Variation and Interpretation of Meanings*. Uppsala: Societas Archaeologica Upsaliensis.

Matt, Nash. 2004. 'A Short History of Progress.' *The Silhouette* 75, no. 13.

Mauss, Marsel. 1066. *The Gift: Forms and Functions of Exchange in Archaic Societies*. Translated by Ian Cunnison. London: Cohen and West.

Mazière, Francis. 1969. *Mysteries of Easter Island; with Photographs by the Author*. London: Collins.

McAllister, Don E., and John E. Randall. 1975. *A New Species of Centrolophid Fish from Easter Island and Rapa Iti Island in the South Pacific*. Publications in Biological Oceanography, No. 8. Ottawa: National Museum of Natural Sciences.

McCall, Grant. 1994. *Rapanui: Tradition and Survival on Easter Island*. 2d ed. Honolulu: University of Hawaii Press.

– 2002. 'Nissology: Something to Think About and Something to Protect – Beyond the Boundaries.' *Proceedings of the IUCN/WCPA-EA-4 Taipei Conference*, 18–23, March 2002, Taipei, Taiwan.

McCarthy, Cameron, and Greg Dimitriadis. 2000. 'All-Consuming Identities: Race and the Pedagogy of Resentment in the Age of Difference.' *Revolutionary Pedagogies: Cultural Politics, Instituting Education, and the Discourse of Theory*, edited by Peter Pericles Trifonas. New York: Routledge.

– 2001. *The Work of Art in the Post-Colonial Imagination: Education in an Age of Globalization*. New York: Teachers College Press.

McClintock, Anne. 1995. *Imperial Leather: Race, Gender, and Sexuality in the Colonial Conquest*. New York: Routledge.

McClintock, Anne, et al. 1997. *Dangerous Liaisons: Gender, Nation, and Postcolonial Perspectives*. Minneapolis: University of Minnesota Press.

McHoul, Alec, and Wendy Grace. 1993. *A Foucault Primer: Discourse, Power and the Subject*. London: UCL Press.

McKeon, Michael. 1987. *The Origins of the English Novel*. Baltimore: Johns Hopkins University Press.

McLaren, Peter. 1994. 'Multiculturalism and Pedagogy of Resistance and Transformation.' In *Between Borders: Pedagogy and Politics of Cultural Studies*, edited by Henry Giroux and Peter McLaren. New York: Routledge.

– 2000. 'Unthinking Whiteness: Rearticulating Diasporic Practice.' In *Revolutionary Pedagogies: Cultural Politics, Instituting Education, and the Discourse of Theory*, edited by Peter Pericles Trifonas. New York: Routledge.

McLaughlin, Shawn. 2005. 'Cannibalism and Easter Island: Evaluation, Discussion of Probabilities, and Survey of Easter Island Literature on the Subject.' *Rapa Nui Journal* 19, no. 1: 30–50.

Métraux, Alfred. 1957. *Easter Island: A Stone-Age Civilization of the Pacific*. Translated by Michael Bullock. [London]: A. Deutsch.

– 1971. *Ethnology of Easter Island*. Bernice P. Bishop Museum Bulletin No. 160. Honolulu: The Museum.

Meyers, Diane Tautens. 1994. *Subjection and Subjectivity: Psychoanalytic Feminism and Moral Philosophy*. New York: Routledge.

Michelsen, Karen. 2004. 'Easter Island.' *Running Room Magazine*, September–October: 51–2.

Mignolo, W.D. 1989. 'Colonial Situations, Geographical Discourses and Territorial Representations: Toward a Diatopical Understanding of Colonial Semiosis.' *Dispositio/n: American Journal of Cultural Histories and Theories* 14, nos. 36–8: 93–140.

- 2000. *Local Histories / Global Designs: Coloniality, Subaltern Knowledges, and Border Thinking*. Princeton: Princeton University Press.

Milet-Mureau, M.L.A., ed. 1797. *Voyage de la Pérouse autour du monde, publié conformément du décret du 22 avril 1791.* 4 vols. Paris: n.p.

Mitchell, W.J.T. 1987. *Iconology, Image, Text, Ideology.* Reprint ed. Chicago: University of Chicago Press.

- 1994. *Picture Theory: Essays on Verbal and Visual Representation*. Chicago: University of Chicago Press.

- 1995. 'Translator Translated (Interview with Cultural Theorist Homi Bhabha).' *Artforum Volume* 33, no. 7 (March): 80–4.

- 1997. 'Gombrich and the Rise of Landscape.' In *The Consumption of Cutlure*, edited by Ann Bermingham and John Brewer. London: Routledge.

Moerenhout, J.A. 1837. *Voyages aux Iles du Grand Ocean, Contenant des Documens Nouveaux ... et des Considerations Generales. ... Par J.A. Moerenhout, Consul General des Etats Unis aux Iles Oceaniennes.* 2 vols. Paris: Arthur Bertrand.

Mohanty, Chandra Talpade. 1994. 'On Race and Voice: Challenges for Liberal Education in the 1990s.' In *Between Borders: Pedagogy and Politics of Cultural Studies*, edited by Henry Giroux and Peter McLaren. New York: Routledge.

Mok, Michael. 1930. 'Explore Weird Island of Death.' *Popular Mechanics*, April.

Monboddo, Lord James Burnett. [1773] 1967. *Of the Origin and Progress of Language*. English Linguistics 1500–1800. Menston: Scholar Press.

Mongia, Padmini. 1996. *Contemporary Postcolonial Theory: A Reader*. London: Arnold.

Moore-Gilbert, B.J. 1997. *Postcolonial Theory: Contexts, Practices, Politics*. London: Verso.

Moore-Gilbert, B.J., Gareth Stanton, and Willy Maley. 1997. *Postcolonial Criticism*. New York: Longman.

Mordo, Carlos. 2002. *Easter Island*. Willowdale: Firefly Books.

Moss, John. 1994. *Enduring Dreams: An Exploration of Arctic Landscape*. Concord, ON: House of Anansi Press.

Moss, Laura, ed. 2003. *Is Canada Postcolonial? Unsettling Canadian Literature*. Waterloo, ON: Wilfrid Laurier University Press.

Mott, Albert J. 1880–1. 'Notes on Easter Island.' *Proceedings of the Literary and Philosophical Society of Liverpool* 35: 159–91.

Mukherjee, Arun. 1998. *Postcolonialism: My Living*. Toronto: Tzar.

Mulloy, William T., and Steven R. Fischer. 1993. *Easter Island Studies: Contributions to the History of Rapanui in Memory of William T. Mulloy*. Oxford: Oxbow Books.

Murrill, Rupert Ivan. 1968. *Cranial and Postcranial Skeletal Remains from Easter Island*. Minneapolis: University of Minnesota Press.

Myrsiades, Kostas, and Jerry McGuire. 1995. *Order and Partialities: Theory, Pedagogy, and the 'Postcolonial.'* Albany: State University of New York Press.

Narayan, Uma, and Sandra Harding. 2000. *Decentering the Center: Philosophy for a Multicultural, Postcolonial, and Feminist World.* Bloomington: Indiana University Press.

Neal, Larry. 1990. *The Rise of Financial Capitalism.* Cambridge: Cambridge University Press.

Newberry, John. 1994a. *Easter Island Rongo-Rongo Hieroglyphics.* Indus and Other Ancient Script Monographs. Vancouver: J. Newberry.

– 1994b. *Easter Island Rongo-Rongo Tablets.* Indus and Ancient Script Monographs. Vancouver: J. Newberry.

Newton, Arthur Percival. [1926] 1967. *Travel and Travellers of the Middle Ages.* Freeport: Books for Libraries Press.

Niranjana, Tejaswini. 1992. 'Politics and Poetics: Deman, Benjamin and the Task of the Translator.' *Siting Translation: History, Post-Structuralism and the Colonial Context.* Berkeley: University of California Press.

Nordquist, Joan. 1998. *Postcolonial Theory: A Bibliography.* Santa Cruz, CA: Reference and Research Services.

Norton, Frank H. 1894. 'The Mystery of Easter Island.' *Illustrated American*, 3 March.

Nugent, Ann. 2000. *Curtain Calls.* National Library of Australia News. Retrieved 3 June 2005 from www.nla.gov.au/pub/nlanews/2000/august00/curtain.html.

Nussbaum, Felicity A. 1997. 'Polygamy, Pamela, and the Prerogative of Empire.' In *The Consumption of Culture*, edited by Ann Bermingham. London: Routledge.

Obeyesekere, Gananath. 1992. *The Apotheosis of Captain Cook.* Princeton: Princeton University Press.

Olson, Gary A., and Lynn Worsham. 1999. *Race, Rhetoric, and the Postcolonial.* Albany: State University of New York Press.

Orliac, Catherine, and Michel Orliac. 1995. *The Silent Gods: Mysteries of Easter Island.* London: Thames and Hudson.

– 1995. *Easter Island: Mystery of the Stone Giants.* Translated by Paul Bahn. New York: HNA Books.

Otto, Ton, and Nicholas Thomas. 1997. *Narratives of Nation in the South Pacific.* Amsterdam: Harwood Academic Publishers.

Outram, Dorinda. 1966. 'New Spaces in Natural History.' In *Cultures of Natural History*, edited by N. Jardine and E.C. Spary. Cambridge: Cambridge University Press.

Panofsky, Erwin. 1955. *Meaning in the Visual Arts*. Chicago: University of Chicago Press.

Parish, Sir Woodbine. 1852. *Buenos Ayres and the Provinces of the Rio De La Plata from Their Discovery and Conquest by the Spaniards to the Establishment of Their Political Independence* ... London: John Murray.

Parry, Jonathan. 1989. 'On the Moral Perils of Exchange.' In *Money and the Morality of Exchange*. Cambridge: Cambridge University Press.

Pateman, Trevor. 1991. 'The Sublime.' In *Key Concepts: A Guide to Aesthetics, Criticism and Arts in Education*. London: Falmer Press.

Patton, L., and R.A. Foakes, eds. 1969. *The Collected Works of Samuel Taylor Coleridge*. Princeton: Princeton University Press.

Pauwels, Louis, and Jacques Bergier. 1972. *The Eternal Man*. Translated by Michael Heron. New York: Avon.

Philip, Franklin, ed. 1994. *Discourse on the Origin of Inequality by Jean-Jacques Rousseau*. New York: Oxford University Press.

Phillips, Ruth B. 1996. *Mapping Men and Empire: A Geography of Adventure*. London: Routledge.

Phillips, Ruth B., and Christopher Burghard Steiner. 1999. *Unpacking Culture: Art and Commodity in Colonial and Postcolonial Worlds*. Berkeley: University of California Press.

Picker, Fred, and Thor Heyerdahl. 1974. *Rapa Nui*. New York: Paddington Press.

Pickles, John. 1992. 'Texts, Maps, and Hermeneutics.' In *Writing Worlds*, edited by Trevor Barnes and James Duncan. London: Routledge.

Picknett, Lynn. 1979. 'The Stone Statues of Easter Island.' In *Mysteries of the World*, edited by Christopher Pick. Secaucus, NJ: Chartwell Books.

Pioch, Nicolas. 2002. *Webmuseum, Paris*. BMW Foundation. 30 June 2005.

Pollock, Nancy. 1993. 'Traditional Foods of Rapanui.' In *Easter Island Studies*, edited by Steven Fischer. Oxford: Oxbow Books.

Polo, Marco. 1958. *The Travels of Marco Polo*. Translated by Ronald Latham. Harmondsworth: Penguin.

Ponting, Clive. 1991. *A Green History of the World*. London: Sinclair-Stevenson.

Porteous, J. Douglas. 2004. 'Rapa Nui: A Hyperbolic Iconography.' *Rapa Nui Journal* 18, no. 1: 17–19.

Porteous, J. Douglas, and University of Victoria, Deptartment of Geography. 1981. *The Modernization of Easter Island*. Victoria, BC: University of Victoria.

Powell, Commodore W. Ashmore. 1899. *Proceedings of the Royal Geographical Society of Australasia, South Australian Branch 1886–1918 Proceedings of the Royal Geographical Society of Australasia, South Australian Branch (Incorporated) 1919–1986*.

Pratt, Mary Louise. 1992. *Imperial Eyes: Travel Writing and Transculturation*. New York: Routledge.

Protter, Eric. 1962. *Explorers and Explorations: Man's Greatest Adventures of Discovery*. New York: Grosset and Dunlop.

Purchas, Samuel. 1613. *Purchas His Pilgrimage, or, Relations of the World and the Religions Observed in All Ages and Places Discovered, from the Creation Unto Present: In Foure Partes, This First Containeth a Theologicall and Geographicall Histoire of Asia, Africa and America, with the Islands Adjacent ... With Briefe Descriptions of the Countries, Nations, States, Discoveries, Private and Publike Customes and the Most Remarkable Rarities of Nature or Humane Industrie in the Same*. London: William Stansby for Henrie Fetherstone. Microform.

Quilley, Geoff. 2004. *William Hodges 1744–1797: The Art of Exploration. 'Cook's Second Voyage.'* National Maritime Museum, UK. Retrieved 10 June 2005 from www.nmm.ac.uk/upload/package/30/voyage.php.

Rabinow, Paul, ed. 1984. *The Foucault Reader*. New York: Pantheon Books.

Radcliffe, S.A. 1997. 'Different Heroes: Genealogies of Postcolonial Geographies. Commentary.' *Environment and Planning* A29: 1331–3.

Ramírez, José Miguel, and Carlos Huber. 2000. *Easter Island: Rapa Nui, a Land of Rocky Dreams*. N.p.: Carlos Huber Schulz.

Raskin, Jonah. 1971. *The Mythology of Imperialism*. New York: Random House.

Reid, Helen Evans. 1965. *A World Away: A Canadian Adventure on Easter Island*. Toronto: Ryerson Press.

Rennie, Neil. 1995. *Far-Fetched Facts: The Literature of Travel and the Idea of the South Seas*. Oxford: Clarendon Press.

Renshaw, F. Stanley. 1993. 'Ancients of Easter Island.' *Amazing Stories* (April): 46–53.

Reuveny, R., and C.S. Decker. 2000. 'Easter Island: Historical Anecdote or Warning for the Future?' *Ecological Economics* 35, no. 2: 271–87.

Reynolds, Kevin, Tim Rose-Price, and Diana Landau. 1994. *Rapa Nui: The Easter Island Legend on Film*. New York: Newmarket Press.

Reynolds, Sir Joshua. [1797] 1959. *Discourses on Art*, edited by Robert R. Wark. New Haven: Yale University Press.

Richards, Thomas. 1993. *The Imperial Archive: Knowledge and the Fantasy of Empire*. London: Verso.

Robinson, Douglas. 1997. *Translation and Empire: Postcolonial Theories Explained*. Manchester: St Jerome.

Rogers, Woodes. [1712] 1992. *Captain Woodes Rogers' Voyage Round the World, 1708–1711*. Edited by Donald Jones. Bristol: Bristol Branch of the Historical Association.

Rojek, Chris. 1992. '"The Eye of Power": Moral Regulation and the Professionalization of Leisure Management from the 1830s to the 1950s.' *Society and Leisure* 15, no. 355: 373.

Rojek, Chris, and John Urry. 1997. *Touring Cultures: Transformations of Travel and Theory.* London: Routledge.

Roman, Leslie G., Linda K. Christian-Smith, and Elizabeth Ann Ellsworth. 1988. *Becoming Feminine: The Politics of Popular Culture.* London: Falmer Press.

Rosaldo, Renato. 1993. *Culture and Truth: The Remaking of Social Analysis.* Boston: Beacon Press.

Rosenblum, Robert. 1971. 'The Dawn of British Romantic Painting, 1760–1780.' In *The Varied Pattern: Studies in the 18th Century,* edited by Peter Hughes and David Williams. Toronto: A.M. Hakkert.

Ross, Rupert. 1992. *Dancing with a Ghost: Exploring Indian Reality.* Markham, ON: Octopus Publishing Group.

Roth, M.S. 1995. *The Ironist's Cage: Memory, Trauma, and the Construction of History.* New York: Columbia University Press.

Routledge, Katherine Pease. 1919. *The Mystery of Easter Island; the Story of an Expedition.* London: Printed for the author by Hazell Watson and Viney.

– 1920. *The Mystery of Easter Island; the Story of an Expedition.* 2d ed. London: Printed for the author by Hazell Watson and Viney and sold by Sifton Praed, 1920.

– 1921. 'Mystery of Easter Island.' *National Geographic* 40 (December): 628–44.

Russell, Nancy. 1997. *A Historical Refutation of Multiculturalism.* Available online from www.socialequality.comwww.wsws.org.

Sahlins, Marshall. 1976. *Culture and Practical Reason.* Chicago: University of Chicago Press.

– 1981. *Historical Metaphors and Mythical Realities.* Ann Arbor: University of Michigan Press.

– 1985. *Islands of History.* Chicago: University of Chicago Press.

– 1993. 'Goodbye to Tristes Tropes: Ethnography in the Context of Modern World History.' *The Journal of Modern History* 65, no. 1: 1–25.

– 1995. *How 'Natives' Think: About Captain Cook, for Example.* Chicago: University of Chicago Press.

– 2000. 'Cosmologies of Capitalism: The Trans-Pacific Sector of the "World System."' In *The Discovery of the True Savage,* edited by Marshall Sahlins. New York: Zone Books.

Said, Edward. 1993. *Culture and Imperialism.* New York: Vintage Books.

– 1994. *Orientalism.* New York: Vintage Books.

Said, Edward W., et al. 1998. *Edward Said on Orientalism.* Northampton, MA: The Media Education Foundation.

Sainthill, Richard. 1870. 'Rapa-Nui, or Easter Island in November 1868. By an Officer of H.M.S. "Topaze."' *MacMillan's Magazine* (London): 449–54.

Sami, David, Chandra Ali, and Multi Mapping Ltd. 1998. *An International Travel Map, Easter Island*. 2d ed. Vancouver, BC: ITMB Publishing.

Sampat Patel, Niti. 2001. *Postcolonial Masquerades: Culture and Politics in Literature, Film, Video, and Photography.* New York: Garland Publisher.

San Juan, E. 1998. *Beyond Postcolonial Theory.* New York: St Martin's Press.

Sanborn, Geoffrey. 1998. *The Sign of the Cannibal: Melville and the Making of a Postcolonial Reader.* Durham, NC: Duke University Press.

Sawicki, Jana. 1991. *Disciplining Foucault.* London: Routledge.

Schwartz, Jean-Michel. 1973. *The Mysteries of Easter Island.* New York: Avon.

'Science.' *Time*, 1 July 1946, 52.

Scott, David. 1999. *Refashioning Futures: Criticism after Postcoloniality.* Princeton: Princeton University Press.

Scott, Jamie S., and Paul Simpson-Housley. 2001. *Mapping the Sacred: Religion, Geography and Postcolonial Literatures.* Atlanta: Rodopi.

Seaver, Joan. 1993. 'Rapanui Crafts: Wooden Sculptures Past and Present.' In *Easter Island Studies*, edited by Steven Fischer. Oxford: Oxbow Books.

Sharp, Andrew. 1970. *The Journal of Jacob Roggeveen.* Oxford: Clarendon Press.

Sharpe, Jenny. 1993. *Allegories of Empire: The Figure of Woman in the Colonial Text.* Minneapolis: University of Minnesota Press.

Shore, Darren. 2005. 'Book of the Week.' *The Link* (Concordia University), 11 January 2005. Retrieved 10 June 2005 from http://thelink.concordia.ca/lit/05/01/10/1659242.shtml.

Sidney, Philip, Sir. [1590] 1987. *The Countess of Pembroke's Arcadia.* Edited by Victor Skretkowicz. New York: Oxford University Press.

Simmel, Georg. [1908] 1997. 'The Sociology of Space.' In *Simmel on Culture: Selected Writings*, edited by M. Featherstone and D. Frisby. London: Sage.

Simon, Roger I. 1994. 'Forms of Insurgency in the Production of Popular Memories: The Columbus Quincentenary and the Pedagogy of Counter-Commemoration.' In *Between Borders: Pedagogy and Politics of Cultural Studies*, edited by Henry Giroux and Peter McLaren. New York: Routledge.

– 2000. 'The Paradoxical Practice of Zakhor: Memories of "What Has Never Been My Fault or Deed."' In *Between Hope and Despair: Pedagogy and the Remembrance of Historical Trauma*, edited by Roger I. Simon, S. Rosenberg, and C. Eppert. Lantham, MD: Rowman and Littlefield.

– 2002. 'Remembrance as Praxis and the Ethics of the Inter-Human.' *Cultural Machine: Generating Research in Culture and Theory* 4. The Ethico Political Issue. Available from http://culturemachine.tees.ac.uk/frm_f1.htm.

- 2003. 'Innocence without Naivete, Uprightness without Stupidity: The Pedagogical Kavannah of Emmanuel Levinas.' *Studies in Philosophy and Education* 22, no. 1: 45–59.
- 2005. *The Touch of the Past: Remembrance, Learning, and Ethics.* New York: Palgrave Macmillan.
Simon, Sherry. 1997. 'Translation, Postcolonialism, and Cultural Studies.' *Meta* 42, no. 2: 462–77.
Simon, Sherry, and Paul St-Pierre. 2000. *Changing the Terms: Translating in the Postcolonial Era.* Ottawa: University of Ottawa Press.
Skottsberg, Carl. 1920. *The Natural History of Juan Fernandez and Easter Island.* Uppsala: Almquist and Wiksells Boktryckeri.
Sluyter, Andrew. 2002. *Colonialism and Landscape: Postcolonial Theory and Applications.* Lanham, MD: Rowman and Littlefield.
Smith, Alan, ed. 2001. *Bright Paradise: Exotic History and Sublime Artifice.* Auckland: Auckland Art Gallery.
Smith, Bernard. 1960. *European Vision and the South Pacific, 1768–1850; a Study in History of Art and Ideas.* Oxford: Clarendon Press.
- 1992. *Imagining the Pacific: In the Wake of the Cook Voyages.* Carlton: Melbourne University Press at the Miegunyah Press.
Smith, Dorothy E. 1999. *Writing the Social: Critique, Theory, and Investigations.* Toronto: University of Toronto Press.
Sontag, Susan. 1971. *On Photography.* New York: Farrar, Straus and Giroux.
Sorley, W.R. 1907–21. *Francis Bacon's 'The Great Instauration.'* Vol. 14 of 18 vols. New York: Putnam.
Sorrenson, Richard. 1997. 'The State's Demand for Accurate Astronomical and Navigational Instruments in Eighteenth-Century Britain.' In *The Consumption of Culture,* edited by Ann Bermingham. London: Routledge.
Spencer, John, and Amanda Prantera. 2002. *The Encyclopedia of the World's Mystical and Sacred Sites.* London: Headline Book Publishing.
Spenser, Edmund. [1596] 1978. *The Faerie Queene.* Edited by Thomas P. Roche, Jr. and Assisted by C. Patrick O'Donnell, Jr. New York: Penguin.
Spinoza, Baruch. 1884. *Chief Works.* Translated by R.H.M. Elwes. 2 vols. London: George Bell and Sons.
Spivak, Gayatri Chakravorty. 1993. *Outside in the Teaching Machine.* New York: Routledge.
Spurr, David. 1993. *The Rhetoric of Empire: Colonial Discourse in Journalism, Travel Writing, and Imperial Administration.* Durham, NC: Duke University Press.
Stafford, Barbara Maria. 1984. *Art, Science, Nature, and the Illustrated Travel Account, 1760–1840.* Boston: MIT Press.
Stepputat, Finn, and Thomas Blom Hansen. 2001. *States of Imagination: Ethno-*

graphic Explorations of the Postcolonial State. Durham, NC: Duke University Press.

Sterne, Laurence. 1768. *A Sentimental Journey through France and Italy.* London: n.p.

Strathern, Marilyn. 1988. *The Gender of the Gift*. Berkeley: University of California Press.

Strauss, Theodore. 1986. *Blind Prophets of Easter Island*. Edited by Jacques Cousteau and Phillippe Cousteau. Warner Home Video.

Stuebe, Isabel Combs. 1979. *The Life and Works of William Hodges*. New York: Garland Publishing.

Sugars, Cynthia, ed. 2004. *Home-Work: Postcolonialism, Pedagogy and Canadian Literature*. Ottawa: University of Ottawa Press.

Sugirtharajah, R.S. 1998. *The Postcolonial Bible*. Sheffield: Sheffield Academic Press.

– 2001. *The Bible and the Third World: Precolonial, Colonial and Postcolonial Encounters*. New York: Cambridge University Press.

Sulzer, Johann Georg. 1771. *Allgemeine Theorie Der Schönen Künste*. Leipzig: n.p.

Sweet, Rosemary. 2004. *Antiquaries: The Discovery of the Past in Eighteenth Century Britain*. London: Hambledon and London.

Swift, Jonathan. 1720. *Miscellaneous Works, Comical & Diverting: By T.R.D. J.S. D.O.P.I.I. In Two Parts. I. The Tale of a Tub; ... & the Battle of the Books; ... Ii. Miscellanies in Prose & Verse, ...* London: Printed by order of the Society de propaganda, &c. [for T. Johnson].

– 1726. *Travels into Several Remote Nations of the World by Lemuel Gulliver*. 2 vols. London: Printed for Benj Motte.

Tallarico, Tony. 1992. *I Didn't Know That! About Strange but True Mysteries*. Chicago: Smithmark Publishers.

Teitelbaum, James, and Sven A Kirsten. 2003. *Tiki Road Trip: A Guide to Tiki Culture in North America*. Santa Monica, CA: Santa Monica Press.

Thomas, Nicholas. 1991. *Entangled Objects: Exchange, Material Culture, and Colonialism in the Pacific*. Cambridge, MA: Harvard University Press.

– 1992. 'The Inversion of Tradition.' *American Ethnologist* 19: 213–32.

– 1994. *Colonialism's Culture: Anthropology, Travel and Government*. Cambridge: Polity Press.

– 1997. *In Oceania: Visions, Artefacts, Histories*. Durham, NC: Duke University Press.

– 1999. *Possessions: Indigenous Art, Colonial Culture*. New York: Thames and Hudson.

Thomas, Nicholas, and Oliver Berghof, eds. [1777] 2000. *A Voyage Round the*

World in His Majesty's Sloop Resolution Commanded by Captain James Cook 1772, 3, 4, 5 by George Forster. 2 vols. Honolulu: University of Hawaii Press.

Thomas, Nicholas, Diane Losche, and Jennifer Newell. 1999. *Double Vision: Art Histories and Colonial Histories in the Pacific.* New York: Cambridge University Press.

Thomas, Sprat. [1667] 1959. *History of the Royal Society.* Edited by Jackson I. Cope and Harold Whitmore Jones. St Louis: Washington University Press.

Thomson, William Juda. 1891. *To Pito Te Henua, or Easter Island. Report of the United States National Museum for the Year Ending June 30, 1889.* Washington, DC: Smithsonian Institution Press.

Tobin Fowkes, Beth. 1999. *Picturing Imperial Power: Colonial Subjects in Eighteenth Century British Painting.* Durham, NC: Duke University Press.

Todd, Sharon. 2001. 'Guilt, Suffering and Responsibility.' *Journal of Philosophy of Education* 35, no. 4 (Fall): 597–614.

Traister, Daniel. 1999. '"You Must Remember This ...," or, Libraries as a Locus of Cultural Memories.' In *Cultural Memory and the Construction of Memory*, edited by Dan Ben-Amos and Liliane Weissberg. Detroit: Wayne State University Press.

Trenchard, John. 1725. *Cato's Letters: Or, Essays on Civil Liberty.* 4 vols. London: J. Walthoe.

Trouillot, Michel-Rolph. 1995. *Silencing the Past: Power and the Production of History.* Boston: Beacon Press.

Tuki-Tepano, Rafael, and Clemente Here-veri-Te'ao. 2004. 'The Protection of Natural, Archaeological, and Cultural Heritage on Te Pito O Te Henua.' Paper presented at the Sixth International Conference on Easter Island and the Pacific, Viña del Mar, Chile, September.

Ullendorff, Edward, and C.F. Beckingham., eds. 1982. *The Hebrew Letters of Prester John.* Oxford: Oxford University Press.

Urry, John. 1995. *Consuming Places.* New York: Routledge.

– 2002. *The Tourist Gaze. Theory, Culture and Society.* 2nd ed. Thousand Oaks, CA: Sage.

Van Loon, Hendrik Willem. 1940. *The Story of the Pacific.* New York: Harcourt, Brace.

Van Tilburg, Jo Anne. 1987. 'Symbolic Archaeology on Easter Island.' *Archaeology* 40, no. 2: 26.

– 1990. 'Respect for Rapa Nui: Exhibition and Conservation of Easter Island Stone.' *Antiquity* 64, no. 243: 249.

– 1994. *Easter Island: Archaeology, Ecology, and Culture.* Washington, DC: Smithsonian Institution Press, and London: British Museum Press.

– 2003. *Among Giant Stones.* New York: Scribner.

Van Tilburg, Jo Anne, and British Museum, Department of Ethnography. 1992. *HMS Topaze on Easter Island: Hoa Hakananai'a and Five Other Museum Sculptures in Archaeological Context*. Occasional Paper, 73. London: Deptartment of Ethnography British Museum.

Vanderbes, Jennifer. 2003. *Easter Island*. New York: Dial Press.

Vazan, Bill. 2005. 'Pacific Prison.' *Canadian Art* (Fall): 110–15.

Veijola, S., and E. Jokinen. 1994. 'The Body in Tourism.' *Theory, Culture and Society* 11: 125–51.

Vetlesen, Arne Johan. 1994. 'The Perception of the Moral.' In *An Inquiry into the Preconditions of Moral Performance*. University Park: Pennsylvania State University Press.

Vidler, Mark. 1998. *The Star Mirror: The Extraordinary Discovery of the True Reflection between Heaven and Earth*. London: Thorsons Harper Collins.

Virgil. 1977. *The Eclogues*. New York: Cambridge University Press.

Von Daniken, Erich. 1968. *Chariots of the Gods? Unsolved Mysteries of the Past*. Translated by Michael Heron. New York: Bantam.

von Saher, Herbert. 1993. 'Roggeveen and Bouman: An Inventory of All the Narratives.' *Rapa Nui Journal* 7 (4): 77–82

Wales, William. 1778. *Remarks on Mr. Forster's Account of Captain Cook's Last Voyage*. London: J. Nourse.

– 1961. 'Journal.' In *The Voyage of the Resolution and Adventure 1772–75*, edited by J.C. Beaglehole. Cambridge: Cambridge University Press for Hakluyt Society.

Wearing, B. 1995. 'Leisure and Resistance in an Aging Society.' *Leisure Studies* 14: 263–79.

Webster, Steven. 1998. *Patrons of Maori Culture: Power, Theory and Ideology in the Maori Renaissance*. Dunedin, NZ: University of Otago Press.

Weedon, Chris. 1987. *Feminist Practice and Poststructuralist Theory*. 2nd ed. Oxford: Blackwell.

Weinstein, Mathew. 1999. *Robot World: Education, Popular Culture, and Science*. New York: Peter Lang Press.

Weir, Alison. 1996. *Sacrificial Logics: Feminist Theory and the Critique of Identity*. New York: Routledge.

Wetherell, J.E. 1927. *Strange Corners of the World*. New York: Thomas Nelson and Sons.

Whitaker, Hervey W. 1889. 'Samoa.' *Century Illustrated Monthly Magazine* 38 (May): 12–25.

White, Geoffrey M., and Lamont Lindstrom. 1997. *Chiefs Today: Traditional Pacific Leadership and the Postcolonial State*. Stanford: Stanford University Press.

White, Richard. 1997. 'The Sublime and the Other.' *The Heythrop Journal* 38, no. 2: 125–43.

Whitehead, Neil. n.d. *The Text and the Flesh – Reading Native Practice in Colonial Literatures*. Madison Cultural Translation Project, University of Wisconsin. Available online from http://polygot.Iss.wisc.edu/ctp/whitehead. shtm12003.

Wilk, Andrew Carl, et al. 1997. 'Mummies Unwrapped.' In *Amazing Planet*, edited by James McKenna and Michael Gross. National Geographic Kids Video.

William, Kathleen, ed. 1975. *A Tale of a Tub and Other Satires by Jonathan Swift*. London: Dent.

Willinsky, John. 1998. *Learning to Divide the World: Education at Empire's End*. Minneapolis: University of Minnesota Press.

Wilson, Kathleen. 1997. 'The Good, the Bad, and the Impotent: Imperialism and the Politics of Identity in Georgian England.' In *The Consumption of Culture: 1600–1800*, edited by Ann Bermingham and John Brewer. London: Routledge.

Windham, Ryder. 2002. *What You Don't Know About Mysterious Places*. New York: Scholastic.

Winny, James. 1957. *The Frame of Order: An Outline of Elizabethan Belief Taken from Treatises of the Late Sixteenth Century*. London: George Allen and Unwin.

Winter, J.M. 1995. *Sites of Memory, Sites of Mourning*. Cambridge: Cambridge University Press.

Wolff, Werner. 1948. *Island of Death; a New Key to Easter Island's Culture through an Ethno-Psychological Study*. New York: J.J. Augustin.

Wozniak, Joan. 1999. 'Prehistoric Horticultural Practices on Easter Island: Lithic Mulched Gardens and Field Systems.' *Rapa Nui Journal* 13, no. 4: 95–9.

Wright, Ian. 1996. *Chile and Easter Island*. London: Pilot Film and Television Productions Ltd.

Wright, Ronald. 2004. *A Short History of Progress*. Toronto: House of Anansi.

Wurgaft, Lewis D. 1983. *The Imperial Imagination*. Middletown, CT: Wesleyan University Press.

Yates, Frances Amelia. 1975. *Astraea: The Imperial Theme in the Sixteenth Century*. Boston: Routledge and Kegan Paul.

Young, Robert. 1990. *White Mythologies: Writing History and the West*. London: Routledge.

– 1995. *Colonial Desire: Hybridity in Theory, Culture, and Race*. New York: Routledge.

– 2001. *Postcolonialism: An Historical Introduction*. Malden, MA: Blackwell Publishers.

Zelizer, Barbie. 1995. 'Reading the Past against the Grain: The Shape of Memory Studies.' *Critical Studies in Mass Communication* 12: 214–39.

Index